THE NATURE OF FIFE

The Nature of Fife

Wildlife and Ecology

EDITED BY
GORDON B. CORBET

Published for
The Scottish Wildlife Trust
(Fife & Kinross Branch)
by
SCOTTISH CULTURAL PRESS
EDINBURGH

First published 1998
Scottish Cultural Press
Unit 14, Leith Walk Business Centre,
130 Leith Walk
Edinburgh EH6 5DT
Tel: 0131 555 5950 ◆ Fax: 0131 555 5018
email: scp@sol.co.uk
http://www.taynet.co.uk/users/scp

British Library Cataloguing-in-Publication Data
A catalogue record for this book is available from the British Library

ISBN 1 84017 008 5

Typeset by Carnegie Publishing, Lancaster
Printed and bound by The Cromwell Press, Trowbridge, Wiltshire

Contents

Part II: The flora and fauna of Fife: an inventory

Editorial Committee

George Ballantyne: botanical editor
Robin Clark: business manager
Gordon Corbet: general and zoological editor
Edith Cormack: SWT Fife & Kinross
June Johnson: picture editor
Anne-Marie Smout: Fife Nature
With maps and line-drawings by June Johnson (except chapters 2 and 4).

Contributors

George Ballantyne (recorder for Fife & Kinross, Botanical Society of the British Isles)

Matt G Bentley (Gatty Marine Laboratory, University of St Andrews)

Gordon B Corbet (formerly Natural History Museum, London)

Robert M M Crawford (Department of Biological Sciences, University of St Andrews)

Norman Elkins (Meteorological Office)

David Fairlamb (Royal Society for the Protection of Birds)

Ruth Ingram (Chairman, Scottish Wildlife Trust, Fife & Kinross Branch)

Alison Irvine (Ranger Service, Fife Council)

Roger T F Larsen (formerly Forestry Commission)

A Roy MacGregor (Department of Geology, University of St Andrews)

J Stewart Pritchard (Scottish Natural Heritage)

Chris Smout (Institute for Environmental History, University of St Andrews)

Frank Spragge (formerly Chairman, Scottish Wildlife Trust)

Sarah Warrener (Farming and Wildlife Advisory Group)

Graeme Whittington (Department of Geography, University of St Andrews)

Foreword

BY THE EARL OF LINDSAY

'Nature' is a broad subject, as this book compellingly demonstrates. It is therefore fitting that this should be a collaborative venture, drawing upon expertise from such diverse sources as the University of St Andrews, Scottish Natural Heritage, Fife Council's Ranger Service, the Farm and Wildlife Advisory Group and the Royal Society for the Protection of Birds.

It is also appropriate that the coordinating body should be the Scottish Wildlife Trust. Since its inception in 1964, the SWT has been striving to harness the interest of the general public and the enthusiasm of committed naturalists to conserve and enhance the wildlife heritage of Scotland. In this context, 'wildlife' includes not only such high-profile species as eagles, ospreys and otters that attract the attention of the media, but also the whole interconnected matrix of plants, animals, fungi and microbes that make up our living world.

In championing wildlife in this broad sense the SWT, as a non-governmental organization with around 15,000 members, works closely with other organizations involved with the management of the Scottish countryside. Although nature reserves still have an important part to play in the conservation of rare habitats and rare species, there has over the last few decades been an increasing awareness, amongst both voluntary and statutory bodies, of the importance of managing the entire countryside including farmland (and indeed our towns) in a way that recognizes the role of natural diversity.

To achieve this it is important to know the extent of this 'biodiversity'. Fife Nature was set up in 1992 to collect and disseminate information on the wildlife and habitats of Fife and is now an integral and valuable part of Fife Council's Planning Service.

The authors would, I am sure, be the first to agree that a work such as this is but a snapshot of current circumstances. The environment is ever-changing, as are the political and economic constraints within which we all operate. The key to conserving and enhancing the natural environment of Fife, as so ably described in the following pages, is surely cooperation between all concerned, from the naturalists and scientists recording the fine details to the planners, politicians, land-owners and land-managers whose decisions will all affect the 'Nature of Fife'.

Preface

BY EDITH CORMACK

(formerly chairman, Scottish Wildlife Trust
Fife & Kinross Branch)

This book has been produced as a result of the enthusiasm, expertise and goodwill of its editor, Gordon Corbet, without whose inspiration the project might well have foundered, and of his co-authors. They have written about Fife from specialist points of view, blending to give a comprehensive account of the plants, animals and environment of this part of Scotland. Their contribution is immeasurable and we are greatly indebted to them.

The book also celebrates collaboration between The Scottish Wildlife Trust and Fife Nature. The SWT, a charity founded in 1964, aims, 'for the public benefit, to conserve the fauna, flora and all objects of natural history interest in trust throughout Scotland'. It seeks to achieve this aim largely through management of nature reserves, the monitoring of wildlife, education, and cooperation with statutory and other non-statutory bodies with similar interests. The staff are supported by considerable numbers of active volunteer members.

Fife Nature, the local authority biological records centre, was founded in 1992 by the Fife Regional Council (now Fife Council). A vast amount of information about the occurrence and distribution of plants and animals in Fife has been, and continues to be, gathered and recorded, providing an envied and invaluable service to all concerned with the environment.

Lists of plants and animals were compiled from records held by Fife Nature, the Scottish Wildlife Trust and Scottish Natural Heritage (Cupar Office), supplemented by information gleaned from libraries and provided by many institutions and private sources as detailed on page 148.

Apart from illustrations provided by the authors, additional colour photographs have kindly been donated by David Bell, Niall Corbet, Richard Cormack, Hugh Ingram, Frank Spragge and Tony Wilson. Line-drawings of plants and animals, and additional maps, have been prepared by June Johnson.

Financial help has been gratefully received from The Carnegie Trust, The Russell Trust, and Fife Council's Nature Conservation Fund.

The Earl of Lindsay has honoured us by agreeing to write the Preface.

Many others, including members of the editorial committee, have willingly played a part in what is recognised as a unique venture, based on an idea mooted by 'ordinary' members of the Scottish Wildlife Trust. Jill Dick of Scottish Cultural Press has provided valuable advice and cooperation during the publication process.

It is a privilege to be given the opportunity to express immense gratitude to all.

Part I

The Environment of Fife

1

Introduction

GORDON CORBET

The snowball rolling over the carpet of white grows enormous, however scanty each
fresh layer be. Even so with truth in observational science: it is built up of trifles
patiently gathered together.
(J H Fabre: *The Life of the Spider*)

'Nature' means many things to different people. To some it conjures images of wild places and their fauna and flora, remote from human influence. Some places in Fife come close to this – the cliffs of the Isle of May with their colonies of raucous sea-birds and tapestry of thrift and sea campion; the sands of Tentsmuir Point with seals hauled out at the water's edge and the muted calls of distant curlews and courting eiders. Others see nature on the most intensively cultivated farmland or the high streets of our towns where wild animals and plants live their lives in spite of or, in some cases, because of the human presence. Nature is indeed everywhere around us and we are part of it.

Fife is one of the most intensively cultivated regions of Scotland, and although conspicuous industry is now localized, few if any corners have remained untouched by human exploitation since Mesolithic people began to influence the landscape eight thousand years ago. Nevertheless fragments of the natural communities that once dominated the landscape survive here and there, many impoverished and all modified to some extent by human activity. The nearest we have to the ancient woodlands that once covered most of Fife are small remnants in some of the steep-sided dens cut into the deep glacial deposits that underlie much of our farmland. Other fragments of nearly natural habitat survive on the more inaccessible parts of the coastline, on cliffs and dunes, and bordering fresh waters in the form of marshes and swamps. The freshwater habitats themselves have been greatly depleted by drainage of lochs and marshes, by straightening of rivers and burns, and their quality impaired by many forms of pollution.

Some apparently natural habitats have in fact been grossly modified or even created by human activity. Loch Ore and its natural-looking surroundings have been recreated on land that was denuded by mining; many of our fine woodlands are the result of planting of exotic trees like larch and sycamore on open ground by 18th-century landowners.

Fife is a peninsula, with the sea forming two-thirds of its boundary. At first sight the shores and the sea might appear to be wholly natural, but here too the impact of man is profound, if less visible. Industrial and sewage effluents have insidious effects on the chemistry and life of coastal waters, while the activity of the fishing industry must have

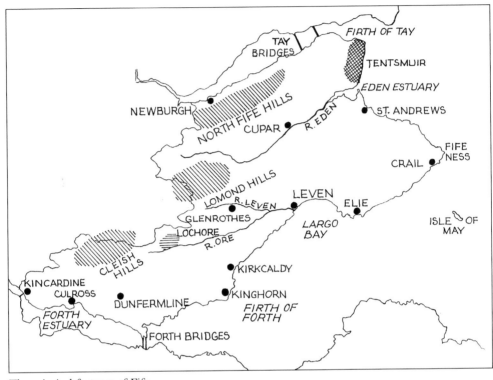

The principal features of Fife.

profoundly changed the ecology of the sea whether or not the level of fishing is sustainable. Nevertheless the communities of animals and plants surviving beneath the waves, in shore pools or even under seemingly lifeless sandy beaches are bewildering in their complexity, and we still have much to learn about them.

The purpose of this book is twofold: Firstly, to encourage Fifers and visitors alike to take a close look at the wildlife around them, to appreciate some of the variety and complexity that exists in every habitat, and to acquire some inkling of how these intricate communities of animals and plants operate. Secondly, to condense and bring together in one place the huge amount of information on the natural environment of Fife that already exists but is widely scattered in published and unpublished documents or indeed in the minds of those who have made it their business to study some aspect of Fife's nature.

It is often said that it is difficult to see the wood for the trees. But to understand a wood it is necessary not only to see it as a whole, to appreciate its shape and to ask what determines its extent; but also to analyze it in detail, to pry into its recesses and discover its diversity. How many kinds of tree are there? Are they native or exotic? Are they varied in age? Is there an underlayer of shrubs? What is growing on the ground? What birds can be seen or heard? Are there mosses and lichens on the trunks? Are there caterpillars feeding on the leaves? What insects are living in the leaf-litter? You may not be able to answer all such questions, but they will never be answered if they are not asked. A wood is not just an assemblage of trees. It is a community of around one to two thousand different kinds of plants, animals, fungi and micro-organisms, all interacting with each other in one way or another. Some interactions are swift and visible, as when a sparrowhawk streaks past in pursuit of a blackbird. Others are too slow to be observed directly and can only be inferred by prolonged observation or historical research, for example to detect the gradual changes in the relative abundance of different trees which, if continued, can totally transform a wood.

Woodland is, on the whole, a discrete and easily recognizable habitat. In the rest of the countryside it is rather more difficult to draw sharp lines between the major habitats that form the subject matter of the following chapters. We are accustomed to seeing a green, open landscape, but how often do we stop to wonder what it is that is green? Very often the answer will be grass. But which grass? Reference to the lists in the second part of this book will show that there are about 80 different species of grasses in Fife. Each of these has its own particular requirements and its own community of associated plants and animals.

In terms of area, farmland dominates the countryside and is the subject of chapter 10. This includes arable land, temporary grassland and permanent grassland that has been substantially altered by reseeding or the application of fertilizer to produce a sward with a greatly reduced variety of grasses and other species of plants. Less altered grasslands, along with heaths (dominated by dwarf shrubs such as heather) are dealt with in chapter 9. However these habitats are still part of the agricultural landscape since they are grazed by sheep or cattle and owe their origin and continued existence to the way they are managed for our use.

Our central aim in this book has been to describe the natural environment of Fife, habitat by habitat as it is now, drawing attention to some of the hidden detail that is not immediately apparent to the casual observer. The living environment is dependent upon the physical environment of climate, rocks and landform and these subjects are dealt with in the introductory chapters. However we can hardly begin to understand what we see without knowing something of its past history. Perhaps the principal lesson of history is that everything has been changing with time and is continuing to change. Some changes are beyond our control. Others are caused by ourselves and we have both the responsibility and, if we put our minds to it, the ability to ensure that the changes we make are for the better and will be seen as such by the next generation who inherit Fife.

Fife, of course, is an administrative rather than a natural entity and has itself changed its boundaries over the centuries. Uniquely amongst the counties and regions of mainland Scotland it has kept its borders virtually intact through the 20th century. However from the point of view of recording natural history it is worth remembering that prior to 1891 the area from Culross to Kincardine, comprising the parishes of Culross and Tulliallan, was a detached part of Perthshire. This is reflected in the 'Watsonian' vice-counties used for biological recording since 1873: most of Fife, along with Kinross, makes up VC 85 – Fife & Kinross – while the Culross-Kincardine section is part of VC 87 – West Perthshire & Clackmannanshire. Earlier still the 'Sherifdome of Fyfe', as shown for example in Blaeu's atlas of 1654, included Kinross as well as pre-1891 Fife, and at that time the parishes of Culross and Tulliallan were in Clackmannanshire. This volume, including the lists of species in part II, is concerned with the current administrative county of Fife.

No single book on the natural history of

Fife has previously been produced. Sir Robert Sibbald included 'an account of the natural products of the land and water' in his *History . . . of the Sheriffdoms of Fife and Kinross* in 1710. Since then many works have dealt with particular aspects of the subject as described in chapter 12, including a volume on the then Kirkcaldy District (now Central Fife Area) published by the Kirkcaldy Naturalists' Society in 1982.

Other parts of Scotland have been dealt with in a variety of ways. Volumes describing the local environment were produced on the occasions of meetings of the British Association for the Advancement of Science, for example in Dundee (1912, 1947, 1968), Stirling (1974) and Glasgow (1901), the last including the most comprehensive listing of the fauna and flora attempted for any region. More recently, volumes in Collins' *New Naturalist* series have dealt very comprehensively with Orkney, Shetland, the Highlands and Islands, and the Outer Hebrides, while many other books have described particular aspects of the wildlife of the Highlands. Lowland Scotland has been less well served. This volume will, I hope, show that although it is very different from the Highlands a lowland region like Fife has many wildlife habitats that are just as rich and awe-inspiring as anywhere in Scotland. They are also very vulnerable and we can all play a part in preserving them for future generations.

Fife: some facts and figures

Area: 1305 square kilometres
             (504 square miles)

Coastline: about 170 kilometres
             (105 miles)

Maximum altitude (West Lomond):
             522 metres (1713 feet)

Population: 351,600 (in 1995)

Eider Duck

2

The shape of Fife: geology and landform

ROY MACGREGOR

Fife forms part of the Central Belt of Scotland, often referred to by geologists as the Midland Valley. This term has been used in preference in this chapter, for reasons explained below.

The geological time scale

The Midland Valley is occupied by layered sedimentary rocks (*strata*) such as sandstone, mostly ranging in age from around 300 million years to around 400 million years. A hundred million years is an immense period of time, indeed inconceivably long compared with our normal time scale or even a historical time scale. During this 100 million years, through gradual subsidence of the land surface, a thickness of some 5000 metres of sediments accumulated in Fife. However, not only Fife but much of the Midland Valley was volcanically active during this immense period and there are substantial thicknesses of lava flows too.

These rocks belong to two periods of geological time (Table, p. 7). The older, called the *Devonian* after the county of Devon, extends from 400 million years ago to 350 million years ago. In many parts of Scotland, because the Devonian rocks are red, the name *Old Red Sandstone* is often used instead of Devonian. The younger period, the *Carboniferous*, named originally because its

rocks contain a lot of coal, extends from 350 million years ago to about 290 million years ago. For brevity this is usually written 290 Ma, thus the Carboniferous Period extended from 350 Ma to 290 Ma.

Igneous rocks

Lava flows from volcanoes form part of a group of rocks, the igneous rocks, which have been molten or liquid, often at temperatures of the order of 1000°C. They have come up from great depths below the surface of the earth, for example from 70 km or more where the rocks are hot enough to melt or at least to partially melt. When this happens the molten rock or *magma* may rise up pipe-like structures or sometimes along cracks or fissures in the rocks. When this magma reaches the surface a volcanic eruption takes place and lava or volcanic ash (*tuff*) may be discharged at the earth's surface. Over millions of years huge thicknesses of lavas can accumulate, for example the 2400 metres of lavas in the Lower Devonian rocks of northeast Fife.

However, sometimes the molten rock or magma coming up from depth squeezes out sideways between the layers of older sedimentary rocks to form thick sheets or sills. This magma cools and solidifies without ever reaching the surface. Such intrusion or emplacement of sills happened twice during the Carboniferous Period, once in the middle of the Carboniferous and a second time right at the end.

The Midland Valley of Scotland

Given the rather varied geological history of accumulation of both sedimentary and igneous rocks we can now turn back to the name Midland Valley within which lies Fife. The Midland Valley is situated between two areas of higher ground, the Scottish Highlands to the northwest and the Southern Uplands to the southeast. There are quite sharp changes in topography in passing from the Midland Valley to the Highlands or the Southern Uplands, because both areas are composed of older rocks more resistant to weathering and erosion than the rocks of the Midland Valley. There is a further reason, however, for their forming high ground. The margins of the Midland Valley are marked by two great fractures or *faults*: the Highland Boundary Fault, which extends southwestwards from Stonehaven to Helensburgh, and the Southern Uplands Fault, extending southwestwards from Dunbar to Loch Ryan. Both fractures are approximately vertical and are known to extend to 10–15 km beneath the surface. The Midland Valley has, relatively speaking, dropped some thousands of metres compared to the old rocks on either side.

The geological evidence indicates that both the Highlands and the Southern Uplands have stood higher than the Midland Valley for a very long time, even during the Devonian and Carboniferous Periods. As a result sediment that has weathered, eroded and then been transported by rivers from the high ground on either side accumulated in the slowly subsiding Midland Valley between the two great faults.

While the geological history of the Mid-land Valley can be broadly regarded from the beginning of Devonian times to the end of Carboniferous times as a history of subsidence, a number of factors complicate the story. Firstly, the subsidence was not at a uniform rate. Secondly it was not evenly spread – some areas subsided more than others. Thirdly, the general subsidence was disrupted by episodes of earth movements in which the previously deposited sediments and lavas were folded by upward arching into *anticlines* (pl. 4) and downfolded into trough-like shapes or *synclines*. This folding was usually accompanied by actual fractures or faults, with uplift on one side and dropping down on the other. Some of these faults extend for many kilometres across country. The south face of the Ochil Hills, especially around Tillicoultry just west of Fife, is one of the most spectacular fault lines in the whole of Scotland. The folded and faulted rocks were also uplifted, often to form mountains, and as a result were eroded.

Lastly as part of the background to all this, in terms of *plate tectonics*, Fife in common with the rest of Scotland lay south of the Equator at the beginning of the Devonian Period, but gradually moved northwards, crossing the Equator during the Upper Carboniferous to lie in the Northern Hemisphere. This northward movement from the subtropics through the tropics and on into the northern subtropics is reflected both in the kinds of sediments that accumulated and in the kinds of soils that formed. The northward migration has continued since the Carboniferous and Fife now lies 56° north of the Equator.

The Geological History of Fife

The Devonian Period
The oldest rocks exposed at the surface in Fife are the volcanic rocks forming the

North Fife Hills (map p. 8), for example Black Craig (NO 329216) or Norman's Law (NO 305203). They are Lower Devonian in age, are very thick, 2400 metres in the Cupar district, and comprise many lava flows of basalt and a similar rock, andesite, erupted on the surface. Individual flows are of the order of 10 metres thick and have rubbly tops and bottoms. The centres of such flows have cooled more slowly after being erupted as a very hot viscous liquid. As a result of shrinkage they have developed *columnar jointing*, the columns being about 50 cm across and ideally hexagonal. Individual flows can sometimes be traced across country for up to 10 km. The rubbly tops of flows led to quite rapid weathering in sub-tropical conditions during the Lower Devonian, and red *laterite* soils developed. This has in turn led to a stepped topography developing on major lava flow successions. The horizontal treads of the steps are co-incident with the tops of the flows and the vertical risers with the massive centres, with columnar jointing perpendicular to the tops and bottoms of the flows.

Stratigraphical succession in Fife

Era	System	Formations etc.			Thickness in metres	Igneous Rocks		Age in millions of years (Ma)	Localities
						Contemp-oraneous	Intrusive		
Quaternary	Recent Pleistocene	Alluvium, Peat Bogs, Raised Beaches, Fluvio-glacial Outwash, Till						1	Kincraig Raised Beaches, Fluvio-glacial sands and gravels- Wormit to Leuchars, Ladybank-Collessie
Tertiary & Mesozoic								225	
Upper Palaeozoic	Permian					Last vents		289	East & West Lomond Hills, Kincraig, Rock & Spindle, Elie Ness
	Carboniferous						Dolerite sills and E-W dykes	296	Sills - North Queensferry, Lomond Hills
		EARTH MOVEMENTS Upper Coal Measures			300	Long			West Wemyss shore
		Middle Coal Measures Lower Coal Measures			800	continued			
		Passage Formation			270	volcanic	Dolerite sills		Dysart-Kirkcaldy shore
		Clack-mannan Group	Upper Limestone Fm.		320	activity			
			Limestone Coal Fm.		430				
			Lower Limestone Fm.		140				Kinghorn-Kirkcaldy shore, Pittenweem-St Monans shore
		Strathclyde Group			2000 +	Burntisland lavas			Burntisland-Kinghorn (vol), Anstruther-Pittenweem, Kingsbarns-Fife Ness
		Inverclyde Group			300			350	
	Devonian	Upper Old Red Sandstone EARTH MOVEMENTS Lower Old Red Sandstone			600 2400+	Very thick lavas	Minor intrusions	400	Dura Den, Bishop Hill Wormit shore ⎫ lavas Norman's Law ⎭ Lucklaw Hill and Forret Hill Intrusions

A summary of the geological history of Fife. This includes a small number of significant ages for geological events and a list of localities where different geological formations can be seen.

FIFE: solid geology

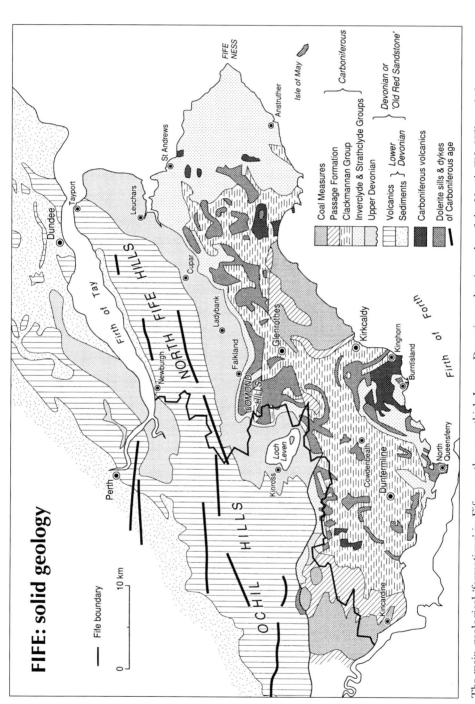

The main geological 'formations' in Fife, e.g. the very thick Lower Devonian volcanic rocks of the North Fife Hills and the Carboniferous Coal Measures northeast of Kirkcaldy.

The lavas of the North Fife Hills were later involved in the Middle Devonian folding, described below, when the Sidlaw Anticline formed (see map). Thus the lavas are no longer lying flat, having been arched over the anticline. In the North Fife Hills they slope down, or *dip*, to the southeast at about 20° to the horizontal. On the other side of the anticline in the Sidlaw Hills similar lavas dip to the northwest also at about 20°. This has a marked effect on the topography. The previously horizontal tops of the flows now dip to the southeast. Because they continue to weather today these surfaces are often seen as grassy fields with good soils. In contrast the columnar jointed centres of the flows, previously with vertical cliffs, now form steep scarp slopes broadly facing northwest, often covered with whins and with little soil, for example on

Glenduckie Hill (NO 2819). *Dip and scarp slopes of this kind are widespread in the North Fife Hills and indeed are to be found all the way from Tayport to Milnathort, into the Ochil Hills and eventually to Stirling.

During quiescent periods between eruptions sand was sometimes washed into hollows on the lava surface and soils developed, but the Lower Devonian was largely a period of eruption and weathering of lava in northeast Fife. There is little sediment.

There are no Middle Devonian sedimentary rocks in Fife nor indeed anywhere in the Midland Valley. Rather it was a time of widespread earth movements, including folding, with the Sidlaw Anticline as the major structure affecting Fife (see map). The line along the centre of the fold, its *axis*, trends northeast to southwest from

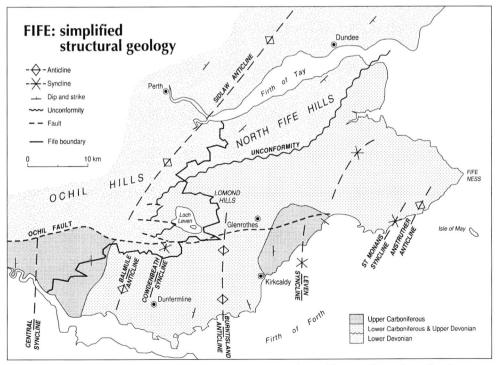

The major folds affecting the underlying 'solid' rocks, together with a small number of major faults, in particular the Ochil Fault. Compare with the section on p. 13.

Montrose through the Sidlaws and Ochils to Tillicoultry. Southeast of this line the sediments or lavas dip or slope down to the southeast at around 20°. The effect of this folding on the Lower Devonian lavas and their land forms has been described above.

Not only were the Lower Devonian lavas folded, they were uplifted and as a result were weathered and eroded so that quite substantial thicknesses of the lava pile were removed before the Upper Devonian sediments were laid down. Consequently the Upper Devonian sediments rest on eroded Lower Devonian lavas. Such a buried erosion surface is an *unconformity*. In Fife this unconformity represents a gap of several million years (map, p. 9).

The Upper Devonian rocks of Fife occupy a narrow strip extending from Leuchars southwestwards up Stratheden past Cupar and Ladybank before sweeping round the north face of the Lomond Hills and south to Bishop Hill and Benarty. They are all sedimentary, with no volcanic rocks, and the sequence has a maximum thickness of 600 m. Sandstone is the dominant rock type, usually fawn-brown, sometimes more cream coloured and sometimes red. From the nature of the bedding in the sandstones – *cross bedding* – it is clear that many of them were deposited by eastward flowing rivers and in places the remains of fresh-water fish occur. Dura Den east of Cupar is well known for its fossil fish, but the locality has long since been worked out, though the sandstones are well displayed in the cliffs (NO 4114). The sediments deposited on either side of the river channels include lime-rich soils, characteristic of subtropical environments today. These are named *cornstones* or *calcretes*.

The highest sediments of the Upper Devonian are again mainly sandstones, but sometimes with well rounded, wind-blown sand grains – 'millet seed' grains. These are

characteristic of desert environments today. They confirm yet again the subtropical setting of the Midland Valley at this time.

The Carboniferous Period
Carboniferous rocks underlie about three-quarters of Fife. They extend from Fife Ness in the east along the south coast past Anstruther and Kirkcaldy, Burntisland and North Queensferry to Kincardine, and indeed continue beyond Fife to Alloa and Stirling. They extend along the northern edge of West Fife, when followed back to the east, into the Cleish Hills, skirt round the south of Loch Leven, then northwards to Bishop Hill and the West Lomond. Thereafter they run along the south side of Stratheden to St Andrews Bay and back to Fife Ness. Within this line the whole of Fife is underlain by Carboniferous rocks.

The Carboniferous environment
The Carboniferous rocks are locally over 4000 m thick yet contain no deep-water sediments; thus they demonstrate that the Midland Valley of Scotland and in particular Fife subsided gradually for around 50 million years to allow the accumulation of this huge thickness of sediments. Unlike the previous Devonian Period the succession includes repeated sequences of sediments deposited in shallow seas – *marine sediments* carrying marine fossils.

Igneous activity occurred too, chiefly as volcanic activity, but on two occasions with the formation of sills. Only in the Burntisland area is there a substantial sequence of lavas. Elsewhere the volcanic activity is now represented only by *vents* or *necks* of old volcanoes. These are filled with volcanic tuffs, for example Largo Law (NO 4204) and Kincraig (NT 4699). The East and West Lomond summits both consist of igneous rock, once molten magma, that solidified in the pipes or vents to form plugs of very resistant *dolerite*, a rock broadly equivalent to the basalt found in the lava flows.

The bulk of the Carboniferous succession found in Fife comprises sedimentary rocks. *Sandstones*, formerly sand, and *shale*, formerly mud or clay, predominate, but both limestone and coal have been economically important. The setting in which these sediments were deposited was very different from that of the Devonian. First of all the Midland Valley was dominated by a huge delta, comparable in size to that of the present-day Mississippi, with the river flowing in from the northeast and carrying a load of sand and mud, again comparable to that of the Mississippi today.

When the speed of the river diminished as it approached the sea the sand was deposited at the mouth of the river, quickly building up to sea level to form the delta top. The fine clay or mud continued seawards until the currents fell away altogether and the clay sank to the sea floor in front of the delta. Remember too that the Midland Valley was in the tropics at this time as Britain crossed the Equator during the Carboniferous.

In a traverse seawards from the delta top the four main rock types are met. Firstly tropical forests and swamps on the delta top went to form thick peat, later to become *coal* – typical leached tropical soils lie beneath many of the coal seams. These forests and soils developed on the top sediment of the delta, namely the sands. Seawards the sands gave way to silt and then clay (now shale following burial, compaction and hardening). Lastly, well offshore, away from the river muds, abundant shells accumulated on the shallow sea floor, eventually to form *limestone*.

As the delta advanced into the sea the shell bed was covered by mud, the mud by silt and then sand, and on top of that a forest grew to produce peat. These sediments in this upward order make up a Carboniferous *cycle*. With long-continued, intermittent subsidence and fluctuating sea level, cycle after cycle formed, some complete, others not, so that well over a hundred cycles can be recognised. Some of these are traceable not only throughout Fife, but over the whole of the Midland Valley.

Within the Carboniferous rocks of Fife a number of major subdivisions can be recognised. Their distribution is shown on the map (p. 8) and their salient features are outlined below in *stratigraphical order*, from the oldest to the youngest (see Table, p. 7).

Inverclyde Group

These beds, the oldest in the Carboniferous, represent a transition from the desert sediments of the Upper Devonian to the delta of the Carboniferous. River (*fluviatile*) sandstones are interbedded with semi-desert lake muds containing evaporite minerals such as gypsum. Cornstone or calcrete soils are also present. The rocks of the Inverclyde Group are not well developed in Fife and they are relatively thin, but they can be seen on the shore 1 km northwest of Fife Ness.

Strathclyde Group

At least 2000 m of cyclic sediments are present in the Anstruther area, one of major subsidence. Despite this only rarely did the sea penetrate to Anstruther and marine limestones are rare. Coal seams are very thin or absent, but soils are commonly present on top of the sandstones. Subsidence was much less around St Andrews where the equivalent strata are only a few hundred metres thick. Again they are cyclic. The Burntisland area was volcanically active and there much of the Strathclyde Group is made up of lava flows. The high ground behind

Burntisland and Kinghorn displays the same kind of dip-and-scarp slopes as occur in North Fife, this time on Carboniferous lava flows. The lavas can be seen on the shore at Kinghorn (pl. 3). Westwards the cyclic sediments were formed when the delta entered not the sea but a very large fresh-water lake which extended southwestwards into the Lothians. The area around the Lomond Hills hardly subsided at all during this time with the result that there are almost no Strathclyde Group sediments there. This illustrates the variable subsidence over Fife at this time – 2000 m at Anstruther and only a few metres in the Lomond Hills.

Clackmannan Group

The lower and upper parts of the Clackmannan Group show the most complete cycles with marine limestones sometimes carrying fossil corals, again pointing to the tropical conditions at the time. The lower part of the Clackmannan Group is very well displayed on the coast from St Monans harbour northeastwards to Pathhead (NO 537021) where the St Monans White Limestone, just below the base of the Clackmannan Group, is virtually a small coral reef of *Lithostrotion.* The limestones pass up into marine shales. The fossils show diminishing marine influence up into the delta shales and silts and no marine content in the delta sandstones. Although the sandstones often end upwards in a soil, significant coals are lacking before the next cycle begins. Nevertheless the middle part of the Clackmannan Group, called the Limestone Coal Formation, carries no marine limestones in its cycles, but on the other hand includes up to 18 worked coal seams, for example those in the Cowdenbeath and Lochgelly coalfields, and the formation has been until recently of immense economic importance.

Passage Formation

This is part of the Upper Carboniferous, a time when any marine influence is almost completely lacking in Fife. In it thick deltaic sandstones alternate with thick shales both in the Kirkcaldy to Leven area and also in west Fife around Kincardine. Largo Law is made predominantly of volcanic ash or tuffs of this age. It was a time of sill emplacement too within the igneous activity, and the Isle of May Sill probably dates from this period (313–296 Ma).

The Coal Measures

Here is the second and indeed the more important sequence of worked coals, centred in the Dysart to Leven area. Formerly worked on land, later a number of mines were driven for considerable distances out under the Firth of Forth. The same coals were also worked immediately west of Kincardine in the Central Coalfield. Although there are few marine beds in the Coal Measures, the rocks are still in good cyclic sequences with shale passing up into sandstone with tropical soils on top and in turn often thick coals.

The highest Coal Measures lack good coal seams and are red, at least in part due to a gradual change in climate. The Midland Valley was now moving north away from the Equator and soils were becoming more subtropical, with reddening taking place often to considerable depths beneath the old land surface. These can be seen on the shore at West Wemyss below the castle.

Carboniferous Earth Movements

So far no attempt has been made to explain the 'patchy' distribution of the various parts of the Carboniferous succession, for example the occurrence of Coal Measures around Kincardine and Leven only. The cause of this distribution is the end-Carboniferous Earth Movements in which the very thick

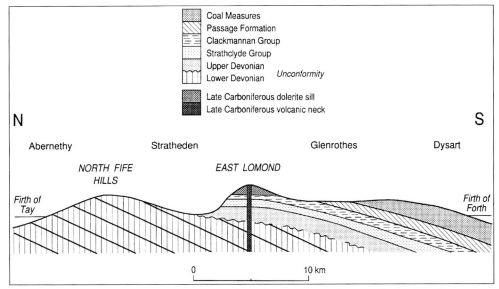

A north–south section from the Firth of Tay through East Lomond to the Firth of Forth, to illustrate the underlying solid geology.

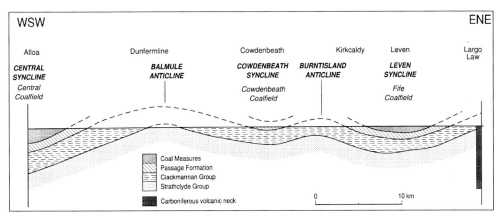

An ENE–WSW section from Largo Law to Alloa, just west of Fife, showing the major folds affecting the Carboniferous rocks. Notice that the major coalfields are in the synclines or downfolds.

sequence of Carboniferous sediments was folded into large anticlines (up-arched) and synclines (down-arched).

The axes or length of these folds run north-south and the strata that have been affected dip east or west off the anticlines into the synclines. The main folds are shown in the section above and the map on p. 9. From east to west the first is the Leven Syncline with the 'young' Coal Measures at the centre. Indeed this syncline extends southwards right across the Firth of Forth to the Lothian Syncline east of Edinburgh. Here too there are 'young' Coal Measures in the centre. Next to the west the Burntisland Anticline brings the 'old' Strathclyde Group rocks up to the surface again, before the Cowdenbeath Syncline brings down the younger Clackmannan Group with its major set of workable coals. Westwards again the Balmule Anticline brings the 'old' lowest part of the Clackmannan Group back up to the surface, and finally, the youngest parts of the Carboniferous reappear between Kincardine and Alloa in the Central or Clackmannan Syncline.

In east Fife the folding is much less clear and trends northeast-southwest. The Anstruther Anticline is the largest fold while the St Monans Syncline is well displayed on the shore. Minor folds are well displayed on the shore east of St Andrews (pl. 4). Inland in both east and west Fife exposures of solid rock are seldom frequent enough to allow folds to be easily seen. (The reason for this lack of exposures is explained in the Quaternary section below.)

The north–south folds in Fife were due to east-west compression during the end-Carboniferous earth movements. As the rocks were compressed from the east and west they extended to north and south. This north-south extension was accompanied by breaking or faulting of the rocks, the faults being at right angles to the extension. They are seen as east-west faults, some of which extend for many kilometres across country, with one side dropping relative to the other sometimes by well over 100 metres.

Late-Carboniferous igneous activity

Following the end-Carboniferous earth movements came the second period of sill emplacement in the Carboniferous of the Midland Valley, in particular the emplacement of the great Midland Valley Sill. This forms the escarpment on Benarty, Bishop Hill and the Lomonds and dies out eastwards at Walton Hill, Cupar. The same major sill is responsible for the headland at North Queensferry, with excellent exposures in both the road and railway cuttings

leading to the Forth Bridges and in the quarries at the nearby Carlingnose Scottish Wildlife Trust reserve. The sill disappears underground in the Coal Measures of the Leven Syncline where it was met in coal mining. It disappears at depth too under west Fife and the Central Syncline but returns to the surface in the Stirling district where it forms the spectacular crags at Stirling Castle and the Wallace Monument.

A small number of vertical fissure-filling east-west *dykes*, often intruded in east-west faults, contain similar dolerite to that of the Midland Valley Sill and are believed to have been 'feeders' for the sill. Several such east-west dykes occur in the North Fife Hills.

The last episode in the igneous history of Fife was yet again one of vulcanicity, seen now as volcanic vents or necks. They appear very similar to those of the earlier Carboniferous, but they have yielded radiometric ages (290–280 Ma) that point to the very end of the Carboniferous or into the early part of the next period, the Permian (Table, p. 7). The East and West Lomonds are the best examples of such necks.

The Mesozoic and Tertiary eras

Almost nothing is known of the geological history of Fife for the next 280 million years. There are no sediments and there are no igneous rocks in Fife to represent this vast period of geological time or to give any direct evidence of what may have been happening during the Mesozoic and Tertiary eras. However, evidence from elsewhere, particularly from the offshore search for oil and gas, shows that the North Sea Basin subsided for most of this time and that most of the sediment that accumulated in the basin was marine. In Fife it is more likely that erosion took place on land, the sediment being transported into the North Sea. While this erosion and deposition were going on

Fife, in common with the rest of the British Isles, was moving steadily northwards from the tropics so that by Quaternary times it lay 56° north of the Equator.

The Quaternary Era

We know from elsewhere that towards the end of the Tertiary Era the climate deteriorated overall and that in the higher latitudes a succession of ice ages or glacial episodes took place. Only the last of these, the *Late Devensian*, has left its mark on Fife, not because earlier glaciations did not occur, but rather because the Late Devensian glaciation swept away the evidence of earlier ones. It lasted from 26,000 BP (years before present) to around 14,000 BP and almost the whole of Scotland was covered by ice.

Till

The main areas of ice accumulation lay to the west of Fife, and ice spread out broadly eastwards across Fife. Evidence for this takes three forms. Firstly the scratch marks or *striae* made by the ice as it dragged rock fragments over the solid bedrock beneath. Secondly the ice picked up any loose fragments from the bedrock and indeed prised off pieces of rock and carried them along until the ice came to rest and melted. These *erratic blocks* may be only traceable in general terms, but in other cases can be very specific, for example two very large glacial erratics lie on the shore at Wormit Bay in north Fife and were almost certainly carried by ice from Glen Lednock, near Comrie, 60–70 km to the west. Thirdly the *till*, the material deposited directly by the ice, includes not only the boulders or erratics but also a relatively fine-grained matrix of clay or sand. This too has been scraped up by the passing ice and also reflects the nature of the underlying bedrock. Over much of Fife this matrix is grey on account of the substantial amount of Carboniferous shale that has been incorporated by the passing ice.

A look at the '*drift*' map overleaf, shows that about two-thirds of Fife has glacial till at the surface. It has been deposited by the eastward moving ice during the late Devensian Glaciation. It is seldom more than about 20 m thick and is often much less, but in many areas it covers the underlying bedrock completely. With its mainly clay matrix it is impermeable and is often poorly drained, even boggy.

Fluvioglacial deposits

As the Late Devensian Glaciation came to an end the ice ceased to advance and melting became increasingly important both on top of and at the front of the ice sheet. The load carried by the ice, and the till accumulated beneath the ice, became reworked by rivers of meltwater to produce fluvioglacial sediments. There are three major areas of such fluvioglacial sands and gravels in Fife, all of them of major economic importance: the Wormit–Leuchars area, the Collessie–Ladybank area, and the Kennoway–Markinch–Leslie area; with an even larger one around Loch Leven in Kinross. They are all well drained on account of the sand and gravel and are characterised by gravel ridges, the courses of sometimes sub-ice streams and rivers, and by depressions or kettle holes. These are the sites of late-surviving isolated ice masses against which the sand and gravel were banked, for example between Wormit and Leuchars.

Raised beaches

When major ice sheets developed, such as the Late Devensian one with which we are concerned, two things happened. The first was a world-wide fall in sea level. Following evaporation from the sea then precipitation

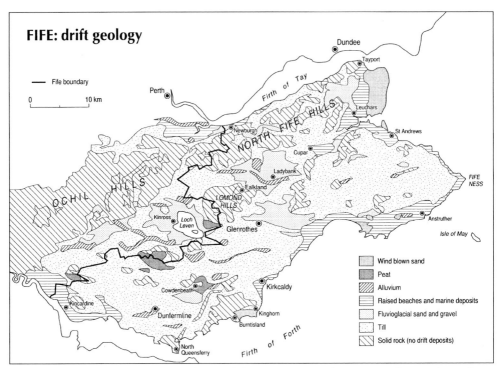

This shows the areas where the underlying solid rocks are exposed at or very close to the surface; and areas where a wide variety of glacial and post-glacial sediments cover the older rocks.

as snow, increasing amounts of water were 'locked up' in the ice sheets. The fall in sea level, worldwide, was around 100 m. The second was the slow sinking of the earth's crust beneath the ice sheets due to the weight of the overlying ice. Where the ice was thickest, in our case west of Fife, the subsidence was greatest.

Melting of the ice sheets was a relatively speedy affair so that sea level rose quite rapidly at the end of the Late Devensian Glaciation; it was much more rapid than the gradual rise of the earth's crust when the ice melted. As a result the sea invaded the depressed, low-lying parts of Fife forming shore lines and beaches, often cut into the glacial till but also into the underlying bedrock. The slow rise of the crust continued, however, and the early postglacial shore lines were lifted above sea level, more so in the west where crustal depression under the

greater load of ice had been greater. Since the ice front retreated westwards by melting, the oldest raised beaches are found only in the east, while younger raised beaches extend successively further westwards.

Raised beaches are particularly well developed in Fife, lying as it does between the two long, east-west estuaries of the Forth and Tay. Their major distribution is shown in the map, but often quite narrow raised beaches can be seen round most of the coast of Fife. Where sediment remains on them it is similar to that on present-day beaches, usually with shelly or pebbly sand. The oldest beaches sometimes yield shells pointing to cold, even arctic conditions at the time of their formation. Later raised beaches have 'temperate' fossils in their sediments.

Much detailed work has been done on the retreat stages of the Late Devensian ice sheet using radiocarbon dating and the elevations and slopes of the many different beaches. Perhaps the best known of all the raised beaches in Fife are those present at the western end of Kincraig Point, Elie at 4 m, 11 m, 22 m and 25 m above sea level. There are also good raised beaches in the Torryburn to Kincardine area of west Fife and indeed they extend westwards far beyond Stirling.

Following upon the disappearance of ice from Fife around 14,000 BP vegetation became established over the land surface. Where bogs developed in hollows, particularly over impermeable till, detailed knowledge of the climate in the post-glacial period has been acquired from a study of the pollen in the successive layers within the peat. The largest areas of such peat in Fife are around Loch Glow in the Cleish Hills, and Moss Morran at Cowdenbeath, with another at Portmoak Moss near Loch Leven, Kinross. Most research has been carried out at Black Loch near Lindores Loch in North Fife and at Bankhead Moss near Peat Inn, a rare surviving raised bog, now a Scottish Wildlife Trust reserve. Yet more recently areas of wind-blown sand have developed, for example at Tentsmuir, Leuchars and Shell Bay, Elie.

The evolution of the landscape on top of all this varied geology, and following deglaciation, is the subject of the next chapter.

Further reading

Text books

Cameron, I B and Stephenson, D (1985). *The Midland Valley of Scotland*, Brit. Reg. Geol., 3rd ed. One of a series of handbooks published by the geological survey, it covers that part of Scotland lying between the Highland Boundary Fault and the Southern Uplands Fault.

Craig, G Y (ed.) (1991). *Geology of Scotland*. Geological Society, London. A major text book covering all aspects of the geology of Scotland.

Gordon, J E and Sutherland, D G (1993). *Quaternary of Scotland*. Chapman and Hall. An up-to-date account of the Quaternary of Scotland with a useful introduction and chapter 15 devoted to Fife and the Lower Tay.

MacGregor, A R (1996). *Fife and Angus Geology, 3nd ed.* Pentland Press. An account of the geology of the area with 14 of the excursion itineraries devoted to Fife.

Whitow, J (1992). *Geology and Scenery in Britain*. Chapman and Hall. A fairly chatty account of the subject with only three pages devoted to Fife.

All these books provide lists of references to papers published in scientific journals on almost all aspects of the geology of Fife.

Geological Survey Memoirs

Armstrong, M, Paterson, I B and Browne, M A E (1985). *Geology of the Perth and Dundee district*. Mem. Br. Geol. Surv., Sheets 48W, 48E and 49. A concise survey memoir covering a large area from Perth to Arbroath and part of north Fife.

Forsyth, I H and Chisholm, J I (1977). *The geology of East Fife*. Mem. Geol. Surv. U.K. A detailed survey memoir covering the geology of East Fife, with extensive lists of fossils for all localities in the area.

Much of the information on West Fife is contained in either old survey memoirs or economic geology memoirs. Reference to these can be found in Craig (1991).

Geological Survey Maps

Fife is covered by the following geological survey maps published on a scale of either 1/50,000 or 1″/1 mile. They are available as 'Solid' maps displaying the pre-Quaternary geology or 'Drift' maps covering the Quaternary geology, i.e. the distribution of till, fluvio-glacial deposits, raised beaches, peat-bogs etc.

Sheets:

32W	Livingston
41	North Berwick
39E	Alloa
48E	Cupar
40	Kinross
49	Arbroath

Acknowledgement

Thanks are due to the Department of Geology of St Andrews University for preparation of the illustrations by G Sandeman.

3

The climate of Fife

NORMAN ELKINS

Being a coastal region between the Highlands and the Southern Uplands, the weather and climate in Fife are largely governed by wind direction, and air-masses are modified markedly by topography and by proximity to the North Sea.

The mountains reduce the strength of winds from directions between S through W to NNW, although the Forth/Clyde valleys tend to funnel the southwesterlies. From seaward directions, there is no protection from the wind's full force. However, the prevailing wind is from WSW, so that there is usually enough protection from the landmass to ensure that gales are not frequent. The strongest winds blow between September and February; the lightest from April to June. In light airflows in summer, E to SE sea breezes are common round the coast, but only rarely penetrate far inland.

The sheltered aspect of the region from directions between N and W ensures that when winds are from these directions the weather is relatively warmer in summer and cooler in winter compared to the west coast. Any winds coming from a seaward direction reverse this seasonal variation, as the sea temperature offshore does not reach its maximum of 14°C until August, while its minimum of 5°C occurs in March. Thus in midwinter cold winds are warmed by the sea, while in midsummer warm winds are cooled. Summer sea breezes therefore lower the temperature along the coast. In

general, average temperatures are lower over high ground such as the Lomonds and the uplands of N and SE Fife, with an average decrease of 0.7°C per 100 metres of altitude.

Its distance from large conurbations generally provides Fife with a clear atmosphere. However, winds off the sea are the most common mechanism bringing fog to the region. This is the haar of early and mid summer, which can be very persistent and unpleasant along the coasts and the outer firths of Tay and Forth, especially in SE Fife, but readily clears inland on a warm day. Fog is also common inland in winter, particularly in valleys where it forms overnight, usually clearing during the morning, although low cloud can give fog for much longer periods where it sits over the higher ground.

Rainfall is at its minimum in spring and also with wind directions between WNW and NE, reflecting the shelter aspect. The wettest months are in midwinter and late summer. Rain (or snow) falls from either shower clouds, or layer cloud formed by fronts (boundaries between air masses). Showery weather in winter is essentially a seaborne type. This means that when showers come from sheltered directions they tend to dissipate over the hills except when driven by strong winds. Showers in Fife thus approach mainly from the southwest, or from the North Sea. In summer, showers are more frequent from landward directions as they develop over the land and move downwind. A noticeable split in the winter tracks of showers occurs in east Fife, where those moving from the west tend to follow the shores of the rivers Tay and Forth, thus missing central areas of Fife. The heaviest showers are often accompanied by thunder storms. Although these occur throughout the year, they are most frequent between May and August, when on average less than two thunderstorms occur per month over the region. Very rarely, associated hail and rain can be heavy and damaging.

Rain from fronts is more frequent in winter than in summer, as the associated depressions take a more southerly track across the Atlantic, and therefore cross near or over Britain more frequently. Such depressions are also much more active in winter, producing more rain-bearing cloud.

The shelter afforded to lowland Fife from prevailing winds means that the area is relatively dry, with the average annual duration of rain and snow less than 7 per cent of the total possible.

Snow is most frequent in January and February, but varies considerably from winter to winter. Only in the severest winters does enough snow fall to make conditions hazardous. Again, the area most prone to snowfall is the higher ground in the west, where snow may lie for more than 20 days during an average winter, in contrast to the 11 days per winter on lower ground and even less on the coastal fringe.

Cloudiness is closely associated with the passage of fronts, and therefore is at its greatest in winter. In the east of Fife, a third of the possible total sunshine is recorded over the year. Understandably most is during the longer summer days, and in midwinter

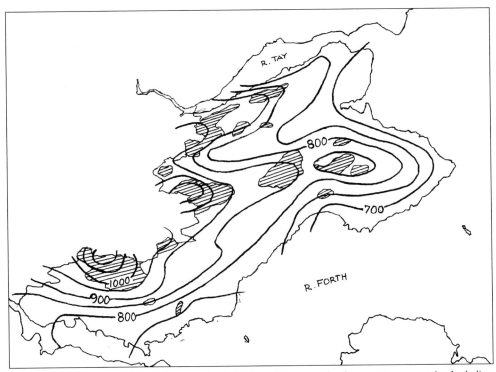

The distribution of rainfall in Fife: annual rainfall in millimetres (land over 200 metres is shaded).

1. Strathmiglo and the Howe of Fife from East Lomond: a scatter of seminatural habitats in a sea of arable farmland. (*Photo: R. M. Cormack.*)

2.. Fife has a varied coastline: the south coast at Earlsferry. (*Photo: R. M. Cormack*)

3. Columnar-jointed basalt on the Kinghorn shore (Lower Carboniferous). The columns, about 30–40 cm across, are ideally hexagonal in section and are perpendicular to the top and bottom of the lava flow. (*Photo: R. MacGregor*)

4. The Saddleback Anticline, Kinkell Braes, near St Andrews. Carboniferous sandstones dip at 30–40° to the SE and NW off the arch-shaped anticline formed during the end-Carboniferous earth movements. (*Photo: R. MacGregor*)

nearly half the days have no sunshine at all. Higher ground has a greater frequency of cloud, while low ground to the lee of hills tends to experience less.

Climate change

Global warming and associated climatic changes are topical subjects. However, there is no evidence that over a tiny area such as Fife any significant change in climate has occurred in recent years other than that naturally expected. Over the centuries there have been major fluctuations in climate which have affected the region, occurring long before man's activities had any influence over the atmosphere.

We know that over the past 1000 years deteriorating climate had profound social effects in the 14th and 15th centuries, when famines in Scotland were almost regular. Further cold and wet periods in the 18th century caused permanent snows on the Cairngorms, and crop failures on lower ground. In the past century, fluctuations have been much smaller, although in living memory we have seen, in Fife, cold and/or snowy winters between 1940 and 1970, and again from 1977 to 1987. In a few of these winters, snow fell as early as November and as late as March, but this is insignificant compared to the late 18th century when notable snows frequently fell between October and May. Warm winters in Fife occurred in the mid 1930s, early 1970s and the 1990s, but have not become significantly more frequent with time.

Summers in Fife have become drier over the past 70 years, with the driest periods being from 1967 to 1984, and again from 1993 to 1997. Indeed, the summers of 1994 and 1995 were the 5th and 3rd driest respectively in 73 years at Leuchars where the average summer rainfall over the 30-year period 1966–1995 was a full 25% lower than that of the previous 30 years. The wettest, and coolest, summers occurred in the late 1920s and the 1930s, and also in the late 1950s and early 1960s.

Spring is the time of growth of plants and invertebrates, with wet and cold seasons having repercussions across the wildlife spectrum. There is no clear pattern of significant change over the last century, although there was a tendency towards warmer springs in mid century, especially in the 1940s, which lasted until the mid 1960s when a cooler, wetter period occurred. The 1950s was also a drier decade than normal. In the past three decades, most dry springs have been followed by dry summers.

For both humans and wildlife, therefore, the climate of Fife is a benign one in which to live, with few extremes, and certainly few major changes over the last century. However, short-term fluctuations in the weather influence one group of organisms to a substantial degree: migrant birds.

Migration weather

Over the past three decades, changes have occurred in spring and autumn weather patterns which influence the arrival of migratory birds from Europe. In spring over the North Sea region, Aprils have become wetter on the prevailing SW winds. May has been the opposite, becoming drier and accompanied by an increase in winds with an easterly component. In autumn, little change has occurred in September, but October has seen more unsettled weather. This time however it has been accompanied by a weakening of the prevailing winds and more frequent winds from easterly directions. This pattern increases the probability of falls of migrant birds in coastal regions, although other factors, such as population fluctuations, are also significant.

Bird migration is extremely complex but, in terms of weather, can be explained fairly simply (Elkins, 1988). Those species that migrate do so to avoid seasonal food scarcity in a region which, in the breeding season, affords rich food supplies for both them and their offspring. In mid and high latitudes, this scarcity occurs in winter due to low temperatures and/or snow and ice cover. Birds use various means to navigate in autumn to their winter quarters, and in spring on their return. All species have an innate sense of time, and longer distance migrants base their navigation on the earth's magnetic field, which they use to obtain bearings from the sun and star patterns. This implies that migration must take place under skies at least partly free of cloud. Suitable winds are also necessary, either light (to avoid drifting from their chosen track) or, if strong, blowing in the correct direction for migration. Strong tail winds reduce flight times and minimize expenditure of energy. Good visibility is also a prerequisite for those migrants that use visual cues such as coastlines, river valleys and mountain ranges.

Strong head- or cross-winds, thick cloud, rain and snow, and poor visibility all serve to hinder rapid passage, and add to the other hazards faced by migrants. Ideal migration weather varies according to species, but for most birds settled weather is most favourable. Depressions and their associated fronts delay migration or, if the birds are already on passage, ground them or drift them off course. Under these conditions, falls of migrants are recorded, particularly if they have encountered adverse weather over the sea and are drifted onto adjacent coasts. Here they will await clearing weather to continue migration.

In Fife, autumn migrants arrive from northerly or easterly directions, while spring migrants approach from between south and east. Normal migration over or into Fife is undertaken by many species from northern Europe and Iceland, e.g. waders, ducks, geese, fieldfares, redwings and wheatears. They prefer fine weather and following winds in order to assist passage over the Atlantic or the North Sea. Many also move SSW in autumn across the North Sea to more distant, even subtropical regions, for example warblers and flycatchers, but the onset of poor weather and strong E–SE winds drifts them west, making landfall on headlands such as Fife Ness and the Isle of May. These birds may also include rare wanderers from as far east as Siberia, such as yellow-browed and Pallas's warblers. It must be stressed that such 'falls' represent only a tiny fraction of the whole migratory population of any one species, with the greater part making a successful journey. Indeed, most autumn falls consist of inexperienced birds of the year.

In spring birds moving north over western Europe are subject to the same delaying weather conditions as in autumn, but falls are usually smaller. Summer visitors to Fife may vary a little in their time of arrival, especially those that are normally early, like the willow warblers, since the later arrivals, such as swifts and spotted flycatchers, encounter weather that is becoming progressively more settled.

Movements are apparent at other times of the year, especially in winter when birds are driven from wintering grounds by severe cold. These include ducks and grebes from the seas around southern Scandinavia, and the departure from Fife of snow-sensitive birds such as lapwings and golden plovers.

Unlike most wildlife, migrant birds found in Fife are therefore subject to atmospheric disturbance well outside the region, and many can be considered as only a peripheral part of the nature of Fife.

Further reading

Elkins, N (1988). *Weather and bird behaviour,* 2nd ed. Poyser, Calton.

Some climatological statistics for Leuchars, 1961–1990

Mean annual temperature	8.3°C
Mean daily maximum in warmest month (July)	18.5°C
Mean daily minimum in coldest month (February)	0.1°C
Maximum temperature recorded (in August)	30.8°C
Minimum temperature recorded (in January)	−14.5°C
Mean annual number of nights with air frost	64
Mean annual rainfall	654 mm
Mean monthly rainfall in wettest month (January)	66 mm
Mean monthly rainfall in driest month (April)	41 mm
Wettest day on record (in August)	62.5 mm
Mean monthly sunshine in sunniest month (June)	190 hrs
Mean monthly sunshine in least sunny month (Dec.)	50 hrs
Mean annual wind speed	19 kph
Mean wind speed in windiest month (January)	22 kph
Maximum gust recorded (in January)	170 kph
Mean annual number of days with gale	8.2

(Statistics kindly provided by the Meteorological Office, Leuchars)

4

Landscape and history

GRAEME WHITTINGTON AND CHRIS SMOUT

By some 13,000 years ago, the final waning of the ice sheet that had earlier covered the whole of Scotland had left Fife with a naked landscape. Using subfossil pollen, it is possible to trace the evolution of the vegetation cover that eventually clothed that nakedness. Although local variations in plant species occurred, depending upon aspect, altitude and different soil development, the earliest vegetation was dominated by herbaceous plants such as grasses, sedges, mugwort, dockens, often accompanied by dwarf willow. Over the next three thousand years, the climate oscillated between warmer and colder periods as the general amelioration of temperature, following the withdrawal of the ice, continued.

In the warmer periods, when July maximum temperatures could reach 16–17°C, tree birch and juniper added variety to the otherwise open landscape, but during the colder phases, tree birch was replaced by the dwarf species, juniper declined almost totally and herbaceous species dominated once more. The last really cold phase occurred between about 11,000 and 10,200 years before the present (BP). At this time glaciers reappeared in some areas of the Highlands. Although this did not occur in Fife, temperatures there were severely depressed with July maxima averaging about 10°C. As a result tree cover disappeared and the only shrubs would be the dwarf varieties of birch and willow. The higher areas would have

resembled the areas of the world that today are classed as tundra.

This cold period lasted nearly one thousand years. From about 10,200 BP temperatures increased rapidly, although minor oscillations still occurred, and the landscape began to take on an entirely different appearance. A start was made to the establishing of a complete woodland cover in Fife (Figure, p. 25). Birch was the pioneer coloniser and had been followed by hazel as a major competitor as early as 9000 BP. Temperatures continued to rise and this allowed elm (by 8500 BP) and oak (by 7880 BP) to supplement hazel and establish a mixed woodland. Even the higher hills, today bearing hardly any trees, were wooded; the Lomond Hills, for example, showing a cover of hazel and birch. This woodland was to survive until about 5000 BP, although it is possible that there may have been some minor interference with it by Mesolithic people. They certainly lived in Fife, as the habitation site at Morton, near Tayport, indicates. There is much debate over the activities, numbers and effects on the landscape of Mesolithic people who provided the population from about 8000 BP.

As a part of north-west Europe, Fife experienced a phenomenon that affected the whole of that area around 5000 BP and about which there is considerable controversy. At that time, evidence from sub-fossil pollen indicates that there was a major interference

A pollen diagram of selected taxa from a sediment core taken from Black Loch, near Lindores, NW Fife. Virtually the whole time period covered by the diagram is dominated by trees. The *Alnus* (alder) would have been local to the loch side, with the main woodland cover provided by *Ulmus* (elm), *Quercus* (oak) and *Corylus* (hazel). The base of the diagram is dated about 9000 BP. At *c.*5000 BP comes the first elm decline, followed by periods of woodland removal (agricultural clearance) and woodland regeneration (agricultural abandonment).

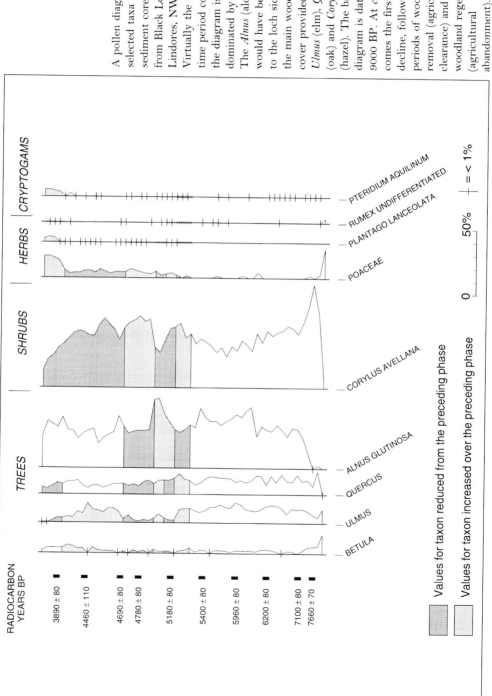

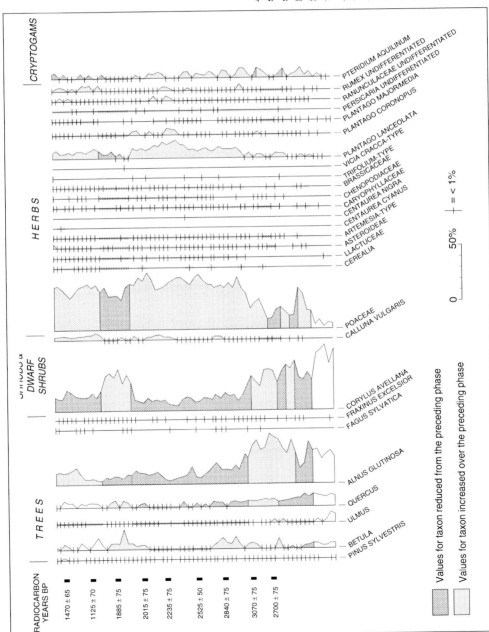

A pollen diagram of selected taxa from a second sediment core from Black Loch, but for a later time period than the last. Alternating periods of woodland clearance and regeneration are again apparent. From *c. 3000* BP–1900 BP, clearance dominates and *Plantago lanceolata* (ribwort plantain) becomes very prominent along with the pollen of cereals and weeds of cultivation.

A pollen diagram of selected taxa from the same sediment core as before covering the first 1500 years of the Christian era. The woodland is greatly reduced but becomes re-established during the Roman period. After that the landscape becomes devoted increasingly to agriculture. Cereal growing is consistently present; weeds especially of the dandelion and corn marigold family are very prominent. The appearance of *Cannabis sativa* (hemp) at *c*. 1050 until *c*. 1300 AD is intriguing; it was probably grown for its fibre, used for the making of such items as ropes, sacks and sailcloth.

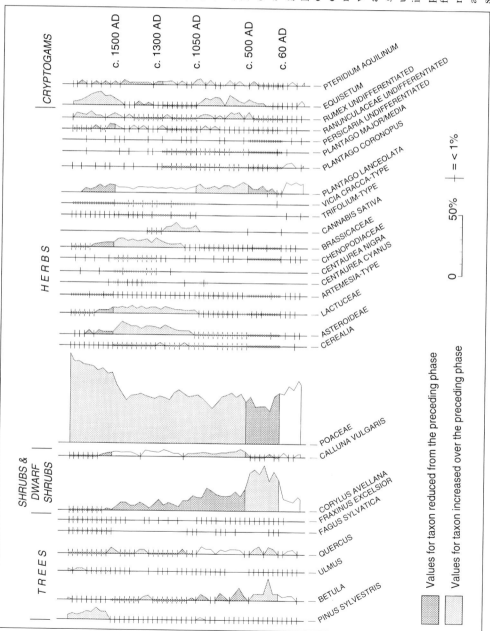

with the elm component of the woodland (p. 25). There are several possible explanations for this. For some, it could be laid at the door of a climatic shift which prevented the elms from flowering; there is, however, little supporting evidence for this theory. More tenable suggestions are that there was an outbreak of disease, akin to the Dutch elm disease of recent times, or that the activities of humans were responsible. The pollen record shows that at the time when the elm decline began other alterations to the vegetation were occurring. Plantain became a consistent and important component, registering as it does the existence of open ground, while the appearance of pollen derived from cereals indicates a fundamental change in the use of the land.

It would seem, therefore, that the elm decline has an association with the development of arable farming by Neolithic people. As a result, it has been suggested that these farmers, recognizing that the elm favoured the better soils, cleared these trees so as to grow their crops, while another suggestion is that they pollarded elms to provide cattle fodder, which would have severely reduced the trees' capacity to flower and liberate pollen. Neither of these suggestions, however, denies the possible influence of disease. The opening up of the woodland, by whatever means, might have allowed a greater degree of access by the beetle responsible for spreading the fungus that causes the disease.

This decline in elm appears to mark the beginning of the removal of Fife's tree cover. It was a long-drawn-out process, marked by different phases of human activity. The evidence suggests that the farmers of the earlier prehistoric periods were only partly sedentary. They seemed to have cultivated the land until such times as soil fertility was reduced; they then moved to another area.

The diagrams on pp. 25 and 26 show the effects this would have had on the landscape. A variable mosaic of trees and open areas would have developed as a result of woodland clearance and woodland regeneration. Over time the periods during which the latter took place became shorter as population grew and pressure on agricultural land became greater. As a result, probably even before the Romans arrived in Scotland, the landscape of Fife would have been as open as it is today. The scene to greet the eye would have been some scattered woodland, fields of barley, pasturing cattle and small groups of circular dwellings.

For some as yet unknown reason, but probably the result of punitive attacks, this picture was to change considerably. In the later phase of the Roman involvement in Scotland, during the 4th century AD, the fossil pollen record shows a strong regeneration of the tree cover and the disappearance of any evidence of arable farming (p. 27). This is a condition that appears to have lasted for about one hundred years and carries the story of the development of Fife's landscape into the period generally known as the Dark Ages.

It was during this time that the Pictish people developed their culture and it has left several features in Fife that help in the understanding of the landscape of that time. Evidence for this comes particularly from place-names because they incorporate terms that precede the speaking of Gaelic on its introduction by the colonising Scots from Ireland. The clearance of woodland has already been noted and that is corroborated by the general lack of place-names that contain a term referring to trees. Such names as there are, for example those including the element *pert* (a copse), indicate only scattered occurrences. What is more important is the place-name element *pit* which gives an

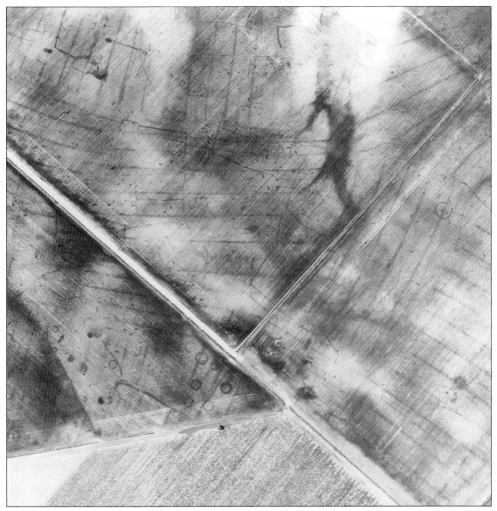

Cropmarks at Leuchars. The lines under the growing corn represent prehistoric hut circles and the rigs of medieval field systems; a vanished landscape comes to light under modern prairie farming. (*Crown copyright: reproduced by kind permission of the Royal Commission on the Ancient and Historical Monuments of Scotland, from the National Monument Record*)

indication of settlement; it can be found across Fife (Figure, p. 30) and indicates a land share. The interesting thing about this place-name element is that it frequently occurs in groups, as for example near Dunfermline and St Andrews and is also found preferentially on the best soils for arable farming and where natural soil drainage was best achieved. The known distribution of Pictish symbol stones and the impressive

tower at Abernethy, where there is a further cluster of *pit* place-names, imply the development of a sophisticated society which must have had a successful economic base that would have been derived from farming. Indeed the fossil pollen record indicates that the landscape was one of farming communities for whom the growing of cereals was very important (p. 27).

By the time the Scots infiltrated Fife in

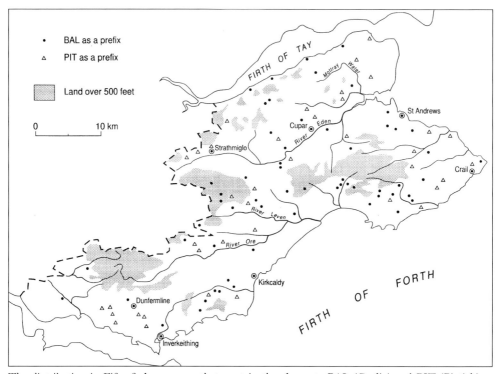

The distribution in Fife of place-names that contain the elements BAL (Gaelic) and PIT (Pictish).

the 9th century and Gaelic superseded the Pictish language, the landscape would most probably have embraced proto-urban settlements, such as the forerunners of St Andrews and Dunfermline, and widespread clusters of houses occupied by farming communities. The development of this settlement pattern continued and some knowledge of its distribution can be gained from the mapping of place-names that contain the element *bal* (see map). This is familiar in Irish place-names where it takes the form *Bally* and it indicated a small agricultural community. An examination of an Ordnance Survey map for Fife shows how frequent such place-names are.

Until the 12th century, there were no settlements that could be considered urban. These did not make an appearance until some locations on the coast received prominence and achieved growth as the result

of royal or ecclesiastical patronage. The earliest of these were where market places or religious foundations were established, bringing into existence such centres as St Andrews, replacing the earlier religious centre of Kinrimund with a planned secular area and a large ecclesiastical precinct, Dunfermline with its royal residence and Inverkeithing with its strategic location on the Firth of Forth.

The replacement of the established religion, which had its origins in Ireland, by one that came through England led to the establishment of monastic centres not only in Dunfermline, Culross and Pittenweem but also in the rural zone, as at Balmerino and Lindores. This resulted in a new influence being brought into the countryside. The monastic orders were provided with land grants which were added to over time by further bequests. In these areas they changed existing agrarian practices by de-manding such improvements as the weeding of crops, the drainage of land and the grow-ing of a variety of crops; non-compliance with these rules led to the imposition of fines. The result of these farming improve-ments was to create contrasting patterns of land-use in the landscape.

On farms in secular ownership farming was strongly compartmentalised. The land nearest the settlement was manured ann-ually with the dung accumulated in the byres over the winter, kept continuously in culti-vation and produced crops of oats and bere (a type of barley). On the outer perimeter of this so-called inbye land, oats were also cul-tivated in patches; these only received the dung of animals penned there during the night. A zone of moorland or rough pasture for the cattle completed the agricultural landscape. It took on a very distinctive ap-pearance because the cultivated land, especially in those areas where the soils were developed on clay, was ploughed into ridges with dividing furrows, often as deep as a metre or more below the crests of the ridges. These provided the only drainage. In addi-tion weeds were rampant, especially corn marigold (*guld* or *gool*).

There would also have been a further con-trast between the more easily worked sandy lands fringing the coast and those of the upland areas; a feature allegedly providing part of the reason Fife was described as 'a beggar's mantle fringed with gold'. On the secular land, the tenurial system was com-plex. Farming was carried out on strips (rigs) in unenclosed fields so that the whole landscape was open. Adjacent strips were cultivated by different land-holders and as more ground was taken into cultivation, farmers could be cultivating strips scattered throughout the settlement's territory. This was inefficient in the use of cultivators' time and frequently led to disputes over bound-aries and access.

As the population grew and further incre-ments were made to the cropped land, this situation worsened. To combat the problem replanning and restructuring of the land-holding units took place with the result that, where once there had been a single unit with one group of houses, two or three distinct and separate farm steadings came into exist-ence. Today this event is still commemorated in the landscape by the existence of place-names, mainly of farms, that are only distin-guished by such prefixes as easter and wester.

By the middle of the 16th century and throughout the 17th, Fife was developing a more pronounced market economy, al-though commercial prosperity was mainly confined to the coastal areas. Coal was being mined, crafts were expanding in the burghs and the development of commercial fishing led to the appearance of fishing quarters in the towns and the creation of salt pans. These activities and the relative landward isolation of Fife from the rest of Scotland placed a great emphasis on the shipping trade, especially across the North Sea. Thus the towns became export–import centres. They also caused a further contrast in the Fife landscape to come into existence. The burghs had substantial stone buildings, es-pecially to be found in the tolbooth (town house) and in the merchants' houses around the market places. Many buildings were of two storeys. In the rural area stone building was rare, with lime mortar largely unused, and the houses could quite accurately be described as hovels. They were thatched and ceilingless, the walls were frequently of turf or clay, dirt floors were normal, there were no chimneys and interior lighting was pro-vided by small glassless apertures which may also have had shutters. Such houses could be gathered around a church (the kirkton) or a mill (the milton), providing a rudimentary village, but more often were in clusters without even these services.

The prosperity of Fife at this period ebbed and flowed with the incidence of war, flourishing in the peaceful reign of James VI, suffering in the disturbances of the civil war and plague under Charles I, and settling at a lower ebb in the second half of the 17th century. It should not be imagined, however, that the Fifers were particularly poor or ill-provided with the necessities of life. The wind-swept, low-yielding farms provided ample oatmeal for a healthy, if monotonous diet, supplemented with bere (barley) and kale for the broth, and wheat and mutton for a treat. The sea-facing towns imported Norwegian wood if the meagre local timber supplies were inadequate, Swedish iron for nails and tools, and Polish flax for the linen weavers. The sea provided fish and salt, and the land itself, peat, turf and coal. Until the middle of the 17th century the alteration of economic experience between generations was not very large, but the landscape provided a strong framework for sufficiency.

In the three and a half centuries since 1650, however, the pace of environmental change has been enormous, accelerating with every generation to a degree that would have astounded previous ages. There was, firstly, a fundamental change in attitudes. Nature, once seen as providing a given and fixed environment into which people fitted themselves as best they could, was increasingly regarded as imperfect, needing to be understood, yet providing a challenge and an opportunity for improvement. One of the earliest in Scotland to express the new attitudes was Sir Robert Sibbald, naturalist, geographer and historian, writing the first systematic account of Fife and Kinross in 1710. 'It will not be accounted an unreasonable digression' he

wrote, half apologetically, 'to give some account of the rise of the moors, mosses and bogs, and how they may be improved to a better value.' Already, he said, the moors and heaths of mid-Fife and the mosses of the west were beginning to be 'improved to good arable or meadow ground', and bog might further be 'converted to useful and profitable ground by draining' or by 'burning it in a drouthy and dry summer'.

The extent of land that was once under heath and bog can be gauged from John Adair's manuscript maps of east Fife from 1684, or from the frequency of place-names such as 'Priormuir', 'Kingsmuir' and 'Mossend'. Lowland heaths and moors have now become rare in Fife, and the peat bogs are under increasing pressure even in the west where they have always been most plentiful. Their decline was, however, at first quite gradual from Sibbald's day. Drainage was difficult until James Smith of Deanston in Stirlingshire invented the mole plough around 1830, although one of Fife's biggest lochs, at Rossie, had been successfully emptied by a canal cut around the middle of the 18th century. The rushes and scrub of Rossie Bog represent a small fraction from its deepest part.

Even as late as 1945 subsoil ploughs could not cope with rocky hillsides; the possibility of pushing conifer crops up the hill has only come with heavy machinery since the Second World War. In the last ten years the farmer's problem has not been water-logged land but the reverse; for example, land in the Tentsmuir area that flooded at every winter storm now suffers from dry topsoil blow in spring, and a need to irrigate in summer. The consequent drop in the water table has been severe.

Drainage was only one aspect of the basic changes in agricultural practice that began in the late 17th and 18th centuries. No less

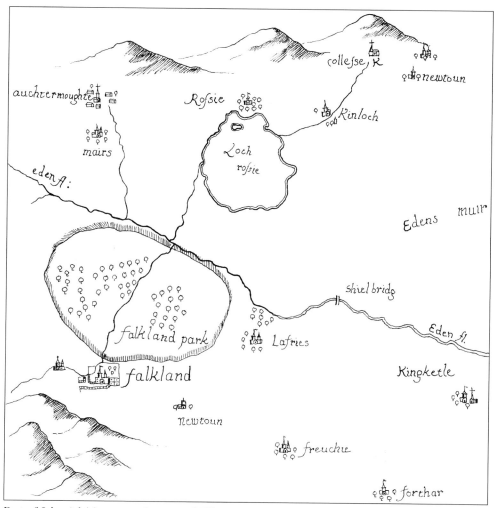

Part of John Adair's manuscript map of Fife, 1684, redrawn. This shows two important features, now disappeared; Falkland Park with its wood of oaks and alders, and Loch Rossie, now reduced to damp grassland and carr. (*From original in the National Library of Scotland.*)

fundamental was the gradual change of the lowland parts of Fife from an open countryside of rig and baulk to an enclosed one of field and dyke. It is possible that in the upland parts fields defined by low dykes of earth and stone, strong enough to prevent the straying of cattle herded by children, had long been the norm, and formal enclosures of a sort round the big houses can also be seen here and there on Adair's map (1684), as around Thirdpart between Anstruther and Crail. The full process of enclosure by

hedge or stone was not, however, completed much before the 1840s. In some places the new patterns barely existed for a century before beginning to be reversed as farmers rooted out hedges, felled hedgerow trees and removed dykes in order to enlarge the fields to accommodate modern agricultural machinery, thus restoring the countryside to something of its ancient treeless and windswept character; but in other places where the cultivation of grain is less important, drystane dykes, hawthorn hedges and lines of sycamore, ash and beech still define the original enclosed fields of the great change.

Similarly, the old farmhouses and steadings were transformed as pantile and slate replaced thatch, and the old settlements where two or more tenants and their cottars might share a joint farm became reduced to single farms with a big house and a row of workers' cottages. So rapid was the increase in the farmers' prosperity between the end of the 18th century and the end of the 19th that some farmhouses might be rebuilt twice within that period, and the ultimate be a great Victorian farm with baronial gables and tall rooms, and with a massive suite of outbuildings incorporating hexagonal horse-mills or even the high chimney of a steam-driven mill.

Around the steadings, it became general to plant a small wood, often of sycamore and elm, that would serve both to break the force of the winds and to provide timber for use about the farm. Such copses were important in a county where the natural woods had long been restricted to a few on poor soils and the stream-sides of the 'dens', but those old woods, too, were often carefully coppiced and managed, as a 17th-century contract relating to the ancient Big Wood of Saline demonstrates. Much more ambitious, of course, were the plantings for profit and ornament around the policies of the gentry and nobility, such as Balcaskie, Balcarres and Cambo in the East Neuk, or at Hill of Tarvit near Cupar, generally incorporating beeches and oak as well as sycamore and elm, and, in modern times, supplemented with extensive estate plantations of larch and spruce. The extensive plantations of Scots pine near Ladybank originated early in the 18th century in the forestry schemes of the Earls of Leven. The dark regiments of coniferous monoculture associated with the Forestry Commission and commercial forestry companies, however, occupy mainly the poor lands of Tentsmuir and the high boggy soils of central and west Fife: they are 20th century developments, but taken with the hardwood planting of the 18th and 19th centuries represent a substantial increase in woodland cover since the days of Sir Robert Sibbald.

The use of beech in these replenishments of Fife's woodland cover raises an interesting feature. The status of beech in Britain has been much disputed and it is generally thought that it did not appear in Scotland until well into the historic period. There are problems with this idea in that beech pollen is found in Scotland as early as the Mesolithic period and with increasing frequency thereafter, as the pollen diagrams (pp. 26, 27) show. This has usually been explained in terms of transport by wind from distant stands of beech, but two factors appear to upset this suggestion. Firstly, beech is a very low and often intermittent producer of pollen, and, secondly, its pollen grains are 'heavy' and not easily taken into the atmospheric circulation.

The impact of the new systems of farming and forestry upon wildlife was ultimately very substantial. Most dramatically, the afforestation of the wide, sandy heathlands of Tentsmuir following the First World War completely altered their botanical and ornithological character, and when the surviving, unforested portion around Earlshall dried out in the 1970s as a result of a falling water table, the remaining interest for breeding wildfowl, waders and ducks evaporated as well. The designation in the 1950s of two National Nature Reserves on the fringes has, in the view of many, largely failed to prevent the loss of interest: Tentsmuir features a lot in this book, but it is a ghost of its former self.

Less obvious but more impelling has been the change in the wider countryside brought about by the use of chemicals, particularly in the last fifty years. In the 18th and 19th centuries more nitrogen and phosphates certainly went into the land than before, but these inputs were achieved by, for example, growing clover or using the manures of animals overwintered on turnips; after 1840 these methods were supplemented by using imported guano from Peru, or nitrates and phosphates from Chile. Ploughing was by horse almost everywhere until 1940 or later, and the first agricultural machines like reapers and binders were small. The impact of these practices on the environment was inconsiderable. Weeds like corn marigold and poppies continued to make the fields colourful in summer, corncrakes and lapwings bred freely in the fields, barn owls were familiar round the steadings feeding on the abundance of rats and mice.

The intensification of farming that followed the Second World War was accompanied by an explosion in the use of artificial fertilisers and the creation of a range of powerful chemical pesticides and herbicides which greatly increased the ability of farmers to produce food. Some of the results were intended: the weeds of cultivation became rare unless they were (like the field pansy) unusually resistant to chemicals; some, like the corncockle and cornflower, disappeared from the landscape. Other results were incidental and aroused regret in some but no action, like the disappearance of the corncrake, the growing rarity of the barn owl and the dwindling flocks of finches and larks or the falling game bags of partridges and hares.

A few consequences were so extreme that action was taken: the discovery of the impact of DDT residues on the food chain in the 1950s led to the banning of a range of pesticides, and the plummeting numbers of raptors like peregrines and sparrowhawks began to recover again, in Fife as elsewhere in the UK. Similarly, in the 1990s part of the Howe of Fife has become so over-supplied with nitrates that questions have been asked about the possible impact on human health; widespread overuse of nitrates has caused many lochs, ponds and streams to suffer from over-enrichment – 'eutrophication' – and some to lose much of their natural life.

Not all the changes in landscape and farming, however, have been to the detriment of wildlife. Wild geese positively gained from the return to huge fields, the coming of profligate spills of grain from the combine-harvested fields and the early flush of nitrogen-enriched grass. The spectacular flocks of pinkfoot and greylag geese that now come to Fife from Iceland in winter are recent phenomena, totally unknown two centuries back and present only on a much smaller scale fifty years ago.

The industrial and commercial development of Fife over the past three centuries has also had a very substantial effect on the natural environment. The beginnings were modest enough; the growth in the 16th and 17th centuries of small-scale coal mining, salt panning and herring fishing for export had few impacts on the environment that can be detected at this distance in time. Far more dramatic were the late-18th century increases in textile manufacture and the Victorian surge in deep mining, engineering and linoleum making, accompanied by a large increase in fishing consequent upon the coming of the deep-sea trawlers, which were largely steam-driven after 1900. The 20th century has seen much decline in the old staples but a rise of light industry and the service trades. The most abiding legacy of this kaleidoscopic economic change has been urbanisation: in 1755 barely one in eight of the population of 81,000 lived in communities of more than 3000, but, in 1995, 351,000 lived in Fife (a four-fold growth), three out of four living in communities of more than 3000. By 1995, the two biggest towns, Kirkcaldy and Dunfermline, together held more people than the whole of Fife in 1755.

The towns not only grew but in due course came to provide more space per inhabitant. Whereas medieval St Andrews and Dunfermline had been close-built yet near to the fields, and the Victorian boom towns

like Leven, Methil, Kirkcaldy and Kelty full of packed tenements and mean cottages, the 20th-century New Town of Glenrothes was planned with generous open green areas, and every town and village came to have council estates (with or without high-rise flats), private housing estates and older villas, all with recreation areas, amenity planting and private gardens. The urban landscapes became, indeed, an important new wildlife habitat, prowled by cats and foxes but also providing a refuge, for example, for butterflies on the

Signs of 19th-century industry in West Fife: Muirbeath Colliery. (*Crown Copyright: reproduced by kind permission of the Royal Commission on the Ancient and Historical Monuments of Scotland, from the National Monument Record*)

Frances Colliery, Dysart, in 1990. A 20th-century landscape of obsolete industry (the colliery waste to the left has been smoothed off prior to reclamation), housing estates, car lots, warehouses and grain farms. The only ground left of much wildlife interest is in the bottom left-hand corner. (*Crown Copyright: reproduced by kind permission of the Royal Commission on the Ancient and Historical Monuments of Scotland, from the National Monument Record*)

buddleias in summer, and for many hard-pressed birds in winter. The householders' red peanut bags feed the tits and sparrows, and the cotoneasters planted around the supermarket car parks feed the visiting wax-wings and thrushes. Such charitable acts towards wild creatures never occurred in Sibbald's day.

With towns and modern industry, how-ever, arrived the first problems of large-scale pollution. By the 1830s, rising population and lack of sanitation led to serious increases in water-borne diseases like typhoid, the new Asian cholera, and typhus, carried by lice in cramped home environments. The Victorian solution was to bring clean water to the towns from country reservoirs and sweep the sewage into the sea. Just how quick sani-tary reform was undertaken depended mainly on the structure and efficiency of local government. St Andrews acted relatively quickly and in doing so removed its picturesque but dirty fishertown in the interests of tourist trade and respectability, as much as of public health. Leven dragged its feet and suffered so badly in the final cholera epidemic of 1866 that it found itself the subject of an excoriating official report on its local council's ineptitude and complacency.

The new reservoirs reflected the size and wealth of the communities. Cameron Reservoir for St Andrews was quite large, but the artificial pools in the hinterland of the East Neuk burghs were tiny because even localities as conjoined as Anstruther Easter and Anstruther Wester could not initially agree to build a common resource. Nevertheless, the many artificial wetlands thus created from end to end of Fife went some way to compensate for those lost by earlier agricultural drainage, though their small-scale and ageing dams make it questionable how many can be retained into the 21st century.

From the towns themselves the sewage flowed untreated into the sea, carried either by pipe or by the rivers themselves, and the burden of the waters carried large quantities of coal washings and textile wastes as well as human ordure. Offshore, increasing numbers of sea ducks, especially scaup and goldeneye, fed at the grosser outfalls on the sea worms and molluscs that in turn fed on the sewage, though their numbers fell abruptly when in the late 20th century the outfalls began to be cleared up. River purification itself made great steps, especially between the 1880s and the 1950s, and no large stream in Fife today replicates the stinking, barren rivers of the industrial areas of one hundred years ago.

Other problems were posed by smoke pollution and the disposing of rubbish through land-fill. Air pollution appears to have restricted the distribution of many lichens in Fife over the past century and a half, as the prevailing winds drove the airborne detritus of industrial central Scotland north-eastwards over the region. Possibly the decline, and now the partial recovery, of the ringlet butterfly was also related to the heavier smoke pollution in the past. Even today, the tall chimneys of the power stations at Kincardine and Longannet are considered to be among the most damaging to local Sites of Special Scientific Interest of any in the country, while the volume of ash and clinker they produce has resulted in considerable land-claim west of Torry, at the expense of the natural mud-flats. In addition their ongoing demand for fuel threatens to devastate an ever-increasing area with opencast mining. 'Restoration' after such operations is, from the perspective of the natural world, often a cosmetic travesty.

Former sites of extractive industry, however, do not have to be devoid of wildlife. Some are among the best sites in the region, thanks either to the long healing processes of time or to inspired modern planning. In the former category, Kilconquhar Loch is a prime example, formed (like the Norfolk Broads) from ancient peat cutting; the pools and bogs at Moss Wood near Kirkcaldy, with their interesting dragonflies, were formed in a similar way. Two of the best Fife woods for their flora and invertebrate life, at Craighall Den and at Cults, occupy early coal and lime works; there are further examples at Torryburn. Some of the coppiced sycamores at Cults may be over 300 years old, the stem wood having once been used for kindling the limekilns. Inspired modern planning has more speedily given prime wetlands on the old coal-mining subsidence at Lochore Meadows, and in the former sand and gravel pits at Birnie Loch near Collessie, both immensely popular with the visiting public yet havens for breeding and wintering wildfowl.

The need for industrial society to dispose of solid waste that could neither be burned nor washed into the sea resulted in many unsightly 'tips' until, in very recent years, a policy of more careful covering and partial recycling has been followed. One consequence was an explosion, in the decades after 1960, in the number of gulls nesting on the Isle of May and frequenting the shores of the Firth of Forth; by scavenging on tips along with rats and crows they increased their ability to support large breeding numbers. Wasteful methods of fishing, throwing back much of the 'by- catch', has helped to keep their numbers up even after the land-fill dumps have come, in the last decade, to be more systematically covered.

The lessons of history are very simple. Ever since earliest times, everything that human beings have done has had an impression upon the natural environment of Fife, and as the centuries have progressed, this effect has become increasingly profound. The landscape gives shelter and sustenance to us all, but how we treat it through our economic and social behaviour determines the fortunes of all those creatures with which we are privileged to share it, and, ultimately, through our good or bad use, determines the fate of ourselves as well.

Further reading

Brooks, N P and Whittington, G (1977). Planning and growth in the medieval Scottish burgh: the example of St Andrews. *Transactions of the Institute of British Geographers*, NS2, pp 278–295.

Sibbald, R (1710). *The history ancient and modern of the Sheriffdoms of Fife and Kinross.* The easiest edition to find was edited anonymously and published in Cupar in 1803.

Sinclair, J (ed.) *The statistical account of Scotland (1791–1803).* By far the most convenient edition, which gathers together the parish accounts for Fife originally scattered in 21 volumes, is that edited by Grant, I R and Withrington, D J for EP Publishing, Wakefield. The volume for Fife is Vol.X by Cant, R G (1978).

The new statistical account of Fife, 1845. A re-survey fifty years later, parish by parish, of the original *Statistical Account.*

Whittington, G (1991). Place-names in North Fife. Nomina 1989–90, 13, pp 13–24.

Whittington, G and Edwards, K J (1990). The cultivation and utilisation of hemp in Scotland. *Scottish Geographical Magazine*, 106, pp 167–173.

Whittington, G and Jarvis, J (1987). Kilconquhar Loch: an historical and palynological investigation. *Proceedings of the Society of Antiquaries of Scotland*, 116, pp 413–428.

Whittington, G, Edwards, K J and Cundill, P R (1991). Late- and post-glacial vegetational change at Black Loch, Fife, eastern Scotland – a multiple core approach. *New Phytologist*, 118, pp 147–166.

Whittington, G, Edwards, K J and Cundill, P R (1991). Palaeoecological investigations of multiple elm declines at a site in North Fife, Scotland. *Journal of Biogeography*, 18, pp 71–87.

5

The landward coast: dunes, salt-marsh and cliffs

ROBERT M. M. CRAWFORD
(ANIMAL LIFE BY GORDON CORBET)

The Fife coast: a north–south meeting place

The Fife coast occupies a unique position, both as a refuge and a meeting place for plants of widely differing geographical distribution. In an age of intensive land management, urbanisation and road building there are few pathways left for the unimpeded migration of plants. Consequently, coastal regions with extensive areas of natural vegetation, such as occur in Fife, are vital for plant migration during periods of biological adjustment to climatic change. Scarcer still are places of refuge where natural communities can preserve their diversity against the unrelenting onslaught of disturbance, pollution and agricultural improvement.

In terms of biodiversity Fife is fortunate in its latitudinal position, as it is climatically capable of supporting plants at their northern limits of distribution as well as being the southerly limit of several arctic and subarctic coastal species. Examples of predominantly northern coastal species, at or near the southern limit of their geographical range, include Scots lovage (*Ligusticum scoticum*), which can be seen in many rock outcrops, particularly on raised beach platforms below the Kinkell Braes and on the West Braes at Crail (see map) as well as between the stones of the Bruce Embankment in St Andrews (pl. 12). The Baltic rush (*Juncus balticus*) has its most southern British locations in the dune slacks at Tentsmuir and St Andrews Links. Tentsmuir also has one of the most extensive populations in Britain of lymegrass (*Leymus arenarius*) which is predominantly an arctic/sub-arctic species although it does extend as far south as Normandy. Southern species approaching northern limits of their east coast distribution in Fife (some of these species extend further north on the west coast) include the seaside and common centaury (*Centaurium littorale, C.erythrea*), sea-wormwood (*Seriphidium maritimum*) (map, p. 42), maiden pink (*Dianthus deltoides*) and sea bindweed (*Calystegia soldanella*).

Coastal habitats in Fife

The Fife Peninsula is environmentally fortunate in having Europe's last major unpolluted water-way, the River Tay, on its north shore and the open Firth of Forth on its southern boundary. Between these two estuaries Fife is bounded by a mainly rocky coast interspersed with a number of extensive sandy bays and salt-marshes. Fife also has Britain's most varied and rapidly developing dune system at Tentsmuir Point

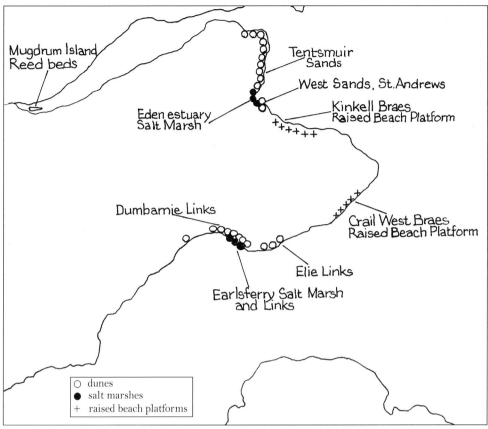

Distribution of some coastal habitats and locations referred to in the text.

National Nature Reserve. As the land rose after the melting of Pleistocene ice sheets, there was left around the Fife coast a series of distinct raised beaches of varying height. These raised beach platforms now lie to seaward of former coastal cliffs. In the vicinity of cliffs they are frequently boulder-strewn with many rocky outcrops. Such protection from being incorporated into fields or golf courses has preserved an extensive zone of raised beach platforms which serve as important species-rich refuges for coast-loving plants.

Fife also has a number of sites where woodland approaches the edge of the sea as where eroded valleys (dens) reach the shore. The seabrae woods between Balmerino and Newburgh stand out as one of the few places in Scotland sheltered enough for mature broad-leaved woods and associated ground flora to grow right down to the saltwater estuary (pl. 5). Comparable sites are the deep inlets of Devon and Cornwall such as the Dart, the Fal and the Fowey. The coasts of Fife therefore provide an excellent opportunity to explore a wide range of coastal habitats with dunes, slacks, raised beach platforms, coastal heaths, machair, salt-marshes, woods and cliffs.

The Fife coast is also a region of continual change. The constant movement of off-shore sand-bars has led to periods of both coastal erosion and accretion. This has contributed to the diversity of the vegetation by

Scottish distribution of sea wormwood (data from the Biological Records Centre).

Sea wormwood.

constantly creating new habitats and altering the degree of exposure to wind, salt spray and flooding. The current predicted rise in sea level of 5 cm per decade is likely to bring about significant changes in the ecology of the coastal communities. The low-lying shores around the Tay Estuary are considered to be particularly vulnerable (Boorman *et al.* 1989). Increased coastal erosion, with the threat of a significant forced retreat of the coastal dune systems, is to be expected and is already visible in certain areas.

However, such physical destruction may not necessarily lead to biological impoverishment as it will also create new opportunities for colonisation of pioneer coastal communities. Rising sea levels can facilitate the growth of salt-marshes, which will be of benefit to both plants and animals (especially birds). The dune systems however will be particularly liable to damage as they are threatened, not only by rising sea levels over which we have little control, but also from increasing drought-stress. Water tables are falling as more and more water is withdrawn from bore holes for irrigating the growing number of coastal golf courses suffering from drought during increasingly frequent dry summers.

Recreational use also has its obvious hazards for the survival of coastal vegetation, such as extensive trampling. However, more insidious and potentially more damaging is the current desire by local authorities for clean beaches which gain European approval certificates. The removal of litter, including washed-up seaweed, prevents dune renewal by removing the organic matter which is essential for the colonisation of fore-shore plant communities and the renewal of the sand dune systems as a whole. A striking example of sand dunes which have no possibility of regenerating due to weekly cleaning throughout the growing season can be seen in the West Sands at St Andrews (pl. 9).

The seaweed on the tide-line also provides the basis for a complex community of animals. The most abundant consumers of the decaying seaweed are the larvae of several species of flies along with amphipod crustaceans – 'sand-hoppers'. These are in turn preyed upon by spiders and beetles, many of which are found only in this habitat. Characteristic birds of the tide-line are pied wagtails, starlings and turnstones, all feeding on these invertebrates of the seaweed community.

Environmental protection depends on us all and it is the aim of this chapter, not just to highlight the natural riches of the Fife coast as it is today, but to examine the ecology of the coastal plants and the conditions necessary for their future survival. Too often irreplaceable habitats and their species are lost through a lack of understanding of ecological processes, even when well-intentioned efforts are being made for their preservation. An informed and caring public is our strongest defence in preserving the biodiversity and ecological well-being of our shores.

Dunes and their hinterland

Dune systems can be divided into those that are formed from acid, shell-deficient sand and those that develop on sand rich in sea shells. Fife is fortunate in having one of the finest examples of a rapidly growing acid sand dune system in the British Isles at Tentsmuir (map, p. 41). On shell-deficient dunes there is a marked change in vegetation from areas of high pH (i.e. alkaline) on the fore dunes to acid dunes, ultimately developing into dune heath in their hinterland. This declining pH gradient creates distinct habitat differences both in the dunes and their intervening depressions, commonly referred to as slacks, or in Scotland sometimes as winter lochs (see diagram). The marked differentiation between the zones in these acid dune systems creates distinct plant communities each with ecologically different species which add to the species richness of the area as a whole.

Biodiversity in sand dune systems
Biodiversity, as it is commonly assessed by ecologists, has two major components: *alpha diversity* which is the number of species in a specific area; and *beta diversity* which reflects differences in species composition between adjoining areas. Due to the varied nature of its hinterland Tentsmuir is particularly rich in having different habitats and therefore beta diversity is higher than in many other sand dune systems. The difference in type of biodiversity becomes apparent when shell-rich sand dune systems in south Fife are considered.

Where sand has a rich shell component there is no rapid fall in pH on moving inland as the shell fragments maintain a high pH, even when the sea salts have been removed

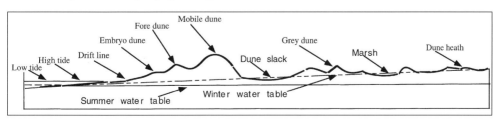

The sequence of plant communities across the dune system in the Tentsmuir National Nature Reserve.

by rainwater. The plant communities that develop on these shell sand dunes and slacks can be species-rich (high alpha diversity), but are more uniform than those on the shell-deficient sand dunes (low beta diversity), as there is no great change in species composition between the inland and shoreward plant communities. These calcium-rich sand dune systems support an un-differentiated but species-rich herb community, and usually erode to form flat, herb-rich plains sometimes referred to as machair (the Gaelic word for a low-lying plain; shell-rich dunes and pastures are a particular feature of the Western Isles). In Fife, and other east coast regions, these areas are sometimes referred to as links, but this term is also used generally for other areas of dunes and slacks, particularly where they have been developed into golf courses.

Differentiation of sand habitat into dunes and slacks must have shaped the development of golf when it was first introduced to Scotland. The first record of playing the game is at St Andrews in 1410. The vegetation of the flood-prone slacks (or winter lochs) dies back in winter and as the flooding also prevents the spread of the coarse tussock grasses from the dunes, this would have provided a natural fairway before the advent of mowing machines.

Acid sand dunes

Between the estuaries of the rivers Eden and Tay at Tentsmuir lies one of the most varied and undisturbed acid sand dune systems in the British Isles. The location of Tentsmuir, with the fortunate provision of a plentiful supply of off-shore sand, has produced a landscape that has been growing ever since the end of the last ice age. Present day rates of accretion at Tentsmuir Point, 7–14 metres per annum, are of the same order of magnitude as those that have operated in the past. The sand, being acidic, is rapidly depleted of mineral nutrients and there is an abrupt rise in acidity behind the unstable, mobile dune systems. This leads to a distinct zonation of vegetation with boundaries that run parallel to the coast line, as the salt-tolerant species of the seaward regions give way in succession to the communities of the fresh-water slacks, grey dunes (dominated by lichens), dune heath and fresh-water marshes (diagram p. 43). Interspersed between these communities are extensive areas of alder, birch and willow. The extensive coastal accretion, coupled with rapid development of diverse habitats, has created a wealth of sites for colonisation by an extensive flora and diverse invertebrate fauna.

The rapid change in plant communities across such a small area as the National Nature Reserve at Tentsmuir Point is all the more surprising, in that the entire biodiversity of the region is supported by the same acid sand-based soil. There are nevertheless physical and chemical differences in the soil which are related to changes in relief, distance from the sea and variation in water table levels. Moving landward, the maritime influence decreases, but the frequency of high water tables increases due to the obstruction of natural drainage channels by the accreting sand. The resulting cross-gradients of flooding stress, nutrient supply and maritime exposure are responsible for the wide diversity of habitats that have developed, despite the soil being a uniform shell-deficient sand across the whole Tentsmuir Reserve.

The floristic diversity of Tentsmuir does not exist just because it is an extensive dune and slack system. The range of environmental variation is greater moving landwards at this site than can be seen in most other Scottish coastal dune systems due to the presence of trees. Areas of woodland with birch and alder that intersperse the dunes and slacks contribute greatly to habitat diversity. Boundary zones between communities are the preferred habitat of many of our rarer species. At Tentsmuir a walk along the boundary between the flood-line alders that inhabit the edges of the slacks and the adjacent grey dunes on one side or slacks on the other can be rewarded with views of many of the rarer plant specialities of the area. One striking example at Tentsmuir is the coral-root orchid (*Corallorhiza trifida*, pl. 11). Thirty years ago Tentsmuir had the largest populations of this species in the British Isles but recently it has declined along with a number of other species that have become less common due to an unfortunate reduction in diversity resulting largely from problems in conservation management (Crawford, 1996).

In many dune areas the succession from sand dunes to dune heath ends with the formation of dune scrub. A typical coastal scrubland can be seen where the Kinshaldy burn enters the sea at Tentsmuir, with extensive stands of sea buckthorn (*Hippophae rhamnoides*) which in autumn produces a colourful display of orange berries.

Before afforestation Tentsmuir, then covering about 23 square kilometres of open land, was a major breeding ground for a variety of ground-nesting birds. Some of these were strictly coastal species like eider, shelduck and the terns: common, arctic and sandwich all bred in large numbers with fewer little and, sporadically, roseate terns. The marshes of Earlshall Moor, at the southern end of Tentsmuir, held a very large colony of black-headed gulls along with a variety of breeding duck – mallard, shoveler and teal. Breeding waders were also well represented, with ringed plover on the shore, redshank and snipe on the marshes,

and golden plover, lapwing, curlew and dunlin on the drier moors.

Of these, dunlin and golden plover ceased breeding in the 1930s, black-headed gulls in the 1970s and all the others have declined drastically. Besides the afforestation, other factors that have contributed to this decline are the lowering of the water-table and the increasing disturbance, especially through vehicle (and thereby dog) access to Kinshaldy Beach.

Some groups of invertebrates have been well recorded at Tentsmuir, especially at Tentsmuir Point Reserve. The diversity of plants is reflected in the diversity of herbivorous insects that are dependant upon them, with about 270 species of moths (all of course herbivorous) and about 140 species of bugs of which the majority are herbivores. Amongst the butterflies, the grayling, a grass-feeder, is abundant, although virtually absent from the rest of Fife. More widespread is the day-flying cinnabar moth whose yellow and black striped caterpillars are conspicuous on ragwort (pl. 7).

The abundance of predatory invertebrates is perhaps more surprising. A study of spiders at Tentsmuir Point recorded 143 species, a remarkable number considering that these are all predatory, presumably each with its own niche in terms of prey species, microhabitat, and diurnal and seasonal activity. Ground beetles, which are predominantly predatory, are also well represented, with about 50 species.

These and many other aspects of the history and ecology of Tentsmuir have been reviewed in greater detail in *Fragile environments: The use and management of Tentsmuir NNR, Fife* (Whittington 1996).

Calcareous sand dunes
On the southern side of Fife there are several areas near Elie and Earlsferry and in Largo

Bay (map, p. 41) where shell sand has come ashore and provided calcium-rich dunes. These have eroded with time to provide pasture which used to be rich in its diversity of herbaceous plants. These were east-coast examples of what is more commonly seen in the Western Isles and west coast of Scotland and referred to as machair. The botanical attraction of these areas is the wide range of flowering herbs that find a habitat in the broad uniform plains of the machair.

Sadly, much of the biodiversity of these coastal areas in south Fife has been lost through grazing improvement. Although these lands may not all have received direct applications of fertiliser, it is sufficient for cattle that have been previously fed on nutrient-rich herbage to be allowed on to the area to transport enough minerals to stimulate the growth of a few rapidly growing species to the eventual exclusion of the less competitive plants. Dumbarnie Links were once home to large populations of cowslips (*Primula veris*) but these have now largely

Cowslip

disappeared as the greater part of the links have become floristically monotonous areas of improved cattle grazing. Some parts of the links, nevertheless, still support a variety of species that are found in few or no other Fife sites, such as the frog orchid (*Coeloglossum viride*), various field and marsh orchids (*Dactylorhiza* spp.), field gentians (*Gentianella* spp.), variegated horsetail (*Equisetum variegatum*), bog pimpernel (*Anagallis tenella*) and lesser hawkbit (*Leontodon saxatilis*). Elsewhere, where grazing improvement has not taken place and where the links have not been subjected to frequent mowing, as in golf courses, there still remain areas of rough ground, as at the caravan site at Shell Bay, that provide viable habitats for cowslips and a number of other coastal herbaceous species.

These south-coast dune systems have always been much narrower than those at Tentsmuir and have never had the large number of breeding birds that were formerly found at Tentsmuir. The level of disturbance, both human and canine, has for long precluded the breeding of terns, and even ringed plovers, with their dispersed and secretive nesting habits, rarely succeed in hatching young and even more rarely succeed in fledging any.

Rabbits are very abundant on these dunes and must play an important part in maintaining the short sward of the dune slacks. Although initially introduced as confined domestic animals – there were royal warrens at Crail by 1264 – they must always have been difficult to contain.

The high calcium content of these sands favours invertebrates with calcareous shells or armour. Terrestrial snails are abundant, the most conspicuous being the ubiquitous brown-lipped banded snail (*Cepaea nemoralis*) and the smaller, more coarsely textured *Candidula intersecta*. On the dunes between

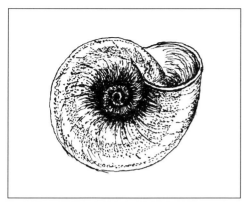

Helicella itala (x2).

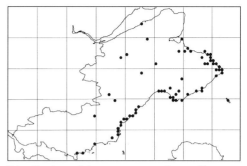

Distribution of the common garden snail, *Helix aspersa*; not so common inland in Fife but abundant on the coast.

Largo and St Monans a third conspicuous snail occurs. This is *Helicella itala*, with a rather flattened shell, a common species along the west and north coasts of Scotland but found nowhere else on the east coast.

Many millipedes are also dependent upon calcareous conditions. The large yellow-striped snake millipede *Ommatoiulus sabulosus* is abundant on the dunes along with several less conspicuous ones.

Salt-marshes

Salt-marshes differ from dune and slack systems in that they develop from the accretion of sediment in tidal areas where there is some degree of shelter from wave erosion. In Fife the best examples are to be found at the estuaries of the River Tay and the River Eden, but there are many smaller patches on the Forth shore, including some on the SWT reserve at Kilminning (west of Fife Ness), at the mouth of the Cocklemill Burn (east end of Largo Bay) and at the Torry Bay Local Nature Reserve in west Fife. The balance between accretion and erosion in these habitats is very delicate and changes in river course, exposure to waves and alterations in sea level all have a profound influence. On rapidly rising coastlines, there is little opportunity for salt-marsh development.

Falling coastlines, or rising sea levels, can allow marsh development provided the change in sea level is not excessive and does not exceed the capacity of the vegetation to consolidate silt and raise the level of the marsh. The sediments that can be anchored in salt-marshes vary from clay-rich muds to sandy gravels.

Particularly effective in raising the shore level in mud flats is the hybrid cord-grass (*Spartina anglica*), a cross between the European *S.maritima* and the American *S.alterniflora* that was first recorded in Southampton Water in 1878. The northern limit of cord-grasses in the northern hemisphere is 57° N and appears to be determined by frost sensitivity. There are only a few colonies of the hybrid cord-grass in Scotland, and the Fife colony, which was planted in the spring of 1948, has managed to establish only a fringe community in the Eden Estuary where it could do much to counteract falling shore levels and erosion to the nearby golf course. Unfortunately, this natural remedy for coastal erosion is being frustrated by the management plan for the Eden Estuary Local Nature Reserve, which actively discourages this species for fear that it might restrict the mud flats available as feeding grounds for wading birds. This fear seems groundless, as at this latitude this polyploid species, although fertile, does not at present reproduce by seed and spread is limited to vegetative propagation. The colony is still confined to a coastal fringe despite 50 years of establishment in the Estuary.

Biogeography of salt-marsh flowering plants
In the British Isles there is a marked distinction between the salt-marsh species of south-eastern regions and those of the north-west. It has been traditional to envisage a line from the Solway to just south of the Firth of Forth as an approximate demarcation of these two biogeographical zones for the distribution of the salt-tolerant (halophytic) flora. Although Fife lies just to the north of this boundary it does contain a number of species that have a predominantly south-eastern distribution. Particularly characteristic of the southern intrusion is sea-wormwood (*Seriphidium maritimum* – p. 42) which reaches its northern British limit in Fife. Thus, the salt-marshes of Fife are of particular interest as they are floristically rich meeting places for species of differing geographical distribution.

Salt-marsh vegetation zonation
Locally, the species composition of salt-marshes is influenced mainly by variations in salinity and inundation. Twice a day, and depending on the season and the lunar cycle, marshes are flooded to varying degrees by salt water. In the lower regions of the marshes nearest to the sea the salinity is rarely greater than that of sea water (3.4%). Higher up the marsh, and particularly as the growing season progresses, the potential for salt-stress increases as evaporation makes the rooting region of the soil progressively more saline. Consequently, there are differences in salt-tolerance, not just between species, but between populations within

species. In red fescue (*Festuca rubra*) and common salt-marsh grass (*Puccinellia maritima*) the up-marsh populations are more tolerant of salt than those that grow lower down the marsh.

Salt-marshes that are bordered by rivers as they enter the sea can be less salt due to flushing by river water. Thus, along the south bank of the River Tay there are extensive reed-beds at Mugdrum Island which extend in patches seawards as far as Balmerino. The maximum concentration of salt that can be tolerated by the common reed is 1 per cent. Similarly, due to the presence of the River Tay, a reduction in coastal salinity allows the development of significant stands of the club-rushes (*Schoenoplectus tabernaemontani* and *Bolboschoenus maritimus*) on the salt-marsh on the Balmerino shore and at Tayport. Frequent inundation encourages these flood-tolerant species, which are not only able to aerate their roots by downward diffusion of oxygen from the shoots, but also have the ability to withstand depletion of oxygen when they are buried for long periods in un-aerated mud. Both these species are also remarkable not just for being tolerant of flooding but for being able to grow new shoots in total absence of oxygen, which is a very rare property in flowering plants.

Salt-marshes provide an excellent opportunity to observe different strategies adopted by plants to limit their exposure to salt. In succulent species such as the sea-sandwort (*Honckenya peploides*) and the sea-milkwort (*Glaux maritima*) the leaves increase in succulence as the growing season progresses and thus effectively dilute the concentration of salt to which their tissues are exposed. In thrift (*Armeria maritima*) and orache (*Atriplex* spp.) salt glands, which can be observed as a mealy texture on the surface of the leaf, actively secrete salt.

The lower salt-marsh

Open mud flats support a large population of diatoms (microscopic algae) which bind the sediment particles together with a copious mucous excretion. The only flowering plants to inhabit these open flats are the eelgrasses (*Zostera* spp.) which are much grazed by wildfowl, especially wigeon. The Eden Estuary is the principal habitat for these plants in Fife where, in common with many other areas of the British Isles, the population declined earlier this century but is now showing good signs of recovery.

Common glasswort or marsh samphire (*Salicornia europaea*) along with annual sea-blite (*Sueda maritima*) are early colonisers of bare mud flats and this is a community that is likely to expand as sea levels rise. There are extensive new colonies of these species forming at present behind the recently accreted sand dunes at the north-eastern extremity of the Tentsmuir Nature Reserve. The most conspicuous species in the lower regions of the marsh is sea-aster (*Aster tripolium*) which can be either annual or biennial. In Britain there is a tendency for the plants in the lower region of the marsh not to flower in their first year of growth whereas in the upper regions the majority of plants do flower in their first year (Adam, 1990).

The upper salt-marsh

In Fife thrift (*Armeria maritima*) is more common on rocky outcrops near the sea but can also be found as a mid-marsh species. Although tolerant of salt, the species as a whole has a wide distribution in environmentally stressed habitats from mountain tops to cliffs and salt-marshes. The species is highly variable and the plants in salt-marshes have broader leaves than those found on Scottish mainland mountains and in the Hebrides. In the upper salt-marsh,

characteristic species are the sea-rush (*Juncus maritimus*) and the salt-marsh rush (*Juncus gerardii*), as well as scurvygrass (*Cochlearia officinalis*) and sea arrowgrass (*Triglochin maritimum*). Typical widespread grasses that also inhabit the upper marsh are creeping bent (*Agrostis stolonifera*), marsh foxtail (*Alopecurus geniculatus*) and salt-marsh grass (*Puccinellia maritima*).

In spite of the inundation by salt water most species of invertebrates on salt-marshes, like the plants, have terrestrial rather than marine affinities, although both are represented. Amongst the most abundant are amphipod crustaceans, related to the familiar sandhoppers of the tide-line. These are mainly *Orchestia gammarellus*, which feed on decaying vegetation and sometimes occur in prodigious numbers. Predatory beetles and spiders are well represented. The wolf-spider *Pardosa palustris* is very abundant on the Cocklemill Marsh at the east end of Largo Bay.

The invertebrates provide food for many species of birds although most salt-marshes in Fife are too small to be of much importance for breeding birds. Several migratory waders are regular visitors, including some of the scarcer ones like green and wood sandpipers and greenshank, as well as the ubiquitous redshanks.

The raised beach platforms

The raised beach platforms left below partially eroded cliffs afford protected habitats for many species on both the north and south coasts of Fife. On the north-facing shore below the Kinkell Braes near St Andrews, the walk to the Rock and Spindle has long been noted for the diversity of plant species that can be seen. The plant communities on these raised beaches can be grouped under two headings, those of wet marsh areas and those of drier banks. The Kinkell Braes raised beach platform has a number of marshy areas where yellow flag (*Iris pseuda-corus*), marsh marigold (*Caltha palustris*), hoary willow herb (*Epilobium parviflorum*), square-stalked St John's-wort (*Hypericum tetrapterum*), water horsetail (*Equisetum fluvi-atile*) and marsh hawk's-beard (*Crepis paludosa*) can still be found where they were recorded at the beginning of the 20th century (Wilson, 1910).

The best development of the drier coastal communities are seen on the southern Fife shore as on the raised beach platform that forms the Crail West Braes. In late spring and early summer a rich collection of herbaceous species can be seen in flower, including lesser meadow-rue (*Thalictrum minus*), purple milk vetch (*Astragalus danicus*) and kidney vetch (*Anthyllis vulneraria*). Saxi-frages are also represented by the annual rue-leaved saxifrage (*Saxifraga tridactylites*) and the perennial meadow saxifrage (*S.gra-nulata*), both of which favour calcareous soils that are well-drained. On the cliffs at Crail there can also be found wild cabbage (*Brassica oleracea*), an introduction but established there for over a hundred years.

Cliffs

Although the cliffs of Fife (with the exception of the Isle of May and Kincraig) are not particularly impressive scenically, they do provide a refuge for those coastal plants that can tolerate sea spray and summer drought but would not survive inundation. Thrift (*Armeria maritima*), sea campion (*Silene uni-flora*), and Scots lovage (*Ligusticum scoticum*) can all be seen on the shore walk from St Andrews to Fife Ness, either in rock crevices on the cliffs or in the boulder-strewn debris below. A number of woodland species also inhabit the cliffs. On the Kinkell Braes

colonies of blackthorn flower profusely in spring while later honeysuckle along with great wood-rush (*Luzula sylvatica*) remind us of the probable existence in the past of a richer coastal woodland.

These patches of scrub provide good habitat for linnets which tend to nest in loose colonies. Although primarily seed-eaters, finding their food amongst the coastal grasslands, like most finches they feed their nestlings partly on insects, found amongst the scrub. Another characteristic bird of coastal scrub, although very much scarcer, is the stonechat. Being entirely dependent upon invertebrate food they are vulnerable to hard winters, and it is doubtful it they still breed on the Fife coast.

West of Elie, parts of the Kincraig cliffs are a veritable rock-garden in spring and early summer with such flowers as rock-rose (*Helianthemum nummularium*) prominent, while species found nowhere else in Fife include sea-kale (*Crambe maritima*) and yellow-horned poppy (*Glaucium flavum*) along with such uncommon plants as henbane (*Hyoscyamus niger*) and wormwood (*Artemisia absinthium*) (pl. 6).

The rock-rose at Kincraig supports a colony of one of our scarcest butterflies, the northern brown argus, which flies in early July (pl. 8). Other less conspicuous insects have their only known Fife sites on these luxuriant south-facing slopes – the tiny lacewing *Psectra diptera* and several beetles, including the leaf-beetle *Mantura mathewsi* which also is dependent upon rock-rose.

Further west, the low cliffs at Pettycur, Kinghorn also support some rarities, notably the only Scottish colony of wild clary (*Salvia verbenaca*). At the SWT reserve at Carlingnose, east of North Queensferry, there are more scarce plants such as the dropwort (*Filipendula vulgaris*), and also a colony of a snake millipede, *Choneiulus palmatus*, otherwise known in Scotland mainly from hot-houses in botanic gardens.

On the Isle of May the cliff-tops offer in early summer a profusion of thrift and sea campion. However, the large increase in nesting gulls in the last 30 years has made the island so nutrient-rich in places that these have been replaced over large areas by a luxuriant growth of common chickweed, nettles, sorrel and hemlock. Remedial action has brought some control over the gull population and the vegetation has in part recovered. Currently, a greater threat to major soil erosion comes from the burrowing activities of the numerous puffins on the higher ground and the large breeding population of grey seals on ground near the shore.

The mainland cliffs do not provide suitable conditions for seabird colonies, although the versatile fulmars nest within a few metres of public paths in St Andrews and Crail, as well as on the volcanic cliffs at Kincraig. There is even an inland site on the old quarry face at Balmullo, 5 kilometres from the nearest salt water. In contrast the islands of the Firth of Forth have major breeding colonies of seabirds and these are dealt with in chapter 6.

Acknowledgements

I am much indebted to Mr R J Banks and Cmdr. E F B Spragge for their experienced help and advice on site visits during the preparation of this chapter and to the botanical recorder for Fife, Mr G Ballantyne for helpful additions and corrections. Fife Nature provided invaluable help with access to their records.

References

Adam, P (1990). *Saltmarsh ecology.* Cambridge University Press.

Boorman, L A, Goss-Custard, J D & McGrorty, S (1989). *Climatic change, rising sea level and the British coast.* Institute of Terrestrial Ecology Research Publ. no.1, HMSO, London.

Crawford, R M M (1996). Tentsmuir Point: A national nature reserve in decline? In Whittington (below), pp 65–88.

Whittington, G (ed.) (1996). *Fragile environments. The use and management of Tentsmuir NNR, Fife.* Scottish Cultural Press, Edinburgh.

Wilson, J H (1910). *Nature study rambles round St Andrews.* Henderson, St Andrews.

6

The shore, the estuaries and the sea

MATT BENTLEY

(BIRDS BY DAVID FAIRLAMB)

The Kingdom of Fife is now readily accessed by road and rail from the south across the Firth of Forth, and from the north across the Firth of Tay. Before these links were completed, the extent of the coast of the Kingdom was much more apparent to the visitor, with Fife being surrounded on three sides by water. Entry to Fife at that time was by way of the Kincardine Bridge, bringing one close to the historic town of Culross on the Forth coast of Fife, or by Newburgh on the Tay to the north. The Fife coast extends about 170 kilometres from Newburgh to Kincardine. Over this distance, the intertidal and marine environments encompass the whole spectrum from very low salinity, muddy, estuarine conditions of the upper Forth and Tay, to exposed sandy beaches and rocky shores around St Andrews and the East Neuk.

This chapter will focus on the nature of the physical environments and of the plant (predominantly algae) and animal species of the eulittoral (intertidal) zone. These species occupy the shore from the mean high water of spring tides (MHWST), that may be covered by the incoming tide on only one or two days a month, down to the extreme low water of spring tides (ELWST), that may be uncovered on only a few of the lowest spring tides in the year. The chapter will also consider the sublittoral environment that is only accessible by diving or sampling from boats.

There will also be consideration given to the inshore sea floor (benthic) environments of St Andrews Bay, and the Firths of Tay and Forth. Finally there will be some discussion of the pelagic fish and fisheries, and the marine mammals and birds that are found around the coast of Fife.

The tidal regime in Fife

Fife, like the entire British coastline, experiences a semidiurnal tidal regime in which there are two low tides and two high tides each day. The tidal range is maximal during periods of spring tides which occur approximately every fortnight and follow immediately after the full or new moon. At the peak of spring tides, around the spring and autumnal equinoxes, the tidal range at St Andrews is in excess of 5 metres. During these periods, species of kelp (predominantly *Laminaria digitata*) of the lower littoral and sublittoral are exposed at low water. Around Fife, low water of spring tides occurs during the first half of the morning. Conversely, low water of neap tides (the smaller tides of the month) occurs during the afternoon. This means that during the summer months, animals and plants that live at the very bottom of the intertidal zone are exposed at a time when they are not subjected to the warmest period of the day. They do, however, face the probability of exposure to very low

5. Sheltered conditions in the Tay Estuary allow close proximity of coastal reed-beds and woodland at Flisk. (*Photo: H. A. P. Ingram*)

6. Kincraig cliffs (Earlsferry) with a striking display of rockrose, bell heather, lady's bedstraw and viper's bugloss. (*Photo: R. M. M. Crawford*)

7. Caterpillars of cinnabar moth on ragwort – a characteristic coastal insect. (*Photo: R. M. Cormack*)

8. Northern brown argus. (*Photo: A.-M. Smout*)

9. Dune-erosion on the West Sands, St Andrews. Regular cleaning of this beach in summer has removed any possibility of fore-dune colonization, and will therefore hasten destruction of the dunes on this famous beach. (*Photo: R. M. M. Crawford*)

10. Creeping willow, a common species in dune-slack communities. (*Photo: R. M. M. Crawford*)

11. Coral-root orchid, once a very common species on the seaward side of the alders at Tentsmuir. (*Photo: R. M. M. Crawford*)

12. Scots lovage, a plant that occurs widely on arctic and subarctic coasts and approaches its southern limit in Fife. (*Photo: R. M. M. Crawford*)

13. The Eden Estuary at low tide; the worm-casts reflect the enormous richness of mudflats for invertebrate life. (*Photo: F. Spragge*)

14. Knotted wrack is the dominant large seaweed in estuarine conditions, as here beside the piers of the old Tay Bridge. (*Photo: M. Bentley*)

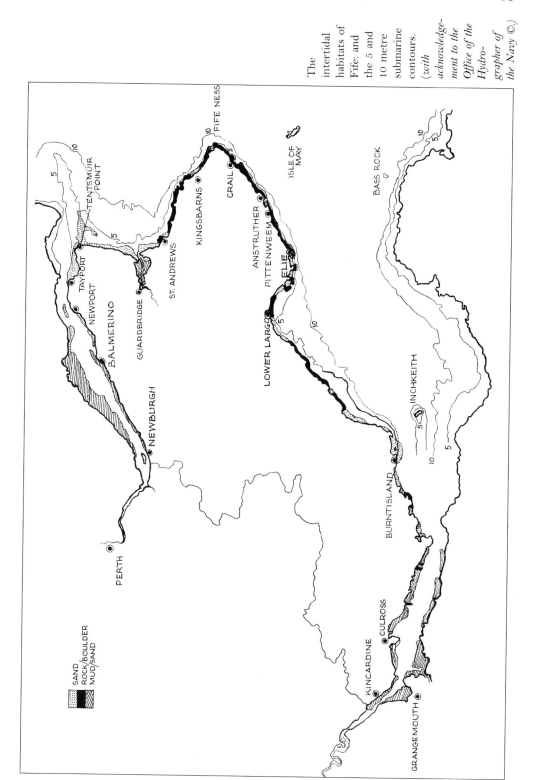

The intertidal habitats of Fife: and the 5 and 10 metre submarine contours. (with acknowledgement to the Office of the Hydrographer of the Navy ©.)

temperatures when exposed to the air early on a winter's day. A number of intertidal algal and animal species have developed a resistance to freezing that enables them to endure such harsh physical conditions.

Salinity and temperature

The salinity of the open coastal waters around Fife (as recorded at St Andrews Bay) is approximately 30 parts per thousand. This is somewhat lower that the typical salinity of the North Sea of around 34 ppt due to the huge volume of freshwater coming from the Forth and the Tay, and to a lesser extent the River Eden which flows into St Andrews Bay just to the north of the town. There is considerable temporal variation in this value, however, with significant lowering following periods of heavy rain. The salinity becomes markedly reduced as one progresses up the estuaries until the marine flora and fauna become replaced by freshwater species. Brackish water could be considered to be any value between 0.5 and 30 ppt.

Inshore sea water temperatures along the open coast of Fife typically reach a maximum of about 15°C in late August and a minimum of about 4°C in February. The maxima and minima vary little from year to year, but the time when sea water temperature declines in the autumn may be delayed following a particularly hot summer. Similarly, there may be delayed warming in the spring following a particularly harsh winter. This may have consequences for the timing of reproduction of a number of marine invertebrates that reproduce in autumn or spring.

Estuaries

The three principal estuaries of Fife are the Eden, the Tay and the Forth. Those of the Tay and the Forth are so large that much of their coastline resembles open exposed coast. The estuary of the River Eden is contained within Fife and extends eastwards to enter St Andrews Bay about 3 km north of the town. The Eden Estuary is an important sanctuary for migratory birds and is normally the most northerly ice-free estuary in Britain.

Estuarine sediments are characterised by a high proportion of silt/clay particles (under 63 μm in diameter) that have been washed from terrestrial soils. Following heavy rain the estuarine water becomes discoloured and plumes of silt are visible being carried out into the sea. The sediments, once settled in the estuary, tend not to be readily re-suspended. They are often further stabilised by secretions from single-celled algae, epipelic diatoms, that live in the surface layer of the estuarine mud. These unicellular organisms migrate to the surface during periods of low tide by exudation of the mucus secretion, to photosynthesise. Their presence on the surface of the sediment is evident by the green colouration that appears. Deeper in the sediment, often from as little as a few millimetres, oxygen is depleted or absent and the sediment is black. Organisms that live at depth in the sediment must either have evolved mechanisms for anaerobic respiration or obtain oxygen from the surface. These are described below.

The upper Forth

The upper Forth estuary has been the subject of a long-term study by staff and students from Stirling University who have focused their attentions on the area around Grangemouth (McLusky, 1987). The estuary was grossly polluted during the 1980s but has made a steady recovery that has seen the re-establishment of a number of typical and important estuarine species. On the Fife side of the estuary opposite Grangemouth, the south facing shore is characterised by a shallow gradient of mud with scattered boulders. The shore is exposed to the sun for considerable periods during summer and may suffer excessive warming. The soft sediment shows evidence of the spiral casts of lugworms (*Arenicola marina*), a species of polychaete worm that is found in soft sediment from middle estuaries down to sandy beaches of open coasts. Scattered boulders carry plants of knotted wrack (*Ascophyllum nodosum*). These fucoid algae are able to withstand desiccation during low water and rehydrate rapidly on re-immersion. Amongst the wrack there are found a number of grazing snails (*Littorina* spp.). The boulders also carry large numbers of the sessile barnacle *Semibalanus balanoides.*

The Tay Estuary

The Fife shore of the River Tay is atypical of an estuary because of its size. Although the Tay is tidal up as far as Perth, most of the upper reaches are characterised by the presence of extensive and ecologically important reed-beds, especially on the north shore. Further east towards Balmerino, the shore becomes more open and is characterised by a pebble substratum. This is exposed to north-westerly winds and the considerable fetch across Invergowrie Bay results in a wave-washed shore. Such a washed pebble shore has relatively little plant life but larger stones carry bladder wrack (*Fucus vesiculosus*) and tufts of the green alga *Enteromorpha intestinalis.*

There is one infaunal animal (i.e. living within the sediment) that deserves a mention with regard to the River Tay. This is the polychaete worm *Marenzelleria viridis.* This is a worm that originates from North America, and is a relatively recent invader of the River Tay. A study in 1987 by Atkins and others showed that at that time it was present in the mud flats around Invergowrie Bay. More recent reports have shown that it is present in the Forth. *M.viridis* inhabits areas of low salinity. It occupies a niche that would normally be occupied by the typical estuarine polychaete in Britain, *Nereis diversicolor* (the harbour ragworm). It is possible that it became established in the Tay following discharge of ship ballast water, and is thought to have been introduced to the Baltic Sea in the same way. It is now common in the Baltic along the coasts of Germany and the Baltic States. There is some concern that it could displace *Nereis diversicolor* from areas where there are specialist bird predators on the ragworm.

The Eden Estuary

The estuary of the River Eden is a valuable resource in Fife. It is used for leisure activities, notably bird-watching, horse-riding and wild-fowling. It is a Local Nature Reserve, with the inner part being a sanctuary area. It has been and still is the focus of scientific research into the ecology of the soft sediment communities and the biology of infaunal species. The estuary has been the subject of a report published by NE Fife District Council (now Fife Council) giving descriptions on plant and animal communities of the estuary.

The upper estuary at Guardbridge has a typical boulder and fine mud substratum. The principal infaunal invertebrate is the burrowing mud shrimp (*Corophium volutator*). This animal is a characteristic member of estuarine mud communities and has a valuable role as a detritivore, feeding on decaying plant matter. It has long anterior appendages that it uses in scavenging food. The other principal upper estuary invertebrate is the polychaete worm *Nereis diversicolor.* This worm feeds by collecting detrital particles at the entrance to its burrow in mucus secretions that it ingests periodically.

Large flat areas of mud in the middle estuary are covered with the bright green seaweed *Enteromorpha intestinalis.* During the summer months the spread of this alga across the surface of the mud can lead to a considerable depletion of oxygen in the sediment surface beneath it. The growth of *Enteromorpha* is encouraged further by the input of nutrient (nitrate, phosphate) from agricultural run-off and drains. Patches of eelgrass, species of *Zostera*, can also be seen in the middle estuary, as can isolated plants of sea lettuce *Ulva lactuca*, a green algae. The surface of the mud is grazed by tiny laver spire snails (*Hydrobia ulvae*). These snails, although small, are present in colossal numbers (over 1000 per square metre) and so represent a considerable biomass that is available to birds, shelduck in particular. Cord-grass (*Spartina anglica*) is present at the upper shore of the middle estuary, above the salt marsh pools, where it was introduced in 1948.

The mud flats of the middle estuary are also inhabited by a number of bivalve molluscs. In particular the peppery furrow shell (*Scrobicularia plana*), the Baltic tellin (*Macoma balthica*) and the cockle (*Cerastoderma edule*). These molluscs live at varying depths in the sediment and feed at the surface. Marks on the surface made by the feeding siphon of *S.plana* are particularly obvious. The cockles live close to the surface and can be collected by raking the surface of the sediment (with a garden rake), although collection and eating of specimens from the Eden estuary is not to be recommended. The middle estuary is traversed by a number of burns carrying freshwater. Flounders are abundant in these channels.

There are large and obvious beds of the edible mussel, raised above the surrounding areas of mud near the river channel in the middle estuary. These were at one time harvested commercially and child labour was employed to transport the mussels across the mud flats and along the old mussel road to St Andrews. The small size of the children allowed them to traverse the mud flats without becoming stuck in the soft sticky sediment. The mussels in the Eden Estuary are slow growing and many reach ten or more years old. They spend a comparatively short time immersed and can only feed when they are under water. This results in the very slow growth rate. A recent application to resume the commercial harvesting of mussels from the Eden Estuary was turned down. Even if permission had been granted, it is doubtful that it could have been a viable proposition. Farmed mussels from the clear Atlantic waters on the west coast of Scotland grow much faster and are cleaner. Many of the Eden mussels carry a small commensal pea crab (*Pinnotheres pisum*) within their shell that would make them unpalatable.

The mussel beds and surrounding mud of the estuary also contain large populations of the king ragworm (*Nereis virens*). These polychaete worms are highly prized by sea anglers, and bait diggers come from afar to collect the Eden ragworms. The impact of these illegal activities is twofold. First it depletes the worm population and secondly it causes disturbance to the sediment. Considerable quantities of shell fragments, for example, are brought to the surface by their digging activities and these provide attachments for algae, thus changing the sediment community. The king ragworms breed only once at the end of their lives and sometimes, following spawning in March, large numbers of moribund male ragworms can be seen on the surface of the mud.

Closer to the estuary mouth the sediment

becomes more sandy and mobile. The outer estuary is dynamic and the path of the river channel changes with time. There are areas of erosion and accretion. The erosion is of particular concern to those with golfing interests in St Andrews because of the proximity of the golf courses to the edge of the sand dune system. The less mobile areas of sediment are inhabited by dense beds of the lugworm *Arenicola marina*. Although this is also a species highly prized for bait, the individuals from the river Eden population tend to be rather small and are not heavily exploited by bait diggers. The lugworms around the coasts of Fife reproduce in the late autumn or early winter. At this time puddles of white sperm can sometimes be seen across the beach at low water. The female sheds her eggs into the burrow and these are fertilised by the sperm when it is diluted by the incoming tide.

The sands of the outer estuary are also occupied by a large bivalve, the sand gaper (*Mya arenaria*). Old shells of these, white and rather chalky in appearance, can frequently be found along the strand line. Also visible along the strand line are empty tubes of the sand-mason worm (*Lanice conchilega*). These are tubes constructed of sand grains cemented to a proteinaceous inner tube. The tube has a fringe at one end. Some living examples of the sand mason worm can be found in the estuary around the edge of the river channel but much more extensive beds occur inside the sand bank at Tentsmuir. When living, the worms live vertically in the sediment with just the fringe of the tube exposed. This fringe slows water currents around the tube and enables food (detrital) particles to be deposited around the worm.

Further out towards Out Head, at the point of the West Sands, the estuary ends and the sediment communities become those of an exposed sandy beach.

Sandy beaches

The open coast of Fife is a mixture of sandy beaches interspersed with rocky shores. Many of the beaches, most notably the West Sands at St Andrews, are exposed to the full force of winter north-easterly gales and are very mobile areas of sediment. As a result, beach topography changes from season to season, and from year to year. This can have a profound influence on the nature of the invertebrate communities in the beach. The extent of seasonal changes that can occur was evident at East Sands, St Andrews during the winter of 1995–96. During this period much of the sand was removed offshore by wave action leaving areas of underlying sandstone exposed.

Mobile exposed sandy beaches such as West Sands and to a lesser extent East Sands at St Andrews have a relatively impoverished invertebrate infauna which is nevertheless much richer than the casual observer might suppose. Some of the largest and most beautiful invertebrates found in sandy beaches are amongst their inhabitants. Many of these can only be found by digging in the sand but evidence of their presence can be seen along the strand line. White tests (skeletal shells) of the heart urchin (*Echinocardium cordatum*) about 5 cm across can be found frequently. The living animals, found at depth in the sediment around and below the low water mark, are much more beautiful being covered with many fine green-gold spines.

Razor shells (especially *Ensis siliqua*) are also found scattered along the strand line. These large bivalves have long parallel-sided valves to their shell and live vertically in the sediment. Their presence in the sand can be detected by a spout of water from the sand surface when an area near the burrow is stood upon. They have a powerful muscular foot and are capable of burrowing down into the sediment faster than one can dig. Following October gales, living specimens are often washed up and can be collected. They are excellent cooked simply in butter with a little garlic. Specimens of another large bivalve, the blunt gaper (*Mya truncata*), also occur around the low water mark and offshore. A number of other beautiful and common bivalve molluscs occur in the sand of open beaches. Amongst these, the tellin *Angulus tenuis*, the banded wedge shell (*Donax vittatus*) and the more robust *Spisula solida* are some of the best known. Specimens of the Baltic tellin (*Macoma balthica*) also occur near the mouth of estuaries.

October gales also occasionally bring large numbers of the sea-mouse (*Aphrodita aculeata*) up onto the shore. This is a large polychaete worm about 10–15 cm in length and several centimetres across. It is so called because of the presence of a covering of fine iridescent hairs (chaetae) that cover the animal's back giving it the appearance of a mouse rather than a worm. Normally these animals can only be collected by dredging in deep water.

In more sheltered areas of these beaches, towards the St Andrews end of West Sands for example, sand casts of the lugworm (*Arenicola marina*) are abundant. Adult individuals from these beaches are much larger than those found in the Eden estuary and are frequently exploited by bait diggers. Nursery beds of lugworm can often be seen much higher up the shore. They can be identified by the presence of fine spiral sand casts similar to those of the adult worm. Casts of adult black lugworms (*Arenicola defodiens*) can also be seen on the beaches of Fife. This worm, only recently described as a separate species, is the preferred target of bait diggers. It lives deeper in the sediment than *A. marina* and the cast produced is often black (due to the sulphide in the sediment at about a metre below the surface).

Isolated specimens of the king ragworm (*Nereis virens*) occur in sandy beaches although they are more common where there is a higher silt content. Their presence can often be detected by the fact that they will pull small pieces of seaweed into the burrow entrance. The white ragworms, *Nephtys caeca*, *N.hombergii* and *N.cirrosa*, are also common. These worms are known as cat-worms because of the pungent odour of tomcats that they emit. The first two species are collected as sea angling bait and are particularly prized by cod fisherman.

Many other smaller invertebrates can be found in sandy beaches including polychaete worms, nematode worms, amphipod crustaceans and nemertines. One representative of these, the nemertine (ribbon-worm) *Lineus longissimus*, is worthy of mention. A specimen

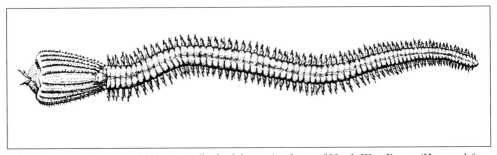

White Ragworm (cat-worm), from *Handbook of the marine fauna of North-West Europe* (Hayward & Ryland, 1995) by permission of Oxford University Press.

of this worm was found at East Sands St Andrews in 1864 that, far from being small, had a length of 55 metres. It is the largest known specimen of this animal.

There are mobile animals that live on the surface of these beaches. The common shrimp (*Crangon crangon*) is one of the most abundant and can be collected with a push net by wading at low water; berried females can be seen carrying eggs during the winter. Juvenile flatfish, plaice and dabs, are common, and greater sand-eels can be found buried in sand at low water.

Areas of sandy beaches that are more sheltered often have more diverse infauna. The beach at Tayport for example is relatively flat, with much overlying water during periods of low tide. There are extensive beds of eelgrass (*Zostera* spp.), cockles are abundant and the peppery furrow shell (*Scrobicularia plana*) is also present. Stones and boulders carry *Fucus vesiculosus* plants and are covered with barnacles. Gammarid crustaceans are abundant under the stones.

In beaches, such as part of Tentsmuir sands, where beds of the sand mason worm (*Lanice conchilega*) are present, they have the effect of stabilising the sediment, allowing invertebrate communities to develop. In addition empty tubes provide a refuge for small invertebrate species. In particular the scale worm *Harmothoe imbricata* is common. This worm is a small predatory species more often associated with the rocky shores. The opalescent coloured polychaete *Ophelia borealis* is another common member of this community.

Rocky shores

Rocky shores around the coast of Fife intersperse the sandy bays and beaches. Most of the rocky shore environments are to be found in the East Neuk between St Andrews

and Elie. Fife Ness is the easternmost point. Algal zonation is less obvious around the coast of Fife than it is elsewhere, on the west coast of Scotland for example. The same suite of algal species is found, however, and they occupy the same relative positions on the shore. On some of the most exposed shores, such as that at Fife Ness, the shore is dominated by barnacles rather than algae.

Channel wrack (*Pelvetia canaliculata*) is the uppermost fucoid alga, being found at the top of the eulittoral. Its distribution is, however, patchy. Just below the *Pelvetia* zone there is the small spiral wrack (*Fucus spiralis*) and below this, covering much of the middle shore, is bladder wrack (*F. vesiculosus*). This is the same alga that colonises boulders on some of the sandy shores. Knotted wrack (*Ascophyllum nodosum*) occurs among the *F. vesiculosus* and sometimes among the *F. spiralis* higher up the shore. Serrated wrack (*F. serratus*) occurs towards the bottom of the eulittoral above the kelp. On open shores, where algal cover is reduced or absent, the rock surfaces are covered with barnacles, *Semibalanus balanoides*. The related *Balanus crenatus* can be found on boulders in the *Laminaria* (kelp) zone.

The eulittoral and sublittoral zones contain a wealth of animal species that are far too numerous to discuss in detail. Some species are well known and easily recognised, the green shore crab (*Carcinus maenas*) for example, but many are concealed in rock crevices or obscured in other ways. Other crab species include the edible crab (*Cancer pagurus*), more reddish than the shore crab and with a characteristic pie-crust edge to its carapace, and the hermit crab (*Pagurus bernhardus*). Kingsbarns beach is a particularly good place to watch hermit crabs in the tide pools. Other tide pool species can also be seen here. Mysid shrimps (*Siriella armata* and *Praunus flexuosus*) can also be seen in the tide pools. Winkles (mainly *Littorina littorea*) can be observed crawling across the bottom of the pools.

A range of echinoderm species can be found on the rocky shore, mainly under stones of the lower shore or amongst the kelp. Occasional specimens of the large urchin *Echinus esculentus* can be found on the shore but the smaller, green *Psammechinus miliaris* are more commonly seen under stones or in tide pools. The common starfish (*Asterias rubens*) is found near the low water mark although juveniles are seen more frequently that adults. The smaller pink-purple *Henricia sanguinolenta* is found under stones. This starfish, unlike *A.rubens*, lays only a few eggs and broods these under the female's arms. Brittle-stars (*Ophiothrix fragilis*) are also found under stones.

Many different shelled and shell-less mollusc species are found on the rocky shore. The edible mussel (*Mytilus edulis*) is common. It is particularly abundant where fresh water runs across the shore. This gives it some protection from its starfish predators that are intolerant of low salinity. On exposed shores the mussels may only be present as juveniles (seed mussel) in fissures of the sandstone. There are a number of periwinkle species, the largest of which, the edible periwinkle (*Littorina littorea*), is still harvested commercially from the shore at Fife Ness. The other easily recognised mobile gastropod is the dogwhelk (*Nucella lapillus*). This white or cream coloured snail is an active carnivore. It predates other molluscs, especially mussels, by boring a hole through the prey's shell with its toothed 'radula' and then eating the contents. There are a number of beautiful shell-less nudibranch molluscs (including *Acanthodoris pilosa*, *Cadlina laevis* and *Goniodoris nodosa*) present on the rocky shore although many of these are cryptic and difficult to spot. They prey upon breadcrumb

sponge (*Halichondria panicea*) and colonies of bryozoan (e.g. *Electra pilosa*) that grow on *Fucus serratus* or *Laminaria digitata*. Evidence of their presence is more easily seen in the form of cream coloured whorls of gelatinous egg strings attached to the lower shore algae.

Gelatinous egg cocoons of a small polychaete worm are also seen attached to fucoid algae. These are the green egg masses of *Phyllodoce maculata* that can itself be observed crawling among the wrack. Many polychaetes are present on rocky shores but many of these are well concealed under stones or in crevices. A few secrete calcareous tubes that provide them with protection from wave action. One of the most obvious is *Pomatoceros triqueter*, a little serpulid fan worm that secretes a white snake-like tube on the surfaces of stones. Another, *Spirorbis spirorbis*, secretes a white flat spiral tube on the fronds of *Fucus* plants. Lifting a few stones or opening a few crevices will reveal a range of brightly coloured and attractive species of polychaete worm. Flat stones that have black anoxic sediment beneath frequently harbour specimens of the bright orange *Cirratulus cirratus*. Scale worms, *Harmothoe imbricata* and *H.impar*, are also found under flat stones in clean gravel, as is the delicate hesionid worm *Kefersteinia cirrata*. Crevices are inhabited by the bright green phyllodocid worm *Eulalia viridis* and the bamboo worm *Nicomache lumbricalis*.

A range of fish species can be found on the rocky shore, either under stones or in tide pools. Amongst the most common are the butterfish (*Pholis gunnellus*), the five-bearded rockling (*Ciliata mustela*), the short-spined sea-scorpion (*Myoxocephalus scorpius*), the shanny (*Lipophrys pholis*) and the viviparous blenny (*Zoarces viviparus*). Occasionally fish species can be found on the shore that would not normally be encountered there. The adult lumpsucker (*Cyclopterus lumpus*), for example, is often seen moribund after spawning in January or February.

Deeper water

The seas around the coast of Fife are relatively shallow. At the Bell Rock, which lies 26 kilometres due east of Tentsmuir Point, the North Sea is still only about 35 metres deep. Much of the shallow water of St Andrews Bay inshore of the Bell Rock is a nursery area for juvenile flatfish, plaice in particular. For this reason, trawling is not permitted in the Bay. Most of the sea bottom around Fife is mud or muddy sand. There are areas of rock and areas of coarser sand, gravel and pebble.

Areas of soft muddy bottom provide refuge for the Norway lobster (*Nephrops norvegicus*). This bottom-dwelling crustacean, more familiar to most as scampi, forms extensive branching burrow systems. Another burrowing crustacean is the much smaller mud shrimp (*Calocaris macandreae*). This species has a particular requirement for a high silt content and where it occurs it is found at high densities. It is a territorial species and is, therefore, evenly distributed across the bottom.

Other invertebrates inhabit the soft muddy sea floor. The sea mouse (*Aphrodita aculeata*), a polychaete worm, crawls actively through the upper layers of sediment seeking out its prey (other polychaetes or small crustaceans) which it catches with an eversible proboscis. A number of species of brittle-star (e.g. *Amphiura filiformis*, *Ophiura* spp.) also occur in the soft sediment.

In areas where the sea floor is more consolidated, being formed of pebble or boulder, a different suite of invertebrate species is found. These show a range of feeding strategies from filter feeders to predators. Echinoderms are well represented. The common starfish (*Asterias rubens*) is abundant as are the edible sea urchins (*Echinus esculentus*). The starfish is a predator whereas the urchin is an omnivore. The common brittle-star (*Ophiothrix fragilis*) occurs in numbers here. This brittle-star is a filter feeder. The large whelk (*Buccinum undatum*) occurs on the hard bottom where it scavenges. The soft

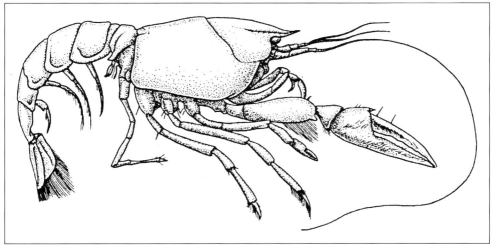

Mud shrimp, from *Handbook of the marine fauna of North-West Europe* (Hayward & Ryland, 1995) by permission of Oxford University Press.

coral (*Alcyonium digitatum*), more commonly known as dead man's fingers, filter feeds whilst being attached to rocks. This coral occurs in two varieties: a white and an orange form. The white form in particular resembles the fingers of a corpse when dredged from the bottom.

Two commercially important crustacean species are common amongst the rock crevices. These are the lobster (*Homarus gammarus*) and the edible crab (*Cancer pagurus*). The large hermit crab (*Pagurus bernhardus*) occupies empty whelk shells, and the colourful red and blue squat lobster (*Galathea strigosa*) also occurs between the rocks.

The lesser octopus (*Eledone cirrhosa*) is a large predatory mollusc that lives around rocky outcrops on the bottom. There it preys upon crabs which it easily disables using its eight arms. The lesser octopus, like other cephalopod molluscs, breeds only once at the end of its life. As a result there is large mortality of the adult population after reproduction in the spring. The dumpling squid (*Sepiola atlantica*) is closely associated with sandy bottoms. It is small but exquisitely marked. When disturbed its colour changes rapidly from red to white and back again. This rapid colour change is controlled by the nervous system.

Many of the bottom-dwelling invertebrates are principal components of the diet of fish that swim close to the bottom, i.e. demersal species. Species of the cod family in particular are closely associated with the sea bottom where there are rocky outcrops.

Fish and marine mammals

Several principal groups of fish inhabit the seas around Fife. There are the bottom-dwelling species, such as the sea-scorpion, that have been mentioned above in the sections on rocky shores. The conger eel is a deeper water bottom dweller. A second group is represented by the flatfishes and demersal gadoids (fish of the cod family), and then there are the pelagic species such as the herring. Many of the fish species are seasonal visitors to the coasts of Fife, others are resident and still others make only occasional appearances from warmer southern waters.

Of the flatfishes, the dabs and flounder are found inshore and venture into estuaries such as the River Eden. Other representatives that are common include the plaice and several species of sole (*Solea solea, Microstomus kitt*). The turbot also occurs frequently. The cod is the best known, and one of the most common gadoids. Cod are found close inshore amongst the sublittoral algae where they are known as kelp cod. Their colouration is quite distinct from the more familiar colour of the deep-water cod seen on the fishmonger's slab. The cod of the kelp beds feed on a variety of invertebrates with the shore crab being one of the principal components of its diet. Cod that forage around the rocky outcrops in deeper water frequently feed on squat lobsters. They are opportunistic feeders, however, and will exploit the seasonal appearance of sand-eels. They also take a range of smaller fish species. The saithe is one of the other common gadoids. The haddock is a much sought-after member of the cod family but this species is less common in shallow water.

Pelagic fishes that occupy upper layers of the water include the herring, the sprat and the mackerel. The herring is much less common now than it used to be. At one time it was the basis for a major fishery in the Forth. The mackerel is a seasonal visitor and is most common around St Andrews Bay and the Firth of Forth during the month of August. An unusual fish worthy of mention is the sparling (*Osmerus eperlanus*). Somewhat resembling the herring, it occurs in the Tay and Forth in the spring when it moves up into the estuaries to spawn. The fish is characterised by a distinct odour of cucumber.

Occasional visitors to the waters around Fife include several members of the shark families. In addition to the resident lesser spotted dogfish (*Scyliorhinus caniculus*), the much larger tope (*Galeorhinus galeus*), the smooth-hound (*Mustelus mustelus*) and the blue shark (*Prionace glauca*) also occur. Several species of skate and ray also occur on the sandy bottom. The cuckoo ray (*Raja naevus*) and the skate (*R.batis*) are the most common.

Sea mammals are common around the coasts of Fife. There are two species of seal: the harbour seal and the grey seal. The harbour seal (also known as the common seal) can be seen hauled out on the sands at Tentsmuir and in the Eden estuary. The harbour seal suffered huge mortality during an outbreak of phocine distemper virus in 1988 but populations have recovered well since. The grey seal was affected little by the virus outbreak. It is the more numerous and occurs in good numbers at the Isle of May where there is a large breeding colony producing about 1300 pups each year. Seals are often blamed for taking large numbers of commercially important fish in their diet. It cannot be denied that their diet undoubtedly includes a number of fish species that are caught commercially for food, but sand-eels, fished for by industrial fishing operations, are also an important component of the diet. The diet of the grey seals at the Isle of May consists of about 25% sand-eels. Fish of the cod family make up the largest component of the diet. Seals in the Eden Estuary feed on flatfishes and salmonids. Seal populations around Britain are monitored by the Sea Mammal Research Unit which is now based in St Andrews.

Whales and dolphins also occur relatively frequently around the coasts of Fife. The story of the Tay whale (a humpback whale that came into the Tay in 1885) is almost legendary, and in March 1997 a sperm whale was stranded and died in the upper Forth estuary. A school of bottlenose dolphins can be seen from time to time in St Andrews Bay and the Firth of Forth. It may be that these are the same individuals that breed in the Moray Firth to the north. Other species of dolphin are infrequent visitors.

Exploitation and conservation

Exploitation of marine life around Fife takes two forms. Local, small exploitation by individuals for their own use or as a small commercial enterprise could be regarded as an artisanal fishery. Large scale fishing by deep water trawlers or industrial fishing represents a much greater threat if not carefully regulated. Many of the local small-scale fisheries have now died out because of changing social trends. Some of the larger operations, most notably herring fishing and salmon netting, have also now ceased due to declining stocks and economic reasons respectively.

Exploitation of the intertidal zone involves harvesting of molluscs and digging of bait for sea angling. Mussel harvesting in the Eden Estuary no longer takes place but edible winkles are collected from the rocky shore around Fife Ness and from some beaches in the Firth of Forth such as Burntisland.

Bait digging for ragworm and lugworm takes place on many beaches including the nature reserve of the Eden Estuary. This activity can cause considerable ecological disturbance. Bait diggers come to the area in organised parties from as far afield as Newcastle where local stocks have suffered heavy bait digging pressure for many years.

Inshore fishing vessels operate from the many small harbours around Fife. The principal quarry is crab and lobsters caught by the use of baited creels. This fishery is closely regulated and monitored by the Scottish Office, and some fishermen are now looking to new forms of revenue. The capture of whelks (*Buccinum undatum*) in baited oil drums full of holes is one such example.

The salmon netting at Newburgh on the Tay ceased in 1996 and this followed the cessation of the net and coble fishery on the River Eden in 1995. There is still a small fishery on the Tay for the sparling. This is not a full time occupation for the fisherman however.

Larger vessels operate out of Anstruther and Pittenweem. They fish mainly in the sea areas within the Firth of Forth and due east of the Forth, although the largest vessels venture much further north and may be away for periods of about a week. Their catch of cod, haddock and scampi is landed and sold through the FMA market at Pittenweem. Crabs are still cooked at the harbour in Crail where they are sold directly to the public.

In 1996 there was considerable concern about the exploitation of sand-eel shoals on the 'Wee Bankie' east of Fife Ness by Danish vessels that sought them for conversion to fish oil products such as margarine. Vessels at Anstruther harbour could be seen flying Greenpeace pennants in support of the conservation group's campaign to prevent the fishing. The sand-eels are important elements of the diet of seabirds, particularly puffins, seals, and also of commercially important fish species such as cod.

There are other specific conservation measures taken in Fife that include the provision of nature reserves and bird sanctuary areas, the Eden estuary being a notable example. One important aspect is that these areas exist alongside other activities such as horse riding, angling and wildfowling. In this way the amenity value of the coast is preserved at the same time as active conservation.

Seabirds of the Forth Islands

There are thirteen islands in the Firth of Forth that support populations of breeding seabirds, from the Isle of May in the east to Inchgarvie under the Forth Rail Bridge. Six of these lie within Fife. At the height of the breeding season these islands hold over 200,000 seabirds of 17 species and were designated as a Special Protection Area (SPA) under the EU Birds Directive in 1990.

Of the cliff-nesting species, guillemots are the most abundant, colonising the other islands away from the Isle of May and Bass Rock from the 1930s onwards. Their diet of small fish, including sand-eels and sprats, crustaceans, molluscs and marine worms, is shared by their other auk relations, razorbills and puffins.

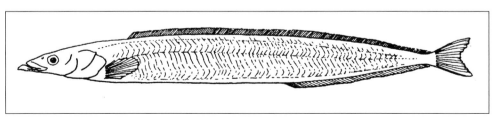

Sand-eel, from *Handbook of the marine fauna of North-West Europe* (Hayward & Ryland, 1995) by permission of Oxford University Press.

Guillemots breed colonially on narrow cliff ledges and atop rock stacks, while razorbills prefer the nooks and crannies within cliff faces. The burrow-nesting puffins have undergone a dramatic expansion since the 1950s, colonising islands as far west as Inchgarvie, although, as with guillemots, the Isle of May remains their stronghold.

Kittiwakes have nested within the Forth since the 1700s, with over half the breeding population on the Isle of May. They use the smallest of cliff ledges for their well constructed nests of plant material bonded together with mud. These oceanic gulls prey upon sprats and herrings during the spring, but are much more dependant on sand-eels as food for their young in summer.

Of the larger predatory gulls, herring gulls are the most numerous. They compete with the migratory lesser black-backed gulls (pl. 18) for nesting sites on the islands and the mainland, including roof-tops in some coastal towns. Great black-backed gulls nest in only small numbers, but are becoming annual breeders on the Isle of May, Craigleith and Fidra. All the predatory gulls have varied feeding habits, including catching or scavenging fish, preying on the eggs and young of other seabirds and increasingly exploiting human food wastage.

Fulmars, often mistaken for gulls, actually belong to the petrel family. The spread of fulmars around the coasts of Britain is well documented, with the first confirmed breeding for the Forth Islands in 1921. As with the large gulls, fulmars also nest on mainland Fife and have attempted breeding at some sites, such as disused quarries, a few kilometres from the coast.

Major factors contributing to the fulmar's successful colonisation of the Forth, and indeed much of the coastline of Britain, has been their catholic diet, including discarded fish offal from trawlers, and their wide range

of nest sites such as cliff ledge, grassy banks and even flat ground.

Small numbers of shags bred on the Isle of May and Bass Rock since the beginning of the 1900s, but it was around the middle of the century when they increased and spread dramatically. However numbers have fluctuated widely since the 1970s. Their close 'cousins', the cormorants, have had only a recent history of nesting on the islands, first recorded breeding on The Lamb in 1957. Since then they have colonised Craigleith, Inchkeith and the Inchcolm outliers.

Cormorants and shags are colonial nesters often constructing huge nests of sticks and seaweed over a period of many years. Both species tend to feed on or around the sea-bed, with the smaller and lighter shags favouring shallow waters. Cormorants can tackle quite large fish including flatfish, whereas shags are far more dependent on smaller fish like sand-eels.

Of the four species of terns that breed on the islands, the sandwich tern, the largest of the British terns, is the most prone to site infidelity. Colonies are known to completely uproot and move to another island during the course of a breeding season. Within the colonies, nests are grouped very close to one another, usually on shingle or sparsely vegetated ground. Numbers of sandwich terns have fluctuated widely over the 20th century from over 1000 pairs to single figures, as at present.

Arctic and common terns often nest in close proximity to each other, as they do on their Forth stronghold on the Isle of May. Taking into account the mainland colonies, common terns are the more abundant in the Forth at present, although numbers have been in overall decline since hitting a peak in the 1940s, with even the Isle of May being deserted for over 20 years until 1979. Arctic terns have had an even more sporadic history, with the Isle of May only being recolonised recently in the 1980s.

Roseate terns have undergone a dramatic decline during the latter half of the 20th century, the Forth colonies mirroring the situation throughout Britain. They usually breed alongside the other terns but prefer to nest under overhanging vegetation or even the entrances to rabbit or puffin burrows.

All the terns feed by plunge-diving into the surface layer of the sea for predominantly small fish such as sand-eels and sprats, but they will also feed on aquatic invertebrates.

The champions of the plunge-divers are the gannets, the largest of the seabirds breeding in Britain, with a wingspan of 180 cm. They plunge headlong into the sea from heights up to 40 metres for their prey, mainly herring, mackerel and sand-eels. Gannets are known to travel up to 300 miles

out from their breeding colonies on fishing trips. The Firth of Forth holds one of the most famous gannetries in the world on the Bass Rock, which in 1994 had just under 40,000 apparently occupied nest sites. This figure represents 15 per cent of the world's breeding population, emphasising the international importance of this colony. Gannets were known to nest on the Isle of May before 1850, but have not bred there since.

Seabird migration through Fife waters

Manx shearwaters are one of the most abundant passage birds seen off the Fife coast during the summer and autumn as they disperse away from their breeding grounds, British birds being known to winter off South America. Of the shearwaters that breed in the southern hemisphere, sooty shearwaters are the only species to be seen

Breeding seabirds of the Forth Islands

	Total number	Number in Fife	% of British population	Year	Counting unit*
Fulmar	1,889	1,100	<1%	1996	aos
Cormorant	385	170	5.5%	1996	nests
Shag	920	538	2%	1996	nests
Gannet	39,571	0	19%	1994	aos
Eider	2,342	1,729	7%	1994	nests
Greater black-backed gull	24	9	<1%	1996	nests
Lesser black-backed gull	7,207	5,559	9%	1994	pairs
Herring gull	13,025	8,978	8%	1994	pairs
Kittiwake	9,947	4,253	2%	1996	nests
Common tern	343	328	2%	1996	nests
Arctic tern	532	532	1%	1996	nests
Roseate tern	5	4	8%	1996	nests
Sandwich tern	2	2	<1%	1996	nests
Razorbill	3,884	3,476	3%	1996	birds
Guillemot	33,474	24,549	3%	1996	birds
Puffin	22,511	20,791	2.5%	1993	aos

* aos: apparently occupied sites

off Fife annually, while Cory's and great shearwaters occur only as scarce vagrants.

The smallest of the seabirds to nest in Britain are storm petrels. Rarely seen by day as they migrate south in autumn to winter off the western and southern African coasts, their presence in Fife waters is often only detected by luring them to the shore at night by playing recorded tapes of their calls.

Often called the pirates of the seabird world, skuas are masters of kleptoparasitism, stealing other seabirds' food. Mainly from July to October four species of skua pass through Fife waters on their way to Biscay, the African coasts or further into the South Atlantic. Arctic and great skuas are the most common on passage, both species actually breeding in Scotland, while pomarine skuas are annual in varying numbers. The smallest and most graceful of the skuas, the long-tailed skua, is not seen every year, although in some years hundreds can be recorded in a single day passing Fife Ness or in the Forth Estuary. Terns and kittiwakes are the main victims of piracy, but great and pomarine skuas have the bulk and build to tackle the larger gulls and even gannets.

In Fife, little gulls are passage migrants, although they have bred in England recently. A true coastal bird outside the breeding season, little gulls are most often seen during the autumn, especially around the Tay and Eden estuaries, where they feed on insects, fish and marine invertebrates. Other migrant gulls include glaucous and Iceland gulls, both winter visitors from their arctic breeding grounds. Both species tend to mix with other gulls, especially around sewage outfalls, fishing harbours and major roost sites.

Winter is also the main season for little auks. These diminutive arctic auks, which feed on plankton, disperse out to sea after the breeding season. Those that reach the North Sea can be seen in varying numbers, moving through Fife waters between November and April. In severe easterly storms many are driven close to shore or inland, ending up on freshwater lochs or even in gardens! Such events are known as 'wrecks' and mortality can be high.

Coastal and estuarine birds

During the autumn and winter the estuaries of the Forth, Tay and Eden play host to over 40 species of wildfowl and waders, with peak numbers estimated at over 140,000 birds.

The Forth is one of the most important estuaries for birds in Scotland. No fewer than 12 species of wildfowl and 10 species of waders reach the level for national importance (regularly comprising at least one per cent of the British population). In addition, the populations of pink-footed geese, shelducks, turnstones, bar-tailed godwits, redshanks and knots qualify as internationally important (regularly comprising one per cent or more of the western European population). On the Fife side of the Forth Estuary, there are major concentrations of birds at Torry Bay, Burntisland to Kirkcaldy coast, Largo Bay, and Ruddon's Point to Fife Ness coast.

The Tay Estuary holds internationally important populations of pink-footed and greylag geese, eiders, sanderlings, bar-tailed godwits and redshanks. Only a section of the southern shore lies within Fife, with the main bird areas including Mugrum Island, Tayport and Tentsmuir.

Although relatively small, the Eden Estuary can still boast three bird species of international importance – shelduck, bar-tailed godwit and redshank – and a further four species of national importance. The main roost site in the inner estuary is on the Guardbridge salt-marsh.

Divers and grebes occur mainly between October and March, although red-throated divers are usually recorded offshore all year round. The Forth is the main British site for red-necked grebes and one of the top sites for slavonian grebes. Divers rely mainly on small fish, while the grebes take a variety of food including molluscs, crustaceans, small fish and worms.

Shelduck are present around the Fife coast throughout the year, breeding in moderate numbers. The wintering population begins to build up in October when birds return from their moulting grounds on the German Waddensee. The main feeding grounds are on the mudflats of the Forth and the Eden which hold their principal prey, the small snail *Hydrobia ulvae*.

The sheltered bays and estuaries of the Fife coast are favoured by sea duck, especially over the winter months. Eider actually breed on the Forth Islands and at a few sites on the Fife mainland, but their numbers swell in the autumn as birds move in from other parts of Scotland. The Tay is their main wintering site, holding in excess of 16,000 birds in some winters. The extensive mussel beds of the outer Tay provide the bulk of the eiders' diet, but they also take other molluscs.

Scaup is another sea duck that favours mussels, but its presence in Fife waters in huge numbers in the 1960s was directly linked to man's activities. The effluent discharges into the Forth of sewage and spent grain from distillary waste provided their main food source. Since new sewage treatment plants have been in operation in recent years, the wintering population in the Forth has fallen from 30,000 in 1969 to 188 in 1994.

Often to be seen in mixed flocks, common scoters, velvet scoters, goldeneyes and long-tailed ducks are most abundant in the bays of Largo and St Andrews and also offshore at Methil, with peak numbers from November through to March. These birds have similar diets of molluscs, crustaceans and small fish (pl. 19).

The size and shape of the bill and feeding behaviour of wading birds varies considerably so that different species can take advantage of a wide variety of food sources, reducing competition and promoting co--existence on their predominantly estuarine feeding grounds.

Numbers of oystercatchers, bar-tailed godwits and redshanks are of national importance on the Forth, Tay and Eden estuaries. Bar-tailed godwits probe the wet sand of the middle and lower shore primarily for lugworms, while ragworms and bivalve molluscs are the main prey for oystercatchers. The feeeding range of redshanks extends to the high shore as they feed on a wide range of estuarine invertebrates. Ringed plovers also use the upper shore, especially sandy areas, where they hunt by sight for worms as they come to the surface, as well as for crustaceans.

The Eden Estuary is the Scottish stronghold for wintering black-tailed godwits, which favour the worms to be found in the mud and sand. Numbers are usually at their highest in spring, up to 270 in recent years, when the winter population is boosted by passage birds. As with the black-tailed godwits, grey plovers on the Eden reach nationally important numbers and use the muddier areas on the Eden where polychaete worms abound.

Knots are specialist feeders on marine bivalve molluscs and their fellow arctic breeders, sanderlings, specialise in small crustaceans found on the outer intertidal sand flats. Dunlins often join these two species in roosting or feeding flocks, probing for ragworms and spire-shells. All three species are to be found in nationally important numbers on the Forth, with peak numbers usually in mid-winter.

Curlews have the longest bill of all British waders, up to 15 cm in females. They can probe deeper than any other wader into the estuarine mud and sand for bivalve molluscs, worms and crustaceans, including crabs.

Two species of waders to be found more on the rocky shores or along standlines are turnstones and purple sandpipers. As their name suggests, turnstones feed by foraging amongst stones and seaweed, pushing them aside to reveal prey items such as shrimps, winkles and barnacles. Purple sandpipers frequently mix with small foraging flocks of turnstones, having much the same diet and feeding behaviour. Both species are of national importance in the Forth, where they can often be encountered on harbour walls and jetties, feeding or roosting.

The Fife shoreline, in particular the estuarine habitat, is used as a staging post by other migratory waders on passage to and from their breeding ground in spring and autumn. Many species appear annually, although in varying numbers, including little stint, curlew sandpiper, ruff, whimbrel, spotted redshank and greenshank.

The mud and sand flats that support these hordes of waders often appear desolate and empty. In fact they are amongst the most productive habitats to be found anywhere. The birds that depend upon them may breed in Siberia or winter in West Africa; we therefore have an international responsibility to ensure that their Fife habitat is secure for the future.

Further reading

Atkins, S, Jones, A and Garwood, P R (1987). The ecology and reproductive cycle of a population of *Marenzelleria viridis* in the Tay estuary. *Proceedings of the Royal Society of Edinburgh*, B 92, pp 311–322.

Gibbons, D W, Reid, J B and Chapman, R A (1993). *The new atlas of breeding birds in Britain and Ireland: 1988–1991*. Poyser, London.

Laverack, M S and Blackler, M (eds)(1974). *The fauna and flora of St Andrews Bay*. Scottish Academic Press, 310 pp.

Lewis, J R (1964). *The ecology of rocky shores*. English Universities Press, London, 323 pp.

Lloyd, C, Tasker, M L and Partridge, K (1991). *The status of seabirds in Britain*. Poyser, London.

McLusky, D S (1987). Intertidal habitats and benthic macrofauna of the Forth Estuary. *Proceedings of the Royal Society of Edinburgh*, B 93, pp 389–399.

Moore, P G and Seed, R (1985). *The ecology of rocky coasts*. Hodder & Stoughton. London, 467 pp

N E Fife District Council. *Eden Estuary Local Nature Reserve management plan*, 136 pp.

Prater, A J (1981). *Estuary birds of Britain and Ireland*. Poyser, Calton.

Sea Mammal Research Unit. *Annual Report 1992–94*. Natural Environment Research Council, 46 pp.

7

Woodland

RUTH INGRAM
(ANIMAL LIFE BY GORDON CORBET;
FORESTRY BY ROGER LARSEN)

Woodland in southeastern Scotland dates back some 10,000 years to the climatic amelioration following the last Ice Age. A succinct account of its probable history is given in chapter 4 based upon evidence from pollen analysis and, for more recent time, documentary evidence. It is therefore unnecessary to do more than summarise the history of woodland in Fife in this chapter.

After the last Ice Age, the initial colonisation by birch-dominated woodland was followed about 9000 years ago by a rapid spread of pine and hazel, and later still by oak, alder and elm. By 7000 years ago a mixed deciduous forest was established which remained relatively stable for about 2000 years until the period of massive forest destruction associated with the establishment of primitive agriculture. Clearance was most easily accomplished on well drained sites, and gradually produced the pattern of bare hillsides and cultivated ground that is characteristic of Fife today.

This change was well established in mediaeval times, when woodland was probably limited to river valleys and badly drained areas such as the forest around Falkland, which by the 15th century was protected as a royal hunting forest. By the 16th century even these areas diminished, though perhaps some woodland for domestic use was main-

tained, particularly where sites were inaccessible in incised river and stream valleys.

Even in the 17th century legislation was passed to encourage tree planting, although most estate planting was from 1700 onwards. Early plantations were usually amenity plantings associated with lairds' houses, and the largest existing areas of mature deciduous or mixed woodland are of this origin, for example, the woods bordering the Tay on Birkhill estate. These plantations may well have incorporated existing relict areas of woodland in small valleys. In any case, they support well established ecosystems and play an important role in maintaining woodland communities in Fife.

Another major factor affecting woodland in Fife has been the establishment of coniferous plantations, either by the Forestry Commission or by private individuals and companies, from the early decades of the 20th century up to the present time. There has been extensive afforestation of this type, such as Tentsmuir Forest, Pitmedden Forest, Devilla and the eastern part of the Cleish Hills.

The approximate extent and location of woodland in Fife can be seen in the series of computer-generated maps below. Figure a) shows the extent of semi-natural woodland in Fife. Figure b) shows the extent of all woodland, most of which is plantation, and

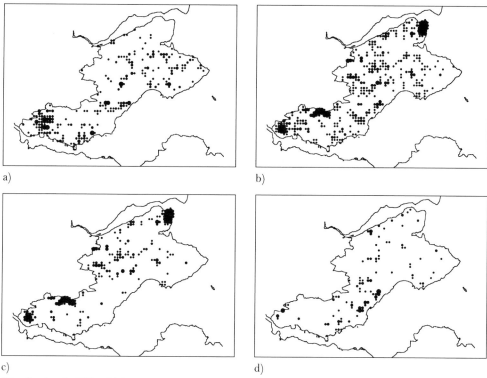

a) b) c) d)

Distribution in Fife of (a) semi-natural broad-leaved woodland; (b) all woodland; (c) coniferous plantation; and (d) mixed plantation. (*Courtesy of Fife Nature*)

Figures c) and d) show the way this is partitioned between coniferous and mixed plantation. The maps are based on information from a recent habitat survey of Fife by the Scottish Wildlife Trust and Scottish Natural Heritage, and have been constructed by Fife Nature, the biological records centre of Fife Council. It is interesting to compare the data on these maps with previous surveys, particularly the comparative survey of Fife carried out by the Nature Conservancy Council as part of the National Countryside Monitoring Scheme (Tudor *et al.* 1994). Though published in 1994, the data for this survey were collected in the 1940s and the 1970s using aerial photography of sample areas.

Trends are apparent from these data which are summarised in the table on p. 73. It can be seen that the overall area of wood-land stayed roughly constant over this 30 year period at about 11 per cent of the total land area. However, this masks the very significant changes that occurred in the composition of the woodland. Broad-leaved and mixed woodland showed a large decrease, compensated for by an increase in coniferous woodland. This is, of course, an over-simplification since it was not a straightforward replacement process, and very often broad-leaved woodland and park-land were lost to arable, whereas conifers were planted on rough grazing and badly drained land. Since the 1970s the trend to-ward coniferous plantations has been slowed by the encouragement of broad-leaved species in planting programmes. However, there is no doubt that there has been an overall loss of natural or semi-natural wood-land this century from a region in which it was already sparse. This is not to say that plantations are without wildlife interest, as will become apparent.

This chapter will discuss the biology of Fife woodlands in three sections:- 1) Long established semi-natural woodland; 2) Long established estate woodland; 3) Modern plantation forestry. These will be followed by a section on the development and practice of forestry in Fife.

Long established semi-natural woodland

These are woodlands that it is reasonable to suppose have some continuity with ancient woodland, or which are known to have existed for at least 150 years, a period within which a mature woodland ecosystem might be expected to develop.

By far the greatest component in this category of woodland consists of the wooded dens which are widespread in Fife. These are very narrow strips of woodland in deeply incised valleys of rivers and burns. Very often the total area of woodland is very small, perhaps as little as 2 hectares, but the linear extent may be considerable, as in Kenly Den, which, with its tributaries, stretches some 8 km inland from Boarhills. In an area that has been largely denuded of native woodland, these dens play a vital role in maintaining habitat diversity and wildlife corridors, as well as acting as reservoirs of woodland species, both plants and animals, from which new plantations can be colonised. The table illustrates clearly the tiny acreage that such long established woodlands occupy, and consequently emphasises their importance.

Wooded dens have probably survived for two reasons: in the first place they are often very steep-sided and difficult of access so that in mediaeval times they were probably

not worth clearing, but instead formed a useful, and renewable, timber resource and provided shelter for livestock; and secondly, in the great era of improvement and mansion-house building of the early and mid 19th century, those that formed part of the policies of such estates were preserved as romantic woodland walks which were suitably improved by the planting of species that were not native to Fife, and sometimes not native to Britain. Sir John Purves, in a talk given in 1980, describing the landscaping of Kinaldy in 1844, stated that the spectacular den was planted and walks constructed. Unfortunately there appears to be no record of the state of the woodland before such fashionable activity was undertaken, nor of the degree of disturbance such landscaping caused. However, the steepest slopes were probably undisturbed, as well as the very wet areas of the stream margins, which are still occupied by native willows and alders. There was thus some continuity of species in both the canopy and the ground flora.

At the present time, the most interesting woodland is found in the larger blocks, especially on private estates with limited access, so that the vulnerable ground flora remains intact. Where access is unrestricted well-made paths help to prevent degradation of the ground flora, although that is difficult to avoid in small or narrow sites such as Cairns Den near St Andrews and Middle Den in Kirkcaldy. In other cases, the woodland has been used as shelter for cattle from neighbouring grassland. Where this is allowed, the ground flora is replaced by grasses, and though the woodland may be ancient it is biologically degraded, and unlikely to regenerate.

The most interesting and biologically rich woodlands are usually separated from adjoining land by old hedges. These give protection from agricultural sprays, and

Estimates of woodland habitat extent and change in Fife from 1940s to the 1970s
(Tudor et al. 1994)

Woodland description	Area (km²) 1940s	Area (km²) 1970s	Net Change Area	%
All woodland & scrub	158.00	156.00	−2.00	−1.0
Broad-leaved woodland	31.39	26.09	−5.30	−16.90
Broad-leaved plantation	3.50	4.97	+1.47	+42.06
Coniferous plantation	54.64	81.18	+26.53	+48.56
Mixed woodland	15.73	10.41	−5.32	−33.83
Young plantation	11.84	9.29	−2.55	−21.54
Felled woodland	2.32	1.84	−0.48	−20.87
Parkland	4.49	1.15	−3.34	−74.39
Scrub, tall	6.20	6.10	−0.10	−1.10
Scrub, low	27.90	14.90	−13.10	−46.70

prevent the incursion of invasive agricultural weeds, so that even in a very narrow woodland strip a woodland ecosystem persists.

The figure on p. 74 illustrates a stylised cross-section of a typical wooded den, such as Dunino Den or Kenly Den. The stream meanders in a deeply incised valley. The edges of the stream itself often form a distinct 'wet-woodland' community.

The more gently sloping parts of the valley floor are reasonably well-drained, and allow the growth of most tree species and the development of a typical mosaic of woodland species in the ground flora. The steeper slopes of the valley are usually wooded, but are extremely sharply drained and sometimes have an unstable surface, particularly where there is disturbance. Seepages from springs form wet flushes at intervals. The boundaries of the den are often formed from old thorn hedges, limiting severe edge effects, though it could be argued the whole den structure is one continuous edge effect, and certainly, as will become apparent later, the ground flora contains many species typical of hedgerows.

Close to the stream, canopy species are alder and willows. The ground flora in shade is often dominated by the opposite-leaved golden saxifrage and lesser celandine, both among the earliest of the spring flowers. Marsh marigold is frequent and reed canary-grass (*Phalaris arundinacea*) forms tall dense stands in less shaded areas. Butterbur may also form dense stands. Mosses and liverworts are very important. Large flat 'thalloid' liverworts are particularly apparent (*Conocephalum conicum* and *Pellia epiphylla*) with their bright green branching fronds covering the bank in places. This type of stream edge community is usually very narrow.

On the valley floor and more gently sloping ground canopy woodland has usually been modified by planting, but some tree species are probably remnants of the primeval woodland. Wych elm (*Ulmus glabra*) has probably always been an important component of the woodland. At present, attack by Dutch elm disease is becoming apparent, and this is already having an important effect on the mature canopy. Sessile oak (*Quercus petraea*) still occurs in some woodland, and is

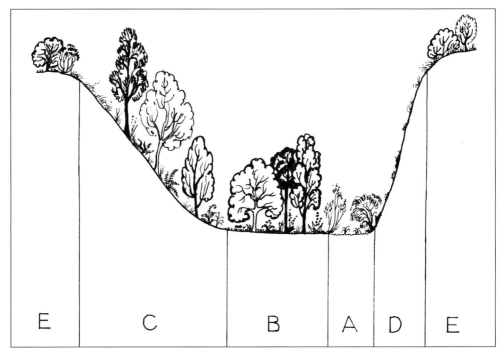

Stylized cross-section of den woodland. A: Stream-edge communities; marshy ground with willows and alders. B: Valley-floor woodland; mixed tree species with well developed woodland ground flora. C: Sharply drained woodland; ground flora with many ferns and grasses. D: Stream-cut cliff; liverworts and mosses dominant in damper parts. E: Boundary hedge.

probably a natural woodland component. However, the pedunculate oak (*Quercus robur*) was widely planted in the last century, and the seed used may not even have been native to Britain. Hybrids between the two species also occur. Beech was also widely planted, and mature trees are found scattered in most policy woodland. It is doubtful if this is a native species in Scotland (see page 34).

Sycamore is certainly a non-native species. The oldest trees in Fife are about 500 years old, but most of the introductions and plantings are much later than this. Sycamore is extremely successful, and is one of the few species that regenerate readily, filling in gaps as they occur, and readily recovering following damage from grazing or any other source. Sycamore coppices easily, regrowing

as multiple stems when cut, and will often survive salt-spray. At Boarhills, the exit of the Kenly Burn is through woodland of sycamore only. At the present time, sycamore is regenerating to the exclusion of almost all other canopy species. Other species play a less important role in the woodland, for example ash (possibly native here), gean (*Prunus avium*) a frequent native tree, and horse-chestnut (always planted). Conifers are always non-native. Larch was sometimes planted as a 'nurse' tree for hardwoods. Small plantings of pine and spruce have also been attempted in some dens.

The understorey may contain holly, hawthorn and blackthorn, along with wild roses and brambles. Hazel and bird cherry are rare in the east but more frequent in the dens of west Fife. This understorey may be derived from and continuous with areas of neglected hedging. The occurrence of snowberry, from North America, usually means that the area concerned has been used for pheasant rearing. Rhododendrons are a pest in some places, particularly *Rhododendron ponticum*, which effectively smothers the ground flora and was frequently planted near large houses. Another North American alien, salmonberry (*Rubus spectabilis*) is spreading rapidly.

The ground flora of the less well drained areas is often a mosaic of wild hyacinths, wood anemones and dog's mercury. Primroses are common on the better drained sites, as is the great wood-rush (*Luzula sylvatica*). Lesser celandines are also very common. Other species that are common are less exclusively woodland denizens, for example, wood avens and water avens, red campion, cow parsley and hogweed. These are essentially hedgerow plants, and indicate a pervasive edge-effect. Nettles are common, and usually indicate nitrate enrichment, for example from fertiliser drift, seepage of nitrate-enriched ground water or from gardens or septic tanks where there are dwellings nearby.

There are other species that are either rare or absent that should be mentioned. Herb paris (*Paris quadrifolia*) is now absent from Fife, though it still occurs in den woodland in Angus and Perthshire and there are old records for Fife too. Sanicle (*Sanicula europaea*) and woodruff (*Galium odorata*) are infrequent, as are moschatel (*Adoxa moschatellina*), lords-and-ladies (*Arum maculatum*), wood stitchwort (*Stellaria nemorum*), and wood sedge (*Carex sylvatica*). Some of these species may be approaching their northern limit here, but there may also have been random loss due to the remnant nature of the habitat.

Ferns are well represented in the ground flora. Broad buckler-fern (*Dryopteris dilatata*)

is usually the dominant large fern followed by male fern (*D.felix-mas*), and more locally, scaly male fern (*D.affinis*). Lady fern (*Athyrium felix-femina*) and hard shield-fern (*Polystichum aculeatum*) are less common. Hart's-tongue is rare in Fife, but does occur in some dens, for example Kenly and Saline, on both natural lime-rich sites and old mortared walls. It seems likely that the climate is generally too dry for this species. Bracken is invasive where there are clearings in well drained areas. Ferns are among the most resilient plants under people pressure, particular male fern and broad buckler fern, and persist in very degraded woodland. However, they are unlikely to reproduce under these conditions.

A list of the most frequent mosses recorded in Kenly Den is probably representative of most den woodlands in which a woodland ground flora is maintained. This is given below. Mosses and lichens are often under-represented in lists of species because of the specialist knowledge required to identify them.

On steep slopes the tree canopy develops from any species that gains rooting space, but the ground layer is often depauperate. Ivy is important, and primroses maintain a foot-hold in places. Where springs occur, and on north-facing slopes, bryophytes become very important. Grasses, such as the meadow-grasses (*Poa trivialis* and *P.nemoralis*), are also prominent and the ferns previously mentioned also occur.

If access is easy, steep slopes are often disfigured by tipping of rubbish of all kinds, including garden rubbish, which can lead to the establishment of daffodils, Welsh poppies, honesty and other exotic species. Some introductions such as few-flowered leek (*Allium paradoxum*) and pink purslane (*Claytonia sibirica*) are threatening the native flora here and there because of their invasive habits.

Bryophytes listed from Kenly Den. This is not an exhaustive list, but gives an indication of the most frequent species recorded. (Courtesy of W Hay.)

Mosses

    Amblystegium serpens

    A.tenax

    Atrichum undulatum

    Brachythecium populeum

    B.rivulare

    B.rutabulum

    Bryum capillare

    Dichodontium pellucidum

    Eucladium verticillatum

    Eurynchium praelongum

    E.striatum

    Fissidens bryoides

    Hypnum cupressiforme var. cupressiforme

    H.cupressiforme var. resupinatum

    H.mammillatum

    Isopterygium elegans

    Isothecium myosuroides

    Mnium hornum

    Orthotrichum pulchellum

    Plagiomnium affine

    P.elatum

    P.undulatum

    Rhizomnium punctatum

    Rhynchostegium confertum

    R.riparioides

    Thamnobryum alopecurum

    Zygodon viridissimus

Liverworts

    Calypogeia arguta

    Conocephalum conicum

    Pellia epiphylla

Woodland regeneration

The health of the woodland community depends not only on its composition at any one time but also on its capacity to maintain itself and regenerate. Thus the structure of a healthy woodland allows for natural death and regeneration of all its components. Openings in the tree canopy due to tree death or coppicing allow the establishment of tree seedlings and a necessary, if temporary, flush of ground flora species. Dead wood from dead trees or brash is necessary as a habitat for decay fungi and bacteria, as well as innumerable species of insects and other invertebrates which both aid the decomposition process and provide food for other wildlife such as birds and small mammals. Recycling of nutrients from dead wood decay is important to the nutrient balance of the woodland.

For all these reasons, excessive tidiness which leads to the clearing of dead wood is a bad management practice, and may be responsible for habitat degeneration in some woodlands. Certainly, in some semi-natural woodlands there is a lack of tree regeneration. Where there is evidence of regeneration, it is often highly biased towards sycamore, though ash is regenerating in some places. It is difficult to disentangle the factors that might be causing these effects. Increased populations of roe deer and rabbits are probably interacting with changing management practices, such as lack of coppicing, to reduce regeneration.

The animals of semi-natural woodland

The diversity of plant species in a long-established woodland provides the basis for a corresponding diversity of animal life. Amongst the mammals, herbivores are few but have an important impact on the vegetation. Roe deer are ubiquitous and since they feed extensively by browsing on shrubs such as bramble and on saplings of trees they can be a limiting factor in regeneration. Rabbits are equally widespread, frequently with their warrens within the edges of woodland. Although much of their feeding takes place on adjacent pasture and cropland, they inevitably feed also within the wood and can seriously affect regeneration of trees. Amongst the rodents, both the native red and the introduced grey squirrel are widespread, the latter usually dominant in broad-leaved woodland. These both feed predominantly upon tree seed, much of it taken while still in the canopy. Of the small rodents, wood mice and bank voles are probably ubiquitous in woodland in Fife, although they have been poorly recorded. Both feed extensively on seeds and nuts, with the bank voles also browsing on leaves of herbs and shrubs, while the wood mice include invertebrates in their diet.

Many birds are also important consumers of seed in woodland; wood pigeons and jays gather acorns and other tree seed from the canopy while in winter siskins specialize on the cones of the stream-side alders. Bullfinches are sparse but feed on buds in spring and on seed, especially ash, in autumn and winter. Chaffinches are dominant amongst the ground-feeding seed-eaters, augmented in winter by their close relatives from Scandinavia the bramblings which are especially partial to beech nuts.

However, in terms of sheer variety and quantity the herbivorous birds and mammals are greatly out-numbered by the insects and other invertebrates. The Lepidoptera (moths and butterflies) in particular dominate the leaf-eating niche, with several hundred species likely to occur in a good wooded den. Some of these occur in prodigious quantity, for example the caterpillars of the oak tortrix moth, *Tortrix viridana*, which can almost defoliate the oaks in early summer before they respond by producing a second crop of leaves.

Sap-sucking insects are also abundant, especially the aphids and many other larger bugs. Aphids are of particular importance since in addition to providing prey for many predators like the tits and hoverflies, they produce huge quantities of sugary faeces – 'honey-dew' – which in turn is used as fuel by a great diversity of flying insects as well as by ants.

Amongst the predatory mammals, foxes, stoats and weasels all hunt in woodland although none are confined to it. In each case voles and mice are the principal prey. Badgers are widespread in north and east Fife but scarce in the west. Their setts are usually situated in woodland, consisting of a series of tunnels that may extend for tens of metres. The tunnels link a number of holes of which only two or three may be used at any one time, indicated by large heaps of freshly excavated earth. Badgers forage both within woodland and on adjacent fields. Earthworms tend to be the dominant prey but they are versatile and will dig out nests of voles and mice as well as bulbs and tubers, for example of pignut.

The principal predatory birds of woodlands work in shifts, with sparrowhawks hunting by day and concentrating on small birds while tawny owls take the night-shift. The owls feed primarily on mice and voles but also on shrews, both common and pygmy, which are themselves predators on the invertebrates of the leaf-litter. Up in the canopy the caterpillars and other insects provide food for many different kinds of birds. Great and blue tits remain throughout the year and supplement their insect diet by seeds in winter, the great tits especially doing much of their foraging on the ground, particularly when beech mast is abundant.

In summer the tits are supplemented by

the migratory warblers which also prey amongst the foliage. The only really widespread one in woodland is the willow warbler, but chiffchaffs, garden warblers and blackcaps all breed locally in Fife woods. That trio of insectivorous migrants so characteristic of oak woods in parts of central and western Scotland, redstart, wood warbler and pied flycatcher, are virtually absent from Fife except for the first two in the far west.

More specialist predators are the spotted flycatcher which catches its prey in flight, the treecreeper which picks tiny insects, spiders and mites from crevices on tree trunks and the woodpeckers which prey upon larvae of insects, especially beetles, in dead wood. Suitable over-mature trees for feeding and nesting of woodpeckers are scarce in Fife and both great spotted and green woodpeckers are only thinly although widely distributed.

Predators are also abundant amongst the woodland invertebrates. All spiders are predatory and many different species occur at all levels from the top of the canopy to the recesses of the leaf-litter. The canopy and undergrowth lend themselves to the stretching of the familiar orb-webs, but only a minority of spiders use this technique although all use silk in one way or another. Predation is common amongst the myriads of species of beetles, especially the ground beetles of the family Carabidae, while in the leaf-litter, dead wood and topsoil several species of centipedes are amongst the dominant predators on small insects.

The decomposers
The autumn leaf-fall in a wood provides a huge source of food for decomposer organisms ranging from fungi and bacteria to a great diversity of invertebrates. The leaf-fall is augmented at other times of year by many other products that contribute to the leaf-litter: bud scales in spring, flowers, twigs and, throughout the summer, a steady rain of frass – caterpillar dung. The tree trunks also contribute to this resource of dead vegetation if they are not harvested – in truly natural woodland there is usually about as much dead wood, fallen and standing, as living trees, resulting in an extremely diverse flora and fauna of decomposers and their attendant predators. It is unlikely that any wood in Fife meets that criterion, but any dead wood makes a very significant contribution to the overall diversity of life in a wood.

The invisible threads or hyphae of fungi are everywhere and along with bacteria are usually responsible for the initial breakdown of dead plant material. It is likely that when the decomposer invertebrates such as snails, slugs, millipedes, woodlice, earthworms and springtails eat dead leaves it is primarily the fungi and bacteria that they are digesting. The composition of this fauna will vary from place to place, depending for example upon the acidity or alkalinity of the soil. Millipedes, woodlice and snails need calcium for their protecting skins and shells. As a result a lime-rich wood like Craighall Den near Ceres has a millipede fauna of at least 15 species compared with only four or five in an acidic oak and birch wood as at Lucklaw Hill.

Not all fungi are decomposers of dead plant material. Many of those with conspicuous toadstools, such as the fly agaric, form intimate 'mycorrhizal' associations with the roots of trees, in this case birch, with both tree and fungus benefitting from the partnership. Some fungi are parasites on trees, some of the most conspicuous being the large woody bracket fungi of the genus *Ganoderma* often found on the lower parts of the trunk of ash and beech.

Less conspicuous but more devastating in its results is the fungus causing Dutch elm disease, *Ceratocystis ulmi*. This grows unobtrusively within the tunnels bored by bark beetles (*Scolytes* spp.) which serve to disperse the spores. Wych elm, which is a prominent element in many semi-natural woods in Fife, especially in the dens, is not quite so susceptible as other elms that have been virtually wiped out in parts of England. Nevertheless a considerable proportion of elms in Fife have already succumbed and many more are showing signs of infection. The ecological results can be difficult to predict. Where the dead trees are left, as at Keil's Den near Largo, it will greatly enhance the diversity of the associated fauna all the way from beetles and hover-flies to woodpeckers and flycatchers. The creation of clearings enhances the herbaceous ground flora as well as encouraging the growth of tree seedlings and saplings. Wych elms are fairly resistant to the disease in the sapling stage and are already filling the gaps at Keil's Den, but in some places they may lose out to competition from sycamore.

Estate woodland

By far the largest areas of broad-leaved and mixed woodland in Fife have survived as policy woodland of mansion houses. Some of these woodlands incorporate den woodland, and may therefore pre-date the 'improvement' era. Even if this is not the case, the policy woodlands of the 18th and 19th centuries are now mature semi-natural woodlands. In some cases the woodlands have outlived the mansion houses they served. This is the case with the Valleyfield Woods, west of Dunfermline. However, their origin as estate woodland is apparent from the presence of exotic deciduous trees such as lime and beech, and exotic conifers such as larch, Douglas and other firs. The presence of *Rhododendron ponticum*, which is now a pernicious weed in some places, is also an indicator of estate woodland.

Estate woodlands were not merely amenity areas, though this was one of their functions, especially near to the mansion house. Timber production was commercially important, and further away from the house, plantations for commercial forestry have always been important. The effect of market forces and government policy on the species grown is discussed later in the chapter. Another aspect of estate forestry was its value for game cover, particularly the rearing of pheasants, and many shelter belts and narrow strips of woodland between fields were planted primarily for game cover. This functional diversity has led to habitat diversity, and great wildlife interest.

An outstanding example of a biologically important estate woodland is Flisk Wood, and other contiguous woodland on the Birkhill estate on the south side of the Firth of Tay in north Fife. This woodland was already established in the mid 18th century when the country was surveyed by General Roy and his colleagues following the 1745 rebellion and is therefore considered to be 'ancient woodland' in the classification used by Scottish Natural Heritage (SNH). The woodland is situated on the steep braes of Tay, and incorporates several steep-sided valleys, incised into the north-facing slope of the estuary. In a recent survey (Robertson 1993) it is suggested that this is the least disturbed area of broad-leaved woodland in Fife. Flisk Wood contains a high proportion of native tree species, such as ash, wych elm, gean and oak (*Quercus petraea*), with a well developed shrub layer and ground flora containing all the species mentioned in the description of den woodland. Despite its native appearance, this wood has probably been supplemented by planting of native species, and it has certainly been modified by the presence of sycamore, which may have been planted, or may have invaded from other areas.

The effect of planting exotics is much more apparent in the woodlands surrounding Birkhill House, where amenity has obviously been the chief priority, and there are mature beech and lime trees as well as exotic conifers. Coniferous plantations, mainly of larch and Scots pine, occur interspersed with the predominant broadleaves. In his Tay Valley study, Robertson records well over 200 species of flowering plants, conifers and ferns in the coastal woodlands in this area. The floral diversity provides habitat diversity for birds, and Flisk Wood itself is now a Site of Special Scientific Interest. It should be noted that there is no public access to Flisk Wood, though there are well trodden paths in the woodland along the Tay near Balmerino, and it is interesting to see the habitat degradation that has resulted. Many other estate woodlands have no public access, and restricted public access has often been a factor in maintaining the biological interest of these sites.

There are many other policy woodlands, or former policy woodlands, dating from the 'improvement' era, which now form important mature woodlands, both from a biological and a public amenity point of view. The Town Wood at Glenrothes (the grounds of Leslie House) is a good example, as are Ravenscraig Park, Dunnikier Park and Milldam at Kirkcaldy, all of which have considerable biological interest.

The management of commercial estate woodland at the present time and the way it is being affected by government policy is discussed in the section on forestry in Fife.

Plantation woodland

Modern plantation forestry began in earnest after the First World War, and therefore the oldest plantations, such as Tentsmuir, are now more than 70 years old, and have become important habitats for wildlife. Many plantations were laid out on areas of rough grazing or moorland. Others replace birch and willow scrub. In the west of the county, these areas usually consist of hill land with peaty soil, such as the eastern part of the Cleish Hills. These plantations are chiefly of spruce and lodgepole pine. The close planting of these large areas and many smaller plantations has largely masked their former moorland or grassland origin, but some pockets of the original habitats remain, and there are several typical den woodlands which persist in the Cleish hills, for example at Meadowhead. Similarly Blairadam plantation contains some remnants of much older broad-leaved woodland planted 200 years ago.

These remnants add vital diversity to the habitat, allowing a much wider range of plants and birds than would otherwise be expected. However, birch and willow scrub is becoming increasingly rare, though pockets are preserved, for example in the SSSI on the upper parts of Glenduckie Hill, where the thin soil supports birch with an extensive ground flora dominated by blaeberry and especially lichens. This site is entirely surrounded by commercial forestry, and may be at risk by seeding from it.

However, these upland plantations do not have the wildlife interest of Tentsmuir Forest, which was planted on a large area of fixed dunes on the south side of the Tay estuary. This land was formerly used as rough grazing and for sport. Prior to 1920 the vegetation consisted of heather moorland with blaeberry and grasses such as sheep's fescue (*Festuca ovina*) and red fescue (*Festuca rubra*). Sand sedge (*Carex arenaria*) was common near the coast. It is interesting to note that stunted Scots pines were recorded on Tentsmuir in the early years of the 20th century (Smith 1900), but it was suggested that they were usually grazed off by sheep. There is some indication, therefore, that without heavy grazing Tentsmuir might well have become open pinewood at that time, and that the afforestation with Scots pine and Corsican pine (*Pinus nigra*) was an entirely appropriate use of the habitat.

At Annsmuir near Ladybank, old lowland heath has survived in the rough areas of the golf course, including the only remaining colony of any size in Fife of the petty whin (*Genista anglica*). In these areas, rabbits are severely controlled, and this has resulted in an open pine-birch wood with an interesting understorey of heather, blaeberry and ferns. Similarly, in the less dense plantations at Tentsmuir, it is possible that the ground flora has persisted and some interesting plants now flourish that were previously suppressed. It seems probable that the large populations of creeping lady's-tresses (*Goodyera repens*) under some areas of both Scots pine and Corsican pine may be an expansion of small populations that were already established before afforestation. There are also flourishing populations of the moss *Ptilium cristacastrensis*, which is an uncommon species characteristic of native pinewoods and has certainly increased at Tentsmuir since afforestation, though it was present in Fife in 1889 (Howie 1889).

More commonly within the less dense pine plantations there is a well developed moss flora, and ferns are prominent, the most frequent being the broad buckler-fern (*Dryopteris dilatata*), the male fern (*D.filix-mas*) and the scaly male fern (*D.affinis*). In some places, heather and blaeberry persist.

Where planting has been more dense, and where stands of Sitka spruce are present, the ground flora is much less well preserved, due to shading.

The animals of coniferous plantations

When plantations are established on open ground the exclusion of domestic stock by fencing results in a lush growth of grasses and other herbaceous vegetation. Herbivorous animals quickly respond and very high densities of field voles are characteristic of recently established plantations. These in turn attract predators such as short-eared owls, kestrels, foxes, stoats and weasels. When the trees reach the shrubby stage, and wild shrubs such as rasp, rose and bramble have established, bank voles usually become dominant and finally as the canopy closes and the ground vegetation disappears wood mice are left as the principal, and sometimes the only, small rodents. However rides, roads and edges maintain residues of the flora and fauna characteristic of the early stages.

Plantations differ from natural woodlands especially in having the trees of uniform age. Although there is usually an abundance of small dead wood, there are few opportunities for species like the woodpeckers, tawny owls and bats that normally rely on old trunks to provide nest holes (and food in the case of the woodpeckers). At Tentsmuir Forest artificial boxes have been supplied for bats and have been successful in attracting pipistrelles, brown long-eared and Natterer's bats. Unlike tawny owls, long-eared owls are not dependent upon tree holes and nest sparsely throughout Fife in coniferous plantations.

Single-species plantations are vulnerable to wildly fluctuating numbers of certain herbivorous insects such as the pine weevils (*Hylobius abietis*), aphids, especially the green spruce aphid (*Adelges abietis*), and the cater-pillars of the bordered white moth (*Bupalis piniaria*). Characteristic insectivorous birds of mature plantations are coal tits and gold-crests which forage in the canopy, while robins and wrens usually manage to survive at ground level.

Coniferous plantations provide the prin-cipal habitat for the red squirrel in Fife and one in which it appears to be able to hold its own against the grey squirrel. Red squirrels feed especially on the seeds of conifers, strip-ping the scales from the cones to get at them and leaving characteristic cores on the ground. However the buds of conifers are also important in their diet in winter and spring, fungi in autumn and the terminal shoots of conifers in winter. The interaction of grey and red squirrels poses one of the more intractable problems of conservation. In every other respect the diversification of conifer plantations with broad-leaved trees is very desirable to enhance the native wild-life and restore at least some of the elements of a natural woodland fauna and flora. On the other hand that is likely to encourage the entry of grey squirrels into the last

bastion of the reds and risk their total re-placement.

Forestry in Fife

The previous sections of this chapter have described the structure and biological im-portance of the woodlands of Fife as they exist at present. This section is concerned with the practical aspects of forestry and its interaction with history, social pressures and government policy, which are the factors that have shaped the present situation, and will determine the future pattern of wood-land in Fife.

State forestry

During the First World War the timber reserves of this country were greatly de-pleted by reason of the German submarine blockade. In 1917 the Acland Committee recommended the formation of a Forestry Commission and the restoration of the fore-stry reserve in order to ensure an adequate strategic timber reserve in the event of an-other war. Three quarters of a million hectares were to be planted, mostly by the

The state forests of Fife: extent and production

		Area	Felling	Thinning
			(Cubic metres per annum)	
1	Pitmeddon	550 ha	8000	1000
2	Weddersbie	125 ha	2000	500
3	Tentsmuir	1550 ha	—	5000
4	Clatto	290 ha	—	1000
5	Ladybank	290 ha	—	1000
6	Blairadam	1335 ha	—	5500
7	Devilla	775 ha	—	4000
8	Bathmoor	216 ha	—	700
9	Cardenden	130 ha	1000	250
	Total	5261 ha	11,000	18,950

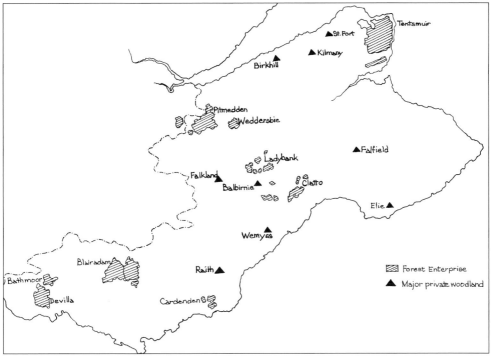

State forests (shaded) and some major private woodlands (triangles) in Fife.

Forestry Commission, who would also grant-aid planting by private owners.

In Fife this resulted in the establishment of Tentsmuir Forest in the 1920s, with an area of 1500 hectares, and later new blocks along the hill slopes of north Fife as well as at Blairadam (see map). Because of the urgency to re-establish reserves quickly, very large planting programmes were carried out from young trees mostly grown at Tulliallan Nursery near Kincardine. The result was large blocks of even-aged conifers, mainly Scots and Corsican pines on the sands of Tentsmuir, and Sitka spruce and lodgepole pine on the peatier soils of Devilla and Blairadam. The spacing between the young trees was initially close, about one metre (to inhibit weeds) and the result was dark plantations with little edge effect and not much holding capacity for wildlife of any sort. This was mitigated to some extent by about 15 per cent of roads, rides, paths and 'waste', giving linear and continuous habitats for shrubs, insects, birds and other wildlife.

In 1958 the national forest policy was amended to include social and economic objectives and in 1963 public recreation and amenity were admitted as desirable functions of forestry. Forest walks were laid out at Devilla and Tentsmuir, and a carpark at Tentsmuir provided the public with access to the woods and the shore.

Foresters have always had a personal inbuilt recognition of the need to include habitat management as part of their work, and work on birds and habitat by Kenneth Williamson, Ian Newton and Dorian Moss, amongst others, lent substance to this, resulting in actual policy changes at the top.

However the primary objective of state forestry is to grow timber for the home market. The table on p. 82 shows the forests of Fife, by area and by estimated annual production from fellings and from thinnings. At approximately 30,000 tonnes per annum this is a significant contribution to the UK requirement – only about 15 per cent of this is home-grown.

Nevertheless the commercial plantations have considerable advantages for wildlife, the foremost of which is shelter. Over the years forest design has improved in that open space, edge effect, and linear conjunction of broad-leaved groups will improve the habitat for a great variety of wildlife as well as benefitting visual amenity and recreational enjoyment. In forests on poorer soils however, such as Tentsmuir, Ladybank and Devilla, replanting will remain primarily as a Scots pine crop, but fellings will be by groups in order to promote diversity of structure.

Private forestry

The Forestry Act of 1919 made grants available for planting trees. Subsequent acts, and changes in the regulations, have changed the number and nature of grants, which are currently available from the Forestry Authority as follows:

1. Woodland Grant Scheme Planting Grant, the amount of which varies with the area and whether conifers or broad-leaved species are used; this may be supplemented for 'Better land' (arable or improved grassland), and 'Community Woodland' (within 5 miles of a town), and for coppice on short rotations.

2. Farm Woodland Premium Scheme, to encourage new woodlands on farms; administered with the Agricultural Departments.

3. Restocking grants for existing woodlands.

4. Annual Management Grant.

5. Woodland Improvement Grants, in three categories.

6. Livestock Exclusion annual premium, for less favoured areas of high environmental value.

In earlier times, grants for tree planting were not unknown: in the 18th century grants were made by way of competition for the best managed oakwoods along the Forth/Clyde Canal. Even earlier, when Charles I visited Fife in the 17th century there was encouragement to plant new oakwoods along the line of the visit.

The nature of privately owned woodlands has changed greatly during the 20th century. Formerly the woodlands provided timber, posts and rails for neighbouring agricultural land and, especially in Fife, for mining timber and for building boats for the local fishing fleets. The location and layout of the woodlands were usually related to the sporting interest, especially pheasant and partridge shooting. Birkhill estate has some plantations of European and Japanese larch, from which hybrid larch seed used to be collected for planting all over Scotland.

Nowadays, pressure for access for public recreation has greatly increased, sometimes giving rise to problems when the various interests overlap. Increasing awareness of the importance of broad-leaved tree species in the landscape (supported by increased rate of grant) is beginning to have an impact. Integration of the needs of timber production, wildlife conservation, public recreation and woodland design was encouraged by the formation of the Farming and Wildlife Advisory Group (FWAG) which also bears on woodlands and forests. Similarly, an annual award for multiple land use in forests, woodlands and farms is administered by the Royal

15. Sharing resources on a rocky shore: dog-whelks (predators), limpets (herbivores) and barnacles (filter-feeders). (*Photo: R. M. Cormack*)

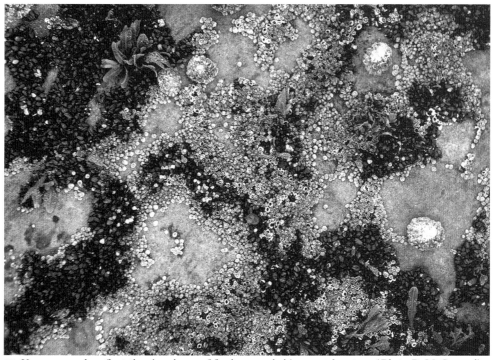

16. Young mussels reflect the abundance of food suspended in coastal waters. (*Photo: R. M. Cormack*)

17. The west cliffs of the Isle of May. (*Photo: A. Wilson*)

18. Lesser black-backed gull, a summer visitor breeding on the Forth islands. (*Photo: N. U. Corbet*)

19. Long-tailed duck: regular winter visitors to the Fife coast, often staying well offshore. (*Photo: D. Bell, ECOS*)

20. Craighall Den, Ceres; a typical 'den', with a deeply incised burn and wooded slopes. (*Photo: H. A. P. Ingram*)

21. Craighall Den; a steep slope with wild hyacinth, dog's mercury, and a good supply of dead wood. (*Photo: H. A. P. Ingram*)

22. Glenduckie Hill; open birch woodland with an understorey of heather and blaeberry. (*Photo: H. A. P. Ingram*)

23. Flisk Wood; ancient woodland modified by estate management. The native oak is mixed with planted beech and exotic conifers. (*Photo: H. A. P. Ingram*)

24. The River Eden near Dairsie. (*Photo: R. M. Cormack*)

Highland and Agricultural Society of Scotland; ownerships in Fife have frequently been successful.

Shelter is perhaps one of the most important benefits woodlands can have for agriculture, particularly in the southern half of Fife where the flatter land is more conducive to the use of heavy machinery and very large fields can give rise to exposure and even loss of top soil. However the planting of shelter belts is not yet particularly noticeable.

Landscape design in planting woodlands is becoming more important, and there are now about 200 approved designed woodland landscapes in NE Fife. At Valleyfield in the south of Fife, the estate where the pioneer landscape gardener Humphry Repton learned his craft, a full-scale landscape design is in being. Of the larger commercial privately-owned woodlands, Balbirnie, Birkhill, Elie, Falfield, Falkland, Kilmany, Raith, St Fort and Wemyss are noteworthy.

In 1980 the Forestry Commission estimated that about 10 per cent of the total area of Fife was under woodland; the 1996 figures are not yet to hand, but it is estimated that the proportion has risen to 15 per cent.

The protection of woodlands and forests
Of the activities by man prejudicial to woodlands, fire, litter and dumping stand out. Fire is by far the most damaging, particularly in young plantations in time of drought and with adverse winds. Whether caused accidentally or maliciously, control can only be by information and education, coupled of course with careful plantation design and layout. The public can be very helpful in reporting outbreaks.

The most important mammal pest in Fife is undoubtedly the rabbit, which eats and damages young shoots and can cause havoc on a large scale. Control is by shooting, snaring and gassing of burrows and, indirectly, by the use of tubes or, in very large areas, by rabbit fencing. Voles can also cause severe damage to young trees at ground level; predators such as kestrels, harriers, owls, foxes and the weasel family can to some extent curb excessive numbers, as can buzzards and most of the afore-mentioned with rabbits. But as is well known, it is the prey population that ultimately controls the numbers of predators, and there has to be a balance between the needs of forestry and those of the sheep farmer and the shooter. Roe, and sika deer in the southwest of Fife, can cause considerable damage by browsing and fraying, and have to be controlled by annual culling. Again careful design of plantations can be of benefit by leaving open spaces both to aid control and to provide browsing opportunities, for example willow beds, as alternatives to valuable tree species. The use of one-metre tubes is now widespread as an alternative to fencing.

Weevils and caterpillars require the use of insecticides – dipping young plants in the case of the weevil, spraying against caterpillars when pupal counts show dangerous increase in numbers. Climatic and other stress factors undoubtedly affect the numbers of these insect pests, and the encouragement of insectivorous predators, for example tits, cannot but be beneficial. This may take the form of increasing edge-effect and extending corridors of broad-leaved tree species between good bird habitats.

Fungal pests include the butt-rot fungus (*Heterobasidion annosum*) and, to a lesser extent, honey fungus (*Armillaria mellea*). These are tackled by treatment of cut stumps with urea and/or a hostile fungus, *Phlebia giganteum*.

Wood industry

Before the Second World War there was not a great deal of mature log-size timber in the country as much of it had been felled in 1914–18. However the coal-mining industry was one of the principal markets, and took large quantities of sawn and round timber for pitprops and chocks. Sheep 'flakes' and potato and hay boxes were in great demand: there was no plastic equivalent in those days. Rustic poles, pallet-wood and fencing timber were also in demand. The war years of 1939–1945 saw a great deal of the remaining larger-size timber felled, and the large plantings between the wars had not yet reached maturity. This situation applied to the whole of the UK, and Fife was no exception. The proximity of the coal mines in the Lothians and Fife was of course advantageous.

Since 1945 progress in the development of the plastics industries has reduced demand for small-wood products, but the advance of techniques for processing pulp, paper, paperboard and wood-based panels has offset this to a great extent, and the subsequent growth of plantations has resulted in sizes suitable for the building industry. Fife is not all that far from board and paper mills at Irvine (Ayrshire) and Cowie (Stirling), and there are several mills for sawn timber in the Lothians.

An important recent feature in British Forestry is the establishment by the Forest Industry Committee of Great Britain (FICGB) of 'Woodmark', a labelling technique whereby growers can indicate to consumers when their product is derived from home-grown timber that has been felled in accordance with Forestry Authority regulations; these include guidance on improving the environment, both for wildlife and visually. It is hoped that this measure, together with schemes such as the Scottish Woods and Forest Awards (sponsored by the Royal Highland and Agricultural Society of Scotland) will do much to improve the habitat of Scotland's woodlands.

Acknowledgements

Our thanks are due for cooperation received from: Mr John Cuthill; Mr Bill Hay; Forest Enterprise, Aberfoyle; and Forest Authority, Perth.

Further reading

Ballantyne, G H and Bease, J B (1982). Forestry and trees, in *The wildlife and antiquities of Kirkcaldy District*. Kirkcaldy Naturalists Society, pp 146–157.

Howie, C (1889). *The moss flora of Fife and Kinross*. Fifeshire Journal Office, Cupar.

Keith, F (1992). *Fife woodlands survey*, vols 1–3. Scottish Wildlife Trust Report. Scottish Natural Heritage.

Purvis, J (1980). Integration of Forestry and Farming Practice, in: Mitchell, R J (ed.) *Trees in the Fife landscape*. University of St Andrews conference report, pp 31–38.

Robertson, J (1993). *Tay Estuary Study (S.side)*. Techn. Rep. Phase 1 Habitat Surveys, Fife Regional Council.

Smith, R (1900). On the seed dispersal of *Pinus sylvestris* and *Betula alba*. *Annals of Scottish Natural History*, January, pp 43–46.

Smout, T C (1997). *Scottish woodland history*. Scottish Cultural Press, Edinburgh.

Tait, A A (1990). *The landscape garden in Scotland 1735–1835*. Edinburgh University Press.

Tudor, G J, Mackey, E C and Underwood F M (1994). *The National Countryside Monitoring Scheme: the changing face of Scotland 1940s to 1970s*. Scottish Natural Heritage.

8

Fresh water

J. STEWART PRITCHARD

Introduction

Fife comprises some of the most intensively managed land in Scotland and the water in Fife's lochs, ponds, rivers and burns must first pass over or through this land. The way in which catchments are managed can greatly influence the variety of fresh-water species and habitats. There is a gradual change in the prevalent farming practices as one travels from the drier east to the wetter west of Fife. The Howe of Fife, the Tay coastal area and the East Neuk have predominantly arable farms on rich soils of glacial origin. To the west, and especially beyond the M90 Perth to Edinburgh motorway, grazing pastures on more clay soils prevail.

Depending upon the soil types, slope, rainfall pattern and state of cultivation, a proportion of fertilisers applied to fields is lost into water courses. In some circumstances, especially where water is running over the soil surface, significant quantities of soil particles, with their adsorbed phosphate and other nutrients, may be washed into these water courses. Apart from the more obvious siltation effects, the unseen nutrients promote increased growth of aquatic plants which can in turn lead to further problems for aquatic life.

Few fresh-waters in Fife can be described as 'undisturbed'. Many show evidence of past alterations and many more are close to paths and roads. Despite these and other pressures, Fife's running and standing fresh waters still provide valuable 'corridors' and 'stepping stones' for wildlife through an otherwise inhospitable environment. It may surprise some readers to learn that Fife still has populations of some of the more retiring aquatic species such as otters and kingfishers. Others, like the fresh-water mussels and water vole, less tolerant of our modern aquatic environment, are in decline, or have already been lost to Fife.

For each water body a riparian zone can be defined. These are the areas of transition from the water's edge extending landwards to the limit of influence of the water body. In natural systems riparian zones might include extensive wet meadows and flood plains. However in Fife these zones are generally narrow to nonexistent and constrained by adjacent land-use practices. The value, even of these impoverished strips, far outweighs that which might be suggested by their extent. In many areas, as hedgerows and woodland edges do elsewhere, they form the only continuous pieces of natural habitat through otherwise relatively inhospitable areas of conurbation or closely grazed or tilled land. Continuity of habitats is very important in facilitating the dispersal of many species and this can be enhanced, at least to a degree, by increasing the width and improving the vegetation structure of the riparian zone. Well established riparian zones, with grassland and tall herbs under an open tree canopy, also have economic benefits through providing improved feeding for fish and protecting banks from erosion and consequent loss of land.

There is insufficient room in this short chapter to provide a detailed ecology of fresh waters and the reader wishing to explore the subject further is referred to the section on page 101. Instead, this chapter aims to highlight the diversity of habitats and aquatic plant species associated with running and standing waters in Fife. Throughout reference will be made to recent and ongoing studies and to more specific examples.

The running waters – rivers and burns

Fife is drained primarily by three rivers. In the north, the River Eden (approximately 31 km from source to the limit of tidal influence) rises in the area between Loch Leven and Glenfarg and flows eastwards through the Howe of Fife villages and farmland, being joined by the burns draining the northern slopes of the Lomond Hills and the southern slopes of the North Fife Hills. East of Cupar, near Dairsie, the Eden is joined by its largest tributary, the Ceres Burn, and a short distance further east, near Nydie, the Eden becomes tidal as it discharges into its estuary.

Whilst the Rivers Leven and Ore (approximately 21 and 19 km respectively between their sources and the limits of tidal influence) also flow eastwards they differ from the Eden in that they pass through significantly larger areas of industrialised and built-up land. The farmland in these catchments tends more towards grazing pastures than the intensive arable farming practised in the Howe of Fife. The River Leven starts as the outflow of Loch Leven

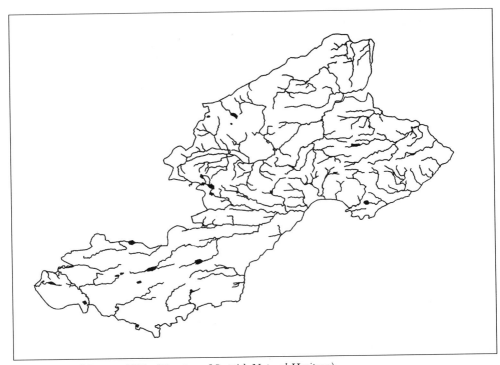

The rivers and burns of Fife. (*Courtesy of Scottish Natural Heritage.*)

which collects the drainage from an intensively arable farming catchment. To Glenrothes it is bordered primarily by arable farmland but in Glenrothes it flows through areas of quiet parkland amidst this busy new town. East of Glenrothes the river flows through mixed farmland before being joined by the River Ore and entering the conurbation of Methil and Leven and discharging into Largo Bay and the outer Firth of Forth.

The River Ore arises as the outflow of Lochore and drains the eastern part of the Fife coalfield. Formed itself as the result of coal mining activities and later landscape restoration in the 1970s, the loch is now the focus of a popular Country Park in which water sports and wildlife areas are accommodated and promoted. Lochore is fed by waters from further west in the Cleish Hills and drains eastwards and northwards past the old mining villages of Cardenden and Thornton to its confluence with the River Leven.

There are also a number of significant burns, including the Kenly Water, and its tributaries the Kinaldy and Cameron Burns, draining the north of the East Neuk, and the Bluther Burn draining the areas west of Dunfermline. The western slopes of the Cleish Hills drain into the Black Devon which flows south and westwards, through neighbouring Clackmannanshire, before discharging into the inner Forth Estuary upstream of the Kincardine Bridge.

The three main river corridors are relatively well known, having been surveyed in 1992 by the then Nature Conservancy Council for Scotland. For every 500 m section, details were recorded of the physical channel profile, substrate type, presence of pools and riffles, riparian and channel vegetation and adjacent land-uses. The Black Devon corridor was similarly surveyed in 1994 for Scottish Natural Heritage. The results highlighted some previously un-noticed differences. The margins of the three rivers are dominated primarily by stands of reed canary-grass (*Phalaris arundinacea*), with or without great willowherb and stinging nettle, and branched bur-reed (*Sparganium erectum*). The shallow margins typically support water forget-me-not (*Myosotis scorpioides*), brooklime (*Veronica beccabunga*) and monkeyflower (*Mimulus guttatus*), an attractive but introduced and now widespread species from western North America.

Unlike the Leven and Ore, the marshy margins of the Eden support large stands of reed sweet-grass (*Glyceria maxima*). Prior to flood defence and associated landscaping works in the early 1990s there was such a stand in Cupar, below Victoria Bridge. Remnants can still be seen here and slightly further downstream. The introduced Indian balsam (*Impatiens glandulifera*) which can be seen in Dura Den near the confluence of the Eden and the Ceres Burn, is frequent along the banks of the upper and middle reaches of the Eden but absent from the Leven and Ore. On the other hand, water-plantain (*Alisma plantago-aquatica*), which has a rather restricted distribution in Fife, is common on the Ore but absent from the Eden and Leven.

These differences, which suggest the rivers have differing nutrient status, are reinforced by a comparison of the submerged, channel vegetation. In the Ore, alternate water-milfoil (*Myriophyllum alterniflorum*) and perfoliate pondweed (*Potamogeton perfoliatus*) occur in the upper reaches, and unbranched bur-reed (*Sparganium emersum*) and fennel pondweed (*Potamogeton pectinatus*) are abundant along much of its length. These species are virtually absent from the Eden and Leven. Stands of water crowfoot (*Ranunculus* spp.) which are abundant in the Eden and present in the Leven, are generally absent from the Ore.

These similarities and differences

together suggest that the Leven and Eden are carrying greater nutrient loads and this seems to be supported by other observations. The Eden has been found to have one of the highest nitrate levels of any Scottish river, almost certainly attributable to diffuse nutrient-rich run-off from its intensive arable catchment, and Loch Leven, from which the River Leven flows, has suffered massive enrichment in recent years. The problems in Loch Leven and its catchment are now being addressed. All sewage discharged into the Loch is now stripped of its phosphate nutrients. Diffuse pollution from the catchment still enters the loch and treated sewage from other lochside villages is diverted around to Scotlandwell where it is discharged at its outflow – which of course does not improve the quality of water in the River Leven!

Where the adjacent land is low-lying relative to the river, or is influenced by ground-water seepage, the riparian zone may extend into areas of marsh or fen. There are few examples of these transitions along the rivers of Fife and one of the best remaining is probably Orebank Marsh, downstream of Bow Bridge, over the River Ore, on the A910 Auchterderran to Lochgelly road.

All three rivers and many of the larger burns were harnessed to provide power and water for past industries. Signs of this historic use remain in the form of the numerous weirs which continue to influence the nature of these rivers and their wildlife. There are some 38 weirs on the three main rivers alone (Eden – 11, Leven – 18 and Ore – 9) and many of these are sufficient to prevent the movement of wildlife, including that of migratory fish. The main rivers are still utilised by today's industries of agriculture, paper making and hydro electricity generation, amongst others.

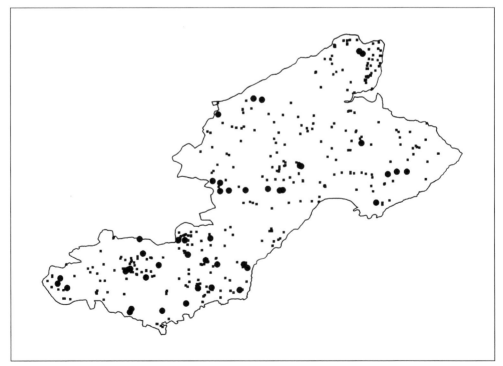

The distribution of standing waters.   ●: over 2 hectares ■: under 2 hectares
(*Courtesy of Scottish Natural History.*)

The standing waters – ponds, lochs and reservoirs

There are in excess of 400 standing waters in Fife (map opposite). These vary in size from tiny ponds, such as the laundry-green pond in Charles Street, Pittenweem, to substantial lochs and reservoirs such as Loch Glow and Cameron Reservoir, and in quality from the peri-urban, litter-strewn and neglected waterway to the near pristine lochans of the Cleish and Lomond Hills.

Ponds

Some ponds may be very ancient features of the countryside whilst others are more recent, transient and sometimes ephemeral in nature. Most ponds in Fife owe their origins to human activities, for example watering ponds for farm animals, abandoned mineral workings or subsidence associated with them, sporting uses such as flight or fish ponds or as landscape enhancements on estates and in parks and gardens. Even on moors and hills the past influence of man is evident. More recently ponds have been established to promote wildlife interests. Many ponds in Fife have been lost due to the cessation of their original purpose and they have subsequently been infilled or left to revert naturally to dry ground by processes of succession.

Ponds have been defined variously as bodies of standing water of up to a certain size, commonly 0.5 or 2 hectares in area. However, this definition fails to take account of their purpose or use which may be equally or more important in determining their value to wildlife. For example, a pond of say 0.25 hectares may be created by an industrialist to provide cooling water to a factory. Such a pond is likely to be constructed to maximise its volume and have steep sides. Similarly, to resist the effects of frequent changes in water level, the sides are likely to be reinforced or constructed with concrete. As a result of its industrial purpose and use this water body, despite being within the size range for a 'pond', is really a 'reservoir'. Ponds, lochs and reservoirs will therefore be considered collectively here and differentiated as appropriate.

Between 1985 and 1993, initially by volunteers as part of the National Ponds and Amphibian Survey for the (then) Nature Conservancy Council and later completed under contract to Scottish Natural Heritage, an attempt was made to survey comprehensively all the standing waters in Fife. Nearly 600 pond sites were identified from maps and visited. Of these, 181 were found to have been lost (an estimated rate of loss of c.5 ponds per annum). It was recognised that, due to their omission from the currently published maps, the numbers of recently created farm and garden ponds was underestimated.

The proximity of ponds to each other is an important factor in determining their value to wildlife. For example, in areas with a greater density of ponds, more tend to be occupied by amphibians. In Fife, pond density (number of ponds per km square) decreases from a high of 0.9 in the southwest to 0.2 (or less) in the east. There are few areas where pond density has not decreased since the 1950s and, in the western extremity of Fife and in the Kirkcaldy to Methil and Newburgh hinterlands, decreases of 50% or more were recorded. Recently there have been pockets of relatively intense pond creation, for example in Tentsmuir Forest and on private land north of Strathmiglo. For Britain, the average overall pond density is 2.6 ponds per square km. For Scotland the overall mean is less than 2 ponds per square km (Swan & Oldham 1989). Fife therefore has a pond density significantly below the national average and remaining ponds should be maintained wherever possible.

The importance of pond density may be related to species' dispersal abilities. However pond density may also reflect local topography, climatic and historic land-use factors and simply creating new ponds without consideration of other habitat requirements would be a futile conservation strategy. In nature, pond losses in one place would often have been compensated for by new ponds developing elsewhere. In the intensively managed Fife countryside, ponds generally only develop where someone has deemed one suitable and funding has been available. The observed rate of pond loss in Fife, as elsewhere in Britain, gives grounds for concern.

In the 1988–93 survey, 13% of ponds were recorded to have more than 75% surface vegetation cover. These ponds are likely to be in their naturally (albeit perhaps accelerated) senescent stages and require management in the near future to prevent the total loss of open water.

The management and care of ponds whose original purpose has now ceased, whether they were watering ponds for working farm animals or header ponds for steam-powered industries, is likely also to have ceased. As a result, many ponds have been infilled. Others have been simply neglected and are now strewn with litter or becoming overgrown. The 1988–93 survey recorded a loss of 181 ponds (c.30%) in the period since about 1950. The main causes of loss were reclamation/infilling (60%) and natural succession (25%). The extent of pond loss in Fife has been significantly greater than the observed loss of 20% for Britain overall since about 1968 (Swan & Oldham 1989). The Fife survey also recorded dumping of refuse as a current or potential threat at 79 ponds.

Many ponds support only sparse submerged vegetation. In the 1988–93 survey, 20% were recorded as having no submerged vegetation and a further 45% as having less than 25% of their bottoms vegetated. Such summary figures obscure a wealth of variation but, in general, poorly vegetated ponds are less likely to support other wildlife. Where ponds are vegetated, they commonly support starworts (*Callitriche* spp.), floating sweet-grass (*Glyceria fluitans*) and the surface floating duckweed (*Lemna minor*). Lack of vegetation can be for a number of reasons including over-shading by trees (26% of ponds in the 1988–93 survey had over 50% shading by trees) and periodic desiccation (at least 26% of ponds were reported to dry out in drought years).

Even where submerged vegetation is lacking, ponds may still support valuable marginal or emergent plant communities. An excellent example is at Red Myre on Weddersbie Hill to the north east of Auchtermuchty (pl. 25). Here the margins are variously dominated by mare's-tail (*Hippuris vulgaris*) and bottle sedge (*Carex rostrata*) with stands of bulrush (*Typha latifolia*). Spreading into more open water are rafts of bogbean (*Menyanthes trifoliata*). The edges of this water body are however very soft and the marginal communities need to be viewed from a distance.

Ponds tend to be hidden away amidst private land making them relatively inaccessible to the casual visitor. Some however can be studied from public access points including Lochore Meadows pond, Cupar Fire Station ponds, the lime kiln pond on East Lomond, the James Street pond in Inverkeithing and the Oriel Road pond in Kirkcaldy. Great care, especially of young children, must always be taken when visiting ponds or other waterways.

Lochs

If lochs are defined as standing waters over two hectares in extent, then there are 45 lochs in Fife; the locations of the largest are shown below. This includes 24 reservoirs which account for most of the larger water bodies but not the two largest – Lochore and Loch Gelly. The passing of the Reservoirs Act 1975 required higher safety standards for reservoirs and subsequently higher maintenance costs. This, and the advent of the Glenfarg, Glenqueich and Glen Devon reservoirs over the border in Perth & Kinross as water supplies for Fife, has placed doubts over the future requirement for many reservoirs in Fife. Already, Lambieletham, south of St Andrews, Coul, north of Glenrothes, and Cullaloe, between Aberdour and Moss Morran, have been decommissioned. A further 11, including Clatto and Loch Glow are now redundant as water supplies and in some cases actions have been taken

to lower water levels to remove them from the requirements of the Act.

Fife Regional Council made an assessment of the nature conservation interests of their reservoirs in 1992/93 with a view to directing resources to managing the most important ones as nature reserves. Cullaloe, with one reservoir drained and another lowered, has already been designated as a nature reserve operated jointly by Scottish Wildlife Trust and Fife Council. Upper Gillingshill near Arncroach, also redundant, is managed as a Community Nature Reserve. Following the restructuring of local authorities in 1996, the responsibility for many of these reservoirs now lies with the East of Scotland Water Authority (ESWA).

In 1905–09 a survey was made of the 'macrophytes' of Fife's lochs, i.e. the larger, predominantly flowering plants as distinct from the 'phytoplankton' comprising the microscopic and filamentous algae (West 1910).

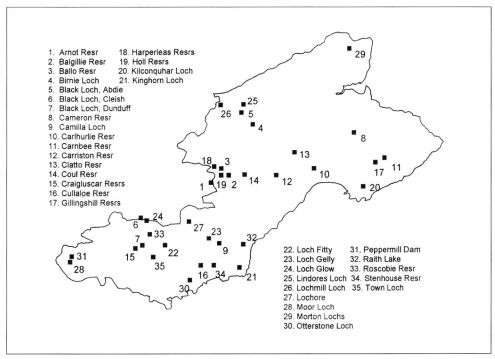

Location of major standing waters in Fife. (*Courtesy of Scottish Natural Heritage.*)

Size distribution of 415 standing waters in Fife. (Derived from Fife and Kinross Pond Survey 1988–93; unpublished, Scottish Natural Heritage.)

Estimated surface area (hectares)	<0.01	0.01 to 0.5	0.51 to 1.0	1.1 to 10	10.1 to 100	101 to 1000
Number of standing waters	60	295	21	38	19	2

Frequency of lochs according to their nutrient status (as determined from three botanical surveys, between 1905/09 and 1991.)

Nutrient Status	Oligotrophic	Oligo-eutrophic	Brackish	Eutrophic
Typical characteristics	Nutrient poor, upland, acidic, influenced by peat, over base poor rocks	Nutrient poor, neutral, over sedimentary rocks, mainly coastal	Lowland, over mainly sedimentary rocks	Nutrient rich, lowland, over sedimentary rocks
West 1910	5	8	5	2
Young & Stewart 1986	4	3	4	8
Bell 1991	3	3	0	19

This was repeated in 1982 (Young and Stewart 1986) and 1991 (Bell 1991). In 1991, 25 lochs were surveyed and details recorded of their substrates, depths and vegetation. Using comparable data from the three surveys, 18 lochs were classified according to the prevailing levels of nutrients (Palmer 1989) and changes over time identified.

The results show, for lochs on low ground, a clear increase of nutrients with time. Associated with this are changes in the species composition of the plant communities and their extent and biomass. There has been a widespread loss of pondweeds (*Potamogeton* spp. and others) and of species more typical of low nutrient conditions such as alternate water-milfoil (*Myriophyllum alterniflorum*) and shoreweed (*Littorella uniflora*). Other species, such as fennel pondweed (*Potamogeton pectinatus*), horned pondweed (*Zannichellia palustris*) and the introduced Canadian waterweed (*Elodea canadensis*), which initially benefit from increased nutrients, had increased in their extent.

In many severely enriched lochs, the final change from macrophyte to phytoplankton dominance can happen suddenly rather than as the result of a long decline. This may already have taken place at Kilconquhar Loch, Otterston Loch and Loch Gelly. Reversal of this 'switching' is rather more difficult to achieve and is subject of considerable research at present.

Fresh-water algae have received relatively little attention and as a result our knowledge of their occurrence, let alone distribution and status, is poor. The microscopic nature of the vast majority of these algae tends to make their study a specialist activity. The Scottish Environment Protection Agency (SEPA) has undertaken some work on the planktonic algae of certain lochs in Fife.

There is however one group of algae, the stoneworts or charophytes, which are more easily studied and for which north-east Fife has been identified as a rich area (Stewart 1996). These are some of the largest and more structurally complex green algae bearing whorls of short 'branches' and superficially resemble higher plants. Stoneworts often form dense stands, creating valuable habitat for small invertebrates which in turn provide food for fish. At least six species have been recorded in Fife (Moore 1986), including the now rare, and attractive, bird's-nest stonewort (*Tolypella nidifica* var. *glomerata*). Only three species were recorded from lochs in 1991 (Bell 1991) of which smooth stonewort (*Nitella flexilis*) was the commonest, occurring in seven lochs including Black Loch (Cleish), Kinghorn Loch and Clatto Reservoir. Rough stonewort (*Chara aspera*), which smells of garlic when handled, was recorded from Town Loch in Dunfermline and fragile stonewort (*C.globularis*) was recorded from Moor Loch and Carlhurlie Reservoir. The shortage of species and records may be attributable in part to the survey having been focused on major lochs and thereby excluding the habitats of other species.

It is encouraging to note that, at least by the above measures, the remote and upland Black Loch in the Cleish Hills of west Fife has not changed significantly this century. The observed changes in the Lomond Hill reservoirs, Ballo and Harperleas, may be more attributable to the direct physical effects of impoundment leading to increased fluctuations in water levels and the consequent loss of marginal and shallow water species, rather than an increase in nutrient status.

Often associated with increasing nutrient levels is the accumulation of organic detritus in, or on, the substrate. Whilst a small proportion, in otherwise sandy or stony substrates, may increase productivity of plants and invertebrates, the impact of increasing organic content soon becomes negative. As the sediment density decreases, this leads to nutrient absorption problems

A stonewort (*Chara aspera*).

for some plants, and other plants and animals are smothered. Where deposition of organic matter exceeds its rate of breakdown, for example where the lower parts of the water column are deprived of oxygen or the water is receiving excessive inputs, a sticky black mud develops. Organic deposits may accumulate in the slower flowing sections of rivers and burns or in sheltered bays and under leeward banks of lochs. This may then lead to a significant, albeit accelerated, stage in the terrestrialisation of the water body and to the development of swamp and then fen communities.

Characteristic of the margins of nutrient-rich lochs are areas of swamp. Swamps tend to comprise single-species stands of tall grasses or sedges in shallow water on organic substrates. Swamps of reed canary-grass are an exception and occur at the upper limit of water levels, on more exposed stony substrates. Downshore of the reed canary-grass are often further swamp communities of water horsetail (*Equisetum fluviatile*) or common spike-rush (*Eleocharis palustris*). Swamps of the tall common reed (*Phragmites australis*) provide an important habitat for many birds including the shy water rail, sedge warbler and reed bunting. Examples can be seen at the western end of Loch Gelly from the A92 road, at Morton Lochs National Nature Reserve near Tayport and the north-western side of Loch of Lindores. Common reed swamp may also develop in more exposed sites and on considerably less organic substrates but tends here to be more open and sparse.

Introduced species

Just as fresh waters provide 'corridors' and 'stepping stones' for the movement of native wildlife, they also facilitate the rapid colonisation by alien and sometimes wholly undesirable species. The giant hogweed (*Heracleum mantegazzianum*) of southwest Asia is an archetypal introduction that has received publicity on account of its sap that burns the skin in sunshine. Established along many stretches of river and burn, including the Kinness Burn in St Andrews and the Cocklemill Burn which drains into the east end of Largo Bay, its often impressive form and size – up to 5 metres – make it hard to overlook wherever it occurs. Similarly, the North American monkey flower (*Mimulus guttatus*) and Indian balsam (*Impatiens glandulifera*) provide eye-catchingly attractive floral displays in late summer.

Less obvious is the insidious spread of submerged aquatic plants including the well known Canadian waterweed (*Elodea canadensis*) or the more recently introduced Australian swamp-stonecrop (*Crassula helmsii*). The former occurs commonly in urban and ornamental ponds as well as in the slower reaches of the Rivers Leven, Eden and Ore. Its robust growth can make it a

major problem in larger lochs where it excludes native species and creates major problems for fishery managers. A small extent of Canadian waterweed was noted in Loch of Lindores in the late 1970s. When surveyed again in 1991 the loch bed was carpeted with this species. Of the 12 species of submerged plants recorded in 1982 only five remained and, with the exception of amphibious bistort (*Persicaria amphibia*) and yellow water-lily (*Nuphar lutea*), these were represented by only sporadic specimens.

Like Canadian waterweed, Australian swamp-stonecrop is easily spread by the movement of stem fragments and is likely to become more widespread. This species forms dense mats around the margins of ponds to the exclusion of other species and is very difficult to eradicate once established. To date, there is only one unconfirmed report from a fire pond in Tentsmuir Forest. Further alien plant species wait in the wings. The South African curly waterweed (*Lagarosiphon major*), for example, is sold widely as an ornamental pond plant and has been introduced to at least one pond west of Auchtermuchty. Where it has been released into larger ponds this species grows vigorously to form dense columns and may continue where the superficially similar Canadian waterweed left off. Like our native pondweeds, these aliens require adequate light to grow and in enriched waters with abundant planktonic growth they too suffer from shading.

The issue of introduced species is not restricted to plants. Amongst Fife's freshwater fish, seven species are known to have been introduced to date although some may not have survived. Anglers were probably responsible for the introduction of tench, roach and bream to improve or create new coarse fisheries. More recently, roach were introduced into Birnie Loch, following its creation in the early 1990s, and carp were introduced into Kinghorn Loch as part of the loch's recovery programme. Carp and tench have also been released into various new ponds and rainbow trout and farmed brown trout are released into, and sometimes escape from, commercial angling waters. The River Eden holds Fife's only population of the introduced salmonid, grayling.

Concern was raised recently following the discovery of a north American signal crayfish (*Pacifastacus leniusculus*) in the River Earn. This highly fertile, invasive species will feed on almost anything from detritus to macrophytes and invertebrates to small fish and their eggs. An unconfirmed record of their release into the Bottom Burn near Auchtertool requires further investigation.

Invertebrates

The abundance and diversity of fresh-water invertebrates strongly reflects the prevailing aquatic conditions. Different assemblages typify running and standing, clean and polluted, hard and soft waters. This measurable factor is used by SEPA to monitor water quality at more than 200 stations along the major rivers and their tributaries in Fife.

Eleven species of damsel and dragonfly have been recorded in Fife. There are concentrations of records around Tentsmuir Forest and Tentsmuir National Nature Reserve and in the Lomond and Cleish Hills. Whilst some species, such as the widespread common blue and blue-tailed damselflies (*Enallagma cyathigerum* and *Ischnura elegans*) will breed in all types of standing and flowing waters, others are more demanding. The common hawker (*Aeshna juncea*) appears to use only small water bodies in areas of seminatural habitat, and the black darter (*Sympetrum danae*) is often associated with peatland pools.

There are no recent records of the large fresh-water mussels in Fife. Three species (*Anodonta anatina*, *A.cygnaea* and *Margaritifera margaritifera*) have been recorded this century. Fresh-water mussels are highly susceptible to pollution and low oxygen conditions. They are also dependent upon good numbers of trout and salmon to act as hosts for their developing larval stages. It is possible that periods of poor water quality may have eliminated these species from Fife.

Fish

Seventeen species of fish have been recorded from Fife's fresh waters. Of some significance, both commercially and as a marker of water quality, are the migratory salmon and sea trout and the resident wild brown trout. The Rivers Eden and Leven and some of the larger coastal burns support stocks of salmon and sea trout. Recent efforts by the Forth District Salmon Fishery Board, in cooperation with local industries, to remove obstacles in the Leven have now enabled migratory fish to move upstream as far as Balgonie power station where a further fish pass is to be installed.

Salmon, trout, grayling and stone loach demand clean, well oxygenated water. Where water quality has been impaired by nutrient or other pollution these species are soon lost. Excessive growths of phytoplankton can, in bright conditions, lead to a depletion of dissolved carbon dioxide and the utilisation of dissolved bicarbonate to fuel photosynthesis. This can cause the pH to rise to levels harmful to juvenile trout. Similarly, during such algal blooms, the demand for oxygen overnight can seriously deplete the levels of dissolved oxygen, leading to fish kills. Stone loach, a widespread species in Fife, now occurs in the Lochty Burn which

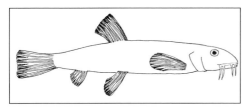

Stone loach

previously suffered extensive pollution. The loach here are likely to have recolonised from a tributary, the Sauchie Burn.

In most parts of Fife, it should be possible to find shoals of minnows or sticklebacks, or catch a glimpse of an eel sliding into cover, in ponds and burns. To observe pike, perch, lampreys or stone loach more specialist methods, such as netting or electro-fishing, are likely to be required.

Pike and perch are widespread in Fife. Perch can be found in the Rivers Leven, Ore and Eden, Loch Glow, Town Loch and together with pike in Lochore. Pike were also discovered during electro-fishing in Holl Reservoir. Perch were previously present in Loch Gelly but have since died out. Recent and ongoing works to reduce the sewage discharges into this loch may facilitate their return. Young flounders will frequently venture from estuaries into freshwaters and may be found some considerable distance from the sea.

Amphibians

Five species of amphibian occur in Fife, most frequently in smaller ponds and lochans. Frogs are the most widespread and use many ephemeral pools as well as more permanent waters. Toad breeding sites appear to be less widespread but this may be due, at least in part, to the lower observability of their spawn strings in comparison with the floating masses of frogspawn. The scattering of records of smooth and palmate newts, as

shown in the atlas produced by Fife Nature (Smout and Pritchard 1995), suggests that newts are grossly under-recorded in Fife and are in fact widespread. Newt recording requires torch-light searches at night, intensive searches for eggs on the leaves of aquatic vegetation or a technique known as funnel trapping.

Until 1996 crested newts were believed to have been forced into extinction in Fife. They had only ever been known from four sites and no crested newts had been observed during several surveys since 1985. Crested newts are generally associated with areas of high pond density and are known to be susceptible to the effects of nutrient enrichment of ponds, perhaps explaining their marginal status in Fife. However, during a nationwide survey of old crested newt localities and nearby ponds in 1996, two positive crested newt egg records were made (Alexander 1997). One was at a previously recorded site which has suffered nutrient enrichment in recent years and the other is a new site on high ground amidst woodland.

All the amphibian species occurring in Fife prefer ponds with substantial growths of submerged vegetation. The 1988–93 survey recorded only 16% of ponds to have between 25% and 75% of their bottoms vegetated and therefore likely to be optimal for amphibians.

Birds

There are few sights as enthralling as seeing flocks of geese coming in to roost at dusk or the flashing iridescence of a kingfisher flying up a burn. Fife can boast opportunities to experience both of these though the latter may take some greater effort and luck.

Large numbers of pink-foot and greylag geese visit Fife's arable farmland each winter and many find secure roosting on the larger lochs and reservoirs. Cameron Reservoir now attracts internationally important numbers of pink-foot geese, peaking annually at c.12,000 in October and November. This is a large site and the geese can be viewed easily, and with little risk of disturbing them, from the public car park at the east end or from the footpath on the north shore. Whilst pink-foot numbers have increased at Cameron, the numbers of greylags there have fallen. Greylag geese now roost predominantly on Kilconquhar Loch, Carriston, Carlhurlie and Ballo Reservoirs and the Eden Estuary.

The larger standing waters also provide important roosting and feeding for other wintering wildfowl including tufted duck, wigeon, pochard and coot. Smaller numbers of these species and others including shoveler, mute swan, great-crested grebe and dabchick also breed around Fife's lochs. Fife's mute swans have been the subject of a long-term study into their breeding status and movements. Swans marked in Fife have been recorded from as far away as Islay, Loch of Strathbeg near Fraserburgh and Yorkshire (A Brown *pers. comm.*).

Where water is flowing quickly over a stony substrate, even in built-up areas, dippers may be found close by. The Lady Burn in Cupar, culverted for much of its length and constrained by high walls along its open stretches, is often frequented by dippers. For most of the time they go largely unseen by passers-by, even when they rise out of the burn to navigate the road junction at the foot of the Lady Wynd! Grey wagtails also frequent the Lady Burn and may be seen on other burns and rivers including the Kinness Burn in St Andrews and in Letham Glen, Leven.

Kingfishers which are seen, and occasionally breed, on the Rivers Leven, Ore and Eden were historically more widespread and

occurred on the Kenly, Ceres and Bluther burns amongst others (Smout 1986). Their population appears to fluctuate significantly and the current low numbers may be attributable to the natural effects of climate or to the reduction in bankside vegetation or changes in water quality this century.

Although frequently seen foraging along rivers and burns, sand martins are more frequently found nesting some distance away, often in sand cliffs of sand and gravel workings. The number of river bank colonies in Fife appears to have diminished but they do still occur on the Black Devon.

Increasing sightings of osprey may herald their return to Fife in the near future. This species has been absent as a breeding bird since the end of the 19th century but is making a significant comeback. It is now a widespread, but still scarce, breeding bird north of the Tay.

Mammals

Mammals are generally secretive creatures and are most active around dusk and dawn. It is not surprising therefore that few people are aware of their presence or that they might be living close to them.

Rivers with tall riparian vegetation provide rich feeding, in the form of large populations of insects, and shelter for bats. Two species of bat are commonly associated with freshwaters in Fife. The pipistrelle can be identified by its erratic flight pattern, relatively small size and emergence close after sunset. The Daubenton's bat (sometimes called the water bat) can be identified by its low, straight and level flight across the flat waters of river pools, lochs and larger ponds, its relatively larger size and, if seen in torch light, by the very white fur on its underside. Both species can be seen on mild evenings in summer on the River

Eden in Cupar, the Ceres Burn in Dura Den between Dairsie and Pitscottie or on the River Leven in Glenrothes Town Park. In other parts of Britain, Daubenton's bats are commonly found roosting in bridges over water. A survey of 90 bridges in Fife and Kinross (Smith and Altringham 1988) found no such activity, although a bridge over the Cameron Burn near Dunino was later found to be used occasionally. To this date few roosts of this species in Fife are known.

Two small mammals are associated with fresh waters in Fife, the water vole and the water shrew, and both appear to be scarce in Fife. Their distributions are represented by only 13 and 5 records respectively between 1980 and 1994 (Corbet and Smout 1994). Elsewhere, water voles are known to have suffered declines in the presence of mink, disappearing from the main river channels and persisting as isolated populations on the smaller tributaries. The current paucity of records may reflect what is a national trend of growing conservation concern.

The fluctuating status of otters in Scotland this century has been well documented (Green and Green 1997) and their distribution surveyed on three occasions. In 'The Otter Survey of Scotland 1977–79' (Green and Green 1980) otters were not considered to be resident on the River Eden, despite

Otter

occasional sightings there over the previous two decades. Only four out of 88 sites surveyed showed signs of otters, these being on the upper River Ore. Further signs were recorded from the upper River Leven just across the border into Perth and Kinross. Fife was then described as 'one of the least suitable parts of Scotland for otters' on account of 'the small scale of the drainage systems, intensive agriculture, a fairly dense human population and extensive industry and mining'. The 1980 report concluded that whilst transient animals might still occur, the otter populations of the Leven and Ore were discreet and likely to become further fragmented by human disturbance.

The report of the third survey between 1991–94 (Green and Green 1997) recorded that otters had extended their range into parts of east and southwest Fife from which they had no previous contemporary records. This survey found otters to be absent from the Dunfermline to Kirkcaldy area and from many of Fife's smaller burns that discharge directly into the sea. In many areas, the return of otters is first detected by the discovery of animals killed on our roads. The death of an otter on the B981 road between Inverkeithing and Crossgates in 1994 may therefore signal that these areas may also be re-occupied.

The recovery of otter can be attributed to several factors including improved water quality and legal protection. In the late 1970s, pollution and eutrophication of rivers was a problem. The River Ore and the Lochty Burn were badly affected by colliery waste residues and iron pollution and the quality of the River Leven, below its confluence, consequently declined. Pollution is still an issue and there are constant threats of new pollution arising from iron laden water from abandoned mine workings. The 1991 survey of the Rivers Eden, Leven and

Ore (Jackson and Harding 1992) identified 48 waste discharges. Improved standards are however increasingly being met and this may explain the encouraging spread of otters in Fife since the late 1980s and their successful recolonization of the Eden.

The feral American mink, often misidentified as otter, has become established in Fife since around the early 1960s. There were fears at one time that mink would compete with otters for food and cause their decline. This has not been proven and the niches of these two species appear to be sufficiently distinct that any impact mink might be having on otters is insignificant compared with poor water quality and the lack of bankside cover and potential holt sites.

The future for Fife's fresh waters

Several significant problems for Fife's fresh waters remain. The old threats of pollution remain. There are still burns, like the Lappie Burn in West Wemyss and the Inverkeithing Burn, suffering pollution from mining related activities which will require the combined effort and co-operation of government agencies, industry and landowners to resolve (pl. 26). Demands for water continue to increase whilst we may be experiencing a change in climate leading to new rainfall patterns and consequent changes to the available resource. Old ponds will continue to disappear in the absence of appropriate management. New introduced species may become established and replace native wildlife.

It is quite likely that Fife will lose further sites and species over the coming decade; however there is good evidence to support an overall optimistic outlook. The extent of good quality waterway has been increasing steadily since the 1970s and major efforts have been made to clean up polluted lochs

such as Kinghorn and Lochore. New ponds are being created every year and some previously scarce species are making recoveries. Grants and other financial incentives are now available to support the management of land in an environmentally sensitive manner. That there is now significant and widespread interest in the environment, and increasing understanding of the problems, is probably the single most important recent development.

There is however no room for complacency and it will take a great deal of co-operative effort by all parties to sustain a long term recovery.

Acknowledgements

I thank Alan Brown of Fife Council for information on reservoirs and mute swans; Alastair Morrison of Scottish Environment Protection Agency for information on pollution, fish and recent fish conservation efforts; and my wife, Jane, for reading drafts of the text and suggesting improvements.

Further reading

Alexander, L (1997). National survey for the great crested newt *Triturus cristatus*. Report to Scottish Natural Heritage.

Bell, D (1991). Fife freshwater macrophyte survey. Report to Nature Conservancy Council for Scotland, Cupar.

Corbet, G B and Smout, A-M (1994). *The mammals of Fife – a provisional atlas*. Fife Nature, Glenrothes.

Green, J and Green, R (1997). *Otter survey of Scotland 1991–94*. The Vincent Wildlife Trust.

Green, J and Green, R (1980). *Otter survey of Scotland 1977–79*. The Vincent Wildlife Trust.

Jackson, A and Harding, T (1992). *Fife river*

corridor survey 1992 (Volume 1, River Eden; Volume 2, River Leven and River Ore). Report to Nature Conservancy Council for Scotland, Cupar.

Moore, J A (1986). *Charophytes of Great Britain and Ireland.* BSBI Handbook No 5. Botanical Society of the British Isles, London.

Palmer, M (1989). A botanical classification of standing waters in Great Britain. *Research and Survey in Nature Conservation*, 19. Nature Conservancy Council, Peterborough.

Smith, G M and Altringham, J D (1988). *Fife and Kinross Bridge Survey.* Report of the Fife Bat Group.

Smout, A-M (1986). *The Birds of Fife.* John Donald Publishers Ltd, Edinburgh.

Smout, A-M and Kinnear, P (1993). *The dragonflies of Fife – a provisional atlas.* Fife Nature, Glenrothes.

Smout, A-M and Pritchard, S (1995). *The amphibians and reptiles of Fife – a provisional atlas.* Fife Nature, Glenrothes.

Stewart, N F (1996). Stoneworts – connoisseurs of clean water. *British Wildlife* 8, pp 92–99.

Swan, M J S and Oldham, R S (1989). Amphibian communities, final report. Report to Nature Conservancy Council, Peterborough.

West, G (1910). A further contribution to a comparative study of the dominant phanerogamic and higher cryptogamic flora of aquatic habit in Scottish lakes. *Proceedings of the Royal Society of Edinburgh* 30, pp 65–181.

Young, C P L and Stewart, N F (1986). *Changes in the aquatic flora of Fife and Kinross lochs.* Report by the Nature Conservancy Council, Cupar.

9

Grassland and moorland

ALISON IRVINE

Grassland is perhaps one of the commonest, most widespread and certainly the most accessible of habitats, not only in Fife, but throughout the country. This chapter will not cover the amenity grasslands or intensive agricultural grasslands which are dealt with elsewhere. Here we shall explore the natural and semi-natural grasslands in all their complexities, ranging from flower-rich calcareous meadows to the marshy grasslands of many hilly areas, along with the logical extension to this habitat – the moorlands and heathlands, both wet and dry. We shall also turn our sights to bogs and fens, areas often associated with grassland and moorland species of plants and animals, but quite special and unique habitats in their own right.

Perhaps it is worth spending some time looking at the definitions of grassland and moorland, and how the two blend into each other. Unimproved grassland can be defined as any grassland which is not intensively managed, often because of low soil fertility, steep slopes or poor drainage, and which consequently has a large variety of native species. Moorlands and heathlands tend to have dwarf shrubs such as heather and blaeberry, but can also have rough grassland and wetter areas scattered through them in a mosaic. For our purposes moorland is taken as being generally above 200 m while heathlands are generally at a much lower altitude.

Almost all grasslands, moors and heaths

in eastern Scotland are 'man-made' habitats, cultural landscapes created by the activities of man, both through clearing of woodlands for fuel and for cultivation, and subsequently through the high level of grazing by domestic animals. Many of the grasslands and moorlands in Fife have had rather a chequered history. Until around 4000 years ago they were mostly derived from woodlands, felled by Bronze-age people. From then on cultivation would be the norm, particularly in the hills, on gentle slopes where poor drainage was not a problem. The Lomond Hills have the remains of several farming settlements dating back around 2000 years. When the sun is low in the west, or when there is a light fall of snow highlighting the subtle walls and ridges, it is easy to see the remains of ancient field systems about Harperleas reservoir or beside the West Lomond track. For hundreds of years these areas were, to all intents and purposes, arable. Then improved drainage freed the marshy lands of the Howe of Fife, and this, combined with climatic changes, moved cultivation down from the hills. The hills became common grazing lands for the villagers surrounding them, and the rough grasslands and moorlands of today began to evolve. So when we talk of these as natural habitats we must remember their varied past, and that the hand of man still dominates their structure and diversity.

Even in recent times moorland and grassland have changed in Fife. Figures published in the National Countryside Monitoring Scheme, which compares areas of each habitat in the 1940s and 1970s, showed a 67 per cent decrease in heather moorland and a 20 per cent decrease in unimproved grassland in Fife during that 30-year period.

Conversely, some grassland habitats have been created in the last few years, although they do not necessarily replace in quantity or quality what has been lost. One example of semi-natural grassland evolving from derelict land is at Lochore Meadows. Following the massive reclamation of mining land in the late 1960s, the area has been largely planted with trees, but some parts have been left as grassland and are slowly developing an interesting and varied grassland flora. They are already good for some of the grassland butterflies such as meadow browns, and the abundance of small mammals such as voles forms the basis of a food chain. In time (a very long time, probably), the shallow reclaimed soils may develop sufficiently to support woodland, but in the meantime this is a good grassland habitat, for fauna if not yet for flora.

Another very under-rated grassland habitat is formed by roadside verges. There are 2235 kilometres of road in Fife, ranging from motorways to single tracks; and assuming a grass verge of at least one metre on either side of the rural roads this represents a minimum of 300 hectares of grassland. Of course the quality of this varies, and this habitat is dealt with in chapter 11.

Moorland

Upland moors

These occur in Fife mostly in the Lomond Hills, the Cleish Hills and on Benarty Hill. There are two main divisions based on soils. Dry, sandy moors, such as on Lacesston

Muir on the north west slopes of the Lomonds, form over free-draining sandstone, while the acid, shallow, peaty moorlands form most often on soils derived from the volcanic dolerite rock. This latter type of moorland is by far the more common in upland Fife.

Moorlands form in conditions that are poor in nutrients. On the sandy heaths, the very free-draining soils allow nutrients to be washed quickly down from the upper layers. The lack of trees means these nutrients are not readily returned to the soil, so nutrient-poor conditions become established. On the dolerite soils, which are again free-draining, similar acidic and nutrient-poor conditions, often over a shallow layer of peat, also favour the moorland habitats. These soil conditions, together with altitude and a generally cold and wet climate, lead to the formation of a moorland habitat.

On these soils the most common plants are heathers. The dominant species is ling (*Calluna vulgaris*), with cross-leaved heath (*Erica tetralix*) in the damper areas and bell heather (*Erica cinerea*) in the drier parts. Other dwarf shrubs are also found, the most common being blaeberry (*Vaccinium myrtillus*), but crowberry (*Empetrum nigrum*) and, at higher altitude, cowberry (*Vaccinium vitis-idaea*) can also be found. These three species are often more prominent where grazing pressure is higher.

The structure and appearance of a heather moorland is very much affected by man's management of the site. Without man's intervention moorland would revert to woodland and scrub, and eventually a natural tree line would develop. But even within a man-managed moor, the appearance depends on the aims of management. Grouse moors, for example, have long angular strips of heather of different ages, created through controlled burning to produce ideal conditions for red

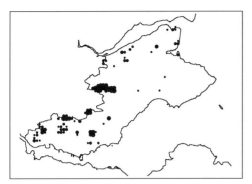

Moorland in Fife. (*Courtesy of Fife Nature.*)

grouse. Areas grazed by sheep change their appearance depending on stocking density and timing of grazing. To understand how this works, it is necessary to understand the natural 'life-cycle' of the heather plants (shown below). Left to their own devices, dense stands of heather would gradually open out and die back, allowing other plants to establish, leading to the return of woodland. An example of this can be seen on East Lomond beside the road to the car park where numerous rowan, Scots pine, beech and willow are invading the heather.

The use of fire or controlled grazing by livestock allows man to prevent heather reaching the degenerate stage, and stimulates the production of new growth from the heather stems. Fire can be used to clear old heather plants and allow regeneration from seed. Heather seeds are very small and are extremely numerous in the leaf litter and soil below heather – seed banks of 100,000 to 10 million seeds per cubic metre can develop. They remain viable for many years (up to

150 years in ideal conditions) and are stimulated to germinate by heat and exposure to light – thus they are perfectly adapted to germinate after a fire. While too frequent burning can lead to great loss of nutrient, fire every 12 to 20 years can maintain a productive heather moorland.

However, it has recently been discovered that some heather stands can naturally maintain themselves, and even in the absence of burning or grazing do not revert to woodland (MacDonald *et al.* 1995). One of the sites studied, which showed the best examples of this, was on East Lomond. From a central plant, horizontal stems often more than a metre long grow out, and where these touch the ground or become buried by moss or leaf litter, adventitious roots develop, and new, fresh plants can eventually be found radiating out from the parent plant. If the parent plant dies back, other plants from surrounding shoots will already be growing in to fill the space. The conditions to achieve a healthy, self-perpetuating stand of adventitiously rooting heather are quite exacting. It occurs best where: a) heather canopy is less than 90 per cent and the stand is more or less even aged; b) there is a high frequency of horizontally growing stems; c) there is a low frequency of mosses and lichens around the stems; and d) there is deep soil, rich in organic material. These conditions are found at their most favourable on the southern and eastern slopes of East Lomond, and are easily seen from the road and tracks in the area.

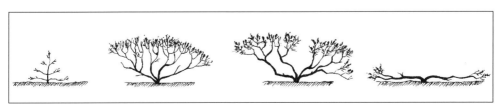

The natural 'life-cycle' of a heather plant; from left to right: pioneer, building, mature, degenerate (after Gimmingham, 1975).

Most of Fife's moorlands are grazed by sheep, usually through the summer months but occasionally into the autumn and winter. At low intensities, sheep grazing is the single most important factor in maintaining moorland. Trees are prevented from re-generating and heather benefits from gentle pruning by the animals. If sheep numbers are too low the animals select the richer, grassier areas, perhaps around springs and flushes, and the moorland can become scrub-bier as the heather grows tall and bushy. If sheep numbers are too high, the heather can-not survive the constant grazing pressure. Typically the plant becomes 'leggy', with just tufts of closely cropped shoots at the tips of the branches (illustrated below).

Sheep choose to eat the tastier grasses and shrubs, and certain species that they avoid can eventually become dominant. One such species is mat-grass (*Nardus stricta*), the main grass found on so-called white moorland (as opposed to the 'black moorland' composed of heather). This coarse grass, which grows in persistent tussocks (see below), has little nutritional value for either livestock or wild-life and has been spreading over Scotland's moors for many decades. Fortunately, in Fife, although mat-grass is found on almost every moorland, it has not on the whole become such a problem as in other parts of Scotland. Where sheep grazing is removed from a 'white moorland', other grass species and heathers can return to their former abundance in time.

The appearance of a moorland is also af-fected by the natural structure of the land. Damp hollows lead to bogs, fens or marshy grassland, flushes may appear on the sides of hills and these wet areas are very rich in plant life.

On the northern slopes of West Lomond, in a series of flushes, plants such as mossy saxifrage, chickweed willowherb, the

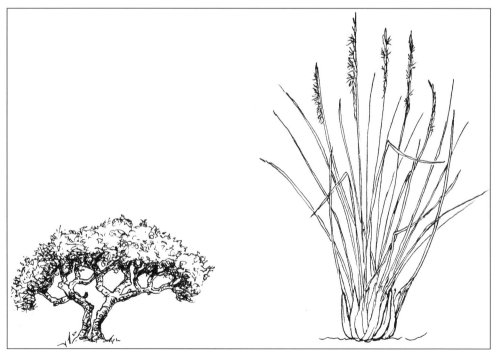

Plants of heavily grazed moorland; heather with closely cropped shoots; mat-grass.

introduced New Zealand willowherb and many attractive mosses such as *Calliergon cuspidatum* and *Bryum pseudotriquetrum* form bright green carpets amongst the heather. Where rocks come close to the surface and the soil is very shallow, small areas of specialist plants resistant to droughts and able to survive in the extreme conditions are found. Examples are hairy stonecrop, common whitlowgrass, and the dwarf grass, *Aira praecox*. Often these small areas closely resemble the calcareous grassland described later in this chapter.

Blanket mire

One particularly rare upland habitat in Fife's moors is blanket mire. This forms in areas of high rainfall, typically more than 2000 mm per year, with over 200 wet days per year.

Blanket mires, or blanket bogs, are basically a carpet of peat covering an area. Peat forms where the rate of production of plant material exceeds the rate of decomposition. Complete decomposition is prevented in water-logged soils and at low temperatures. The water-logging means that the soils are anaerobic (low in oxygen), and without oxygen the soil fungi and bacteria needed for decomposition cannot survive. In addition, the acidic soil water conditions, often enhanced or entirely created by bog-mosses, species of *Sphagnum*, also restrict the growth of soil micro-organisms. So in essence the more rain there is, the more water-logged the soil, which encourages the growth of sphagnum mosses, and results in the deposition of deep layers of peat. As the water-logging is caused by excessive rainfall rather than by water accumulating in a hollow, blanket bogs can actually form on slopes and hill tops which look as if they should be free-draining.

A characteristic of blanket mire is the formation of hummocks and hollows. Large clumps of *Sphagnum* can grow up from the surface of the bog, rising above the water table and creating drier conditions on these hummocks which are colonised by heather, grasses and mosses including other species of *Sphagnum*. Between the hummocks are hollows of lower lying *Sphagnum* species, often completely water-logged and forming pools. On a timescale of about 10 to 20 years the surface of a bog is constantly changing as large hummocks die back or collapse under the weight of colonising vegetation, or of a passing large animal, and new ones grow from hollows round about.

Fife has very little upland with the amount of rainfall needed to create blanket bog so it is a correspondingly scarce habitat. Even these areas of peatland that exist, particularly in the Cleish Hills, have generally been modified by some form of management in the past, such as digging of peats, or ploughing for drainage or forestry.

Some areas of bog to the south of Loch Glow in the Cleish Hills are the only remaining unafforested examples of upland blanket bog in Fife. Even here, much of the bog has been heavily affected by drainage and no longer shows the characteristic hummock-hollow profile. Some of the typical plants of the bogs in Fife's uplands are, of course, heather, with the cottongrasses *Eriophorum angustifolium* and *E.vaginatum*, and cross-leaved heath, over a carpet of *Sphagnum* mosses, of which up to 10 species can be found. Scattered throughout the bog sedges will be found, such as star sedge (*Carex echinata*) and common sedge (*C.nigra*), and occasionally less common plants such as sundew and butterwort. These are insectivorous plants which meet their nutrient requirements by catching and digesting insects.

Where the bogs have been drained, degraded blanket bog is found, dominated by purple moor-grass (*Molinia caerulea*), with smaller proportions of heather and cross-leaved heath, and with the drainage channels lined by rushes.

Acid grassland
This habitat has the same under-lying acid geology as moorland, but is created by moderate to heavy sheep grazing. The grassland is characterised by mat-grass and wavy hair-grass (*Deschampsia flexuosa*) depending on the intensity of grazing, with red fescue (*Festuca rubra*), sheep's fescue (*F.ovina*) and some common bent (*Agrostis capillaris*) also frequent. Much of the Cleish Hills, Knock Hill, Saline Hill, Benarty Hill and the Lomonds support this type of habitat. The grassland tends to be species-poor, typical associates being heath bedstraw, tormentil and occasionally harebell (Scottish bluebell). Much of the accessible acid grassland in Fife has been 'improved' by the use of artificial fertilisers, but almost any walk in Fife's hills will show examples of typical acid grassland.

In essence then, much of Fife's moorland is a mosaic of vegetation types with heather, blaeberry and acid grassland being particularly common. The majority of these dry dwarf-shrub/acid grassland moors are not botanically rich in themselves. There are the common acid grasses, such as wavy hair-grass, but the acid soil conditions limit the variety of species that will grow. Mosses such as *Pleurozium schreberi* and *Hylocomium splendens* and occasional *Cladonia* lichens are to be found, more commonly amongst blaeberry, which, being deciduous, allows light to reach these plants during the winter.

Despite the lack of variety of plant species, animal life on upland moorland can be rich and varied. Sheep are not the only herbivores on moorland. Many wild creatures choose to live there, though there are no mammals entirely dependent on heather moorland in Fife – there are no mountain hares nor red deer in the county. Field voles are common on moorlands, where they prefer rough grassland, both for shelter and food. They burrow through the base of grass tussocks and the surface soil, and eat the young grass shoots, destroying more than they eat. Mice are also found on moorland, though far less frequently than voles. Rabbits can create extensive warrens in the cover provided by dwarf shrubs, but they need to be close to grassland as their main source of food. Roe deer are often to be found browsing on moorland, especially if it is adjacent to forest plantations.

On a different scale, invertebrate herbivores are very common on moorland. Several spectacular moth species are restricted to moorland. One of these is the emperor moth which flies in the late evenings in June. Its wings have vivid eye spots to scare off potential predators. Equally amazing, and certainly a lot easier to find, are its caterpillars, which feed on heather and are found in August. Up to 5 cm long, these Disneyesque creations of bright green and black stripes, with pink spots and tufts of hair, are often found in the heather beside footpaths in the Lomonds. Later in autumn on many of Fife's moors the large, dark brown, hairy caterpillars of the fox-moth can be seen as they seek out a sheltered spot to hibernate. They feed on heather, blaeberry and various herbaceous plants, and are well protected by their dense coat of irritant hairs. They emerge from hibernation in the spring, often sunning themselves in sheltered spots before pupating and emerging as the adult moths in June.

Moorlands carpeted with heather flowers are a great attraction for nectar-seekers. This fact is exploited by Fife's beekeepers, some of whom move their hives of honeybees to the moors of Glenvale and elsewhere during the summer months. The natural nectar seekers are, of course, the bumble-bees, especially the white-tailed *Bombus magnus,* which is confined to this habitat. Easily confused with these is the slightly less hairy cuckoo bumble-bee, *Psithyrus bohemicus,* which lays its eggs in bumble-bee nests and, cuckoo-like, fools the bumble-bees into feeding its larvae.

There is one bird species that is entirely dependent on heather moorland: the red grouse. Red grouse feed almost exclusively on heather, though blaeberry can be taken. They need young heather shoots to eat, and long, mature heather in which to nest and shelter. Grouse chicks have an insectivorous diet for the first few days of their lives, and that is best provided on a varied moorland, with wet flushes and boggy pools. There are almost no well managed and productive grouse moors, as previously described, to be found today in Fife. Intensive grazing, public pressure, the increase in forest plantations and subsequent fear of burning heather close by, and the reduction in active gamekeeping have reduced the number of grouse, perhaps back to their natural numbers prior to grouse shooting becoming fashionable. On an estate in the Lomond hills, bags of between 50 and 80 brace were not uncommon in the 1930s. Now shooting takes place only occasionally and it is likely that there are no more than 15 to 20 pairs of grouse on their moorland now. Since 1995, red grouse numbers have recovered slightly in the Lomonds, perhaps due to a partial resumption of moorland management by the estates. The grouse around the radio mast on East Lomond are conspicuous and easily watched, especially in early mornings in February and March as they claim their territories with much displaying and calling.

The other native grouse, the black grouse, is on the verge of extinction in Fife but can still be found in very small numbers in the Cleish Hills. It may even have benefited from recent afforestation since it favours woodland edge rather than open moorland. In winter the grouse are joined on the moors by flocks of bullfinches when up to 40 of these birds can be found feeding on heather seed, even when there is snow around. They generally occur not too far from woodland edge, or where trees are starting to grow through heather. One can almost guarantee to see them around East Lomond radio mast and several other moorland sites during the winter months.

Feeding on this myriad of moorland herbivores are an equally varied array of predators. Research carried out in the North Yorkshire moors, many of which are similar to Fife's moors, has shown that an amazing 20 per cent of all known species of spiders in Britain and 15 per cent of species of ground beetle are to be found in the moorland habitat.

On the dry sandy moorland of Lacesston Muir, on the north slopes of West Lomond, green tiger beetles sun themselves on the paths. When approached, they move with a lumbering flight, often alighting further up the path. Both adults and larvae are fierce carnivores, the larvae digging a small burrow in which they lie in wait for their prey.

Most of the bird species of moorland are insectivorous. Many species come to Fife's moors to breed, either from low ground and coastal sites in Britain and Europe, or from Africa. Curlew are often back in the hills of Fife by early March, calling and giving display flights to claim a territory. They need long old heather or tussocky grassland for their nest, and the young birds feed on the rich invertebrate fauna of the moorland. Skylarks and meadow pipits are also back in the hills by early March, breeding in areas of shorter, tussocky vegetation. By early April the wheatears have arrived from Africa. This species has been declining in recent years, though no accurate estimate of the number of pairs using Fife's moorland has been made. They nest in crevices in old walls, and their white rumps makes them conspicuous as they fly along a wall in front of walkers before making a wide circuit round and back when they reach the end of their territory. The paths of East and West Lomond, flanked by boulder dykes, are good places to look for them.

Whinchats have always been less common than wheatears in Fife, but they too have declined. For example, there was an estimated 20 pairs breeding in the Lomond Hills in 1983, but in 1995 there were only one or two pairs. Whinchats need some scrub or bracken in which to build their nest.

Many of these species that are found breeding on upland moors were once frequent also in the lowlands, where they are now increasingly restricted by modern farming techniques, as all of them feed predominantly on insects and other invertebrates, at least in the summer.

Mammal predators are common on moorland though none are entirely dependent on this habitat for their survival. Foxes have been increasing in many areas despite constant control measures by landowners. The foxes have benefited from the abundance of forestry plantations giving them a safe refuge from which they can hunt over neighbouring land. Stoats and weasels are both found in the moorland habitat, often associated with old walls or the stony remains of long abandoned farms or settlements. Peregrine falcons occasionally hunt for red grouse in Fife although they prefer pigeons. Hen harriers are autumn and spring visitors to Fife's moors, passing through on their annual migrations.

Finally at the end of the food chain are the decomposers, essential in recycling the limited nutrients of the moorland habitat.

Many fungi are found on moorland, for example, horse-hair fungus (*Marasmius androsaceus*) growing on old heather stems. Millipedes, which feed on and help to break down decaying vegetation, have been shown by a recent study in the Sidlaw Hills (Corbet 1997) to be very abundant on moorland, the commonest species being *Ommatoiulus sabulosus* and *Julus scandinavius*.

Lowland heaths

Lowland heaths, heathland occurring below about 200 m, were once plentiful in Fife. Created in nutrient-poor, outlying land or low hills, which were grazed by commoners' cattle and sheep, almost every village had its associated 'muir'. From the very start of the agricultural revolution in the late 17th century, these moors were amongst the first areas to be reclaimed. Many old title deeds to small holdings in Fife include the words '… entitled to that area of land worked from the muir in one year.' or '… together with the right to cut turves or peats from the muir.'

In more recent times, afforestation of huge areas such as Tentsmuir and Edensmuir have reduced the area of lowland heath, and the great drive to increase agricultural production after the Second World War carried on the trend of reclaiming lowland heath. Now the most sizeable remaining areas of heath are on the North Fife Hills, particularly around Glenduckie and Norman's Law, although small fragments survive on the coast as at the Kilminning Coast SWT reserve near Fife Ness. Typical heathland vegetation can be similar to moorland and consists of dwarf shrubs such as heather and blaeberry with acid grasses such as wavy hair-grass. Often they can be found in association with some peatlands or as fragments within birch woodland, or in a mosaic with gorse scrub or tall grassland

and bracken. Usually, Fife's lowland heaths are more intensively grazed than the moorlands, which further restricts the variety of vegetation.

Mixed through the dwarf shrubs and acid grasses are tormentil, heath bedstraw and harebell. These flowers can help to make the heathlands an important area for invertebrates. Typical, and quite common in Fife, is the small heath butterfly. Its caterpillars feed on grasses and the small orange-brown butterfly is to be found in June and July. Bumble-bees are also numerous, with similar species as on Fife's moorlands. Grasshoppers are abundant, with the common green grasshopper (*Omocestus viridulus*) being found in longer grass and the mottled grasshopper (*Myrmeleotettix maculatus*) the commonest in short, dry grass.

The commonest birds are meadow pipits and skylarks. However, in early summer large noisy flocks of young starlings descend on the short heath vegetation, feeding on the numerous insects. Similar flocks of rooks and jackdaws can also be seen, though they tend to concentrate their feeding on the insects on dung from grazing animals. Kestrels hovering over the open heaths confirm the presence of field voles.

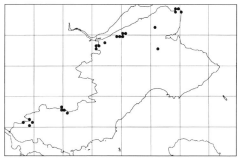

Distribution of green hairstreak butterfly – a localized species whose caterpillars feed mainly on blaeberry. (*Fife Nature.*)

Lowland bogs

Lowland raised bogs are another 'heathery' type of habitat, but they are formed in a totally different fashion. They are found on level areas which have impeded drainage, often over infilled glacial lakes where layers of boulder clay or fine silt restrict free drainage of rain water. The resulting waterlogged conditions, if maintained for long enough each year, allow peat to form, and this can eventually accumulate into a raised dome several metres high over the original area of impeded drainage. Water in these bog systems tends to flow around the edges of the main peat dome, forming a lagg stream with associated swamp and fen. Finally

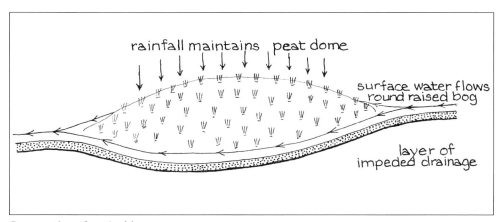

Cross-section of a raised bog.

lagg woodland develops on the drier heath habitats.

Raised bogs can be found across Fife. However, most have been modified as a result of agricultural activity and peat cutting. Extensive deposits of peat occur at Moss Morran, the largest raised bog in Fife. Here peat overlies a series of small basins and intervening ridges to a maximum depth of 8 metres. However, as a result of peat cutting, most of the surface vegetation has been removed, leaving only a few species typical of raised bogs. A good example of a raised bog is the SWT reserve of Bankhead Moss near Peat Inn. This reserve is open to the public and is worth visiting. Raised bog is a wet, dwarf-shrub heath system. Typical species of raised bogs are heather, cross-leaved heath, bog asphodel and *Sphagnum* mosses, with the rarer cranberry (*Vaccinium oxycoccus*) at some western sites. At Bankhead Moss a series of lint holes, dug in the last century for soaking flax, now have excellent examples of heathland pool vegetation, including *Sphagnum* and sundew.

As with most of Fife's raised bogs, man's influence can be felt at Bankhead. Drainage of surrounding farmland has dried the edges of the bog, allowing birch to colonise in large numbers. Over the years attempts have been made to control the birch, which by its very existence further dries out the bog and threatens its survival. It is likely to be a long, on-going battle with the trees.

Lowland raised bogs such as Bankhead Moss are particularly good habitats for insects; the lint pools in particular provide breeding sites for dragonflies and damselflies. Several species are found at Bankhead, including common blue damselfly, blue-tailed damselfly and common hawker dragonfly. Frogs, toads and newts are also resident in the moss.

Fens

Fens are a distinct community on peat soil where the water supply is not just from rainwater, but is largely by seepage from surrounding mineral soils or rocks. The peat soil is enriched by the addition of minerals and the vegetation is usually richer than that on a raised bog which is fed only by rainwater. The exact nature of the fen vegetation depends on the type of surrounding soil and rock, but typical species include bottle sedge (*Carex rostrata*), brown sedge (*C.disticha*), the cotton-grasses (*Eriophorum*), common marsh bedstraw and marsh cinquefoil. Heather and other dwarf shrubs are not often found on fens.

Fens are often found at the margins of lochs or ponds where they may merge into swamp. They are transitional habitats, changing towards willow carr, or even to bog if rainfall is high and tree growth is prevented. Often they are found in very small areas in a variety of other wetland or bog habitats. Good examples in Fife can be seen at the SWT reserve of Barnyards Marsh near Kilconquhar, at Miller's Loch in the Lomond Hills, at Star Moss near Markinch and at Dalbeath Marsh near Cowdenbeath. Miller's Loch includes examples of quaking or floating fen, where the vegetation forms a mat on top of the water surface.

Lowland grassland

Semi-natural grasslands consist of a mixture of grasses, sedges, broad-leaved plants and mosses. The main factors that determine the composition of a grassland are geology, soil type, water table, climate and management. An important feature of grasslands in temperate regions is that more than 90 per cent of the plant species are perennials and many have long life spans, often over 100 years (Lowday and Wells 1977). Seed production can be very variable and is affected by climate as well as by management. Many broad-leaved plants in grassland have adapted by regularly reproducing vegetatively, which has allowed them to persist at isolated old sites without necessarily spreading to new sites nearby. Their long life span means that even if unsympathetic management has prevented flowering for many years, if the correct conditions arise, flowers can appear as if by magic on apparently uninteresting grassland. Grass and sedge plants are adapted to withstand grazing or cutting as their growing point is at the base of the plant just above the roots.

There are many different types of grassland; they can be divided into groups according to soil type. Calcareous grasslands usually occur on limestone or similar rocks which give rise to 'basic' soils with a high content of calcium carbonate. Acidic grasslands occur on a variety of soil types, but the common factor linking them is their low pH value. Neutral grasslands are found on soils which are neither markedly acidic nor basic, such as clays or loams. A further commonly described type is marshy grassland, found where the water table is high, often at or very near the soil surface for much of the year.

Calcareous grassland

In Fife, calcareous grasslands are fairly unusual, and tend to be found in localised base-rich patches associated with rock outcrops of limestone and steep volcanic ridges. They are very rich in plant species and include grasses such as downy oat-grass (*Helictotrichon pubescens*), meadow oat-grass (*H.pratensis*), quaking-grass (*Briza media*) and crested hair-grass (*Koeleria macrantha*). In summer, when flowers are out, the large

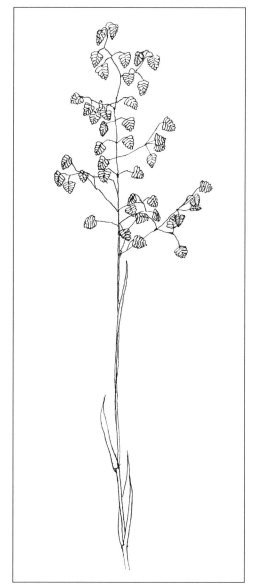

Quaking-grass

variety of broadleaved plants in calcareous grassland gives rise to a sea of colour. Typical species include wild thyme, rock-rose, purging flax (*Linum catharticum*) and lady's bedstraw.

One quite accessible calcareous grassland is Craigmead Meadow in the Lomond Hills. It is best viewed from the footpath towards

East Lomond, from where the thousands of mountain pansies (*Viola lutea*) can be seen, as well as the rarer species such as mountain everlasting (*Antennaria dioica*). More difficult to find are two very unusual ferns, adder's-tongue (*Ophioglossum vulgatum*) and moonwort (*Botrychium lunaria*). Growing to around 5 to 10 cm high, these ferns are an indicator of the importance of this grassland. Most of Fife's good calcareous grasslands are actually found around the coast and further examples are given in chapter 5.

Springs and flushes are often associated with rich calcareous type vegetation. They occur where mineral-rich water seeps out of the ground, providing small areas of base-rich soil. They often have a very good moss flora, including such attractive species as *Calliergon cuspidatum*. Rare plants in Fife such as dioecious sedge (*Carex dioica*), butterwort (*Pinguicula vulgaris*), and the nationally rare hairy stonecrop (*Sedum villosum*) can be found in these springs and flushes, particularly along the northern slopes of the Lomond Hills.

These floristically rich habitats support a correspondingly rich invertebrate community. Many butterfly and moth caterpillars that have very specific food plant requirements are to be found in calcareous grasslands. In particular, the chimney-sweep moth, whose caterpillars feed on pignut, and six-spot burnet moth, on bird's-foot-trefoil, can be found on many of these grasslands. Butterflies such as small copper and common blue are also found there.

Grazing is an essential process for maintaining a grassland, and rabbits, hares and voles are important. At the East Lomond limekiln, rabbit grazing is almost sufficient in itself to maintain the grassland sward, but in most other grasslands sheep or cattle are important. Being rich in calcium these grasslands often have a good population of snails

and slugs. Many grassland snails are small (less than 5 mm) and are associated with ground debris or grass clumps. Typical species are the slippery snail (*Cochlicopa lubrica*), and the chrysalis snail (*Lauria cylindracea*).

The wild herbivores are preyed upon by a variety of predators, ranging from the ubiquitous kestrel, hovering overhead, to the many grassland birds such as skylark and meadow pipits which feed their young on the abundance of caterpillars, spiders and insects. Where the grasslands are relatively close to water, amphibians such as frogs and toads also hunt, especially when they have just developed from tadpoles. Grassland offers them shelter from sun and predators and rich feeding on the multitude of small invertebrates.

The decomposers to be found on calcareous grassland depend to some extent on the management of the area as this will influence how much dead plant material is on site, and whether there are animal droppings to be found. Some of the commonest and most attractive grassland fungi are the wax-caps. In Fife grasslands it is worth looking for the dull orange meadow waxcap (*Hygrocybe pratensis*), the pure white snowy waxcap (*H.nivea*), and even the pale blue-green of the parrot waxcap (*H.psittacina*). Grasslands are of course the place to hunt for mushrooms, both the field mushroom (*Agaricus campestris*), and the horse mushroom (*A.arvensis*), though they are mainly found where the grassland has been grazed by farm animals. All these fungi are not confined to calcareous grassland but are found on the other types as well.

Underground, semi-natural grassland can have very large populations of earthworms and roundworms living on the decomposing plant materials. Up to 500 earthworms per square metre have been recorded, or 5 million per hectare! As well as breaking down organic material, increasing soil fertility and aerating and draining the soil with their burrows, earthworms are also a very important food for many grassland animals such as moles, songbirds and even badgers which come onto grassland areas specifically to hunt for worms.

Neutral grassland

Neutral grasslands are generally found on soils with a pH of around 5.5 to 7.0, that is, neither acidic nor basic. In Fife, these grasslands tend to be on enclosed land, with deeper soils, and they have been generally improved by the use of fertilisers or by ploughing and reseeding or draining. Today, unimproved neutral grassland communities are probably most common on waste ground, small uncultivated corners of fields or on roadside verges. Often the vegetation is quite tall or tussocky, but it can be grazed or cut. Common grass species are meadow foxtail (*Alopecuris pratensis*), false oat-grass (*Arrhenatherum elatius*) and cock's-foot (*Dactylis glomerata*). Broad-leaved plants are abundant, though not as varied as those in calcareous grassland. Typically found are knapweed, field scabious, tufted vetch, red campion and melancholy thistle (*Cirsium heterophyllum*).

The SWT reserves of Lielowan, near Saline, and Cullaloe, near Aberdour, have a variety of grassland types including good examples of neutral grassland. At Cullaloe the banks of the old reservoir dam have bugle, crosswort, knapweed, lady's-mantle, violets and ox-eye daisy. Further east at the Cullaloe site the flat land between the current loch and the old reservoir has also developed into an interesting knapweed-crested dog's-tail grassland which is particularly unusual in Fife. From the car park at Holl reservoir in the Lomond Hills it is possible to see large numbers of fragrant orchid, red clover, burnet-saxifrage (*Pimpinella saxifraga*) and yellow rattle, to name but a few. The yellow-rattle is a semi-parasitic plant, which, although capable of surviving on its own if necessary, normally has its roots growing into those of a neighbouring flower from which it takes some of its nutrients. It is an annual plant which must grow from seed each year, and its semi-parasitic habit allows it to survive in the perennial-dominated grasslands as the seedlings do not need to grow their own roots, but merely use those of another plant.

As with calcareous grasslands, a good semi-natural neutral grassland is rich in invertebrates, including butterflies, moths, grasshoppers, beetles and spiders of many different species. In many respects the fauna of neutral and calcareous grasslands are very similar.

One species worth highlighting is the ringlet butterfly, which was confined to the east of Fife until the 1980s. Since then it has spread dramatically westwards so that it can now be found around Dunfermline. The butterflies lay their eggs on grasses, hence the species' close association with neutral grassland, especially quiet roadside verges. The caterpillars hibernate and do most of their feeding in the spring when the grasses are young and tender, before pupating in late spring and emerging as the adult butterflies at the end of June.

Marshy grassland

A distinctive grassland habitat is found where the water table is close to the surface for much of the year and water logging or flooding can occur. These grasslands can have a high proportion of rush species, as well as sedges, meadowsweet, buttercups, valerian and even marsh marigold. In Fife, these marshy grasslands very often show signs of having been affected by drainage or fertilising. Many upland farms in the Lomond and Cleish Hills have marshy pastures, and interestingly, in west Fife, much of the land reclaimed from coal mining and returned to agricultural grassland has developed a marshy characteristic. Although these reclaimed grasslands are not rich in plant species, they are nevertheless an important sector of the marshy grasslands in Fife. The fields around Star Moss and Bankhead Moss are interesting marshy grasslands despite repeated and continuing attempts to drain them. Though they are now no doubt much drier than in the past, they still support tussocky areas of soft rush (*Juncus effusus*), jointed rush (*J.articulatus*), sharp-flowered rush (*J.acutiflorus*), tufted hair-grass (*Deschampsia cespitosa*), hairy sedge (*Carex hirta*) and both creeping and meadow buttercups. Mosses are not a very significant feature of marshy grasslands as the taller grass and herb vegetation tends to dominate and deprive them of light.

Marshy grasslands have their own associated fauna. Herbivores such as field voles are common as they can live in the tussocks of grass. Rabbits are less frequent as they cannot burrow in wet areas, but they will happily graze the wet grassland if there are suitable burrowing sites nearby. One butterfly closely associated with this habitat is the green-veined white, whose caterpillars feed on a variety of plants including cuckoo-flower and water-cress, both common marshy grassland plants.

On any damp day, numerous black slugs (*Arion ater*) will be found in wet grassland and snails such as *Trichia hispida* and *Nesovitrea hammonis* actually prefer these wetter areas.

In Fife, marshy grassland is of critical importance for breeding and feeding waders, especially lapwing, redshank and snipe. These birds use their long bills to probe into the soft muddy soil, feeling for worms and other invertebrates. All three species require the tussocky wet grassland for breeding. Redshank and snipe lay their eggs in a sheltered, half hidden position, while lapwings make a scrape, usually on bare ground, in which to lay their eggs. This preference of the lapwings explains why they so often choose to nest in ploughed fields with usually fatal consequences. However the chicks of all three species do best if they have a marshy, semi-natural grassland where they can feed on the multitude of small invertebrates. These three species have been declining across Britain, but seem to be suffering particularly badly in Fife where the development of roads, intensive agriculture and forestry plantations has severely reduced their preferred marshy grassland habitat.

One predator often associated with marshy grassland is the short-eared owl. This species does not breed regularly in Fife, but over-winters in a few areas where it is often seen flying low and slowly over tussocky wet grassland hunting for voles.

Decomposition of dead vegetation on marshy grassland can be slow, depending on how much of the year it is waterlogged. However, earthworms are still generally abundant, though usually of different species from those in drier grassland.

Lielowan Reserve has typical marshy grassland, and large areas of the rough grazing in the Lomond Hills, especially south of Ballo reservoir, are also good places to see this habitat, and the variety of plants and animals associated with it.

The future for Fife's moors, heaths and grasslands

Economic pressures on farmers and landowners, and the effects of the European

25. Red Myre, Weddersbie Hill; the foreground dominated by bogbean. (*Photo: R. M. Cormack*)

26. Water polluted by mining spoil. (*Photo: D. Bell, ECOS*)

27. Common blue damselflies breed in still and slow-flowing water with abundant marginal vegetation. (*Photo: R. M. Cormack*)

28. Heather moorland, Lomonds. (*Photo: Fife Ranger Service*)

29. The Devil's Burdens, W. Lomond: a mosaic of acid grassland and heather. (*Photo: Fife Ranger Service*)

30. A flower-rich meadow with common spotted orchid – Holl Meadows, Lomonds. (*Photo: Fife Ranger Service*)

31. Adder's tongue – an elusive little fern of calcareous grassland. (*Photo: R. M. Cormack*)

32. A species-rich road verge.
(*Photo: S. Webster*)

33. Uncut hedges: a rich habitat for both plants and animals. (*Photo: R. M. Cormack*)

34. Beetle bank; the uncultivated strip provides nesting habitat for birds and a reservoir of predatory insects that help control pests on the adjacent crops. (*Photo: S. Warrener*)

Common Agricultural Policy, continue to have a very large part to play on the habitats in Fife's countryside. The introduction of the Countryside Premium Scheme, which offers financial support to protect and enhance certain habitats, will hopefully have a benefit in the near future. In Fife, targeted habitats for the Countryside Premium Scheme include heaths, moors and semi-natural grasslands, so it is possible that these habitats may receive more sympathetic management. However, there will always be a danger that moors and grasslands on farmed land will be lost as economics and farming policy change.

On nature reserves and other protected sites it is important to be able to continue with the management which has led to the creation of the high quality moor or grassland, whether it is a precise grazing regime or the annual removal of a crop of hay. These often take a lot of effort, enthusiasm and money and can be difficult to maintain.

As man-made habitats, moors, heaths and grasslands will always be vulnerable to change whenever man's use of the area changes, and constant monitoring will be necessary to protect these habitats in Fife.

Acknowledgements

I would like to thank Dr Hugh Ingram and Stewart Pritchard for their suggestions on fens and mires, and Caroline Gallacher for her help with the section on moors and grassland. I would also like to thank Caroline for checking the manuscript and making several helpful changes. Thanks also to Ian Christie for the use of his computer and for his assistance with typing the chapter.

Further reading

British Gas (1988). *Heathland restoration. A handbook of techniques.* Camelot Press, Southampton.

Corbet, G B (1997). Myriapods of moorland habitats in the Sidlaw Hills, Angus. *Bulletin of the British Myriapod Group* 13, pp 4–13.

Gimmingham, C H (1975). *An introduction to heathland ecology.* Oliver & Boyd, Edinburgh.

Hester, A J *et al.* (1994). *Heaths and moorland – cultural landscapes.* HMSO.

Lowday, J E and Wells, T C E (1977). *The management of grassland and heathland in country parks.* Countryside Commission Publication 105.

MacDonald, A J, Kirkpatrick, A H, Hester, A J and Sydes, C (1995). *Regeneration by natural layering of heather* (Calluna vulgaris): *frequency and characteristics in upland Britain.* Journal of Applied Ecology 32, pp 85–99.

Rodwell, J S (1991). *British plant communities, volume 2. Mires and heaths.* Cambridge University Press.

Rodwell, J S (1992). *British plant communities, volume 3. Grasslands and montane communities.* Cambridge University Press.

Tansley, A G (1939). *The British Islands and their vegetation.* Cambridge University Press.

10

Farms and fields

SARAH WARRENER

Fife has been farmed since prehistoric times and the biggest changes probably took place at the time of the agricultural revolution in the mid 18th to 19th centuries and more recently since the Second World War. Although the changes during the 18th and 19th centuries undoubtedly had a big impact on wildlife at the time, most of the methods used were what we regard as traditional, for example the use of crop rotations, mixed farming systems and improvement of fertility by the use of natural products such as animal manures and leguminous plants like clover.

The changes wrought since the Second World War have been quite different, with the use of chemicals and large machinery being particularly important. Although farmers and landowners have carried out the changes, these have generally been dictated by political policies. During the war 'dig for victory' led to huge areas of previously unploughed land becoming tilled, much of which has continued to be farmed intensively. Grants were available to farmers for 'improving' their land — removing hedgerows, draining wet areas and reseeding old pastures. Britain aimed to become as self sufficient in food production as possible and our farmers were immensely successful at it.

When Britain entered the Common Market in 1972 domestic policies were taken over by European policies. The price support system changed from one that was basically market-led to one that guaranteed sales of produce regardless of demand. The result was the European milk lakes, beef and grain mountains etc. of the 1970s and 1980s. The European Common Agricultural Policy still dictates what farmers do on their land but in the 1990s the emphasis has altered. Arable farmers are required to set-aside land, dairy farmers have quotas, and sheep and beef producers are expected to have set levels of stock per forage hectare — all to reduce production. Inevitably these political policies affect wildlife.

The intensive use of chemicals has probably had the most profound effect on wildlife. In the 1960s tremendous damage was done with the widespread use of the insecticide DDT which transferred up the food chain and caused numbers of top predators such as otters and sparrowhawks to crash. Although modern chemicals are less harmful in a direct way, they have their impact in indirect ways. It is unusual to see fields with poppies, cornflowers and other arable weeds these days. Less weedy crops provide less food for herbivorous insects which provide less food for insectivorous birds, mammals and other predators.

Farmland in Fife covers 75 per cent of the county, comprising about 98,600 hectares spread over 1277 holdings. Of this about 60,000 ha consist of arable or vegetable ground, including set-aside, and 34,800 ha are of grassland, including rough grazings.

The remainder comprises woodland, roads, yards and other cultivated land. (These figures are rough averages for the first five years of the 1990s.) Farmland is therefore very important in the context of Fife's wildlife.

Average area of crops grown in Fife 1991–1995 (hectares) (figures supplied by the Scottish Office Agriculture, Environment and Fisheries Department)

Wheat	16,122
Barley	21,885
Oats	1,062
Oilseed rape	6,466
Potatoes	2,833
Veg for human consumption	2,745
Set-aside	6,480
Other crops	2,191
Grass	27,865
Rough grazing	5,142

Average numbers of livestock in Fife 1991–1995 (figures supplied by the Scottish Office Agriculture, Environment and Fisheries Department)

Dairy cows	6459
Beef cows	13,889
Other dairy breeding cattle	3,539
Other beef breeding cattle	3,894
Fattening cattle	14,692
Total sheep	122,419
Total pigs	27,445
Total poultry	2,633,007
Other livestock	2,676

The type of farming system has a strong bearing on both the appearance of the landscape and on the wildlife found within it. About 500 of the holdings specialise in cereals and general cropping, whilst about 130 comprise mixed crop and livestock holdings.

Most of the rest specialise in livestock or in forage and grass. Only about 60 holdings involve dairying either as specialist or mixed units. This shows that there has been a move away from the traditional mixed farming into more specialised operations, particularly larger arable units.

Large areas of Fife, especially within the north-east of the county, are dominated by arable and field vegetable enterprises, for example in the East Neuk and the Howe of Fife. These are almost certainly the places that have changed most since farming became more intensive. Despite the general belief that these areas are wildlife deserts they are actually important for arable specialists, for example seed-eating birds, many invertebrates and annual plants such as corn marigold, common poppy and field pansy.

Farmland birds have declined seriously over the last twenty-five years. Some parts of Britain have hardly any skylarks or linnets, both of which are still relatively numerous in Fife. Other seriously declining farmland birds include the grey partridge, corn bunting, reed bunting and rook. Rooks are omnivorous, feeding both on invertebrates such as worms and leatherjackets, and on seed, including spilled grain. They have declined in many areas of arable

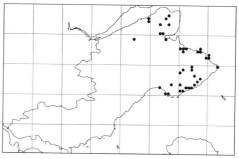

Distribution of corn bunting in the breeding season – a declining species with a precarious hold on the arable lands of east Fife (*Fife Nature*).

farming. Although they are still numerous throughout Fife they are clearly vulnerable to changes in farming practice.

One of the main causes of the decline of all these farmland birds is thought to be the change from spring- to winter-sown cereal crops and the consequent loss of winter stubbles that provide a source of food. More intensive farming means that there are fewer rough areas left where ground-nesting birds such as grey partridge can breed. Clean crops mean little insect food for chicks and consequently fewer survive to breed themselves.

New techniques have been developed to try to arrest some of these changes, and where farmers are sufficiently interested they can achieve excellent results. For example the introduction of wide grassy field margins, beetle banks (grassy strips up the centre of arable fields) and conservation headlands (the outer part of the arable crop which receives a reduced spraying regime) increased the number of grey partridge from 122 to 220 at Gilston, near Largoward in four years. The grass margins and beetle banks simply provide additional nesting areas. The peripheral part of the crop with a good population of annual arable weeds acts as a food supply for insects, which in turn feed chicks during the vital first two weeks of life.

The introduction of wider field margins and beetle banks obviously requires the farmer to give up some croppable land, but the use of conservation headlands interferes very little with normal farm practice and results in minimal crop loss because the end-riggs are naturally the lowest yielding parts of a field. There is an added bonus that conservation headlands and beetle banks provide reservoirs of predatory insects like ladybirds which in turn help reduce crop pests.

Field margins dominated by 'natural' vegetation, i.e. native grasses and herbs as opposed to agricultural grasses that have been bred specifically for high production, can support a surprisingly diverse community. This is especially the case where herbicides have not obliterated some of the more sensitive grassland plants such as field scabious. Even some of the ranker field margin vegetation, for example that dominated by creeping thistle and stinging nettle, can support a very diverse invertebrate fauna. Examples of species frequently found are small tortoiseshell and meadow brown butterflies and the common green grasshopper, all of which may breed in field margins. Of course beneficial insects such as bumble-bees and hoverflies may be found where there are nectar-rich plants. These may be crops such as oilseed rape or green cover such as the mauve-flowered phacelia from California which has recently been sown on set-aside areas. The structure of vegetation is often more important to invertebrates than its composition. This is especially the case for predatory species such as spiders and ground beetles. Field margins often remain unmanaged and thus provide relative stability, although they can be subject to catastrophic actions such as mowing or spray drift. Fortunately the use of insecticides on cereal crops in Scotland is almost unheard of, although vegetable crops often receive regular doses.

Field margins are important for many small mammals such as common shrews and field voles. They are also important for their predators including stoats, weasels and kestrels. Unfortunately some predators typically associated with farmland such as barn owls are now very rare both in Fife and in Britain. Barn owls not only need significant areas of good rough grass for hunting, but also need suitable nesting sites. Often the two do not marry, although it is possible to erect nest boxes and barrels in areas where hunting habitat is good and nest sites scarce. The current trend for conversion of old steadings or simply demolishing unused buildings has greatly reduced nest sites not only for barn owls but also for other typical steading birds such as swallows.

Set-aside was first introduced in the late 1980s as a voluntary scheme. This was then changed and all units with arable land were obliged to put down a specified percentage of set-aside. Although this started off as quite a sizeable amount, the proportion has slowly reduced to the 5 per cent required in 1997. Set-aside is widely disliked especially by the farming community, but it has had benefits for wildlife, especially arable special-ists. The most useful type of set-aside is naturally regenerated stubble, which sup-ports a wide range of arable weeds beneficial to seed-eating birds and invertebrates. The relative lack of disturbance also means that ground-nesting birds such as lapwing, oys-tercatchers and skylark are more able to raise broods successfully.

Lapwing

It is often difficult to detect trends in mammal populations but the brown hare seems to be increasing across most of Fife following a country-wide decline in the 1970s and 80s. This may be connected to the increasing amounts of new farm wood-lands, which provide ideal breeding areas in the early years. Set-aside also seems to at-tract them with as many as six having been seen at once in one field near Crail.

Rabbits have increased enormously dur-ing the 1990s and farmers are being forced to fence fields or take other actions to mini-mise crop damage. Associated with the increased rabbit population is an increase in buzzards. Other species that seem to be very successful are carrion crows and, in west Fife, magpies, which are expanding east-wards. Carrion crows in particular are known to predate the nests of ground-nest-ing farmland birds such as lapwings and other waders. They are frequently associated with herds of outdoor pigs, for example near Guardbridge, owing to the easily available pig food.

Wood pigeons are another successful pest associated with farmland. In the past their numbers were controlled by the scarcity of food during the winter. The advent of winter-sown oilseed rape has meant that there is an abundant winter food source upon which they now feed so their natural control mechanism no longer applies. Many farmers expend a great deal of effort trying to control wood pigeons or at least scare them off crops because of the damage their feeding does.

Reseeded pastures, both short-term and longer-term leys, are usually extremely poor with respect to plant species diversity. The grasses sown are normally agricultural strains developed to give maximum produc-tion. These frequently have little value for wildlife except in providing structurally suitable habitats for some species, especially invertebrates. Examples of invertebrates that live in large numbers in such grasslands are leatherjackets (the larvae of craneflies) and earthworms, both of which provide a food source for many species as diverse as rooks, lapwings, badgers and common shrews.

Some species prefer improved pastures for feeding, providing the grass is of a suitable length. Examples are flocks of wild geese, especially greylag and pink-footed geese, for which Fife holds significant proportions of the British wintering populations. These birds will also feed on arable crops and do huge amounts of damage, especially during spring on winter-sown cereals that are just starting to grow well. Some species of geese may be shot outside the close season and licences may be issued within the close season to prevent serious damage to agricultural crops in problem areas.

Improved pasture is not only grown for grazing but also provides winter stock feed. Traditional hay making has largely been replaced by silage production. The timing of cutting is crucial to farmers because they need to maximise the food value of the crop as well as the yield. As a consequence some breeding wildlife, hares for example, may suffer. Many farmers now cut their fields in strips rather than working from the outside in, so that birds and animals within the crop have a better chance to escape.

Within the intensively farmed areas there are pockets of unimproved habitat. These are often associated with uncultivatable areas such as rockheads or wet flushes. Unfortunately these areas are often uneconomic to manage in the best interests of wildlife and as a result many small pockets are lost to scrub or suffer from the effects of ill directed sprays and fertilisers.

Locally rare plants such as maiden pink (*Dianthus deltoides*) may be found on rock-

Maiden pink

heads along with more common but equally attractive dry-grassland species such as lady's bedstraw and eyebright. Providing the correct food plants are available and the areas are large enough, less frequently seen butterflies such as small copper and common blue may also be found.

Damp flushes may support populations of orchids, both common spotted (*Dactylorhiza fuchsii*) and northern marsh orchid (*D.purpurella*), along with commoner wetland plants such as lady's smock. These areas may also provide habitats for amphibians, especially if they are close to or connected to nearby breeding ponds. Wetland areas with vegetation of a suitable length and type may support breeding snipe and redshank if they are large enough; both species have seriously declined as breeding birds in Fife.

Field boundaries provide places for many species of wildlife to live and breed. Even the most tumble-down old dyke has crevices for small mammals and invertebrates such as spiders and woodlice to hide in. Dykes may also provide habitat for interesting ferns, such as polypody, mosses and lichens. In addition they can support ivy which is an excellent habitat for a range of invertebrates, birds and mammals. Ivy is particularly useful as a late food source for nectar-seeking insects in autumn and provides a crop of berries in late winter.

Besides considering the habitats and species above ground level it is also important to take account of those that live below the surface. Earthworms are a vital part of the natural nutrient-recycling system. They are numerous in fields that have been regularly treated with farmyard manure or inorganic fertiliser. They are also abundant within grass fields, especially permanent pasture. Earthworm densities of 50 kg per hectare are normal in arable fields and up to 220 kg per hectare have been recorded in

permanent pasture. High densities are usually dependent upon the length of time a field remains undisturbed. Earthworms are an extremely important food source for many species including badgers, foxes, shrews, amphibians, thrushes and waders. Gulls and rooks following the plough in autumn are a very common sight.

The introduced New Zealand flatworm (*Artioposthia triangulata*) preys upon earthworms and is a potential threat to worm populations. However, although it is widespread in gardens, it does not yet appear to have colonised arable farmland in Fife to any great extent, in contrast to the wetter west of the country where it is a more serious problem.

As long as cultivated land comprises a mosaic of different crops interspersed with field boundaries and features that are able to provide a refuge for wildlife, it can support a surprisingly high number of species. Like all habitats it needs to be managed carefully to maximise its value for its specialists. In modern times that is largely

Hedgerow and treelines in Fife; changes between 1940 and 1970 (kilometres) (from National Countryside Monitoring Scheme, Scottish Natural Heritage, 1993)

Hedgerows	North & east Fife	Central & west Fife	Fife
1940s	1751	1365	3184
1970s	1175	940	2171
Gains	177	171	171
Losses	754	596	1382
Net change	−576	−425	−1014
Percentage change	−32%	−31%	−32%
Treelines			
1940s	643	682	1356
1970s	541	525	1083
Gains	123	185	324
Losses	226	342	596
Net change	−102	−156	−272
Percentage change	−16%	−23%	−20%

associated with careful selection and use of agrochemicals and the uptake of techniques developed to increase wildlife habitat without having too high an impact on the agricultural business.

Hedgerows

Hedgerows are an intrinsic part of the agricultural landscape in Britain, and Fife is no exception to this. The hedgerow was originally invented by farmers and landowners for two specific purposes: to keep stock enclosed and to mark boundaries between properties. Other benefits such as the provision of shelter, creation of wildlife habitats and adding to the attractiveness of the landscape are all incidental to these original purposes.

Although Fife has been farmed since prehistoric times, most of the agricultural changes have occurred since the mid 18th century, especially during the 19th century. It was during this period of great change that most of the enclosures took place. Most of the boundaries of this period enclosed fields of regular shapes and were made of stone or hedging shrubs. It can be surmised that there are relatively few truly ancient hedges surviving in Fife, unlike parts of England where some boundaries date back to the 13th century.

The most popular species of hedging plants in the 19th century were hawthorn and beech, although it has to be said the former is far more suitable as an encloser of stock than the latter. Many hedges were planted with evenly spaced trees that were allowed to grow up into standards. Popular species were ash, wych elm, oak and sycamore, although on some estates the range of species included lime and horse-chestnut. These old trees are often all that remain of the old enclosures. The pace of agricultural

change has accelerated during the past fifty years and as a consequence many fields have been combined in order to make larger and more economically viable blocks. Stone dykes and hedges have been lost as a result, although owing to the comparative lateness of enclosure Fife has possibly suffered less than those parts of Britain that had a basically mediaeval field pattern.

Although wildlife habitat creation was not in the forefront of the minds of the enclosers, hedges have become a vital part of farmland ecology. A great variety of species of plant and animal life – mammals, birds and invertebrates – can be found using them, and many of these are almost entirely dependent upon hedgerows as habitat.

The basis of any hedgerow is the shrub component, although the grassy strips that are usually adjacent form an integral part of the hedgerow habitat. Usually the diversity of plants within a hedge increases with age, although modern hedge planting often includes a great many more woody species than those planted in the 19th century. These tended to be dominated by a single shrub species and one or two tree species.

The range of shrubs found within Fife's hedges can be great, although those most commonly found are beech, hawthorn and elder, with dog-rose, bramble and tree species such as ash following behind. Sometimes undesirable garden escapes such as snowberry can smother out the more traditional species – a particularly notable example can be found between Freuchie and Newton of Falkland. On some estates rhododendron hedges are fairly usual especially in connection with policy woodlands. Less common shrubby species found within Fife hedges are holly, hazel and blackthorn, although these are all considered normal hedging species.

Non-woody plants associated with hedges

are many and varied. Many are more commonly associated with other habitats such as woodlands and grasslands, for example primrose, wild hyacinth, field scabious and common knapweed. Others however are considered typical hedgerow species, for example cow parsley, hogweed and red campion. It is normally accepted that a greater diversity of plants, especially native plants, leads to a greater diversity of other wildlife since the basis of the food web is plant life.

Hedgerows and adjacent grassy strips support a huge diversity of insects and other invertebrates. Human activities can play an enormous part in dictating the composition of these populations at a given time since hedge cutting and spraying in adjacent fields can bring about great changes very quickly. The diversity of invertebrates is frequently related to the presence of certain plants since many are dependent upon one or two species for breeding. Common hedgerow butterflies are ringlet and meadow brown, both of which breed on grasses. The small tortoiseshell, another common hedgerow butterfly, breeds on nettles so almost certainly has suffered from the practice of spraying weeds out of hedge bottoms – fortunately few farmers do this now.

Many of the invertebrate species living within hedgerows can be useful to farmers as agents of biological control. For example ladybirds and carabid beetles prey upon aphids and other crop pests. Slugs and snails of many different species are common in hedges. These feed mainly on decaying vegetation although some will eat fresh plants quite happily, especially if they take the form of cultivated crops such as lettuce and oilseed rape. Molluscs are an important part of the diet of many hedgerow mammals and birds, notably hedgehogs and song thrush.

Fourteen species of British lowland mammals are commonly found in hedges. Each of these is also known to breed within hedgerows, although it has to be said this is within Britain as a whole rather than just Fife. Nevertheless eleven species can reasonably be assumed to breed commonly in hedgerows in Fife. Examples of these are bank vole, stoat and common shrew. Common rats may also be present but usually only where the hedge is accompanied by a wet ditch.

About fourteen species of Britain's resident birds commonly breed within hedgerows along with many summer visitors. Research has shown that the density of birds on farmland rises from 8.3 per 1000 yards of boundary to 20.5 when hedges are present. Common hedgerow/farmland birds are blackbird, dunnock, chaffinch, robin, whitethroat and yellowhammer. Of course the structure of the hedge will determine its value and its ability to support a narrow or wide range of wildlife. For example a hedgerow with occasional old, large trees will also provide habitat for hole-dwelling species such as blue tits, tree sparrows, pipistrelle and brown long-eared bats.

In turn the structure of a hedge is determined by the way it is managed. The advent of tractor-mounted hedge-cutting machinery has led to a general decline in hedges of good structure, although in recent years the tide has started to turn, with farmers taking more interest in wildlife and consequently the state of their hedges. This is largely due to the efforts of the Farming and Wildlife Advisory Group who have raised the profile of hedges in Fife by running a campaign to improve their management.

Good wildlife hedges need to be wide and tall and twiggy. Ideally they should be cut between Christmas and March after most of the berries have been consumed by birds and other wildlife. Careful cutting practices such as leaving several inches of the new growth on the hedge allows some flowering and fruiting to occur the following season since many shrubs including hawthorn only flower on seasoned wood. For preference hedges should be cut every other year so that there is always a profusion of flowers and fruits on some of them.

No cutting at all can be as bad as too much cutting since the bottoms become gappy and the plants open out thus offering less shelter. Sometimes more drastic management is required, such as coppicing (i.e. cutting close to the ground), in order to bring a poor hedge back into better condition. Unfortunately farmers are often castigated for doing this because people frequently assume they are removing a hedge whereas in fact they are simply managing it.

Hedgerow trees are slowly being replaced either by new plants or by allowing saplings to develop into standards instead of being cut. There is still some antipathy to hedgerow trees because they are seen as pigeon roosts and they shade out crops. Farmers are more likely to accept them when they run in a line north-south or are adjacent to tracks where they are less of a nuisance.

The recent trend towards conservation-friendly grant schemes and initiatives will doubtless continue the trend in improved management. The Countryside Premium Scheme, launched in the spring of 1997, is the first scheme available throughout Scotland that encourages farmers to manage their hedges and other habitats to the benefit of wildlife. As yet it is too early to estimate take up, but indications are that many farmers are showing interest.

Further reading

Andrews, J and Rebane, M (1994). *Farming and wildlife. A practical management handbook*. RSPB.

Dowdeswell, W H (1987). *Hedgerows and verges*. Allen & Unwin.

Institute of Terrestrial Ecology (1993). *Managing set-aside land for wildlife*. HMSO.

Lack, P (1992). *Birds on lowland farms*. HMSO.

Mellanby, K (1981). *Farming and wildlife*. Collins, London.

O'Connor, R J and Shrubb, M (1986). *Farming and birds*. Cambridge University Press.

Watt, T A and Buckley, G P (eds) (1994). *Hedgerow management and nature conservation*. Wye College Press.

11

Living with man

GORDON CORBET AND GEORGE BALLANTYNE

Previous chapters have shown that many environments that appear predominantly natural in fact owe their present condition to the way in which they have been managed, or indeed created, by human intervention. Woods have been planted, pasture has been created by the draining of marshes, fields have been made out of all sorts of original habitats. All of these have rich and varied wildlife, which reflects, in some degree, that of the parent habitat. However the more conspicuously man-made environments of towns, villages, factories, quarries, roads and railways also have their own suites of plants and animals, which can be surprisingly diverse although not so obviously related to natural habitats.

Buildings

The insides of our houses might seem the least likely wildlife habitat, and indeed any non-human animal that is not a pet tends to be ejected or killed, either by the house-holder or a professional pest-controller. However most houses and other buildings contain a community of plants and animals that do not necessarily conflict with our own interests although there are often con-spicuous exceptions.

The more damaging indoor species such as dry-rot fungus and the wood-boring beetles are now much less prevalent than before because of the efficiency of modern chemical treatment of timber. Woodlice, es-pecially *Porcellio scaber*, are frequent indoors but harmless, usually living in the under-floor space and emerging through the air-bricks to feed on dead leaves in the gar-den, but occasionally coming instead through a crack in the floor-boards into a centrally heated room where they soon die of desiccation. Silverfish (*Lepisma saccharina*), which are wingless insects, are widespread, feeding on spilled food, wall-paper paste etc. Most houses contain three or four resident species of spiders, all dependent upon insects for food, sometimes including one of the lar-gest of British spiders, *Tegenaria saeva*. House mice are probably a diminishing species in domestic premises but houses with

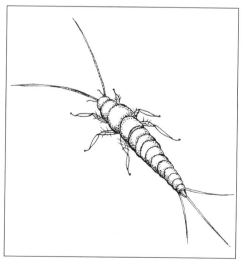

Silverfish, a fairly harmless insect of warm buildings (c.12 mm without appendages).

gardens are often invaded by wood mice in autumn.

The outsides of buildings support a very specialized flora. Roof tiles are frequently encrusted with lichens: the grey *Lecanora conizaeoides* and the orange *Xanthoria parietina* are common in towns, being resistant to air pollution. The latter especially benefits from fertilization provided by birds on the rooftops. Mosses are less resistant to desiccation but flourish in ill-maintained rones as well as in cracks in paving. The dominant urban ones are *Ceratodon purpureum* and *Bryum argenteum*, the latter getting its name from the silvery hair-tips on its leaves. Water squeezed from the mosses will be found to contain a complex community of microlife: diatoms, ciliate protozoans, amoebae and rotifers, as well as water-bears (tardigrades) which, although complex multicellular animals, can form resting stages that are highly resistant to drought.

Walls are a mini-habitat supporting a small but typical flora, especially those that are old and have not been too well maintained. In addition to lichens such as *Lecanora campestris* and *L.dispersa* and the

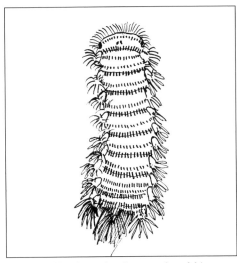

Bristly millipede, a tiny (2–3 mm) and bizarre millipede found locally on lichen-covered walls.

moss *Tortula muralis*, two frequent ferns are wall-rue and common spleenwort. Flowers favouring walls include ivy-leaved toadflax and yellow corydalis. Some invertebrates are found almost exclusively on walls. One of the more conspicuous is the zebra spider (*Salticus scenicus*), a striped black and grey jumping spider which hunts actively on walls by day. Other spiders like the widespread *Segestria senoculata* live in crevices and dash out to grab prey that touch the 'trip-wires' of silk. The rare and bizarre bristly millipede (*Polyxenus lagurus*) can be seen on the churchyard walls at Leuchars and Auchtermuchty in bright sunshine, conditions that would send any other millipede scurrying for somewhere moist and dark.

There is a characteristic community of flowering plants in heavily built-up areas. The most ubiquitous is the annual meadow-grass (*Poa annua*) whose seeds are everywhere – you probably pick up some on the soles of your shoes every time you go out. Other common annuals are chickweed and groundsel. At the other extreme the butterfly-bush (*Buddleja davidii*) has a remarkable capacity to grow in cracks in masonry and often acts as a magnet for butterflies in otherwise impoverished areas.

Houses provide nesting or resting places for many animals that forage out-of-doors. Pipistrelle bats are widespread in Fife and form nursery colonies during the summer months in crevices behind wall-cladding or under tiles. Contrary to common belief they are just as likely to be in modern houses as in ancient church belfries. They cause no damage and consume huge quantities of insects on their nightly forays so they should be welcomed – indeed they are legally protected provided they are not in the living-space of a house. Swifts are not so densely colonial and they need deep crevices for their nests. They therefore nest more commonly on larger public buildings but are entirely dependent upon such artificial nest-sites. Although house martins mostly nest under the eves of buildings, a few still nest in natural sites such as the Kincraig Cliffs near Elie.

In recent years herring and lesser black-backed gulls have nested on roofs in the middle of towns including Kirkcaldy, where passers-by have been 'dive-bombed' regularly after the chicks have hatched. Since the 1950s fulmars have colonized every available sea-cliff (and some inland), and have taken to nesting on the old window-ledges of Ravenscraig Castle at Kirkcaldy. A more bizarre example of birds nesting on buildings is the recent colonisation of the flat rooftops of Glenrothes by nesting oystercatchers. The chicks have then to be fed until they fledge instead of being able to forage for themselves from an early age.

House sparrows are still common in towns and villages although they have declined considerably in the countryside in recent years. The adults are basically seed-eaters, but they are versatile enough to thrive on dropped chips and hamburgers and other human refuse; however they feed their chicks mainly upon caterpillars and therefore perform a useful service in keeping the more damaging insects under control.

Gardens and parks

All gardens, urban and rural, have the potential to harbour rich and diverse communities of wildlife that are entirely compatible with productive gardening. The great variety of cultivated plants in gardens influences wildlife in a number of ways. For one thing many plants have escaped from gardens and colonised the countryside. These are mostly exotic species such as the thicket-forming Japanese knotweed which has invaded mainly disturbed land like road and rail verges, or the (also Japanese) *Rosa rugosa* which is colonising large areas of the Largo dunes. Most garden plants however are highly selected cultivars and hybrids which are much less able to compete with natural vegetation. Nevertheless, many either get cast-out or escape into the countryside and are increasingly encountered in unexpected places; examples are columbine, dame's-violet, honesty and Welsh poppy.

No two people will agree on what exactly constitutes a garden weed, but most if not all would include such annuals as chickweed, groundsel and shepherd's-purse, together with aggressors like creeping thistle, dockens and nettles – all are 'plants growing where they are not wanted'. But not a few incomers to our gardens add variety and colour and do little harm if an eye is kept on them, poppies, gowans, feverfew and mayweed among them. It is surprising how many plants cultivated in other gardens, some far away, appear in one's own garden of their own accord. Peach-leaved bellflower and purple toadflax are two that commonly infiltrate, and others include borage, red valerian and ivy. With the planting of many berried shrubs both in gardens and open spaces, species such as cotoneasters and tutsan are cropping up uninvited, along with the occasional seedling tree, for example rowan and whitebeam and even conifers like western hemlock.

Garden plants provide food for a huge array of insects and other invertebrates. The most conspicuous are the butterflies, bees and hoverflies that frequent the flowers for pollen and nectar. Few of these are fussy as to the kind of flower they visit, provided nectar is available. However some species of bumble-bees, such as the white-tailed *Bombus hortorum*, have long tongues adapted to long-tubed flowers like honeysuckle,

Bumble-bees

while others have short tongues and these often specialize in composite flowers like Michaelmas daisies. One of these is the red-tailed *Bombus lapidarius* which has only recently spread to become widely distributed throughout Fife.

Tortoiseshells are usually the most abundant of garden butterflies. Although the adults can feed from a large variety of nectar-producing flowers, with *Buddleja* and *Aster* amongst their favourites, the caterpillars are much more specialised, being entirely dependent upon stinging nettles. Patches of nettles in the corners of gardens or parks can therefore play an important part in maintaining good populations of these magnificent insects.

Decomposer invertebrates are important in gardens, consuming dead vegetation and creating humus-rich soil, both in the compost heap and generally wherever leaves are left on the ground. Earthworms predominate but millipedes and woodlice are also widespread. The pill-woodlouse (*Armadillidium vulgare*), which can roll into a ball as its names imply, is of special interest. Although a common garden species further south (and the one woodlouse most often seen by day), it is at the extreme northern edge of its range in Fife where records so far are confined to a few coastal sites and the Botanic Garden at St Andrews.

All these invertebrates, as well as the less welcome aphids, caterpillars and slugs, provide a rich resource of food for predators.

Hedgehogs are frequent while blackbirds find worms in even the smallest urban garden. Tits – blue, great and coal – are also widespread, especially if the provision of nest-boxes enables them to stay in summer to feed on aphids after being fed on peanuts all winter. One specialized predator that has only recently spread throughout Fife is the New Zealand flatworm (*Artioposthia triangulata*), which preys upon earthworms. This has been in Fife at least since the early 1980s, at first predominantly in large rural gardens and garden-centres, but increasingly colonising small gardens.

With the decline of ponds in the countryside, garden ponds are becoming increasingly important for aquatic life. Even the smallest pond can develop a surprisingly diverse community of plants and animals, often without any help. It comes as a surprise to many that water beetles can and do fly, and some species quickly colonise new ponds. Although many invertebrates can coexist with fish, the exclusion of fish, especially in a small pond, will greatly enhance the variety of invertebrates and improve the chances of successful breeding of frogs, toads and newts.

Urban and suburban parks have many of the features found in small gardens, with the addition of large areas of mown grass. Whereas in a very small garden it may not be practical to have both a mown lawn and an area of long grass, this is a realistic option in public parks, and one that can be very rewarding in diversifying wildlife.

Not that closely mown lawns need be deficient in wildlife interest. Provided they are not treated with weed-killer, they can carry a surprising variety of wild plants and animals. Daisies and dandelions can stand frequent mowing and in many lawns are supplemented by slender speedwell (*Veronica filiformis*), an introduction from Turkey, forming superb patches of delicate blue in spring. Mosses can add to the variety of colour and texture and are entirely compatible with a lawn provided it is not subjected to hard wear. Invertebrates are plentiful and attract a variety of birds – blackbirds feeding upon earthworms, starlings probing for leather-jackets (the larvae of crane-flies) and pied wagtails chasing tiny flies on the surface.

Where areas of less frequently mown tall grass can be left in larger gardens and parks an entirely different and complementary community is created. Tall herbs such as knapweed, thistles and campions supplement the grass and provide a three-dimensional habitat with a flora and fauna that is distinct from that on short grass. Field voles find shelter as well as food (grass); butterflies and grasshoppers find both breeding and feeding sites as well as shelter from wind and predators.

Recent years have seen a great increase in amenity planting with all sorts of verges, plots and odd corners filled with plants, mostly shrubs and small trees. As well as familiar species such as hawthorn and roses, many new varieties have been introduced, especially cotoneasters, brooms, alders and willows. Some of these are already becoming self-sown in neighbouring natural spots and they seem likely to continue to spread and become part of the Fife flora.

Sports-fields

A different kind of grassland is that of sports-fields. The grasses used must be those that can best withstand trampling, especially rye-grass, and other plants may be scarce. However earthworms and leather-jackets are often abundant. Especially in winter, playing fields can be important feeding grounds for a whole host of birds:

blackbirds and thrushes (including the winter redwings and fieldfares); black-headed and common gulls; oystercatchers, lapwings and curlews; rooks, jackdaws and starlings.

Out of town, the dominant 'sports-fields' are the golf courses, which have even greater potential for doubling up as wildlife reserves. Fife has 40 courses, with others in various stages of development, occupying at least 2000 hectares (i.e. 20 square kilometres). Of that area, about 45 per cent is used for play, leaving a huge area of 'rough' and associated habitat with considerable potential for wildlife. The Scottish Golf Course Wildlife Group, led by the Scottish Golf Union, is currently preparing a database of information on the kinds and quality of habitat on golf courses throughout Scotland. They aim to encourage the managers of courses to prepare Integrated Management Plans to realize the potential of courses for wildlife without compromising enjoyment of the game.

The earliest courses, as at St Andrews and Elie, were developed on dune slacks and can, with sympathetic management, retain much of the botanical diversity of the original natural vegetation, as described in chapter 5, especially in the roughs. They can also harbour rarities. St Andrews Links – the collective name for the five courses – have long been known for the curved sedge (*Carex maritima*), now unhappily much diminished owing to the removal of its favoured damp turf, while also present is a small colony of Baltic rush (*Juncus balticus*). An unexpected but long-established denizen of the Links is tree lupin. The rough at the home of golf and elsewhere supports a considerable number of plants, among them eyebrights, bluebell (harebell), cowslip and occasional orchids. As there is little disturbance other than the hacking out of an odd errant ball, the flowers have the chance to flourish, and parts of several courses merit conservation status.

Industry

The traditional heavy industry of Fife, especially coal-mining, made large areas of land very inhospitable to wildlife. It also introduced its own curiosities like the emergence from imported pit-props of giant 'wood-wasps' (wood-boring sawflies of the family Siricidae) which were reported to have alarmed the miners of Muiredge near Buckhaven in 1872.

Derelict land resulting from the decline of the coal-mining industry has considerable potential for restoration of a variety of wildlife habitats, although it is a fallacy to believe that the more natural habitats can be removed and restored quickly. A rich semi-natural woodland for example is likely to take centuries to recover its full suite of associated species.

The most ambitious project of this kind was undertaken by Fife Regional Council in the 1970s when a huge area of dereliction at Lochore was transformed into a Country Park. A variety of habitats was created, ranging from open water through marginal swamps and fens to woodland and grassland, and with a planned level of human activity

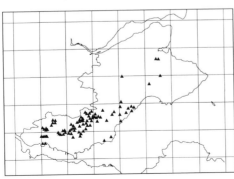

Location of former coal mines.
(*Courtesy of Fife Nature.*)

from active water-sports to secluded bird-watching.

There are many other areas of derelict land in Fife. On the initiative of the Scottish Wildlife Trust a survey was conducted in 1979 and 1980 for Fife Regional Council (Crichton *et al.* 1980). This identified 442 sites of which 73 per cent by area resulted from mining and 16 per cent from quarrying.

Many derelict sites on the urban fringe have subsequently been reclaimed for light industry, parks or sports fields. However many of the former mining sites are rural and have either been left to natural recolonisation or have been planted with trees, which is usually a more productive option than attempting to restore agriculture.

Most disturbed land, if left to its own devices, becomes clothed in vegetation, although this usually includes a greater complement of exotic plants than is found in undisturbed natural habitats. Annual weeds such as the mouse-ears and thale cress intermingle with dandelions, buttercups and dead-nettles, often accompanied by weld. On bare ground, especially old crumbling concrete bases, biting stonecrop is often present, occasionally partnered by shining crane's-bill. Grasses soon move in and it is not long before such bushes as whin and broom appear, usually followed by birch and willows; the last are particularly prevalent on and by old railways and pit bings.

Quarries

With its great geological diversity, Fife has for long been extensively quarried. The earlier pattern of small local quarries has gradually been replaced by fewer larger ones, leaving many abandoned. Some of these have been filled leaving no trace, but many remain and provide interesting and rare habitats. Although calcareous rocks are

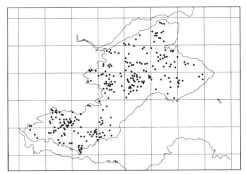

Location of disused quarries.
(*Courtesy of Fife Nature.*)

widespread in Fife they are mostly covered by such a deep layer of glacial till that they have little effect on the surface. Quarrying has brought this rock to the surface at many places, the largest being around Charlestown and Limekilns in west Fife where quarrying ceased in 1898 although mining of limestone continued for some time later. Another major site is on the ridge of Cults Hill on the high spine of east Fife south of the Eden, where quarries are still active.

The export of lime was a major industry at Charlestown and led to the introduction and establishment of several 'calciphile' plants and animals in ballast. The snail *Cernuella virgata* is likely to have arrived in this way along with black horehound (*Ballota nigra*).

Sites of smaller limestone quarries can often be identified by surviving limekilns. One at Craigmead on the south slope of East Lomond has been restored, while a massive one in Craighall Den near Ceres is surrounded by evidence of a limy past in the form of a rich fauna of snails and millipedes.

Surviving quarry faces and floors develop communities of lichens and mosses, and a varied mix of wild flowers. In late spring many tiny annuals show themselves, including whitlowgrass and early forget-me-not followed by cudweeds and wild thyme. Old faces and ledges have a wide spectrum of inhabitants, ranging from ubiquitous daisies through meadow saxifrage to scarce species such as bloody crane's-bill.

Transport

Road verges provide an exceptionally valuable but also vulnerable wildlife habitat. Many are of great antiquity and have preserved remnants of once more widely distributed communities of plants and animals that have been reduced by intensive agriculture and urbanization. The history of Fife's roads has been ably described by Silver (1987). In the late 18th century the new coaching roads were provided with wide verges for security. Many modern roads also have very extensive verges, for example in motorway cuttings and to provide sightlines on bends. A more typical verge however is around one or two metres wide.

On rich soils the dominant vegetation usually consists of tall grasses such as false oat-grass and cock's-foot along with tall herbs such as cow parsley, hogweed and rosebay willow-herb. However many other flowers can be present when conditions are right – field scabious and bird's-foot trefoil on drier banks, restharrow on sandy verges near the coast, and cowslips and a variety of orchids on the lime-rich verges on Cults Hill.

Rural verges are cut by Fife Council's Roads Division for purposes of road safety. Usually the front metre only is cut in early summer and again in autumn, with the remainder cut in autumn as necessary to control the growth of shrubs. For most roads this produces a useful diversity of vegetation, with low-growing plants encouraged at the front of the verge. In other cases an early summer cut would remove some of the scarcer flowers before seed has been set. To prevent this some verges of

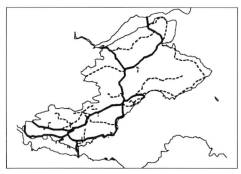

Location of used and disused railways.
(*Courtesy of Fife Nature.*)

special interest have been identified by the Scottish Wildlife Trust. These are marked with posts and by agreement with the Roads Division they are not cut during specified periods.

Many of the broader verges of motorways and some new trunk roads have been planted with predominantly native trees and shrubs, which will provide the basis for a diverse flora and fauna in the future. The broader grassy verges and banks provide ideal habitat for field voles which are in turn preyed upon by kestrels which are a familiar sight as they hover over the verges.

All roads of course provide hazards as well as benefits to wildlife. Salt spray in winter can reduce the range of plants that can survive on verges although it can also lead to communities more reminiscent of salt-marshes. On some motorways Danish scurvygrass (*Cochlearia danica*) produces spectacular displays of mauve on the central reservation and verges in spring, as on the A90 exit from the Forth Road Bridge.

Animals living on road verges are, like ourselves, vulnerable to accidents. Birds especially at risk are owls (both tawny and, where they occur, barn), pheasants, yellowhammers and the thrushes, including blackbirds. Although rooks are a familiar sight as they forage for dead insects and grit on the edge of the road they are remarkably smart

at avoiding the traffic; regrettably hedgehogs are not so adept. Amongst other mammals rabbits dominate the road-kills and in turn provide food for crows as well as magpies, gulls, foxes and other scavengers.

Rail verges have much in common with road verges. However cuttings and embankments are more common and provide unstable ground that favours some plants such as Japanese knotweed. Since the demise of steam power rail verges are less prone to burning, so that shrubs and trees can colonize more readily. Sycamore is usually the first tree to take advantage.

Abandoned railways are widespread in Fife, both former multi-purpose routes like the coastal line from Leven to Leuchars and many 'mineral' lines associated with the coal industry. The survey of derelict land recorded 238 km of disused railways in Fife. Although some have disappeared entirely under the plough, as in the approaches to Elie, many remain as valuable and varied habitats for wildlife, especially dry grassland and scrub. One particular plant seldom found other than on old railway lines is small toadflax (*Chaenorhinum minus*). A relative, common toadflax (*Linaria vulgaris*), and common St John's-wort (*Hypericum perforatum*) sometimes turn long stretches of line-side yellow in summer. Some of these are 'local' plants; others, like Oxford ragwort, have certainly arrived *via* the railway. Butterflies frequently thrive in these conditions – the old Leuchars to Tayport line along the western edge of Tentsmuir, incorporating the car-park at Morton Lochs, is a prime site for butterfly-watching.

Railway sidings such as the Kirkland Sidings on the left bank of the river at Leven also produce distinctive wildlife communities. The substrate is normally ash (from steam engines) without the stony ballast of normal railway tracks. Legumes such as melilots and garden lupins along with hawkweeds (*Hieracium* spp.) thrive during the early stages of colonization, often followed by birch and sallow.

Apart from their value as habitats in their own right, roads and railways provide corridors linking larger areas of seminatural habitat, making it easier for species to recolonise if they have become locally extinct.

In the heyday of Fife's coal export trade, ships from the continent arrived at the county's many harbours 'in ballast', that is laden with stones and rubble which were dumped nearby, in time forming what became known as 'ballast banks'. This led to the appearance of many foreign plants (and to an influx of botanists!), although most lasted only for a season or two. However one or two persist today, for example wall rocket (*Diplotaxis tenuifolia*) in the Inverkeithing area. A more recent parallel is the import of grain for malting, the spillage of which at places like Kirkcaldy harbour resulted in the springing up of several alien species. A few may still be seen, notably Oxford ragwort and hoary cress (*Lepidium draba*) along with widespread white melilot (*Melilotus alba*).

Waste disposal

Some aspects of the disposal of both liquid and solid waste have been touched upon in chapter 4 (p. 39). As the amount of domestic waste has gradually increased, so has there been a centralization of waste-disposal. At one time a great deal of domestic and farm waste was dumped in small quarries and in the wooded dens. In the case of quarries it can be argued that they are man-made holes and filling them is a process of restoration. Against this is the fact that many quarries develop near-natural communities of wildlife that are generally scarce and therefore worth fostering. An example of a quarry that has

been used for waste-disposal and has then been developed for nature conservation is at West Quarry Braes near Crail. This is now a reserve operated by the Scottish Wildlife Trust in cooperation with Fife Council, especially as a refuge for arriving migrant birds, but with considerable value as an island of woodland in an area where such habitat is scarce.

The use of wooded dens for the disposal of rubbish is quite indefensible. As shown in chapter 7 many of these contain priceless remnants of near-natural habitats. Rubbish not only affects the ecology of the den directly, for example by polluting water and encouraging rats; it also hinders public appreciation of the enormous value of these sites for nature conservation. In spite of the public provision of waste-disposal services this is a continuing problem.

In recent years the disposal of domestic waste has shown some encouraging trends. Recycling has reduced the volume, although there is a long way to go in that direction. Land-fill sites are covered more quickly with topsoil, but problems of contamination of water remain.

Industrial waste produces different problems and different solutions. A continuing source is the 'pulverised fuel ash' from Longannet power station on the upper Forth Estuary. This has for long been dumped in lagoons – the Valleyfield Lagoons – in Torry Bay. The new land thus created now covers almost two square kilometres and is within the Torry Bay Local Nature Reserve established in 1996. Such ash is initially alkaline and salty and the first colonizers are salt-marsh grasses, orache and other salt-tolerant plants. As the salts are washed out, other plants colonize, although some persistent toxic salts, especially of boron, limit the species that can cope. Finally thickets of alder and willows have developed, but with some interesting and rare associates such as the wood small-reed (*Calamagrostis epigejos*), a tall grass albeit shorter than the common reed (*Phragmites australis*). The Valleyfield Lagoons are the site of a major experiment in sewage treatment using beds of common reed .

Such projects require major professional and political decisions. But our personal attitudes and actions with regard to litter can also harm or benefit wildlife. Litter on roadsides and hedgerows, and in parks and other public places, can harm wildlife directly – shrews become trapped in discarded bottles and cans, birds get their bills and feet tangled in plastic and in metal ring-pulls. But perhaps even more important is the effect on public perception of wild plants and wild places. When a wild rose bush is draped with plastic shopping bags it is all too easy to condemn the rose rather than the litter-lout. The answer is to find ways to control the litter rather than to throw the baby out with the bath-water by converting wild land to closely mown grass.

The management and creation of urban habitats

Even more than in rural situations, to realize the wildlife potential of urban sites often requires active management or even creation of habitat, but the rewards can be correspondingly great in terms of public awareness and educational potential. When the Glenrothes Development Corporation was wound up in 1994 all the existing woodland within the town, comprising 24 woods covering 254 hectares, was donated to the Woodland Trust for management as a public amenity. A further 110 hectares of farmland at Formonthills on the northern edge of Glenrothes was made available to the Woodland Trust for planting as a Community

Woodland. Many other smaller Community Woodland projects are underway throughout Fife, sponsored by Forest Enterprise in conjunction with Fife Council.

A further habitat creation project, 'Grounds for Learning', encourages schools to develop wildlife gardens in their own grounds or on nearby land. Sponsored by Fife Council, Fife Enterprise and Scottish Natural Heritage, the scheme already has over a hundred active projects in schools throughout Fife.

There was a time when urban and industrial land was virtually ignored by those involved with nature conservation. There is now an increasing realization of the importance and potential of such land, perhaps associated with the parallel realization that most of the wider countryside also owes its present condition to the interaction of man and nature. The Scottish Wildlife Trust is promoting an 'Urban Greenspace' campaign to encourage appreciation of the wildlife, existing and potential, in towns and villages. Although initially focused upon the larger cities the message is equally relevant for the smallest village – wildlife is everywhere and we and it are interdependent.

Further reading

Chinery, M (1977). *The natural history of the garden*. Collins, London.

Crichton, J, Roper-Lindsay, J and Taylor, P (1980). *Derelict land survey; final report*. Fife Regional Council, 109 pp.

Gilbert, O L (1989). *The ecology of urban habitats*. London, Chapman & Hall, 369 pp.

Scottish Natural Heritage (no date). *Golf's natural heritage*, 32 pp.

Silver, O (1987). *The roads of Fife*. Edinburgh, Donald.

Walters, M (1993). *Wild and garden plants*. HarperCollins, London.

12

The study and conservation of Fife's natural heritage

FRANK SPRAGGE

It is a truism that one cannot undertake or even contemplate any plan of conservation, either of habitats or of species, without some knowledge of what went on in the past, so it is appropriate that this chapter starts with a brief review of the literature available to us.

At the very beginning we must touch our cap with great respect to Sir Robert Sibbald, whose seminal book *The History, Ancient and Modern, of the Sheriffdoms of Fife and Kinross* (1710) is the first printed work to give any account of the flora and fauna of Fife. This was followed by the First (1790s) and Second (1840s) Statistical Accounts, which offered sporadic and anecdotal mention of natural history in some parish descriptions. A Third Statistical Account was published after the Second World War, in 1952. This contains a comprehensive chapter on the geological and geomorphological basis of the county, but otherwise deals chiefly with the economic development of Fife: for a practicing conservationist it is no less interesting for that, for a knowledge of past land use and exploitation is essential if we are to understand the present picture of our natural history resource and how it came about. For the real purpose of this exercise, however, we may take as our starting point the end of the 19th century, when the first thorough floras and faunas began to flow from the

pens of amateur naturalists of the late Victorian era.

The great 'Vertebrate Fauna' series of Harvie-Brown and Buckley (1887–1906), for example, covered most of central and northern Scotland, and is still used to this day as a reliable account of our 19th century species distribution and abundance (or rarity). They were based on river catchment areas, and for

William Evans (1851–1922), a pioneer naturalist of the 'Forth Area'.

Evelyn V. Baxter and Leonora Jeffrey Rintoul, pioneers of Scottish Ornithology who were the first to study bird migration on the Isle of May. (*Courtesy of Scotttish Ornithologists' Club.*)

Fife the volume covering the Tay Basin and Strathmore (1906) takes in the whole of the northern part of the county, and gives us a marvellous baseline for that area. However, a corresponding volume covering the Forth catchment (and hence the south and west of Fife) was never published, although much of the data for it had been put together by the distinguished Edinburgh naturalist William Evans. It was not till 1935 that *A Vertebrate Fauna of Forth* was written, following a similar format, by Leonora Rintoul and Evelyn Baxter, combining Evans's material with their own observations, thus completing the Fife picture. Indeed, no account of conservation in Fife (or in Scotland) could be considered complete without acknowledging the huge debt that we owe to these two Fife ladies. Most of the ornithological advances of this century can be traced back to their pioneering work, including early migration

studies on the Isle of May from 1907 onwards.

For the botanist, trying to establish a baseline from which to work is far less easy. True, there were numerous field-workers in the 19th and early 20th centuries making detailed observations on a species or site basis (Howie's *Moss Flora of Fife and Kinross* (1889) is an example of this) but their results were published – if at all – in obscure or inaccessible journals, or tucked away in the libraries or herbaria of St Andrews and Edinburgh Universities. Recognising this, William Young put together all the data he could find, and in 1936 published *The Flowering Plants and Ferns from Fife and Kinross* as part of the Transactions of the Botanical Society of Edinburgh. Although helpful, this slim volume hardly qualifies as a definitive Flora of Fife, which is currently in preparation by the present long-serving

Botanical Recorder for the Fife and Kinross vice-county.

At much the same time there was an upsurge in the formation of Natural History Societies. Those within Fife included the Dunfermline and Kirkcaldy Naturalists, supplemented from across their respective estuaries by those from Edinburgh and Dundee, who could gain access to the Kingdom via the newly-built railway bridges. These bodies organised lectures and field outings, and performed the valuable functions of encouraging an interest in the natural sciences, allowing members to share their knowledge and fostering a greater enjoyment of their own locality. With the exception of the Edinburgh N.H.S. they published little or nothing, although the Kirkcaldy N.S., to mark their centenary in 1982, produced a substantial volume entitled *The Wildlife and Antiquities of Kirkcaldy District* which brought all modern and historic records of one district together for the first time.

From only a cursory perusal of this book it is apparent how much we owe to that brilliant and tireless all-round naturalist William Evans of Edinburgh, who has already been mentioned in this chapter. Evans died in 1922, and were it not for his detailed, accurate records, we would still be wringing our hands over huge gaps in our knowledge, particularly over much of our invertebrate fauna. A wonderful challenge exists for enthusiastic field naturalists to bring his records, many of which are a century old, up to date.

We should not neglect our marine environment, for Fife has a diverse coastline of some 170 km. The doyen of marine biologists must be W C McIntosh, an amateur (he was a doctor of medicine) who started publishing his observations in 1864. He later became Professor of Natural History and head of the new St Andrews Fisheries Laboratory in 1883, which was expanded to become the Gatty Marine Laboratory in 1896. From these early beginnings the Laboratory has continued to contribute to our knowledge of marine wildlife, both around Fife, and beyond. In 1996 the formidable battery of biological and natural science departments which make up the School of Biological and Medical Sciences at St Andrews University was augmented by the nationally important Sea Mammal Research Unit, previously based at Cambridge.

From this necessarily short review it can be seen that up to the turn of the century – indeed up to the Second World War – the picture of conservation in Fife, as elsewhere, consisted largely of skilled and enthusiastic individuals, amateurs and academics, following their own interests with no attempt at co-ordination or management. This was not surprising, as the means and methodology to do this on a national scale were yet to be devised.

Professor W C McIntosh (1838–1931), founder of the Gatty Marine Laboratory at St Andrews. (*Photograph courtesy of St Andrews University Library.*)

Once the War was over, however, things began to change. A massive leap forward proved to be the establishment of the Nature Conservancy in 1949; for the first time ever there was a body responsible to and funded by Government, charged with setting up and maintaining nature reserves, and providing scientific advice on the conservation of Britain's flora and fauna. For Fife, this led in the 1950s to the declaration of three National Nature Reserves.

The first of these, in 1952, was Morton Lochs near Tayport. Originally created as a series of shallow ponds for trout-fishing at the beginning of the century, they lie athwart the East coast migratory flyway and had developed into a wonderful ornithological site where many species of waders and wildfowl paused to feed and rest. Unfortunately their small size (24 hectares of which only a small proportion is open water), the proximity of growing forest up to the reserve boundary, and changes in the water regime from adjacent farmland have meant that the Lochs have silted up over the last 45 years. In spite of an extensive and prolonged management effort by the Conservancy (now Scottish Natural Heritage) it is doubtful whether Morton Lochs would be considered nowadays for NNR status. It is worth mentioning, in passing, that Scotland's only breeding of golden oriole took place on this NNR in the early 1970s.

The next NNR to be declared (1954) was Tentsmuir Point, at the mouth of the Tay. This is one of the most mobile coastlines on the eastern seaboard, and a line of anti-tank blocks put in place in 1940 can now be traced several hundred metres inland at one point, and elsewhere have vanished, undercut and disintegrated by the scour of the currents. The evolving development of the dune and slack systems leads to much

botanical interest, and the fact that the NNR is shielded from intensive farming practices by a large area of commercial forest means that Tentsmuir is by far the most outstanding entomological site in Fife. The offshore Abertay Sands, part of the NNR, are used as a haul-out by both grey and common seals, countable at times in their hundreds.

The third NNR on Fife's list is the Isle of May in the Firth of Forth. Long known as a supreme migrant stopover, an observatory and ringing station has been operating on the island since 1934. The May is also a spectacular seabird breeding site with its west-facing cliffs covered with auks and kittiwakes and its surface with puffin burrows. During the 1950s and 60s the gull population built up to such an extent that the tern colonies, at their peak in 1946–47 at 6000 pairs of common and 550 pairs of arctic terns, had dwindled to nil, and a major gull culling programme took place in the early 1970s. The vegetation has been slow to recover but the terns are back in increasing numbers; this proved to be a classic example of the dictum that conservation sometimes involves difficult decisions and hard, unpleasant work. A substantial breeding population of grey seals has developed recently, producing about 1300 pups annually, and both seals and seabirds cross-migrate freely between here, the Farne Islands and elsewhere round our coastline.

The 1960s was the decade that saw the growth of County Wildlife or Nature Conservation Trusts throughout the U.K. Their purpose was to harness the detailed local knowledge of local people, and to give some focus to the growing environmental movement by establishing nature reserves of regional importance, conducting surveys, monitoring planning applications and so on. The Scottish Wildlife Trust was formed in 1964, and the foresight of the founding fathers in insisting on a Scotland-wide body has been vindicated time and again. Local branches were created as soon as membership reached critical mass, and in May 1967 the Fife, Kinross and Clackmannanshire Branch came into being. (Clackmannanshire was transferred to the new Central Region Branch when local government was reorganised in 1975.)

The new Branch immediately set about its priorities, which included a study of the management requirements of Bankhead Moss, its first reserve near Peat Inn. A tiny gem of a raised bog, the Moss sits in its little valley like an upturned saucer on an ashet, and holds within its few hectares a depth of at least seven metres of peat. This had been dug in the first half of the 19th century to provide lint-holes for retting locally-grown flax, but for the last century and more, once disused, these have been colonised by an interesting community of sphagnum species, adding to the reserve's importance. The centre of the Moss has been inexorably drying out, though, and much recent management effort has been put into attempting to prevent a total encroachment of birch seedlings over the open heather surface. The reasons for this are far from clear, and are probably a combination of more than one circumstance. A contributory factor, it has been suggested, could be an early manifestation of global warming: if so, it means that nature can detect and react to minute changes in the climate long before we humans become aware of them or of their significance.

At this time, too, the Branch was busy surveying and reporting on the wildlife of the Lomond Hills for the County Planning Department and putting together a detailed analysis of the conservation importance of Fife's coastline. This was the time that North Sea oil was being discovered, and

hasty exploitation plans were being made. Those involved in conservation at that time will recall the vast amount of effort that went into monitoring the unprecedented scramble for facilities both ashore and offshore, to make sure that the least possible permanent damage was done to valuable wildlife resources. Fife ended up with one substantial rig-building yard at Methil, and a smaller one at Burntisland. Neither of these were greenfield sites, and both brought badly needed work to the county. The petrochemical site at Moss Morran was built on farmland in the late 1970s, and both it and the related marine terminal at Braefoot Bay were very closely scrutinised to ensure that the possibility of pollution was kept to a minimum. A network of pipelines carrying natural gases and oils through and across the countryside all had to be checked to make sure they avoided SSSIs and similar sites of conservation value. Few, apart from those who were directly involved, can now detect where these systems run.

At the same time that the infrastructure to exploit new sources of energy was being planned and built, much effort was being put into replacing the dereliction left behind by a defunct source. The end of the coalmining industry had left a legacy of worked-out mines, bings, mineral railways and the like throughout central and west Fife, and nowhere was this more apparent than at Lochore. In 1971 the County Council embarked upon an ambitious programme of reclamation, turning a barren moonscape of slurry ponds, smouldering clinker hills and pools of stagnant polluted water into what is now a hugely popular Country Park. In the course of this, the Fife and Kinross Branch of the SWT was invited to create a new nature reserve at the west end of Lochore Meadows. At that time it was given to few conservation bodies to devise a quality wildlife site from literally nothing, and it proved a magnificent challenge. While the main contractors and earthmoving equipment were still on site it was possible to divert the river Ore, make islands in the subsidence pools, stabilise water levels with a weir, and plant over 35,000 trees and shrubs to create a mosaic of spinneys and open spaces. Twenty-five years later those ten hectares or so have developed into a most exciting component of Lochore Meadows Country Park, and have long since surpassed the intentions of their designers.

The rest of the 1970s and 1980s proved to be a period of steady consolidation, and it was during this time that many of Fife's SSSIs were designated. A Site of Special Scientific Interest is selected by SNH under rigorous national criteria and a minimum aim is to represent all the different habitats and species that are present in each county or region of the country by at least one example of each. For many habitats the minimum will not be enough and a guiding principle is that, as rarity or special value increases, so does the need to notify a larger proportion of the remaining areas. SNH is empowered to offer the owners of SSSIs financial and technical help in managing their sites, for it is clearly unjust to expect them to bear the full cost of looking after these very special areas of land on behalf of the community. At the present count there are 59 SSSIs in Fife, from upland grassland and heather moor to coastal salt-marsh, freshwater lochs, herb-rich meadows, and woodland; and coastal and inland geological features. Within this wide variety of habitat types there are parallel designations such as National Nature Reserves, Ramsar sites (internationally important wetlands) and Special Protection Areas (designated under the European *Birds Directive*).

An important step forward was the appointment in 1976 of the first member of the Fife Ranger Service, run by the local authority. Initially recruited to manage the new Country Park at Lochore, this quickly expanded to take in the Lomond Hills Regional Park. At first confined to Fife Region, the Ranger Service soon spread to the Districts, in particular to North East Fife. This local authority had declared the Eden Estuary a Local Nature Reserve in 1978 under the National Parks and Access to the Countryside Act (1949), primarily to regulate the wildfowling in winter, and a Ranger was appointed to run the LNR and administer the bye-laws. This has been a successful partnership between a number of countryside activity bodies, individuals and others (including the Ministry of Defence).

More recently Dunfermline District took Rangers onto their staff too but Fife had to wait until 1996 for its second LNR. This is at Torry Bay, in the upper Forth estuary, and extends along a six-mile stretch of the foreshore between Longannet and Crombie. Both LNRs are internationally or nationally important for a variety of wildfowl and waders as well as interesting for other branches of natural history, and hold much potential for recreational activities.

In 1985 another national voluntary organisation, the Woodland Trust, acquired its first holding in Fife. This was a small area of Dura Den, where the Ceres Burn cuts through the soft sandstone to join the river Eden near Kemback. But it was in 1994 that the Woodland Trust was really able to get to work in Fife, when it became the owner of 330 hectares of woodland or unplanted land in and around Glenrothes. This was as a result of the decision by the Scottish Office to wind up the New Town Development Corporations and transfer their assets to the neighbouring local authorities or, as in this case, to suitable charitable bodies. This admirable arrangement will lead over the next generations into the 21st century's equivalent of the great public parks of the Victorian era; large areas managed for amenity, landscape and wildlife.

In 1986, too, the Farming and Wildlife Advisory Group (FWAG) appointed its first advisor for Fife and Kinross, thus preparing the ground for a more effective partnership between the farming community and sources of conservation advice and best practice.

The 1990s have been notable for the massive rearrangement of the statutory bodies responsible for conservation in the United Kingdom. In Scotland the old Nature Conservancy Council has metamorphosed into Scottish Natural Heritage, subsuming the Countryside Commission for Scotland in the process. The River Purification Boards (which were responsible for many quiet, unsung improvements in our natural ecosystems) have amalgamated with other Government bodies to form the Scottish Environment Protection Agency. It is these two organisations, funded by the Scottish Office, that will lead us into the third millennium.

In 1992 Fife Regional Council, recognising that a detailed knowledge of our natural environment is an essential planning tool, set up 'Fife Nature' biological records centre within the Department of Economic Development and Planning. There is no doubt that this will be regarded by future commentators as an enlightened and farseeing step, and has been carried forward by the reorganised Fife Council. Not simply a computerised database of species, plant communities, sites and habitats, it has begun to produce a series of booklets summarising Fife's wildlife in a precise and up-to-date form, including distribution maps, and the data are available to all who wish to make use of them.

We have achieved much in the last thirty or forty years. Nowadays central government has been rightly persuaded that a clean sustainable natural environment is essential for our well-being. Our local authority in Fife has long had a Charter for the Environment and is leading the way in preparing a Biodiversity Action Plan for the county. At the present tally there are well over twenty nature reserves of various sorts, and scores of other sites where the public can go to study and enjoy our flora and fauna, including Regional and Country Parks and long-distance coastal footpaths. There are opportunities for individuals of all ages and interests to further their knowledge, start new hobbies, or help their local wildlife through numerous voluntary bodies and societies; from lectures and demonstrations to real welly-boot mud-and-sweat outdoor work. Employment in conservation-related jobs can be counted in dozens. There is a growing shelf of literature which provides up-to-date information for resident and visitor alike. Very little, if any, of this was available a generation ago.

Fife is a fertile, well-farmed part of Scotland, and much of what is not farmed is industrial or urban. Yet there are plenty of wildlife sites of high quality and interest, although they tend to be small and need searching out. But there is one factor that has not changed at all over the period of this review. Constant vigilance is still vital. Central and local government and their statutory bodies can only do so much, and in any case are driven by different imperatives, with different timescales, and always within the constraint of the Treasury's iron grip. The voluntary organisations and the private citizen must work in partnership with government, for each needs the encouragement and stimulus of the other, a state that will not change for generations.

These days we know so much more about our surroundings than our forebears, and as our knowledge expands, so do our expectations. If we have learnt one immutable lesson, it is that mankind is but one element of the world's great natural ecosystem, and it is only a matter of enlightened self-interest to look after it in basic terms of minimum pollution and maximum sustainable diversity. For the sake of our children and grandchildren we are all environmentalists now.

Ivy-leaved toadflax

Part II

*The flora and fauna of Fife:
an inventory*

The flora and fauna of Fife: an inventory

Estimates of the numbers of different kinds of organisms living in Scotland are necessarily rather vague for some of the lesser known groups, but suggest the presence of about 25,000 species of animals, about 3000 non-microscopic plants, several thousand fungi and lichens; and several tens of thousands of micro-organisms. In the course of preparing this book we have attempted to compile an inventory of all the extant species that have so far been recorded in Fife. We cannot claim that the search is complete but around 8000 species have been listed. Since a bare list of names would be of little interest, we have briefly annotated each species to give some indication of habitat, distribution, rarity or ecological niche.

In the following lists, two different treatments have been used:

• For the better known groups like the flowering plants, the vertebrates and others that can, generally, be identified in the field, all species are listed.

• For groups of species that are microscopic or that need microscopic examination for identification, a sentence has been included to draw attention to their existence and diversity, but the individual species are not listed, or only a few of the more conspicuous or better known ones are named. However the full list of species is available on disc from Fife Nature in a variety of computer-readable formats (see p. 223).

The extent to which the list for any particular group is a complete record of what is actually living in Fife varies greatly from group to group. For some, such as the birds, the list is virtually complete, or as nearly so as is practicable given the inevitable delay in publication and the dynamic nature of life. Some lists are very incomplete. This may be because the organisms are small, difficult to identify and have never attracted the attention of more than a few specialists anywhere in the country; but chance has also played a part in determining whether a specialist in the group has recorded in Fife.

Many species, especially amongst the smaller invertebrate animals, mosses and fungi, are listed only on the basis of one or two old records and their current status is not known. However no such list can be final: species become locally extinct; species that have previously been overlooked are discovered; new species colonize from elsewhere or are accidentally or deliberately introduced; what was considered a single species may, by the use of modern technology, be found to comprise two or more independent species; others may prove not to justify recognition as distinct species. The most we can achieve is a snapshot indicating what has been observed in the past and what might be out there now.

Specialized surveys have not been undertaken specifically for this book – the aim has been to bring together in one place lists of species recorded to date and thereby to draw attention to gaps that remain to be filled. The amount of information given with each species has had to be minimal. However records of all terrestrial and fresh-water species have been added to the 'Recorder' database held by Fife Nature at Glenrothes, along with details of locality, habitat, date, recorder etc. and, where relevant, the bibliographic reference from which the record has been taken. Marine species, and some microscopic groups, are not yet included in the 'Recorder' system, but paper copies of all these sources are held by Fife Nature.

In the case of marine species no fixed line has been used as the limit of 'Fife waters'. In the Forth and Tay estuaries a midline has been used to include or exclude localized records, but others from below shore level simply recorded as 'Tay' or 'Forth' have also been included. In St Andrews Bay the basis of the lists is *The fauna and flora of St Andrews Bay* (Laverack and Blackler, 1974) which includes some records from well offshore although distances are not specified; records on the shore are all likely to be in Fife, but for offshore records St Andrews Bay was defined as extending from Fife Ness to Arbroath. Other major sources of marine and estuarine records are, for the Tay, Alexander (1932) and Khayralla and Jones (1975); and for the Forth, Leslie and Herdman (1881), Kingston (1980), Bennett (1989) and unpublished reports by the Scottish Environmental Protection Agency (SEPA).

The following abbreviations and conventions have been used for marine species:

F: Forth (not specified in greater detail)
IF: Inner Forth (above Forth bridges: the estuary
OF: Outer Forth (below Forth bridges: the firth)
S: St Andrews Bay (Fife Ness to Tentsmuir Point)
T: Tay Estuary
HW: high water mark
LW: low water mark
Offshore: in contrast to 'on shore', i.e. including inshore waters.

Authors of scientific names are not given. These, along with synonyms and other details, can be found in the relevant checklists, handbooks etc. which are quoted in the accompanying disc, except in the case of most aquatic invertebrates for which the following works have been followed: marine – Hayward and Ryland (1990, 1995); freshwater – Maitland (1977).

Other abbreviations and conventions:

[ ] round whole entry: extinct, or occurrence in Fife doubtful.
[ ] round part of entry: information not confirmed in Fife.

Corrections and additions to these lists are welcome and should be addressed to Fife Nature, Fife House, Glenrothes, KY7 5LT.

Our sincere thanks are due to the following individuals who have helped to compile or referee sections of the list:
Keith Bland (Lepidoptera, agromyzid flies)
Helen Caldwell (lower plants)
Garth Foster (water beetles).
Adam Garside (beetles)
Bill Hay (bryophytes)
David Horsfield (flies)
Peter Maitland (fish)
William Penrice (freshwater and terrestrial molluscs)
Anne-Marie Smout (birds)
Geoff Swinney (fish)
Ken Watt (hoverflies)
Tony Wilson (fungi)

Members of the following organizations have kindly provided data:
Dundee Museum: Adam Garside.
Fife Nature: William Penrice, Anne-Marie Smout
Game Conservancy: John Hughes.
Royal Botanic Garden, Edinburgh: Brian Coppins (lichens), David Long (bryophytes), David Mann (marine algae), Roy Watling (fungi).
Royal Museum of Scotland (including the Scottish Insect Records Index): Susan Chambers, David Heppell, Graham Rotheray, Mark Shaw, Andrew Whittington.
Scottish Environmental Protection Agency: Richard Park.
Scottish Natural Heritage: David Horsfield, David Phillips.

35. Lochore Meadows, before reclamation. (*Photo: Courtesy of Fife Council*)

36. Lochore Meadows, after reclamation.
(*Photos: F. Spragge*)

37. Bankhead Moss Reserve from the air. The original reserve consisted of the pale-coloured birchwood with the open heathery centre, but was later augmented by the darker pinewood beyond and the rough field with the open water. (*Photo: F. Spragge*)

38. The cull of gulls on the Isle of May, 1972. One day's cull of herring and lesser black-backed gulls being checked for rings before incineration. (*Photo: F. Spragge*)

Synopsis of lists

PLANTS

Vascular plants

The wild flowers and ferns of Fife have been well collected and documented over the last two hundred years. An attempt at compiling a full list was made by Young (1936) but this overlooked many sources and contained many errors. Recent detailed information for some parts of Botanical Vice-County 85 may be found as follows: Kirkcaldy district: Ballantyne (1970, 1982); west Fife: Ballantyne (1990); Balmerino area: Ballantyne (1991); Kinross: Ballantyne (1978/85).

The following list excludes many species considered to be casual only, i.e. occurring once only or for a very short period, such as those brought in by ships' ballast or imported in grain from abroad. Quite a number that are not native to Fife are mentioned, including garden plants that have either escaped or have been cast-out into the wild and have subsequently become established. Habitats of the commoner species have not been included as they may be ascertained from any reputable field guide, while localities are sparingly given as most may be found in the works mentioned above. Some additional species, including introductions that have become extinct, rare hybrids, erroneous published records, and microspecies of brambles, dandelions and hawkweeds, are included on the Fife Nature disc (p. 223). Names follow Stace (1991).

Herbs and dwarf shrubs

Trees and large shrubs are listed separately below (p. 167).

Lycopodiopsida: clubmosses and quillworts

Huperzia selago, Fir Clubmoss. Rare, Lomonds.

[*Lycopodiella innundata*, Marsh Clubmoss. Long extinct]

Lycopodium clavatum,

Stag's-horn Clubmoss. Becoming uncommon, somewhat ephemeral.

[*Diphasiastrum alpinum*, Alpine Clubmoss. Long extinct]

Selaginella selaginoides, Lesser Clubmoss. Very local.

Isoetes lacustris, Quillwort. Very rare, Loch Glow.

Equisetopsida: horsetails

Equisetum hyemale, Rough Horsetail. Very rare.

E.variegatum, Variegated Horsetail. Rare, on sand dunes.

E.fluviatile, Water Horsetail. Common.

E.x litorale, Shore Horsetail.

Uncommon, edges of ponds and waysides.

E.arvense, Field Horsetail. Very common, including damp areas.

E.pratense, Shady Horsetail. Uncommon, hillsides and shady places.

E.sylvaticum, Wood Horsetail. Locally common.

E.palustre, Marsh Horsetail. Local.

E.telmateia, Great Horsetail. Very rare, West Wemyss.

Pteropsida: Ferns

Ophioglossum vulgatum, Adder's-tongue. Very local, declining.

Botrychium lunaria, Moonwort. Very local, rather ephemeral.

Osmunda regalis, Royal Fern. Extinct as a native; very rarely planted.

[*Cryptogramma crispa*, Parsley Fern. Extinct.]

Pilularia globulifera, Pillwort. Now very rare.

Hymenophyllum wilsonii, Wilson's Filmy Fern. Probably extinct.

Polypodium vulgare, Polypody. Common on walls and rocks.

P.interjectum, Intermediate Polypody. Scarce.

Pteridium aquilinum, Bracken. Very common.

Phegopteris connectilis, Beech Fern. Uncommon.

Oreopteris limbosperma, Lemon-scented Fern. Local on moorland.

Phyllitis scolopendrium, Hart's-tongue. Local in dens and on walls; doubtfully native.

Asplenium adiantum-nigrum, Black Spleenwort. Local on walls, never in quantity.

A.marinum, Sea Spleenwort.

Uncommon, on rocks by sea.

A.trichomanes, Maidenhair Spleenwort. Common on walls and shady rocks.

A.ruta-muraria, Wall-rue. Very common on walls.

Ceterach officinarum, Rustyback. Very rare intro.; not persisting?

Matteuccia struthiopteris, Ostrich Fern. Occasional in old estates, intro.

Athyrium filix-femina, Lady Fern. Common in woodland and damp spots.

Gymnocarpium dryopteris, Oak Fern. Scarce.

Cystopteris fragilis, Brittle Bladder-fern. Local on shady walls and rocks, ocasionally intro.

Polystichum aculeatum, Hard Shield-fern. Local in dens.

Dryopteris filix-mas, Common Male Fern. Very common.

D.affinis, Scaly Male Fern. Local in open woods and old moors.

D.carthusiana, Narrow Buckler-fern. Local in damp shady woods; declining?

D.x deweveri (*carthusiana* x *dilitata*). Occasional, not always with parents.

D.dilatata, Broad Buckler-fern. Very common.

Blechnum spicant, Hard Fern. Somewhat local, usually in moory woods.

Azolla filiculoides, Water Fern. Rare, short-lived, intro.

Magnoliopsida: flowering plants

Nymphaceae: water-lilies

Nymphaea alba, White Water-lily. Uncommon, decreasing.

Nuphar lutea, Yellow Water-lily. Local.

N.x spenneriana, Hybrid Water-lily. Very rare, Black L (Cleish).

Ceratophyllaceae: hornworts

Ceratophyllum demersum, Rigid Hornwort. Rare in ponds.

Ranunculaceae: buttercups etc.

Trollius europaeus, Globe-flower. Rare, decreasing.

Caltha palustris, Marsh Marigold. Common.

Helleborus foetidus, Stinking Hellebore. Very rare, intro.

H.viridis, Green Hellebore. Very rare, intro.

Eranthis hyemalis, Winter Aconite. Uncommon, naturalised.

Aconitum napellus, Monk's-hood. Rare, intro.

Anemone nemorosa, Wood Anemone. Common.

Ranunculus acris, Meadow Buttercup. Common.

R.repens, Creeping Buttercup. Very common.

R.bulbosus, Bulbous Buttercup. Local.

R.sardous, Hairy Buttercup. Rare casual.

R.arvensis, Corn Buttercup. Casual.

R.auricomus, Goldilocks Buttercup. Very local.

R.sceleratus, Celery-leaved Buttercup. Local.

R.lingua, Greater Spearwort. Rare, sometimes intro.

R.flammula, Lesser Spearwort. Common.

R.reptans/R.x levenensis, Creeping Spearwort. Very rare.

R.ficaria, Lesser Celandine. Very common.

R.hederaceus, Ivy-leaved Crowfoot. Local, often on mud.

R.trichophyllus, Thread-leaved Water-crowfoot. Rare.

R.peltatus, Pond Water-crowfoot. Common.

R.fluitans, River Water-crowfoot. Rare.

R.circinatus, Fan-leaved Water-crowfoot. Rather local.

[*R.aquatilis* (s.s.), Common Water-crowfoot. Very rare, requires confirmation.]

[*R.baudotii*, Brackish Water-crowfoot. Extinct.]

Aquilegia vulgaris, Columbine. Rare, escape.

Thalictrum minus, Lesser Meadow-rue. Local.

Papaveraceae: poppies

Papaver orientale, Oriental Poppy. Very rare, escape.

P.somniferum, Opium Poppy. Rare, escape.

P.rhoeas, Corn Poppy. Local, less so in NE Fife.

P.dubium, Long-headed Poppy. Very common.

P.argemone, Prickly Poppy. Very local, apart from NE Fife.

Meconopsis cambrica, Welsh Poppy. Locally naturalised .

Glaucium flavum, Yellow Horned Poppy. Very rare.

Chelidonium majus, Greater Celandine. Rare, escape.

Fumariaceae: fumitories

Dicentra formosa, Bleeding-heart. Very rare, intro.

Pseudofumaria lutea, Yellow Corydalis. Common on walls.

Ceratocapnos claviculata, Climbing Corydalis. Very local.

Fumaria capreolata, White Ramping-fumitory. Rare, near sea.

F.bastardii, Tall Ramping-fumitory. Very rare.

F.muralis, Few-flowered Fumitory. Common weed.

F.purpurea, Purple Ramping-fumitory. Very rare.

F.officinalis, Common Fumitory. Very common weed.

F.densiflora, Dense-flowered Fumitory. Very local away from NE Fife.

Urticaceae: nettles

Urtica dioica, Common Nettle. Very common.

U.urens, Small Nettle. Common.

Parietaria judaica, Pellitory-of-the-Wall. Local on old buildings.

Chenopodiaceae: Goosefoots etc.

Chenopodium bonus-henricus, Good King Henry. Very local, often near old buildings.

C.glaucum, Oak-leaved Goosefoot. Very rare on north Eden shore.

C.rubrum, Red Goosefoot. Local on mud or as a weed.

C.album, Fat-hen. Very common weed.

Atriplex prostrata, Spear-leaved Orache. Common on shore.

A.glabriuscula, Babington's Orache. Common on shore.

A.littoralis, Grass-leaved Orache. Common on shore.

A.patula, Common Orache. Very common weed.

A.laciniata, Frosted Orache. Local on shore.

Beta vulgaris ssp.*maritima*, Sea Beet. Extinct?

Salicornia europaea agg., Glasswort. Rather local in bays.

Suaeda maritima, Annual Sea-blite. Uncommon in saltmarshes.

Salsola kali, Saltwort. Rather local by sea.

Portulacaceae

Claytonia perfoliata, Spring Beauty. Locally common, often near sea.

C.sibirica, Pink Purslane. Well naturalised in woods.

Montia fontana, Blinks. Common in damp spots.

Caryophyllaceae: campions etc.

Arenaria serpyllifolia ssp.*serpyllifolia*, Thyme-leaved Sandwort. Common.

A.serpyllifolia ssp.*leptoclados*, Small Thyme-leaved Sandwort. Rather rare?

A.balearica, Mossy Sandwort. Ocasionally naturalised on exposed tree roots.

Moehringia trinervia, Three-nerved Sandwort. Common.

Honckenya peploides, Sea Sandwort. Common.

[*Minuartia verna*, Spring Sandwort. Long extinct.]

Stellaria nemorum, Wood Stitchwort. Rather local except in west.

S.media, Common Chickweed. Very common weed.

S.pallida, Lesser Chickweed. Rare on sand dunes.

S.holostea, Greater Stitchwort. Common.

S.palustris, Marsh Stitchwort. Rare.

S.graminea, Lesser Stitchwort. Very common.

S.uliginosa, Bog Stitchwort. Common.

Cerastium arvense, Field Mouse-ear. Common.

C.tomentosum, Snow-in-summer. Frequently naturalised.

C.fontanum, Common Mouse-ear. Very common.

C.glomeratum, Sticky Mouse-ear. Very common.

C.diffusum, Dark-green Mouse-ear. Rather local, mainly coastal.

C.semidecandrum, Little Mouse-ear. Common in bare places.

Sagina nodosa, Knotted Pearlwort. Rather local.

S.subulata, Heath Pearlwort. Uncommon.

S.procumbens, Procumbent Pearlwort. Very common.

S.apetala ssp.*apetala*, Annual Pearlwort. Common.

S.apetala ssp.*erecta*, Fringed Pearlwort. Common.

S.maritima, Sea Pearlwort. Local by sea.

Scleranthus annuus, Annual Knawel. Rather local.

Spergula arvensis, Corn Spurrey. Common arable weed.

Spergularia media, Greater Sea-spurrey. Local near sea.

S.marina, Lesser Sea-spurrey. Local near sea.

S.rubra, Sand Spurrey. Local on light soils.

Lychnis flos-cuculi, Ragged Robin. Common.

L.viscaria, Sticky Catchfly. Very rare.

[*Agrostemma githago*, Corncockle. Former weed.]

Silene vulgaris, Bladder Campion. Common.

S.uniflora, Sea Campion. Common.

S.noctiflora, Night-flowering Catchfly. Rare weed in East Neuk.

S.latifolia, White Campion. Common.

S.x hampeana, Hybrid Campion. Local.

S.dioica, Red Campion. Very common.

[*Silene nutans*, Nottingham Catchfly. Long extinct.]

Saponaria officinalis, Soapwort. Rarely naturalised.

Dianthus deltoides, Maiden Pink. Rare, probably declining.

Polygonaceae: knotweeds etc.

Persicaria wallichii, Himalayan Knotweed. Uncommon, intro.

P.bistorta, Common Bistort. Local, often in graveyards.

P.amplexicaulis, Red Bistort. Very rare, intro.

P.vivipara, Alpine Bistort. Rare except on Lomonds.

P.amphibia, Amphibious Bistort. Common on ponds and as a weed.

P.maculosa, Redshank. Very common weed.

P.lapathifolia, Pale Persicaria. Local weed.

P.hydropiper, Water-pepper. Uncommon in damp places.

Polygonum oxyspermum, Ray's Knotgrass. Very rare by sea, ephemeral.

P.arenastrum, Equal-leaved Knot-grass. Local, usually on tracks.

P.aviculare, Knot-grass. Very common.

Fallopia japonica, Japanese Knotweed. Commonly naturalised.

F.sachalinensis, Giant Knotweed. Rare, intro.

F.balschuanica, Russian Vine. Rare, intro.

F.convolvulus, Black Bindweed. Common weed.

Rheum x *hybridum*, Rhubarb. Occasional escape, persisting.

Rumex acetosella, Sheep's Sorrel. Very common on bare ground.

R.acetosa, Common Sorrel. Very common.

R.pseudoalpinus, Monk's Rhubarb. Locally naturalised.

R.longifolius, Northern Dock. Somewhat local.

R.x propinquus. Uncommon.

R.x hybridus. Common.

R.hydrolapathum, Water Dock. Rare, Kinshaldy area.

R.crispus, Curled Dock. Very common.

R.x pratensis. Common.

R.conglomeratus, Clustered Dock. Local in damp spots.

R.x abortivus. Very rare.

R.sanguineus, Wood Dock. Common.

R.x dufftii. Rare.

R.obtusifolius, Broad-leaved Dock. Very common.

R.maritimus, Golden Dock. Very rare, casual.

Plumbaginaceae

Armeria maritima, Thrift. Common.

Clusiaceae (Hypericaceae): St John's-worts

Hypericum androsaemum, Tutsan. Occasionally naturalised.

H.perforatum, Common St John's-wort. Common, often by railways.

H.maculatum, Imperforate St John's-wort. Uncommon.

H.tetrapterum, Square-stalked St John's-wort. Local in damp ground.

H.humifusum, Trailing St John's-wort. Very local.

H.pulchrum, Slender St John's-wort. Common.

H.hirsutum, Hairy St John's-wort. Common, often in wooded parts.

H.montanum, Pale St John's-wort. Very rare, near Kirkcaldy.

Malvaceae: mallows

Malva moschata, Musk-mallow. Occasionally naturalised by roads and railways.

M.sylvestris, Common Mallow.
Rather local.
M.neglecta, Dwarf Mallow.
Uncommon.

Droseraceae: sundews

Drosera rotundifolia,
Round-leaved Sundew. Very
local in bogs.
[*D.longifolia,* Great Sundew.
Long extinct.]

Cistaceae: rock-roses

Helianthemum nummularium,
Common Rock-rose.
Common on banks and cliffs.

Violaceae: violets

Viola odorata, Sweet Violet.
Locally naturalised, usually
in woods.
V.hirta, Hairy Violet. Very
local.
V.riviniana, Common
Dog-violet. Very common.
V.canina, Heath Dog-violet.
Uncommon, on moors and
dunes.
V.palustris, Marsh Violet. Local.
V.lutea, Mountain Pansy. Local
on grassy knowes and hills.
V.tricolor, Wild Pansy. Very
local, ?declining.
V.arvensis, Field Pansy. Very
common.

**Brassicaeae (Cruciferae):
cabbages etc.**

Sisymbrium altissimum, Tall
Rocket. Occasional on waste
ground.
S.orientale, Eastern Rocket.
Occasional, increasing on
waste ground.
S.officinale, Hedge Mustard.
Common.
Descurainia sophia, Flixweed.
Rare on waste ground.
Alliaria petiolata, Garlic
Mustard. Common.
Arabidopsis thaliana, Thale
Cress. Common.

Bunias orientalis, Warty
Cabbage. Occasional, usually
near railways.
Erysimum cheiri, Wallflower.
Locally naturalised on old
buildings.
Hesperis matronalis,
Dame's-violet. Locally
naturalised, usually by water.
Barbarea vulgaris,
Winter-cress. Common.
B.intermedia, Early
Winter-cress. Occasional,
increasing on waste ground.
Rorippa nasturtium-aquaticum,
Water-cress. Uncommon.
R.x sterilis, Hybrid
Water-cress. Common.
R.microphylla, Narrow-fruited
Water-cress. Uncommon.
R.palustris, Marsh
Yellow-cress. Local.
R.sylvestris, Creeping
Yellow-cress. Occasional
weed.
Armoracia rusticana,
Horse-radish. Uncommon
escape or cast-out.
Cardamine amara, Large
Bitter-cress. Local by burns,
commoner in west.
C.raphanifolia, Greater
Cuckoo-flower. Very rare,
naturalised in Dunfermline
Glen.
C.pratensis, Cuckoo-flower.
Common.
C.flexuosa, Wavy Bitter-cress.
Common by shady burns.
C.hirsuta, Hairy Bitter-cress.
Very common weed.
Arabis caucasica, Garden
Arabis. Rarely naturalised
on old walls.
A.hirsuta, Hairy Rock-cress.
Local on dry banks and
cliffs.
Aubrieta deltoidea, Aubretia.
Rarely naturalised on old
walls.
Lunaria annua, Honesty.
Occasional escape.

Draba muralis, Wall
Whitlowgrass. Rare weed.
Erophila verna, Common
Whitlowgrass. Common.
Cochlearia officinalis, Common
Scurvygrass. Common by
sea.
C.danica, Danish Scurvygrass.
Local on bare gound near
sea.
Capsella bursa-pastoris,
Shepherd's-purse. Very
common weed.
Teesdalia nudicaulis, Shepherd's
Cress. Uncommon in NE
Fife.
Thlaspi arvense, Field
Penny-cress. Common in
arable fields.
Lepidium campestre, Field
Pepperwort. Very local.
L.heterophyllum, Smith's
Pepperwort. Local.
[*L.latifolium,* Dittander.
Extinct.]
L.draba, Hoary Cress. Locally
common and invasive,
spreading.
Coronopus squamatus,
Swine-cress. Rare, near sea.
C.didymus, Lesser Swine-cress.
Casual.
Diplotaxis tenuifolia, Perennial
Wall-rocket. Very rare, in
Inverkeithing area.
D.muralis, Annual Wall-rocket.
Occasional weed.
Brassica oleracea, Wild
Cabbage. Very rare, on cliffs
at Crail.
B.napus, Rape. Increasingly
common.
B.nigra, Black Mustard. Casual.
Sinapis arvensis, Charlock. Very
common.
S.alba, White Mustard.
Occasional, sometimes as a
crop.
Cakile maritima, Sea Rocket.
Common.
Crambe maritima, Sea-kale.
Very rare.

Raphanus raphanistrum, Wild Radish. Local in arable ground.

Resedaceae: mignonettes

Reseda luteola, Weld. Common.
R.lutea, Wild Mignonette. Uncommon.

Empetraceae

Empetrum nigrum, Crowberry. Local, on moors and hills.

Ericaceae: heathers

Calluna vulgaris, Heather. Common.
Erica tetralix, Cross-leaved Heath. Common.
E.cinerea, Bell Heather. Local on dry rocks.
Vaccinium oxycoccos, Cranberry. Local in bogs.
V.vitis-idaea, Cowberry. Uncommon, usually upland.
V.myrtillus, Blaeberry. Common.

Pyrolaceae: wintergreens

Pyrola minor, Common Wintergreen. Local in woods.
[*P.media*, Intermediate Wintergreen. Extinct.]
[*P.rotundifolia*, Round-leaved Wintergreen. Extinct.]

Monotropaceae

Monotropa hypopitys, Yellow Bird's-nest. Very rare, Tentsmuir.

Primulaceae: primroses etc.

Primula vulgaris, Primrose. Common.
P.veris, Cowslip. Locally common, especially near sea.
P.x polyantha, False Oxlip. Occasional.
Lysimachia nemorum, Yellow Pimpernel. Local in woodland.
L.nummularia, Creeping-Jenny. Very local.

L.vulgaris, Yellow Loosestrife. Very local, probably an escape.
L.punctata, Dotted Loosestrife. Rare escape.
Trientalis europaea, Chickweed Wintergreen. Widespread, locally common.
Anagallis tenella, Bog Pimpernel. Very rare.
A.arvensis, Scarlet Pimpernel. Very local, decreasing.
A.minima, Chaffweed. ?Extinct.
Glaux maritima. Sea-milkwort. Common in salt-marshes.
[*Samolus valerandi*, Brookweed. Extinct].

Crassulaceae: stonecrops

Umbilicus rupestris, Navelwort. Very rare, intro.
Sedum telephium, Orpine. Local.
S.spurium, Caucasian Stonecrop. Rare escape, naturalised at Pettycur.
S.forsterianum, Rock Stonecrop. Rare escape.
S.acre, Biting Stonecrop. Common.
S.album, White Stonecrop. Rather local, escape.
S.anglicum, English Stonecrop. Uncommon, on rocks by sea.
S.villosum, Hairy Stonecrop. Uncommon, chiefly on Lomonds.

Saxifragaceae: saxifrages etc.

Saxifraga x *urbium*, London Pride. Local, naturalised.
S.x geum, Scarce London Pride. Rare escape, or ?error.
S.x polita, False London Pride. Rare escape.
S.hirsuta, Kidney Saxifrage. Rare escape.
S.granulata, Meadow Saxifrage. Local on dry banks and knowes, also in woods.
S.hypnoides, Mossy Saxifrage. Rare, on the Lomonds.
S.tridactylites, Rue-leaved

Saxifrage. Uncommon, rather ephemeral.
Tolmiea menziesii, Pick-a-back-plant. Local, naturalised by burns.
Tellima grandiflora, Fringe-cups. Rare escape.
Chrysosplenium oppositifolium, Opposite-leaved Golden-saxifrage. Common in damp spots.
C.alternifolium, Alternate-leaved Golden-saxifrage. Very local by some western burns.
Parnassia palustris, Grass of Parnassus. Rare.

Rosaceae: roses etc.

Filipendula vulgaris, Dropwort. Rare, N Queensferry-Aberdour area.
F.ulmaria, Meadowsweet. Very common.
Potentilla palustris, Marsh Cinquefoil. Common.
P.anserina, Silverweed. Common.
P.argentea, Hoary Cinquefoil. Very rare, not seen for several years.
P.norvegica, Ternate-leaved Cinquefoil. Very rare, intro. at Newmills.
P.neumanniana, Spring Cinquefoil. Rare, declining.
P.erecta, Tormentil. Very common.
P.anglica, Trailing Tormentil. Rare, often by forest tracks.
P.x mixta, Hybrid Cinquefoil. Rare.
P.reptans, Creeping Cinquefoil. Local.
P.sterilis, Barren Strawberry. Common.
Fragaria vesca, Wild Strawberry. Common.
F.x ananassa, Garden Strawberry. Rare escape.
Geum rivale, Water Avens. Common.

G.urbanum, Wood avens. Very common.

*G.*x *intermedium*, Hybrid Avens. Local.

Agrimonia eupatoria, Agrimony. Local.

A.procera, Fragrant Agrimony. Very rare.

Sanguisorba minor ssp.*minor*, Salad Burnet. Rare.

Alchemilla conjuncta, Silver Lady's-mantle. Rare escape.

A.xanthochlora, Lady's-mantle. Common.

A.filicaulis ssp.*vestita*, Lady's-mantle. Very local.

A.glabra, Lady's-mantle. Common.

A.mollis, Garden Lady's-mantle. Rare escape.

Aphanes arvensis, Parsley-piert. Uncommon.

A.inexpectata, Slender Parsley-piert. Very common.

Fabaceae (Leguminosae): vetches etc.

Astragalus danicus, Purple Milk-vetch. Local, in short turf near sea.

A.glycyphyllos, Wild Liquorice. Rare, near sea.

[*Oxytropis halleri*, Purple Oxytropis. Extinct.]

Anthyllis vulneraria, Kidney Vetch. Common.

Lotus corniculatus, Common Bird's-foot-trefoil. Common.

L.pedunculatus, Large Bird's-foot-trefoil. Common in damper places.

Ornithopus perpusillus, Bird's-foot. Uncommon on moors and bare ground.

Securigera varia, Crown Vetch. Rare escape.

Vicia cracca, Tufted Vetch. Common.

V.hirsuta, Hairy Tare. Common.

V.sepium, Bush Vetch. Common.

V.sativa ssp.*nigra*, Narrow-leaved Vetch. Common.

V.sativa ssp.*segetalis*, Common Vetch. Local.

V.lathyroides, Spring Vetch. Local in short grass by sea.

[*V.lutea*, Yellow Vetch. Extinct.]

Lathyrus linifolius, Bitter-vetch. Local.

L.pratensis, Meadow Vetchling. Very common.

L.tuberosus, Tuberous Pea. Rare escape; ephemeral?

L.grandiflorus, Two-flowered Everlasting-pea. Rare escape.

L.aphaca, Yellow Vetchling. Casual.

Ononis repens, Common Restharrow. Common.

Melilotus altissimus, Tall Melilot. Casual.

M.albus, White Melilot. Occasionally established, as near W Wemyss.

M.officinalis, Ribbed Melilot. Occasionally established.

Medicago lupulina, Black Medick. Common.

M.sativa ssp.*falcata*, Sickle Medick. Very rare escape.

Trifolium repens, White Clover. Very common.

T.hybridum, Alsike Clover. Local, sometimes as a relic.

T.campestre, Hop Trefoil. Local.

T.dubium, Lesser Trefoil. Very common.

T.micranthum, Slender Trefoil. Very rare, lawns in St Andrews.

T.pratense, Red Clover. Very common.

T.medium, Zigzag Clover. Local.

T.striatum, Knotted Clover. Uncommon, often by sea.

T.scabrum, Rough Clover. Rare by sea.

T.arvense, Hare's-foot Clover. Local.

T.ornithopodioides, Bird's-foot Clover. Very rare, casual?

Lupinus arboreus, Tree Lupin.

Locally naturalised, as on St Andrews Links.

*L.*x *regalis*, Russell Lupin. Local escape.

Genista anglica, Petty Whin. Very rare, Annsmuir.

Haloragaceae

Myriophyllum spicatum, Spiked Water-milfoil. Local in ponds and reservoirs.

M.alterniflorum, Alternate Water-milfoil. Uncommon in more acid water.

Lythraceae

Lythrum salicaria, Purple-loosestrife. Uncommon by freshwater.

L.portula, Water Purslane. Uncommon on mud.

Onagraceae: willowherbs etc.

Many hybrids occur occasionally.

Epilobium hirsutum, Great Willowherb. Common.

E.parviflorum, Hoary Willowherb. Local.

E.montanum, Broad-leaved Willowherb. Very common.

E.obscurum, Short-fruited Willowherb. Local.

E.roseum, Pale Willowherb. Local.

E.ciliatum, American Willowherb. Very common.

E.palustre, Marsh Willowherb. Common.

E.alsinifolium, Chickweed Willowherb. Rare, on Lomonds.

E.brunnescens, New Zealand Willowherb. Locally naturalised.

Chamerion angustifolium, Rosebay Willowherb. Very common.

Oenothera spp., Evening-primroses. Occasional, sometimes on dunes.

Circaea lutetiana, Enchanter's-nightshade. Local in open woodland.

C.x intermedia, Upland Enchanter's-nightshade. Very rare on Lomonds.

Euphorbiaceae: spurges etc.

Mercurialis perennis, Dog's Mercury. Very common.

Euphorbia helioscopia, Sun Spurge. Common weed.

E.peplus, Petty Spurge. Common weed.

Linaceae

Linum catharticum, Fairy Flax. Local.

[*Radiola linoides*, Allseed. Extinct]

Polygalaceae

Polygala vulgaris, Common Milkwort. Very local.

P.serpyllifolia, Heath Milkwort. Local.

Oxalidaceae

Oxalis corniculata, Procumbent Yellow-sorrel. Occasional weed.

O.acetosella, Wood-sorrel. Common.

Geraniaceae: crane's-bills etc.

Geranium sylvaticum, Wood Crane's-bill. Rather local except in west.

G.pratense, Meadow Crane's-bill. Common.

G.sanguineum, Bloody Crane's-bill. Local, often on rocks near sea.

G.columbinum, Long-stalked Crane's-bill. Rare.

G.dissectum, Cut-leaved Crane's-bill. Common weed.

G.x magnificum, Purple Crane's-bill. Rare escape.

G.pyrenaicum, Hedgerow Crane's-bill. Local, naturalised.

G.pusillum, Small-flowered Crane's-bill. Very local.

G.molle, Dove's-foot Crane's-bill. Very common.

G.lucidum, Shining Crane's-bill. Local.

G.robertianum, Herb-robert. Very common.

G.phaeum, Dusky Crane's-bill. Rare escape.

Erodium cicutarium, Common Stork's-bill. Common.

Balsaminaceae

Impatiens parviflora, Small Balsam. Very rare, St Andrews.

I.glandulifera, Indian Balsam. Locally abundant by freshwater.

Araliaceae

Hedera helix ssp.*helix*, Common Ivy. Very common.

H.helix ssp.*hibernica*, Irish Ivy. Occasional escape.

Apiaceae (Umbelliferae): umbellifers

Hydrocotyle vulgaris, Marsh Pennywort. Common.

Sanicula europaea, Sanicle. Local in woods.

[*Eryngium maritimum*, Sea Holly. Extinct.]

Chaerophyllum temulum, Rough Chervil. Common.

Anthriscus sylvestris, Cow Parsley. Very common.

A.caucalis, Bur Parsley. Local, by sea.

Scandix pecten-veneris, Shepherd's Needle. Casual.

Myrrhis odorata, Sweet Cicely. Common by roads and tracks.

Smyrnium olusatrum, Alexanders. Local, near sea.

Conopodium majus, Pignut. Common.

Pimpinella saxifraga, Burnet-saxifrage. Local.

Aegopodium podagraria, Bishopweed. Very common.

Berula erecta, Lesser Water-parsnip. Rare.

Oenanthe fistulosa, Tubular Water-dropwort. Extinct?

O.crocata, Hemlock Water-dropwort. Local, usually near sea.

[*O.aquatica*, Fine-leaved Water-dropwort. Extinct.]

Aethusa cynapium, Fool's Parsley. Local weed.

Meum athamanticum, Spignel. Very rare.

Conium maculatum, Hemlock. Common.

Apium graveolens, Wild Celery. Very rare escape.

A.repens, Creeping Marshwort. Very rare, Kinghorn Loch.

A.inundatum, Lesser Marshwort. Local, on muddy margins.

Petroselinum crispum, Garden Parsley. Very rare escape.

Cicuta virosa, Cowbane. Very rare.

Ligusticum scoticum, Scots Lovage. Local, by sea.

Angelica sylvestris, Wild Angelica. Common.

Peucedanum ostruthium, Masterwort. Rare, naturalised.

Pastinaca sativa, Wild Parsnip. Rare, naturalised.

Heracleum sphondylium, Hogweed. Very common.

H.mantegazzianum, Giant Hogweed. Locally abundant by burns.

Torilis japonica, Upright Hedge-parsley. Common.

T.nodosa, Knotted Hedge-parsley. Very rare, coastal.

Daucus carota, Wild Carrot. Very local, on sea braes.

Gentianaceae: gentians, etc.

Centaurium erythraea, Common Centaury. Local.

C.littorale, Seaside Centaury.
Very rare, Tentsmuir.
Gentianella campestris, Field
Gentian. Rare.
G.amarella, Autumn Gentian.
Very rare.

Apocynaceae

Vinca minor, Lesser Periwinkle.
Local, naturalised.
V.major, Greater Periwinkle.
Rare escape.

Solanaceae: nightshades etc.

Atropa belladonna, Deadly
Nightshade. Very rare.
Hyoscyamus niger, Henbane.
Rare, including I of May.
Solanum dulcamara,
Bittersweet. Local, by burns
and waysides.

Convolvulaceae: bindweeds

Convolvulus arvensis, Field
Bindweed. Common.
Calystegia soldanella, Sea
Bindweed. Very rare.
C.sepium, Hedge Bindweed.
Common.
C.pulchra, Hairy Bindweed.
Rare.
C.silvatica, Large Bindweed.
Uncommon.

Menyanthaceae

Menyanthes trifoliata, Bogbean.
Local in marshes.

Polemoniaceae

Polemonium caeruleum,
Jacob's-ladder. Rare escape.

Boraginaceae:
forget-me-nots, etc.

[*Lithospermum arvense*,
Common Gromwell. Extinct
cornfield weed.]
Echium vulgare, Viper's
Bugloss. Local, in sandy
soils.
Pulmonaria officinalis,
Lungwort. Rare escape.

P.'Mawson's Blue',
Narrow-leaved Lungwort.
Rare escape, as at Balbirnie.
Symphytum officinale, Common
Comfrey. Very local, centred
on Inverkeithing area.
S.x uplandicum, Russian
Comfrey. Very common.
S.tuberosum, Tuberous
Comfrey. Common.
S.grandiflorum, Creeping
Comfrey. Very rare escape.
S.orientale, White Comfrey.
Very rare escape.
Anchusa arvensis, Bugloss.
Common weed.
Pentaglottis sempervirens, Green
Alkanet. Common,
naturalised.
Borago officinalis, Borage.
Occasional escape.
Trachystemon orientalis,
Abraham-Isaac-Jacob. Very
rare escape.
[*Mertensia maritima*,
Oysterplant. Extinct.]
Myosotis scorpioides, Water
Forget-me-not. Common by
burns.
M.secunda, Creeping Forget-
me-not. Local in more acid
places.
M.laxa, Tufted Forget-me-not.
Common in marshes.
M.sylvatica, Wood Forget-me-
not. Local, naturalised.
M.arvensis, Field Forget-me-
not. Very common.
M.ramosissima, Early Forget-
me-not. Local in short turf
and bare ground.
M.discolor, Changing
Forget-me-not. Common.
Omphalodes verna, Blue-eyed
Mary. Very rare escape,
Valleyfield.
Cynoglossum officinale,
Hound's-tongue. Very local,
by sea.

Lamiaceae (Labiatae):
dead-nettles etc.

Stachys officinalis, Betony. Very
rare, not seen for several
years.
S.sylvatica, Hedge Woundwort.
Common.
S.x ambigua, Hybrid
Woundwort. Local.
S.palustris, Marsh Woundwort.
Common.
S.arvensis, Field Woundwort.
Local arable weed,
decreasing.
Ballota nigra, Black
Horehound. Rare, near sea.
Lamiastrum galeobdolon
ssp.*argentatum*, Yellow
Archangel. Increasing
escape in woodland.
Lamium album, White
Dead-nettle. Common.
L.maculatum, Spotted
Dead-nettle. Rare escape.
L.purpureum, Red Dead-nettle.
Very common.
L.hybridum, Cut-leaved
Dead-nettle. Local.
L.confertum, Northern
Dead-nettle. Uncommon,
possibly only in East Neuk.
L.amplexicaule, Hen-bit
Dead-nettle. Common.
Galeopsis speciosa, Large-
flowered Hemp-nettle. Local.
G.tetrahit, Common Hemp-
nettle. Common.
G.bifida, Bifid Hemp-nettle.
Local.
Phlomis russeliana, Turkish
Sage. Very rare escape,
Balmerino area.
Marrubium vulgare, White
Horehound. Very rare,
Inchcolm.
Scutellaria galericulata,
Skullcap. Very local in
damp ground.
Teucrium scorodonia, Wood
Sage. Common.
Ajuga reptans, Bugle. Common.

Glechoma hederacea, Ground-ivy. Common.

Prunella vulgaris, Selfheal. Common.

Clinopodium vulgare, Wild Basil. Uncommon.

Origanum vulgare, Wild Marjoram. Uncommon, scattered.

Thymus polytrichus, Wild Thyme. Common.

Lycopus europaeus, Gipsywort. Uncommon, NE Fife only.

Mentha arvensis, Corn Mint. Local arable weed, decreasing.

*M.*x *verticillata*, Whorled Mint. Local, by freshwater.

M.aquatica, Water Mint. Common.

*M.*x *piperita*, Peppermint. Local, in ditches and by burns.

M.spicata, Spear Mint. Local,on waste ground.

*M.*x *villosa*, Apple-mint. Local, on waste ground.

*M.*x *villosonervata*, Sharp-toothed Mint. Uncommon, on waste ground.

Salvia verbenaca, Wild Clary. Very rare, Kinghorn/Pettycur.

S.verticillata, Whorled Clary. Very rare.

Hippuridaceae

Hippuris vulgaris, Mare's-tail. Local in lochs and reservoirs.

Callitrichaceae: water-starworts

Callitriche stagnalis, Common Water-starwort. Very common.

C.hermaphroditica, Annual Water-starwort. Local in lochs and reservoirs.

C.platycarpa, Various-leaved Water-starwort. Common.

C.hamulata, Intermediate Water-starwort. Local in pools and burns.

Plantaginaceae: plantains

Plantago coronopus, Buck's-horn Plantain. Common, by sea.

P.maritima, Sea Plantain. Common, by sea.

P.major, Greater Plantain. Very common.

P.media, Hoary Plantain. Very rare escape, Hill of Tarvit lawn.

P.lanceolata, Ribwort Plantain. Very common.

Littorella uniflora, Shoreweed. Locally dominant around lochs and reservoirs.

Scrophulariaceae: figworts etc.

Verbascum thapsus, Great Mullein. Local, ephemeral.

V.lychnitis, White Mullein. Very rare, Newburgh area.

Scrophularia nodosa, Common Figwort. Common.

S.auriculata, Water Figwort. Very rare.

S.umbrosa, Green Figwort. Locally common in NE Fife.

S.vernalis, Yellow Figwort. Local in open woods.

Mimulus moschatus, Musk. Very rare escape.

M.guttatus agg., Monkeyflower. Common by burns.

Limosella aquatica, Mudwort. Uncommon on exposed mud.

Antirrhinum majus, Snapdragon. Uncommon escape.

Chaenorhinum minus, Small Toadflax. Very local, decreasing; on railway tracks.

Cymbalaria muralis, Ivy-leaved Toadflax. Common on walls.

Linaria vulgaris, Common Toadflax. Common by roadsides and railways.

L.purpurea, Purple Toadflax. Increasing escape.

L.repens, Pale Toadflax. Very rare escape.

Digitalis purpurea, Foxglove. Very common.

Erinus alpinus, Fairy Foxglove. Rare escape, on walls.

Veronica serpyllifolia, Thyme-leaved Speedwell. Common.

V.officinalis, Heath Speedwell. Common.

V.chamaedrys, Germander Speedwell. Very common.

V.montana, Wood Speedwell. Uncommon, less so in west.

V.scutellata, Marsh Speedwell. Local.

V.beccabunga, Brooklime. Very common.

V.anagallis-aquatica, Blue Water-speedwell. Local.

V.catenata, Pink Water-speedwell. Rare?

V.arvensis, Wall Speedwell. Very common.

V.agrestis, Green Field-speedwell. Common weed.

V.polita, Grey Field-speedwell. Uncommon weed.

V.persica, Common Field-speedwell. Common weed.

V.filiformis, Slender Speedwell. Common on lawns and playing fields.

V.hederifolia, Ivy-leaved Speedwell. Common.

Melampyrum pratense, Common Cow-wheat. Very rare, Lethan's Den (Saline).

Euphrasia arctica ssp.*borealis*, Eyebright. Common.

E.tetraquetra, Eyebright. Rare, coastal.

E.nemorosa, Eyebright. Local?

E.confusa, Eyebright. Uncommon in short grass.

E.scottica, Eyebright. Uncommon in flushes.

Odontites vernus, Red Bartsia. Common.

Rhinanthus minor, Yellow-rattle. Common.

Pedicularis palustris, Marsh Lousewort. Local.

P.sylvatica, Lousewort. Very local, on moors.

Orobanchaceae: broomrapes etc.

Lathraea squamaria, Toothwort. Very rare, Lethan's Den (Saline).

Orobanche alba, Thyme Broomrape. Very rare.

O.minor, Common Broomrape. Casual.

Lentibulariaceae: butterworts etc.

Pinguicula vulgaris, Common Butterwort. Local in upland damp areas.

[*Utricularia vulgaris*, Greater Bladderwort. Extinct.]

[*U.intermedia*, Intermediate Bladderwort. Extinct.]

[*U.minor*, Lesser Bladderwort. Extinct.]

Campanulaceae: bellflowers

Campanula lactiflora, Milky Bellflower. Very rare escape.

C.persicifolia, Peach-leaved Bellflower. Increasing escape.

C.glomerata, Clustered Bellflower. Rare.

C.latifolia, Giant Bellflower. Common in woods.

C.trachelium, Nettle-leaved Bellflower. Very rare escape, St Andrews.

C.rapunculoides, Creeping Bellflower. Rare escape.

C.rotundifolia, Bluebell. Common.

Rubiaceae: bedstraws etc.

Sherardia arvensis, Field Madder. Local in dry, grassy places.

Galium odoratum, Woodruff. Local in woodland.

G.uliginosum, Fen Bedstraw. Local.

G.palustre, Common Marsh-bedstraw. Common.

G.verum, Lady's Bedstraw. Common.

G.mollugo, Hedge Bedstraw. Very local.

G.saxatile, Heath Bedstraw. Very common.

G.aparine, Sticky Willie. Very common.

Cruciata laevipes, Crosswort. Local.

Adoxaceae

Adoxa moschatellina, Moschatel. Uncommon in shady places.

Valerianaceae: valerians

Valerianella locusta, Common Cornsalad. Local in dry, barish spots.

V.carinata, Keeled-fruited Cornsalad. Very rare, Wormit area.

Valeriana officinalis, Common Valerian. Common.

V.pyrenaica, Pyrenean Valerian. Locally naturalised by burns.

Centranthus ruber, Red Valerian. Locally naturalised on walls.

Dipsacaceae: scabiouses etc.

Dipsacus fullonum, Wild Teasel. Local in waste ground.

Knautia arvensis, Field Scabious. Common.

Succisa pratensis, Devil's-bit Scabious. Common.

Asteraceae (Compositae): daisies etc.

Arctium minus, Lesser Burdock. Common.

Carduus tenuiflorus, Slender Thistle. Uncommon, coastal.

C.crispus, Welted Thistle. Common on waste ground.

C.nutans, Musk Thistle. Rare, ephemeral.

Cirsium vulgare, Spear Thistle. Very common.

C.heterophyllum, Melancholy Thistle. Very local.

C.palustre, Marsh Thistle. Very common.

C.arvense, Creeping Thistle. Very common.

Onopordum acanthium, Scotch Thistle. Rare casual.

Centaurea scabiosa, Greater Knapweed. Local.

C.montana, Perennial Cornflower. Occasional escape.

C.cyanus, Cornflower. Very rare.

C.nigra, Common Knapweed. Very common.

Cichorium intybus, Chicory. Rare, intro.

Lapsana communis, Nipplewort. Very common.

Hypochaeris radicata, Cat's-ear. Very common.

*H.*x *intermedia*, Hybrid Cat's-ear. Very rare, Tentsmuir.

H.glabra, Smooth Cat's-ear. Very rare, Tentsmuir.

Leontodon autumnalis, Autumnal Hawkbit. Common.

L.hispidus, Rough Hawkbit. Rare, ephemeral.

L.saxatilis, Lesser Hawkbit. Rare, on sand dunes.

Tragopogon pratensis, Goat's-beard. Local.

Sonchus arvensis, Perennial Sow-thistle. Common.

S.oleraceus, Smooth Sow-thistle. Very common.

S.asper, Prickly Sow-thistle. Common.

Lactuca virosa, Greater Lettuce. Very rare, Newburgh area.

Cicerbita macrophylla, Common Blue-sow-thistle. Locally naturalised.

Mycelis muralis, Wall Lettuce. Very local.

Taraxacum officinalis agg., Common Dandelion. Very common.

Crepis paludosa, Marsh Hawk's-beard. Local except in west.

C.capillaris, Smooth Hawk's-beard. Common.

[*C.mollis*, Northern Hawk's-beard. Extinct.]

Pilosella officinarum, Mouse-ear Hawkweed. Common.

P.aurantiaca ssp.*carpathicola*, Orange Hawkweed. Occasional escape.

P. flagellare, Hawkweed. Rare escape.

Hieracium vulgatum agg., Hawkweed. Common.

Filago vulgaris, Common Cudweed. Uncommon in dry grassy places.

F.minima, Small Cudweed. Very local on barish ground.

Antennaria dioica, Mountain Everlasting. Uncommon, on Lomonds.

Gnaphalium sylvaticum, Heath Cudweed. Uncommon on moorland.

G.uliginosum, Marsh Cudweed. Common.

Inula helenium, Elecampane. Very rare escape.

Solidago virgaurea, Goldenrod. Local.

S.canadensis, Canadian Goldenrod. Local escape.

S.gigantea, Early Goldenrod. Rare escape.

Aster tripolium, Sea Aster. Local in salt-marshes.

*A.*x *versicolor*, Michaelmas-daisy. Locally naturalised.

A.novi-belgii, Michaelmas-daisy. Locally naturalised.

*A.*x *salignus*, Michaelmas-daisy. Locally naturalised.

[*Erigeron acer*, Blue Fleabane. Extinct.]

Bellis perennis, Daisy. Very common.

Tanacetum parthenium, Feverfew. Common.

T.vulgare, Tansy. Locally common.

Seriphidium maritimum, Sea Wormwood. Very local, in East Neuk.

Artemisia vulgaris, Mugwort. Common.

A.absinthium, Wormwood. Rare, scattered.

Achillea ptarmica, Sneezewort. Local in damp ground.

A.millefolium, Yarrow. Very common.

Anthemis arvensis, Corn Chamomile. Rare arable weed.

Chrysanthemum segetum, Corn Marigold. Local arable weed.

Leucanthemum vulgare, Oxeye Daisy. Very common.

*L.*x *superbum*, Shasta Daisy. Occasional escape.

Matricaria recutita, Scented Mayweed. Rare arable weed.

M.discoidea, Pineapple Weed. Very common.

Tripleurospermum maritimum, Mayweed. Uncommon by sea.

T.inodorum, Scentless Mayweed. Very common.

Senecio jacobaea, Common Ragwort. Very common.

S.aquaticus, Marsh Ragwort. Uncommon in marshes.

S.squalidus, Oxford Ragwort. Local in built-up areas.

S.vulgaris, Groundsel.Very common.

S.sylvaticus, Heath Groundsel. Local on dry, acid banks.

S.viscosus, Sticky Groundsel. Common by railways and waste ground.

Doronicum pardalianches, Leopard's-bane. Locally naturalised in woodland.

*D.*x *willdenowii*,

Leopard's-bane. Occasionally naturalised.

*D.*x *excelsum*, Leopard's-bane. Occasionally naturalised.

D.plantagineum, Plantain Leopard's-bane. Occasionally naturalised.

Tussilago farfara, Colt's-foot. Very common.

Petasites hybridus, Butterbur. Common, often by water.

P.japonicus, Giant Butterbur. Very rare, intro.

P.albus, White Butterbur. Locally naturalised in woods.

P.fragrans, Winter Heliotrope. Locally naturalised on banks.

Galinsoga parviflora, Gallant Soldier. Casual.

Bidens cernua, Nodding Bur-marigold. Rare, damp places.

B.tripartita, Trifid Bur-marigold. Casual.

Eupatorium cannabinum, Hemp-agrimony. Uncommon, coastal.

Alismataceae:
Water-plantains

Alisma plantago-aquatica, Water-plantain. Local.

[*Baldellia ranunculoides*, Lesser Water-plantain. Extinct.]

Hydrocharitaceae

Elodea canadensis, Canadian Waterweed. Common.

Lagarosiphon major, Curly Waterweed. Very rare, intro.

Jungacinaceae

Triglochin palustris, Marsh Arrowgrass. Local in marshes.

T.maritima, Sea Arrowgrass. Local in saltmarshes.

Potamogetonaceae:
pondweeds

Potamogeton natans, Broad-leaved Pondweed. Common.

P.polygonifolius, Bog
    Pondweed. Local, on acid
    soils.
*P.*x *zizii*, Long-leaved
    Pondweed. Uncommon.
P.gramineus, Various-leaved
    Pondweed. Very local.
*P.*x *nitens*, Bright-leaved
    Pondweed. Very rare, Ballo.
P.alpinus, Red Pondweed. Very
    local.
P.praelongus, Long-stalked
    Pondweed. Rare, Black L
    (Cleish).
P.perfoliatus, Perfoliate
    Pondweed. Local.
P.pusillus, Lesser Pondweed.
    Common.
P.obtusifolius, Blunt-leaved
    Pondweed. Local.
P.berchtoldii, Small Pondweed.
    Common.
P.crispus, Curled Pondweed.
    Common.
P.filiformis, Slender-leaved
    Pondweed. Local.
*P.*x *suecicus*, Swedish
    Pondweed. Very rare, L
    Fitty.
P.pectinatus, Fennel Pondweed.
    Common.
[*P.lucens*, Shining Pondweed.
    Extinct.]

Zannichelliaceae

Zannichellia palustris, Horned
    Pondweed. Local.

Zosteraceae: eelgrasses

Zostera marina, Eelgrass. Rare,
    Eden Estuary.
Z.angustifolia, Narrow-leaved
    Eelgrass. Uncommon.
Z.noltii, Dwarf Eelgrass.
    Locally common.

Araceae

Arum maculatum,
    Lords-and-ladies. Local;
    naturalised?
A.italicum, Italian Lords-and-
    ladies. Rare escape.

Lemnaceae

Lemna minor, Common
    Duckweed. Common on still
    water.
L.trisulca, Ivy-leaved
    Duckweed. Local in pools.

Juncaceae: rushes

Juncus squarrosus, Heath Rush.
    Local on moors.
J.tenuis, Slender Rush. Rare,
    probably increasing.
J.gerardii, Saltmarsh Rush.
    Local.
J.bufonius, Toad Rush.
    Common.
J.articulatus, Jointed Rush.
    Common.
J.acutiflorus, Sharp-flowered
    Rush. Common.
J.bulbosus, Bulbous Rush. Local
    in ponds.
J.maritimus, Sea Rush. Very
    rare, near St Andrews.
J.balticus, Baltic Rush. Rare,
    Tentsmuir.
J.inflexus, Hard Rush. Local.
*J.*x *diffusus*. Rare.
J.effusus, Soft Rush.Very
    common.
J.conglomeratus, Compact Rush.
    Common.
Luzula pilosa, Hairy Wood-
    rush. Local on shady banks.
L.sylvatica, Great Wood-rush.
    Common.
L.luzuloides, White Wood-
    rush. Rare escape.
L.campestris, Field Wood-rush.
    Common.
L.multiflora, Heath Wood-rush.
    Common.

Cyperaceae: sedges etc.

Eriophorum angustifolium,
    Common Cottongrass.
    Common in bogs.
E.latifolium, Broad-leaved
    Cottongrass. Very rare,
    Waltonhill.
E.vaginatum, Hare's-tail
    Cottongrass. Local in bogs.

Trichophorum cespitosum,
    Deergrass. Very local,
    upland.
Eleocharis palustris, Common
    Spike-rush. Common.
E.uniglumis, Slender Spike-
    rush. Uncommon, coastal.
E.quinqueflora, Few-flowered
    Spike-rush. Uncommon.
E.acicularis, Needle Spike-rush.
    Local, around some
    reservoirs.
[*E.multicaulis*, Many-stalked
    Spike-rush. Extinct.]
Bolboschoenus maritimus, Sea
    Club-rush. Local, by sea.
Scirpus sylvaticus, Wood Club-
    rush. Local, less so in west.
Schoenoplectus lacustris,
    Common Club-rush. Local
    by freshwater.
S.tabernaemontani, Grey Club-
    rush. Local, mainly coastal.
Isolepis setacea, Bristle Club-
    rush. Very local.
Eleogiton fluitans, Floating
    Club-rush. Very rare.
Blysmus rufus, Saltmarsh
    Flat-sedge. Very local.
[*Schoenus nigricans*, Black
    Bog-rush. Extinct.]
Rhynchospora alba, White
    Beak-sedge. Very rare,
    Lockshaw Moss.
Carex paniculata, Greater
    Tussock-sedge. Local.
C.diandra, Lesser Tussock-
    sedge. Rare.
C.otrubae, False Fox-sedge.
    Local, coastal.
C.spicata, Spiked Sedge. Very
    rare.
C.muricata, Prickly Sedge.
    Uncommon, ephemeral.
C.arenaria, Sand Sedge.
    Common on dunes.
C.disticha, Brown Sedge.
    Common.
C.maritima, Curved Sedge.
    Very rare, now almost
    extinct.

C.remota, Remote Sedge. Local, in woods and dens.

C.ovalis, Oval Sedge. Common.

C.echinata, Star Sedge. Common.

C.dioica, Dioecious Sedge. Local in marshes.

C.curta, White Sedge. Local in bogs.

C.hirta, Hairy Sedge. Common.

C.lasiocarpa, Slender Sedge. Very rare.

C.acutiformis, Lesser Pond-sedge. Local.

C.riparia, Great Pond-sedge. Uncommon.

C.rostrata, Bottle Sedge. Very common.

C.vesicaria, Bladder-sedge. Rare.

C.pendula, Pendulus Sedge. Rare, intro.

C.sylvatica, Wood-sedge. Local.

C.flacca, Glaucous Sedge. Very common.

C.panicea, Carnation Sedge. Very common.

C.laevigata, Smooth-stalked Sedge. Very rare.

C.binervis, Green-ribbed Sedge. Local, on moorland.

C.distans, Distant Sedge. Local, coastal.

C.extensa, Long-bracted Sedge. Very local in salt-marshes.

C.hostiana, Tawny Sedge. Local in flushes.

C.viridula ssp.*brachyrrhyncha*, Long-stalked Yellow Sedge. Local.

C.viridula ssp.*oedocarpa*, Common Yellow Sedge. Common.

C.viridula ssp.*viridula*, Small-fruited Yellow Sedge. Very rare, Tentsmuir.

C.pallescens, Pale Sedge. Very local in open woods.

C.caryophyllea, Spring Sedge. Common.

C.pilulifera, Pill Sedge. Common.

C.magellanica, Tall Bog-sedge. Very rare, Cleish Hills.

C.aquatilis, Water Sedge. Locally common.

C.nigra, Common Sedge. Very common.

C.pulicaris, Flea Sedge. Local in flushes.

[*C.pauciflora*, Few-flowered Sedge. Extinct.]

[*C.limosa*, Bog-sedge. Extinct.]

Poaceae (Gramineae): grasses

Nardus stricta, Mat-grass. Local on moors and hills.

Milium effusum, Wood Millet. Local.

Festuca pratensis, Meadow Fescue. Very local.

F.arundinacea, Tall Fescue. Local.

F.gigantea, Giant Fescue. Local in woodland.

F.arenaria, Rush-leaved Fescue. Rare, coastal.

F.rubra, Red Fescue. Very common.

F.ovina, Sheep's-fescue. Common.

F.filiformis, Fine-leaved Sheep's-fescue. Uncommon, on dry banks.

[*F.altissima*, Wood Fescue. Very rare (or error?)]

[x *Festulolium loliaceum*, Hybrid Fescue. Extinct.]

Lolium perenne, Perennial Rye-grass. Very common.

L.multiflorum, Italian Rye-grass. Local, usually intro.

Vulpia bromoides, Squirrel-tail Fescue. Local.

V.myuros, Rat's-tail Fescue. Rare.

Cynosurus cristatus, Crested Dog's-tail. Common

Puccinellia maritima, Common Saltmarsh-grass. Local.

P.distans ssp.*distans*, Reflexed Saltmarsh-grass. Very local.

P.distans ssp.*borealis*, Northern Saltmarsh-grass. Uncommon.

Briza media, Quaking-grass. Local in unimproved grassland.

Poa annua, Annual Meadow-grass. Very common.

P.trivialis, Rough Meadow-grass. Common, by freshwater and as a weed.

P.humilis, Spreading Meadow-grass. Common.

P.pratensis, Smooth Meadow-grass. Very common.

P.angustifolia, Narrow-leaved Meadow-grass. Rare, on dry banks.

P.chaixii, Broad-leaved Meadow-grass. Locally common, intro.

P.compressa, Flattened Meadow-grass. Casual.

P.nemoralis, Wood Meadow-grass. Common.

Dactylis glomerata, Cock's-foot. Very common.

Catabrosa aquatica, Whorl-grass. Local.

Catapodium rigidum, Fern-grass. Very local, often near sea.

C.marinum, Sea Fern-grass. Uncommon, by sea.

Glyceria maxima, Reed Sweet-grass. Locally common.

G.fluitans, Floating Sweet-grass. Common.

G.x pedicellata, Hybrid Sweet-grass. Rare

G.declinata, Small Sweet-grass. Local.

G.notata, Plicate Sweet-grass. Local.

Melica uniflora, Wood Melick. Very local in dens.

Helictotrichon pubescens, Downy Oat-grass. Local.

H.pratense, Meadow Oat-grass. Local.

Arrhenatherum elatius, False Oat-grass. Very common.

Avena fatua, Wild Oat.
Uncommon.
Trisetum flavescens, Yellow
Oat-grass. Local.
Koeleria macrantha, Crested
Hair-grass. Locally common.
Deschampsia cespitosa, Tufted
Hair-grass. Very common.
D.flexuosa, Wavy Hair-grass.
Common on moors.
Holcus lanatus, Yorkshire-fog.
Very common.
H.mollis, Creeping Soft-grass.
Very common.
Aira caryophyllea, Silvery
Hair-grass. Local.
A.praecox, Early Hair-grass.
Common.
Anthoxanthum odoratum, Sweet
Vernal-grass. Very common.
Phalaris arundinacea, Reed
Canary-grass. Common.
P.canariensis, Canary-grass.
Casual.
Agrostis capillaris, Common
Bent. Very common.
A.gigantea, Black Bent. Local,
increasing, a weed.
A.stolonifera, Creeping Bent.
Very common.
A.canina, Velvet Bent. Local.
A.vinealis, Brown Bent.
Uncommon?
Calamagrostis epigejos, Wood
Small-reed. Local, coastal,
West Fife.
Ammophila arenaria, Marram.
Common.
Alopecurus pratensis, Meadow
Foxtail. Common.
A.geniculatus, Marsh Foxtail.
Common.
A.myosuroides, Black-grass.
Rare, ephemeral.
Phleum pratense, Timothy.
Very common.
P.bertolonii, Smaller Cat's-tail.
Very common.
P.arenarium, Sand Cat's-tail.
Rare on sand dunes.
Bromus hordeaceus
ssp. *hordeaceus*, Soft Brome.

Common.
ssp. *ferronii*, Sea Soft Brome.
Rare.
*B.*x *pseudothominei*, Lesser Soft
Brome. Rare, intro.
Bromopsis ramosa, Hairy
Brome. Local in or by
woods.
B.erecta, Upright Brome. Rare,
coastal.
Anisantha sterilis, Barren
Brome. Common.
Brachypodium sylvaticum.
False-brome. Common.
Elymus caninus, Bearded Couch.
Uncommon in woodland.
Elytrigia repens, Common
Couch. Very common.
*E.*x *laxa*, Hybrid Couch. Rare,
coastal.
E.juncea, Sand Couch. Local,
on shore.
Leymus arenarius, Lyme-grass.
Common, coastal.
Hordeum murinum, Wall
Barley. Local.
H.jubatum, Foxtail Barley.
Rare, intro.
Danthonia decumbens,
Heath-grass. Local.
Molinia caerulea, Purple
Moor-grass. Local on moors
and hills.
Phragmites australis, Common
Reed. Common.
Spartina anglica, Common
Cord-grass. Very rare, intro.
on Eden Estuary.

Sparganiaceae: bur-reeds
Sparganium erectum, Branched
Bur-reed. Common by
freshwater.
S.emersum, Unbranched
Bur-reed. Local, except for
R Ore.
S.angustifolium, Floating
Bur-reed. Uncommon, L
Glow.
[*S.natans*, Least Bur-reed.
Extinct.]

Typhaceae
Typha latifolia, Bulrush.
Common.
T.angustifolia, Lesser Bulrush.
Very rare, Lindores L.

Liliaceae: daffodils etc.
Narthecium ossifragum, Bog
Asphodel. Very local in bogs.
Gagea lutea, Yellow Star-of-
Bethlehem. Very rare, intro.
Tulipa sylvestris, Wild Tulip.
Rare, intro.
Lilium martagon, Martagon
Lily. Rare escape.
L.pyrenaicum, Pyrenean Lily.
Very rare escape.
Convallaria majalis, Lily of the
Valley. Very rare escape.
Polygonatum multiflorum,
Solomon's Seal. Very rare,
intro.
*P.*x *hybridum*, Garden
Solomon's Seal. Rare, intro.
[*Paris quadrifolia*, Herb Paris.
Extinct.]
Ornithogalum angustifolium,
Star-of-Bethlehem. Local
escape.
Hyacinthoides non-scripta, Wild
Hyacinth. Common.
H.non-scripta x *hispanica*,
Garden Hyacinth. Locally
naturalised, increasing.
Muscari armeniacum, Garden
Grape-hyacinth. Rare escape.
Allium triquetrum,
Three-cornered Garlic. Very
rare, intro.
A.paradoxum, Few-flowered
Garlic. Locally common,
spreading.
A.ursinum, Ramsons. Common
in dens.
A.carinatum, Keeled Garlic.
Uncommon, North Fife.
A.scorodoprasum, Sand Leek.
Very local, scattered.
A.vineale, Crow Garlic. Local,
mostly coastal.
Leucojum vernum, Spring
Snowflake. Very rare, escape.

Galanthus nivalis, Snowdrop.
Commonly naturalised.
Narcissus poeticus, Pheasant's
Eye. Occasional escape.
N.pseudonarcissus
ssp.*pseudonarcissus*, Wild
Daffodil. Locally naturalised.
Narcissus sp., Garden Daffodil.
Common escape.

Iridaceae: irises etc.

Iris pseudacorus, Yellow Iris.
Common.
I.foetidissima, Stinking Iris.
Rare escape, in woodland.
Crocus vernus, Crocus.
Occasional escape.
Crocosmia paniculata,
Aunt-Eliza. Rare escape.
C.x crocosmiiflora, Montbretia.
Locally naturalised.

Orchidaceae: orchids

[*Cypripedium calceolus*, Lady's
Slipper. Planted.]
[*Cephalanthera longifolia*.
Narrow-leaved Helleborine
Extinct.]
Epipactis helleborine,
Broad-leaved Helleborine.
Local.
Neottia nidus-avis, Bird's-nest
Orchid. Uncommon.
Listera ovata, Common
Twayblade. Locally common.
L.cordata, Lesser Twayblade.
Very rare, Tentsmuir.
Goodyera repens, Creeping
Lady's-tresses. Rare,
Tentsmuir.
[*Hammarbya paludosa*, Bog
Orchid. Extinct.]
Corallorhiza trifida, Coralroot
Orchid. Rare, Tentsmuir.
Platanthera chlorantha, Greater
Butterfly-orchid. Local.

P.bifolia, Lesser
Butterfly-orchid. Very rare.
Anacamptis pyramidalis,
Pyramidal Orchid. Very rare.
[*Pseudorchis albida*,
Small-white Orchid.
Extinct.]
Gymnadenia conopsea, Fragrant
Orchid. Very local.
Coeloglossum viride, Frog
Orchid. Uncommon.
Dactylorhiza fuchsii, Common
Spotted-orchid. Common.
D.x venusta. Occasional.
D.maculata, Heath
Spotted-orchid. Uncommon
on moors.
D.incarnata, Early
Marsh-orchid. Uncommon.
D.purpurella, Northern
Marsh-orchid. Common.
Orchis mascula, Early-purple
Orchid. Local.

Trees and shrubs

The following lists include those species that are likely to be seen in the countryside, whether it be by roads and tracks, by field edges, in woods or in old estates and also in built-up areas, notably parks that have formerly been the grounds of old mansion-houses. Not many species can be regarded as being truly native - not one of the conifers is - but many appear in natural or semi-natural habitats and may now rightly be treated as part of the wild landscape, particularly those that reproduce by one means or another (termed 'selfing' below). A number of introductions are now very common, a few to the extent of becoming pests. Others have been planted recently, especially in community and amenity areas, on roadside banks, at edges of older plantations, etc., and it is anticipated that some of these (particularly berried shrubs) will increasingly appear in wild situations, including plants not listed here.

Conifers

Abies alba, Silver Fir. Rare.
A.grandis, Grand Fir.
Occasional mature tree, now
sometimes in forestry
plantings.
A.nordmanniana, Caucasian Fir.
Small scale plantings.
A.procera, Noble Fir.
Occasional.
Araucaria araucana, Monkey
Puzzle. Fairly frequent.
Cedrus atlantica, Atlas Cedar.
Quite common.
C. deodara, Deodar. The
commonest true cedar.

C. libani, Cedar of Lebanon.
Quite common.
Chamaecyparis lawsoniana,
Lawson's Cypress. Common,
including forestry (several
vars.)
C.nootkatensis, Nootka Cypress.
Occasional.
C.obtusa, Hinoki Cypress. Rare.
C.pisifera, Sawara Cypress.
Rare.
Cryptomeria japonica, Japanese
Red Cedar. Occasional.
x *Cupressocyparis leylandii*,
Leyland Cypress.
Increasingly planted.
Cupressus macrocarpa, Monterey
Cypress. Rare.
Gingko biloba, Maidenhair
Tree. Rare.
Juniperus communis, Common
Juniper. Very rare:
Tentsmuir; occurred in

distant past as a native but no 20th century records.

J.chinensis, Chinese Juniper. Occasional.

Larix decidua, European Larch. Common as individuals and in forestry, selfing.

L.x *marschlinsii*, Hybrid Larch. Common, increasingly planted.

L.kaempferi, Japanese Larch. Common in forestry.

Metasequoia glyptostroboides, Dawn Redwood. Rare.

Picea abies, Norway Spruce. Very common especially in forestry, selfing.

P.brewerana, Brewer Spruce. Rare.

P.omorika, Serbian Spruce. Rare.

P.sitchkensis, Sitka Spruce. Very common especially in forestry, selfing.

P.smithiana, Morinda Spruce. Rare.

Pinus contorta, Lodgepole Pine. Occasional in forestry.

P.nigra var.*nigra*, Austrian Pine. Quite common.

P.nigra var.*maritima*, Corsican Pine. Occasional in forestry.

P.radiata, Monterey Pine. Rare.

P.strobus, Weymouth Pine. Rare.

P.sylvestris, Scots Pine. Common as individuals, very commonly planted, selfing widely.

P.wallichiana. Bhutan Pine. Rare.

Pseudotsuga menziesii, Douglas Fir. Common as individuals and in forestry, occasionally selfing.

Sequoia sempervirens, Coast Redwood. Quite common.

Sequoiadendron giganteum, Giant Sequoia. Occasional.

Taxus baccata, Yew. Very common, selfing.

Thuya plicata, Western Red Cedar. Occasional.

Tsuga heterophylla, Western Hemlock. Occasional as individuals, increasingly planted, occ. selfing.

Broad-leaved trees and large shrubs

These are defined as being roughly 4 metres (13 feet) and over in height although some individual shrubs may not always attain this.

Acer campestre, Field Maple. Occasionally long established; recently planted here and there.

A.platanoides, Norway Maple. Increasingly planted and selfing.

A.pseudoplatanus, Sycamore. Very common, often an undesired weed.

Aesculus carnea, Red Horse Chestnut. Rare.

A.flava, Yellow Buckeye. Very rare.

A.hippocastanum, Horse Chestnut. Common, seldom selfing.

Alnus cordata, Italian Alder. Occasional.

A.glutinosa, Common Alder. Native, very common; increasingly planted.

A.incana, Grey Alder. Occasional, spreading at Tentsmuir (plus hybrid with last).

A.viridis, Green Alder. Rare.

Betula pendula, Silver Birch. Native; common.

B.pubescens, Downy Birch. Native; very common.

B.x *aurata*, Hybrid Birch. Common when the above parents grow together.

Carpinus betulus, Hornbeam. Uncommon.

Castanea sativa, Sweet

Chestnut. Single trees here and there.

Corylus avellana, Hazel. Native; common in west, rare in east.

Cotoneaster frigidus, Tree Cotoneaster. Occasionally self-sown.

C.x *watereri*, Waterer's Cotoneaster. Occasionally self-sown.

Crataegus monogyna, Hawthorn. Native but widely planted; very common.

C.oxyacantha, Midland Hawthorn. Rare.

Euonymus europaeus, Spindle-tree. Rare.

Fagus sylvatica, Beech. Very common, occasionally selfing.

Fraxinus excelsior, Ash. Native, widely planted; very common.

Ilex aquifolium, Holly. Perhaps originally native; very commonly planted and selfing.

I.x *altaclarensis*, Highclere Holly. A rare escape.

Juglans regia, Walnut. Rare.

Laburnum anagyroides, Laburnum. Occasional.

L.x *watereri*, Voss's Laburnum. Rare.

Malus domestica, Apple. Common; seldom the true crab apple.

M.hupehensis, Hupeh Crab. Very rare.

Nothofagus menziesii, Silver Beech. Very rare.

Platanus x *hispanica*, Plane. Rare.

Populus alba, White Poplar. Common, suckering.

P.x *canadensis*, Black Italian Poplar. Common, several varieties.

P.candicans, Balm of Gilead. Occasional.

P.x *canescens*, Grey Poplar. Rare.

P.tremula, Aspen. A very rare native, occasionally planted.

P.trichocarpa, Western Balsam Poplar. Increasingly planted.

Prunus avium, Gean. Rare native; commonly planted, selfing.

P.cerasifera, Cherry Plum. Rare.

P.domestica, Plum. Occasional.

P.laurocerasus, Cherry Laurel. Common, selfing.

P.lusitanica, Portugal Laurel. Quite common, occasionally selfing.

P.padus, Bird Cherry. Local, probably native in the west; increasingly planted.

P.serrulata, Japanese Cherry. A common ornamental.

Pyrus communis, Pear. Rare.

Quercus cerris, Turkey Oak. Rare.

*Q.*x *pseudosuber*, Lucombe Oak. Very rare.

Q.ilex, Holm Oak. Occasional.

Q.petraea, Sessile Oak. Originally native?; uncommon.

Q.robur, Common Oak. Originally native?; widely planted and very common.

*Q.*x *rosacea*, Hybrid Oak (between last two). Commonly planted.

Rhododendron arboreum Tree-rhododendron. Very rare.

Robinia pseudoacacia, False Acacia. Very rare.

Salix alba, White Willow. Common by rivers and the broader burns.

S.caprea, Pussy Willow. Native; very common.

S.cinerea, Sallow, Saugh. Native; very common.

S.daphnoides, Violet Willow. Increasingly planted.

S.fragilis, Crack Willow. Common; several varieties.

S.pentandra, Bay Willow. Uncommon.

S.purpurea, Purple Willow. Uncommon, usually by water.

*S.*x *reichhartii* (hybrid between *caprea* and *cinerea*). Common.

*S.*x *sepulcralis*, Weeping Willow. Occasional.

S.viminalis, Osier. Common, selfing.

(N.B. Several willow hybrids occur that are not listed here.)

Sambucus nigra, Elder. Native; very common.

S.racemosa, Red-berried Elder. Occasional by plantations and roadsides, increasing.

Sorbus aria, Whitebeam. Fairly common, selfing.

S.aucuparia, Rowan. Very common, both native and planted.

S.intermedia, Swedish Whitebeam. Common, selfing.

S.latifolia, Broad-leaved Whitebeam. Very rare.

*S.*x *thuringiaca*, Hybrid Service-tree. Very rare.

Syringa vulgaris, Lilac. Occasional, suckering.

Tilia cordata, Small-leaved Lime. Occasional.

*T.*x *vulgaris*, Common Lime. Common, not selfing.

T.platyphyllos, Large-leaved Lime. Rare.

Ulmus glabra, Wych Elm. Native, widely planted and selfing; in some areas affected by disease.

U.procera, English Elm. Rare.

Viburnum lantana, Wayfaring-tree. Rare.

V.opulus, Guelder-rose. Occasional.

Medium and small shrubs

Defined as being roughly 1 metre (about 3 feet) to 4 metres (13 feet) in height. Thus the lowest shrubby plants such as the heathers are not included; one or two species listed below may not always reach the minimum, especially in exposed places.

Aucuba japonica, Spotted-laurel. Frequent in shrubberies.

Berberis darwinii, Darwin's Barberry. A very rare escape.

*B.*x *stenophylla*, Hedge-barberry. A very rare escape.

B.vulgaris, Barberry. Occasional in hedges or as an odd bush.

Buddleja davidii, Butterfly-bush. Now common in waste ground and on walls, increasing.

Buxus sempervirens, Box. Occasional in old shrubberies/estates, not selfing.

Clematis vitalba, Old-man's-beard. Very rare, long established near Burntisland.

Cornus sericea, Dogwood. Not infrequent, often near water, suckering freely.

Cotoneaster bullatus. A rare escape.

C.dielsianus. A rare escape.

C.horizontalis, Wallspray. Occasional on rocks.

C.integrifolius, Rockspray. Occasional on rocks, long established in places.

C.simonsii, Khasia-berry. Increasingly bird-sown.

C.sternianus. A rare escape.

*C.*x *suecicus*. A rare escape.

Cytisus scoparius, Broom. Very common native, also planted.

Daphne laureola, Spurge-laurel. Uncommon, occasionally long established.

Ficus carica, Fig. Very rare on cliffs; Kirkcaldy & I of May.

Fuchsia magellanica, Fuchsia. A rare escape/cast-out.

Hebe x *franciscana*, Hedge-veronica. Occasional by sea shores.

Hippophae rhamnoides, Sea Buckthorn. Common at Tentsmuir; increasingly planted by sea.

Humulus lupulus, Hop. A rare escape.

H.calycinum, Rose of Sharon. Now rare in shrubberies.

Leycesteria formosa, Himalayan Honeysuckle. Rare in old estates.

Ligustrum ovalifolium, Garden Privet. Occasionally cast-out/planted.

L.vulgare, Privet. Uncommon, sometimes selfing.

Lonicera nitida, Wilson's Honeysuckle. Rarely planted.

L.periclymenum, Honeysuckle. Native; common.

L.xylosteum, Fly Honeysuckle. Rare in old estates.

Lycium barbarum/chinense, Chinese-teaplant. Rare escape; coastal.

Mahonia aquifolium, Oregon-grape. Occasional clumps in old estates.

Philadelphus coronarius, Mock-orange. Rare.

Physocarpus opulifolius, Ninebark. Very well established near Ladybank.

Prunus domestica ssp.*insititia*, Bullace. Occasional extensive thickets.

P.spinosa, Blackthorn. Native; common.

Rhododendron ponticum, Rhododendron. Too common in old woodland, etc. (N.B. Several other rhododendrons occur, especially in old estates.)

Ribes alpinum, Mountain-currant. Occasional in old estates.

R.nigrum, Black-currant. A not infrequent cast-out/escape, especially in damp places.

R.rubrum, Red-currant. Ditto.

R.sanguineum, Flowering-currant. Frequently planted, increasingly selfing.

R.uva-crispa, Gooseberry. A common native and/or escape.

Rosa arvensis, Field-rose. Rarely planted or established.

R.caesia, Glaucous Dog-rose. Native; common.

R.canina, Dog-rose. Native; very common.

R.mollis, Soft Downy-rose. Native; common.

R.pimpinellifolia, Burnet-rose. Native, local; now being increasingly planted.

R.rubiginosa, Sweet-briar. Native, local; occasionally planted.

R.rugosa, Japanese Rose. Rarely established on dunes; now frequently planted.

R.sherardii, Sherard's Downy-rose. Native; common.

Rubus fruticosus, Bramble. Native, very common; over 30 microspecies in Fife.

R.idaeus, Rasp. Native; very common.

R.saxatilis, Stone Bramble. Native; very rare.

R.spectabilis, Salmonberry. Very well established in a few old estates, spreading.

Ruscus aculeatus, Butcher's-broom. Occasional bushes in old estates

Salix aurita, Eared-willow. Native; rather local.

S.myrsinifolia, Dark-leaved Willow. Native; rare.

S.phylicifolia, Tea-leaved Willow. Native; very rare.

S.repens, Creeping-Willow. Native on moors; uncommon.

Sambucus ebulus, Dwarf Elder. Very rare; long known at Inverkeithing.

Spiraea douglasii, Steeplebush. Rarely planted.

*S.*x *pseudosalicifolia*, False Bridewort. Occasional escape/planted, suckering.

Symphoricarpos albus, Snowberry. Common, suckering freely.

*S.*x *chenaultii*, Pink Snowberry. Very rare.

Ulex europaeus, Whin. Native; very common.

U.gallii, Western Gorse. Probably intro., very rare.

U.minor, Dwarf Gorse. Probably intro., very rare, N Queensferry.

Viburnum tinus, Laurustinus. Occasional in old estates.

Bryophyta: mosses, liverworts and hornworts

Bryophytes are common all over Britain although the drier east tends to have fewer species. This is true of Fife, which also suffers by being intensively cultivated and not having much high ground. Of about 1100 species in the UK, Fife probably has about 500 or roughly 45%. Little investigation of Fife's bryophytes was carried out until about 1850 when Charles Howie began collecting, resulting in the publication of his *The moss flora of Fife and Kinross* in 1889. Liverworts were not included, but this was rectified to an extent by one or two naturalists, chiefly William Evans, around the turn of the century. Thereafter not much field work was carried out until after 1960, when there was a resurgence of interest begun by Dr Helen Caldwell. This work updated, expanded and added to many of the earlier records and also brought to light several probable extinctions; nevertheless, many areas have not been revisited or indeed checked at all, so that there remains scope for considerably more recording to be done.

Musci: mosses

Sphagnopsida: bog-mosses

16 species recorded, all in *Sphagnum*, ranging from the common *S.cuspidatum* to the rare *S.magellanicum* and *S.papillosum*. With the drainage of many bogs and pools, both in past and recent years, they have declined considerably but may still be found in such places as Bankhead Moss and Moss Morran.

Andreaeopsida

Form blackish or dark red-brown patches on rocks, mainly in mountainous country.
Andeaea rupestris. On many of the lower hills.
A.rothii. Lomonds 1854, but not since.

Bryopsida

The majority of the mosses.

Tetraphidales

2 species, notably the rare *Tetrodontium brownianum.*

Polytrichales

Polytrichum: 10 species, including *P.commune*, a common plant of acid habitats.
Atrichum: 2 species.
Oligotrichum hercynicum. Possibly extinct.

Buxbaumiales, Archidiales

1 species of each.

Dicranales: fork-mosses (in part)

A large order, including:
Ditrichum: 3 species.

Ceratodon purpureus. Very common.
Dicranella: 8 species.
Dicranum: 8 species including two rare on Tentsmuir.
Campylopus: 5 species
Leucobryum glaucum. A distinctive species, declining on moors and bogs.

Fissidentales

Fissidens: 5 species, including the frequent *F.bryoides.*

Encalyptales

Encalypta: 4 species, including:
E.rhaptocarpa. Rare, on dunes.

Pottiales: screw-mosses (in part)

Tortula: 9 species including the very common *T.muralis.*
Pottia: 7 species, including the halophyte *P.heimii.*
Barbula: 11 species, including the widespread *B.fallax.*
Weissia: 3 species, including the tiny *W.controversa.*
Tortella: 4 species.

Grimmiales

Schistidium: 3 species, including the exclusively maritime *S.maritimum.*
Grimmia: 11 species, including the recently discovered *G.montana.*
Rhacomitrium: 8 species, including the unusual woolly moss, *R.lanuginosum.*
Ptychomitrium polyphylum. Local.

Funariales

11 species, including:

Funaria hygrometrica. Common on burnt and waste ground.
Splachnum: 2 rare species on dung on moors.

Bryales

Pohlia: 9 species.
Bryum: 22 species, including:
B.capillare. Abundant.
B.alpinum. I of May.
Mnium hornum. Very common in woodland.
Plagiomnium: 6 species.
Aulacomnium palustre. Wet places.
Philonotis fontana. Wet places.
P.calcarea. Wet places.
Amblyodon dealbatus. On dunes.

Orthotrichales: mostly epiphytic

Orthotrichum: 11 species.
Ulota: 3 species.
Zygodon: 3 species.

Isobryales:

includes:
Fontinalis antipyretica. Submerged willow moss.
Climacium dendroides. Damp shady places.
Thamnobryum alopecurum. Damp shady places.

Hookeriales, Thuidales

A small group mainly comprising 5 species of *Thuidium.*

Hypnobryales

Cratoneuron: 3 species.
Campylium: 4 species.
Amblystegium: 6 species.
Drepanocladius: 7 species including:

D.lycopodiodes. Tentsmuir; nationally rare.
D.vernicosus. Dumbarnie Links; nationally rare.
Isothecium: 3 species.
Homalothecium: 3 species.
Brachythecium: 8 species, including

B.rutabulum. Abundant.
B.plumosum. Very rare.
Eurynchium: 4 species.
Rhynchostegiella: 2 rare species.
Plagiothecium: 4 species.
Isopterygium: 2 species.
Taxiphyllum wissgrillii. Rare.
Hypnum: 4 species, including:

H.cupressiforme. Very common.
Rhytidiadelphus: 3 species, including:
R.squarrosus. Very common.
Hylocomium splendens. Very common.
Ptilium crista-castrensis. Common in woodland.

Hepaticae: liverworts

Liverworts range from tiny, leafy fronds that are easily over-looked amongst moss and grass, to prominent flat 'thalloid' fronds that can cover large areas of wet rocks.

Jungermanniales: leafy liverworts

87 species recorded of which the following are common:
Lepidozia reptans. On rotten wood and humus.
Calypogeia fissa. In bogs and acid soils.
C.muelleriana. On acid peaty banks.
Cephalozia bicuspidata. In woods.
Nowellia curvifolia. On decaying wood.
Barbilophozia floerkei. Rock ledges.
B.attenuata. Rotten wood.
Lophozia ventricosa. On old wood, acid soils.

Gymnocolea inflata. On acid heaths.
Nardia scalaris. Moorland.
Diplophyllum albicans. On acid soils.
Scapania compacta. Dry banks.
S.irrigua. Marshes.
S.undulata. Rocks in burns etc.
Lophocolea bidentata. On wet grass, walls etc.
L.cuspidata. On decaying logs, banks etc.
L.heterophylla. On decaying logs, sandy rocks.
Chiloscyphus polyanthos, var.*polyanthos.* On wet soil.
Plagiochila asplenoides. Wooded dens.
Radula complanata. Tree trunks, shady rocks.
Ptilidium ciliare. Moorland.
Porella obtusata. Exposed coastal rocks.
Frullania tamarisci. On ground, trees etc.

Metzgeriales: thalloid liverworts

15 species recorded of which the following are common:
Pellia epiphylla. Damp shady banks.
P.endiviifolia. Wet calcareous places.
Metzgeria furcata. On living trees, and rocks.

Marchantiales: thalloid liverworts

11 species recorded of which the following are common:
Lunularia cruciata. Garden paths etc.
Conocephalum conicum. Moist walls and rocks.
Marchantia polymorpha. Riverbanks, gardens etc.
Riccia sorocarpa. Arable and garden soil.

Anthocerotales: hornworts

Lobed green rosettes growing on damp soil.

Anthocerus punctatus. Rocky ledge, I of May.

Phaeocerus laevis ssp.*laevis.* On mud, I of May.

Algae: seaweeds etc.

A large group of plants in the sea, in fresh water and in damp places on land. Below are detailed those forming 'macro-scopic' plants, i.e. those with plant-like fronds or branches. Many other groups contain only microscopic forms (e.g. desmids and diatoms) or filamentous forms (e.g. the blacket-weeds such as *Spyrogyra*). The presence of the Gatty Marine Laboratory at St Andrews has ensured that Fife has been in the forefront of research and recording of marine algae. The *Fauna and flora of St Andrews Bay* (Laverock and Blackler 1974) listed 362 species of algae; although nominally dealing only with the waters around east Fife, in fact nearly every alga known in Fife is mentioned. More recent work has covered areas in the Firth of Forth including around the Isle of May.

Phaeophyta: brown seaweeds

Predominantly marine algae, mostly forming large fronds.

Ectocarpales

Forming branched filaments or encrusting, often on other algae; 31 species recorded, including:
Spongionema tomentosum. Tufts of filaments on wrack.
Ralfsia verrucosa. Purplish crust on rocks.

Dictyosiphonales

Small filamentous fronds on other seaweeds; 14 species recorded, including:
Dictyosiphon foeniculaceus. On other seaweeds, especially *Chordaria.*

Scytosiphonales

Tubular or spherical fronds; 5 species recorded, including:
Colpomenia peregrina. Thin, hollow spheres on other algae.
Scytosiphon lomentaria. Unbranched tubular fronds on rocks.

Desmarestiales

Large, leathery fronds.
Desmarestia aculeata. Sublittoral, perennial.
D.viridis. Smaller, annual.

Laminariales: kelp etc.

Chorda filum, Sea-lace. Cord-like fronds up to 3.5m.
C.tomentosa. Smaller and furry.
Laminaria digitata. Palmately branched, flat.
L.hyperborea. Branched fronds, in deeper water.
L.saccharina. Abundant at LW; unbranched, crinkly fronds.
Alaria esculenta. Greenish fronds with midribs; abundant offshore.

Tilopteridales

Tilopteris mertensii. In sandy pools.

Sphacelariales

Small tufts, mostly on other algae; 11 species recorded.

Dictyotales

Small, with flat, branched fronds.
Dictyota dichotoma. Mainly sublittoral.
Taonia atomaria. Sublittoral.

Fucales: wrack

The dominant, large brown seaweeds of the shore.
Ascophyllum nodosum, Knotted wrack. Midshore, including estuaries.
Fucus serratus, Serrated wrack. Mid-shore.
F.spiralis, Twisted wrack. Mid-shore, including salt-marshes.
F.vesicularis, Bladder-wrack. Abundant, including estuaries.
Pelvetia canaliculata. Upper shore.
Himanthalia elongata, Thongweed. Lower shore and offshore.
Halidrys siliquosa. Pools and offshore.

Rhodophyta: red algae

Predominantly marine algae, forming delicate thin fronds, tufts and calcified filaments and crusts.

Nemaliales

Small, tufted algae, many growing on other seaweeds; 17 species recorded.

Gigartinales

Fronds flat or thread-like; 14 species recorded, including:
Cystoclonium purpureum. Soft bushy tufts, abundant in rock pools.
Chondrus crispus, Carragheen. Common in lower pools and offshore.
Gigartina stellata. Common at LW; used to produce agar for culturing bacteria.

Cryptomeniales

Includes red algae with flat fronds as well as species forming crusts on rocks and on other seaweeds; 22 species recorded, including:
Dilsea carnosa. Large, flat fronds; in pools and amongst kelp.
Dumontia incrassata. Common annual in pools.
Corallina officinalis. Calcified,

segmented tufts; common in pools.

Lithothamnion lenormandii. Calcified crust on rocks in pools.

Rhodymeniales

Fronds leafy or cylindrical; 4 species recorded, including:

Rhodymenia palmata, Dulse. Common, especially on stems of kelp.

Lomentaria articulata. Common

on rock on lower shore; with beaded fronds.

Ceramiales

Diverse, including bushy tufts; 49 species recorded, including:

Ceramium rubrum. Common on other algae.

Callithamnion arbuscula. Common on shore.

Bostrychia scorpoides. On salt-marsh, under grass.

Polysiphonia lanosa. Tufts on wrack, especially *Ascophyllum.*

Goniotrichales

Goniotrichum alsidii. St Andrews, on other algae.

Bangiales

Fronds membranous or filamentous; 11 species recorded, including:

Porphyra umbilicalis, Purple laver. Common at all levels of shore.

Chlorophyta: green algae

Mostly microscopic in fresh water, some filamentous (including some of the blanket-weeds) and a few forming larger plants of characteristic form. Only the last are detailed below.

Ulotrichales

Flimsy flat fronds, tubular or filamentous; 18 species recorded, including:

Enteromorpha intestinalis. On rock and in pools, including salt-marsh.

Ulva lactuca, Sea-lettuce. On rocky shores and in salt-marsh.

U.rigida. On rock and on other seaweeds.

Monostroma grevillei. Widespread on shore, starting as hollow 'balloons' which become split.

Chaetophorales

Filamentous green algae, many in fresh water, others growing in or on seaweeds; 12 species recorded.

Acrosiphonales

Filamentous algae; some on other algae; 4 species recorded, including:

Acrosiphonia arcta. Common on sand-covered rocks, binding the sand.

Cladophorales

Filamentous green algae, both fresh-water and marine; 11 marine species recorded, including:

Cladophora rupestris. Dense tufts or turf-like swards.

Siphonales

Branched, sometimes feathery fronds.

Bryopsis plumosa. Feathery fronds, usually amongst mussels.

Codium fragile. Velvety cylindrical fronds, common in pools.

Charales: stoneworts

Fresh-water algae, resembling vascular plants; 6 species recorded, including:

Chara aspera, Rough stonewort. Town L, Dunfermline.

Nitella flexilis, Smooth stonewort. Widespread.

Tolypella nidifica, Bird's-nest stonewort. Rare.

Fungi

Fungi show every gradation from those with conspicuous fruiting bodies, e.g. the toadstools, to those that exist only as diffuse, microscopic threads (hyphae) in the soil etc. Only those groups that can be easily detected, if not always identified, in the field are included here.

Basidiomycetes

Includes the majority of fungi with large fruiting bodies, but also the less conspicuous rusts and smuts.

Hymenomycetes

Mushrooms, toadstools etc. with exposed spore-bearing surface; 496 species recorded in Fife.

Agaricales

With gills; 141 species recorded, including:
Agaricus campestris, Field mushroom. Common on grassland throughout.
Coprinus comatus, Shaggy ink-cap. On grass and disturbed ground.
Gymnopilus penetrans. Common on dead conifers.

Pluteales

Toadstools with gills; 21 species in Fife, including:
Pluteus cervinus. Common on dead wood.

Russulales

Toadstools with gills, often of a brittle texture; 63 species recorded, including:
Lactarius deliciosus, Saffron milk-cap. Common in pine woods, edible.
Russula emetica, Sickener. Common in pine woods; poisonous.

Tricholomatales

Toadstools with gills; 160 species recorded, including:
Amanita muscaria, Fly agaric. Common in birch and pine woods.
Armillaria mellea, Honey fungus. Common parasite of trees.
Lepista saeva, Common on meadows.

Boletales

Toadstools with pores instead of gills on the underside of the caps; 37 species recorded, including:
Boletus edulis, Cep. Common in coniferous woods.
Suillus luteus, Slippery Jack. Common in coniferous woods.

Cantharellales

Spores borne on gills or tooth-like projections; 17 species recorded, including:
Cantharellus cibarius. Chanterelle. Common in woods.
Hydnum repandum, Hedgehog fungus. Common in woods.

Fistulinales

Fistulina hepatica, Beefsteak fungus. Common on oak.

Ganodermatales

Woody brackets; 3 species recorded, including:
Ganoderma applanatum, Artist's fungus. Common on deciduous trees, esp. beech.

Gomphales

Erect, branching tufts.
Ramaria stricta. Uncommon on tree stumps.

Hericiales

2 species recorded, including:
Auriscalpium vulgare, Ear-pick fungus. On buried pine cones.

Hymenochaetales

Mostly small, bracket-shaped fungi; 4 species recorded, including:
Inonotus hispidus. Widespread on ash; parasitic.

Poriales

Bracket fungi; 27 species in Fife, including:
Polyporus squamosus, Dryad's saddle. A common parasite of deciduous trees.

Schizophyllales

2 species in Fife, including:
Schizophyllum commune, Split-gill. Uncommon, on dead wood.

Stereales

Flattened, leathery fungi, mostly on dead wood; 13 species recorded, including:
Stereum hirsutum. Common.

Thelephorales

4 species in Fife, including:
Thelephora terrestris, Earth fan. Common on sandy soil in conifer woods and heaths.

Gasteromycetes: puffballs etc.

Spore-bearing surface enclosed (exposed eventually in stink-horns).

Lycoperdales: puffballs

With rounded fruiting bodies on the ground; 11 species recorded, including:
Lycoperdon perlatum, Common puffball. Common in sandy woodland.
Langermannia gigantea, Giant puffball. Uncommon near hedges and woods.

Schlerodermatales

2 species recorded, including:
Scleroderma citrinum, Common earthball. Common in woods.

Phallales

Stinkhorns; 3 species in Fife, including:

Phallus impudicus, Stinkhorn. Common in woodland.
Mutinus caninus, Dog stinkhorn.

Heterobasidiomycetes: jelly fungi, rusts and smuts

Auriculariales: jelly fungi

Auricularia mesenterica, Tripe fungus. On dead wood.
Hirneola auricula-judea, Jew's ear. Common, especially on elder.

Darycymycetales

3 species recorded, including:
Calocera viscosa. Common on conifer stumps.

Tremellales

Convoluted fungi, many gelatinous; 5 species recorded, including:
Tremella mesenterica, Yellow brain fungus. Common on dead deciduous branches.

Tulasnellales

Uthatobasidium fusisporum.

Ascomycetes: cup-fungi etc.

Very variable, most with cup-shaped fruiting body, a small minority toadstool-like but without gills; the majority are associated with algae to form lichens and these are dealt with separately below. Yeasts and many common moulds also belong here.

Clavicipitales

Many parasitic on plants and insects; 6 species recorded, the best known being:
Claviceps purpurea. On grasses, the cause of ergot (St Anthony's fire).

Diaporthales

8 species recorded.

Diatrypales

6 species recorded, including:
Diatrype disciformis. On bark of dead wood, especially beech.

Dothideales

Many produce galls; 24 species recorded.

Elaphomycetales

Elaphomyces muricatus. Subterranean in the topsoil of pinewoods, rare.

Erysiphales:

Powdery mildews etc. Parasitic on plants; 19 species recorded.

Eurotiales

Amylocarpus encephaloides.

Gymnoascales

Onygena corvina.

Helotiales

Cup-shaped fungi, usually on dead wood; 51 species recorded, including:
Bulgaria inquinans, Black bulgar. Common on oak branches.

Hypocreales

Small, rounded, often colourful; 5 species recorded, including:
Nectria cinnabarina, Coral-spot. Common on dead wood, esp. sycamore.

Laboulbeniales

Parasitic on insects.
Laboulbenia vulgaris.

Pezizales: cup fungi and morels

With cup-shaped fruiting bodies on the ground; 27 species recorded, including:
Aleuria aurantia, Orange-peel fungus. Widespread in open areas.
Morchella esculenta. An edible morel found in woodland.

Polystigmatales

2 species in Fife.

Rhytismatales

Parasitic on plants; 6 species recorded, including:
Rhytisma acerinum, Tar-spot fungus. Common on sycamore.

Sordariales

3 species in Fife.

Sphaeriales

Hard, black or brown fruit bodies on decaying wood; 19 species recorded, including:
Xylaria hypoxylon, Candle-snuff. Common on dead wood.
Daldinia concentrica, Cramp-balls. Common on dead wood.

Taphrinales

Parasitic on plants; 5 species recorded, including:
Taphrina betulina. Causes witches' broom on birch.

Lichens

Most lichens prefer dry situations and clean air, and are very slow-growing. Their presence or absence is an indicator of air pollution and partly for this reason Fife is among the more poorly represented regions in Scotland. Early records are scarce, but collecting was carried out in the 1970s in Kirkcaldy District by Dr Helen Caldwell and in the Dunfermline area by Dr Brian Coppins, who has compiled an up-to-date list for Fife. This approaches 350 species and although not comprehensive is a good baseline for future field work. The following species are common.

Acarospora fuscata. Acid rocks and stonework.

Anisomeridium nyssaegenum. Trees.

Buellia punctata. Trees and coastal rocks.

Caloplaca citrina. Calcareous rocks and stonework, and trees.

C.marina. Coastal rocks.

Candelariella aurella. Calcareous rocks and stonework.

C.vitellina. Rocks and tree bases.

Catillaria chalybeia. Acid rocks and stonework.

Cladonia macilenta. Acid rocks, tree bases and stumps.

Diploicia canescens. Trees, rocks and stonework.

Evernia prunastri. Trees.

Hypogymnia physodes. Trees, acid rocks, stonework.

Lecania erysibe agg. Calcareous rocks and stonework.

Lecanora albescens. Calcareous rocks and stonework.

L.conizaeoides. Trees, timberwork and acid stonework.

L.dispersa agg. Trees and rocks.

L.expallens. Trees and timberwork.

L.muralis. Rocks and stonework.

L.polytropa. Acid rocks and walls.

L.rupicola. Acid rocks and walls.

Lecidella scabra. Rocks, walls and trees.

Lepraria incana. Trees and acid rocks and walls.

Micarea prasina. Trees and stumps.

Ochrolechia parella. Rocks and walls.

Parmelia glabratula spp.*fuliginosa.* Acid rocks and stonework.

P.saxatilis. Trees, acid rocks and stonework.

P.sulcata. Trees, rocks and stonework.

Phaeophyscia orbicularis. Trees, rocks and stonework.

Physcia adscendens. Trees, rocks and stonework.

P.caesia. Calcareous or nutrient-enriched rocks and stonework.

P.tenella. Trees, rocks and stonework.

Placynthiella icmalea. Acid turf and shaded sandstone.

Platismatia glauca. Trees and acid rocks and walls.

Porpidia crustulata. Acid rocks and walls.

P.soredizodes. Acid rocks and walls.

P.tuberculosa. Acid rocks and walls.

Protoblastenia rupestris. Calcareous rocks and stonework.

Pyrenocollema halodytes. On barnacles.

Rhizocarpon reductum. Acid rocks and stonework.

Rinodina gennarii. Calcareous stonework and sea-shore rocks.

Scoliciosporum chlorococcum. Branches, heather stems etc.

S.umbrinum. Acid rocks and stonework.

Trapelia coarctata. Acid rocks and stonework.

T.involuta. Acid rocks and stonework.

Verrucaria maura. Coastal rocks.

V.mucosa. Coastal rocks.

V.muralis. Calcareous stonework.

V.nigrescens. Calcareous rocks and stonework.

Xanthoria parietina. Trees and rocks.

Slime-moulds: myxomycota

These exist as a slimy wet scum on dead wood and soil but under certain conditions produce fruiting bodies – 'sporangia' – which are often distinctive and colourful. In Fife 51 species have been recorded and probably many more occur.

Mammals

Most species of mammals have had a very direct interaction with human activity in one way or another: as objects of the hunt for food, furs or sport; as pests threatening his domestic stock, crops and stored food; or simply taking benign advantage of his structures as in the case of bats roosting in houses or barns. For distribution in Fife see Corbet and Smout (1994).

Non-marine mammals

Hedgehog, *Erinaceus europaeus.* Widespread.

Mole, *Talpa europaea.* Widespread.

Common shrew, *Sorex araneus.* Widespread.

Pygmy shrew, *S.minutus.* Widespread.

Water shrew, *Neomys fodiens.* Local in wetlands but probably under-recorded.

Pipistrelle, *Pipistrellus pipistrellus.* Widespread.

Long-eared bat, *Plecotus auritus.* Widespread.

Daubenton's bat, *Myotis daubentonii.* Local, especially wetlands.

Natterer's bat, *M.nattereri.* Local.

Rabbit, *Oryctolagus cuniculus.* Widespread, a serious pest of agriculture.

Brown hare, *Lepus europaeus.* Widespread but patchy, mainly on arable land.

[Mountain hare, *L.timidus.* Doubtfully on the Cleish Hills.]

Red squirrel, *Sciurus vulgaris.* Widespread in conifer and mixed woodlands but in danger of replacement by grey squirrel.

Grey squirrel, *S.carolinensis.* Widespread in all but pure coniferous woodlands.

Bank vole, *Clethrionomys glareolus.* Widespread in woodland and hedgerows.

Field vole, *Microtus agrestis.* Widespread in rough grass.

Water vole, *Arvicola terrestris.* Local and perhaps declining in wetlands.

[Musk rat, *Ondatra zibethicus.* Escapes from fur farms established in 1930s, subsequently exterminated.]

Wood mouse, *Apodemus sylvaticus.* Widespread and abundant in woods, hedges and gardens, and, especially in winter, in houses.

House mouse, *Mus musculus.* Widespread in towns, villages and farms.

Harvest mouse, *Micromys minutus.* Known from one site, the northernmost in Britain.

Common rat, *Rattus norvegicus.* Widespread pest in towns and on farms.

Ship rat, *R.rattus.* Present only on Inchcolm.

Fox, *Vulpes vulpes.* Widespread.

[Pine marten, *Martes martes.* Extinct since c.1878.]

Stoat, *Mustela erminea.* Widespread.

Weasel, *M.nivalis.* Widespread.

[Polecat, *M.putorius.* Extinct since 1880s.]

Mink, *M.vison.* Widespread in wetlands.

Badger, *Meles meles.* Widespread.

Otter, *Lutra lutra.* Sparse, on all rivers.

Feral cat, *Felis catus.* Widespread.

[Wildcat, *F.silvestris.* Extinct since c.1903.]

Roe deer, *Capreolus capreolus.* Widespread.

[Red deer, *Cervus elaphus.* Extinct probably since 17th C.; now only on deer farms.]

Sika deer, *C.nippon.* In Devilla Forest (since 1890) and on Lomonds.

[Fallow deer, *Dama dama.* Introduced probably in Mediaeval period; extinct since late 18th C?]

Marine mammals

Common seal, *Phoca vitulina.* Widespread, breeding at Tentsmuir and Eden Estuary.

Grey seal, *Halichoerus grypus.* Widespread, breeding on I of May.

Common porpoise, *Phocoena phocoena.* Widespread.

Bottle-nosed dolphin, *Tursiops truncatus.* Off E and S coast in summer.

White-beaked dolphin, *Lagenorhynchus albirostris.* Regular offshore.

White-sided dolphin, *L.acutus.* Regular offshore.

Common dolphin, *Delphinus delphis.* Sporadic offshore.

Striped dolphin, *Stenella coeruleoalba.* 3 stranded Aberdour Feb.1996.

Risso's dolphin, *Grampus griseus.* Occasional offshore.

Long-finned pilot whale, *Globicephala melas.* Regular offshore.

Killer whale, *Orcinus orca.* Sporadic offshore.

False killer whale, *Pseudorca crassidens.* 7 stranded near St Andrews 1935.

Bottle-nosed whale, *Hyperoodon ampullatus.* C.50 in Tay 1937; 1 in Forth 1978.

Sowerby's beaked whale, *Mesoplodon bidens.* Occasionally stranded.

Sperm whale, *Physeter macrocephalus.* Occasional offshore.

Minke whale, *Balaenoptera acutorostrata.* Occasional offshore.

Fin whale, *B.physalis.* Last stranded 1903 (Kirkcaldy).

Blue whale, *B.musculus.* One stranded Aberdour 1858.

Birds

The birds are by far the most intensively recorded group of animals. Of the 318 species listed here (excluding extinct, doubtful and escaped birds) 111 breed regularly and a further 19 breed occasionally, or have bred, or have been suspected of breeding (in 20th century). For further detail see Smout (1986) and the annual *Fife Bird Report*, (Fife Bird Club) and *Isle of May Bird Observatory Report* (Isle of May Trust). Terminology used:

Vagrant: fewer than five records ever.

Occasional: five records or more, but still very rare.

Rare: not every year.

Regular: recorded yearly, even if only once.

Uncommon: very small numbers.

Resident: around all year and breeding.

Red-throated diver, *Gavia stellata*. Common winter visitor and passage migrant; occasional in summer.

Black-throated diver, *G.arctica*. Regular winter visitor and passage migrant.

Great northern diver, *G.immer*. Regular winter visitor in small numbers.

White-billed diver, *G.adamsii*. Winter vagrant.

Little grebe, *Tachybaptus ruficollis*. Common resident on lochs, often moving to coast in winter.

Great crested grebe, *Podiceps cristatus*. Present all year; breed on many lochs and winters in the Forth and off Tentsmuir.

Red-necked grebe, *P.grisegena*. Regular winter visitor in small numbers.

Slavonian grebe, *P.auritus*. Regular winter visitor, especially off Tentsmuir and in Largo Bay.

Black-necked grebe, *P.nigricollis*. Regular winter visitor; have bred in small numbers.

Black-browed albatross, *Diomedea melanophris*. Vagrant.

Fulmar, *Fulmarus glacialis*. Common resident on coastal cliffs; one inland colony in quarry.

Cory's shearwater, *Calonectris diomedea*. Occasional visitor to the Forth.

Great shearwater, *Puffinus gravis*. Occasional visitor to the Forth.

Sooty shearwater, *P.griseus*. Regular visitor, especially on autumn passage.

Manx shearwater, *P.puffinus*. Regular visitor, sometimes in large numbers in summer.

Mediterranean shearwater, *P.yelkouan*. Occasional autumn visitor to the Forth.

Storm petrel, *Hydrobates pelagicus*. Tape-lured regularly in August to I of May and elsewhere in small numbers.

Leach's petrel, *Oceanodroma leucorhoa*. Occasional visitor to the Forth.

Gannet, *Sula bassana*. Common; breed on the Bass Rock (Lothians).

Cormorant, *Phalacrocorax carbo*. Locally common on the coast and inland; breed on the Haystack and other islands in the Forth.

Shag, *P.aristotelis*. Present all year, sometimes in thousands; breed in numbers on the I of May.

Bittern, *Botaurus stellaris*. Rare visitor; last record 1925.

Little bittern, *Ixobrychus minutus*. Spring vagrant.

Night heron, Nycticorax nycticorax. Occasional; most but perhaps not all from the free-living colony in Edinburgh Zoo.

Little egret, *Egretta garzetta*. Vagrant.

Grey heron, *Ardea cinerea*. Common resident.

White stork, *Ciconia ciconia*. Vagrant.

Glossy ibis, *Plegadis falcinellus*. Vagrant; not since 19th century.

Spoonbill, *Platalea leucorodia*. Rare visitor.

Mute swan, *Cygnus olor*. Common resident.

Bewick's swan, *C.columbianus*. Regular winter visitor in small numbers, especially to central Fife and the Lomond Hill reservoirs.

Whooper swan, *C.cygnus*. Common winter visitor in varying numbers.

Bean goose, *Anser fabalis*. Uncommon winter visitor and passage migrant; has become rarer since 19th century when it was common.

Pink-footed goose, *A.brachyrhynchus*. Winter visitor in thousands; Cameron reservoir can be a spectacular roost site.

White-fronted goose, *A.albifrons*. Uncommon winter visitor; both Greenland *A.a.flavirostris* and European *A.a.albifrons* races occur.

Greylag, *A.anser*. Common winter visitor.

Snow goose, *A.caerulescens*.

Irregular winter visitor; origins uncertain.

Canada goose, *Branta canadensis*. Regular passage migrant; otherwise rare.

Barnacle goose, *B.leucopsis*. Regular winter visitor in small numbers, and passage migrant.

Brent goose, *B.bernicla*. Regular winter visitor in small numbers, especially to the Eden estuary; was formerly more numerous; both dark-bellied *B.b.bernicla* and light-bellied *B.b.hrota* races occur.

Ruddy shelduck, *Tadorna ferruginea*. Vagrant; origins uncertain.

Shelduck, *T.tadorna*. Local resident and common winter visitor.

Mandarin, *Aix galericulata*. Rare feral visitor to lochs; all probably descendants of a naturalised population established in the R Tay at Perth.

Wigeon, *Anas penelope*. Common winter visitor; has bred.

American wigeon, *A.americana*. Rare winter visitor; origins uncertain.

Gadwall, *A.strepera*. Breed in small numbers; common on passage, rare in winter.

Teal, *A.crecca*. Uncommon breeder, common on passage and in winter; the N American race (green-winged teal *A.c.carolinensis*) is an occasional winter visitor.

Mallard, *A.platyrhynchos*. Abundant resident; winter in large numbers.

Pintail, *A.acuta*. Regular winter visitor in small numbers, especially to the Eden; has bred.

Garganey, *A.querquedula*. Uncommon summer visitor.

Shoveler, *A.clypeata*. Breeds locally; commoner on passage.

Red-crested pochard, *Netta rufina*. Rare visitor to lochs, mostly in autumn; origins uncertain.

Pochard, *Aythya ferina*. Resident; in winter may gather in large flocks.

Ring-necked duck, *A.collaris*. Vagrant; origins uncertain.

Tufted duck, *A.fuligula*. Common resident.

Scaup, *A.marila*. Declining winter visitor; flocks in St Andrews Bay and off Levenmouth dwindling since new sewage works installed; occasional on lochs.

Eider, *Somateria mollissima*. Common resident; breed in large numbers on I of May; winter in very large numbers, especially in Tay estuary.

King eider, *S.spectabilis*. Casual winter visitor; may return year after year to same location, e.g. off Tayport.

Long-tailed duck, *Clangula hyemalis*. Winter visitor in varying numbers on coast; occasional inland.

Common scoter, *Melanitta nigra*. Winter visitor, sometimes in large numbers, especially off Tentsmuir, St Andrews and in Largo Bay; small numbers in summer; has bred.

Surf scoter, *M.perspicillata*. Has become a regular winter visitor to St Andrews Bay and Largo Bay in small numbers since 1980s

Velvet scoter, *M.fusca*. Winter visitor; locally common especially off Tentsmuir, St

Andrews Bay and Largo Bay.

Goldeneye, *Bucephala clangula*. Common winter visitor both at sea and inland, rare in summer.

Smew, *Mergus albellus*. Regular winter visitor in very small numbers.

Red-breasted merganser, *M.serrator*. Locally common throughout the year; does not breed.

Goosander, *M.merganser*. Uncommon throughout the year; a flock moults off Tayport in August.

Ruddy duck, *Oxyura jamaicensis*. Has increased substantially in recent years; now breed on several lochs; rare in winter; feral origin from English escapes.

Honey buzzard, *Pernis apivorus*. Occasional, mostly at I of May.

Red kite, *Milvus milvus*. Rare visitor at any time of the year; numbers have increased since reintroduction schemes elsewhere in Scotland.

White-tailed eagle, *Haliaeetus albicilla*. Vagrant, not since 19th century.

Marsh harrier, *Circus aeruginosus*. Uncommon summer visitor and passage migrant; increasing.

Hen harrier, *C.cyaneus*. Regular passage migrant and winter visitor in very small numbers, probably decreasing.

Goshawk, *Accipiter gentilis*. Rare resident, from reintroduced feral population.

Sparrowhawk, *A.nisus*. Common resident.

Buzzard, *Buteo buteo*. Has colonised Fife since 1980s

and become a widespread resident.

Rough-legged buzzard, *B.lagopus.* Winter vagrant.

Golden eagle, *Aquila chrysaetos.* Vagrant.

Osprey, *Pandion haliaetus.* Regular summer visitor and passage migrant in small numbers.

Kestrel, *Falco tinnunculus.* Common resident and passage migrant.

Red-footed falcon, *F.vespertinus.* Vagrant.

Merlin, *F.columbarius.* Winter visitor in varying numbers; probably declining.

Hobby, *F.subbuteo.* Uncommon passage migrant.

Gyrfalcon, *F. rusticolus.* Vagrant, record only accepted for I of May.

Peregrine, *F.peregrinus.* Winter visitor and passage migrant; has bred.

Red grouse, *Lagopus lagopus.* Resident on Lomonds and Cleish Hills; probably declining.

Black grouse, *Tetrao tetrix.* Resident in very small numbers in W Fife.

Capercaillie, *T.urogallus.* Introduced to Tulliallan 19th century, now extinct there; a small population at Tentsmuir throughout the 1980s is now thought to be extinct.

[Chuckar/red-legged partridge, *Alectoris chukar/rufa.* Birds, usually hybrids, are released for sporting purposes throughout Fife.]

Grey partridge, *Perdix perdix.* Common resident; was declining, but sensitive management by farmers such as the introduction of 'beetle-banks' has greatly increased population.

Quail, *Coturnix coturnix.* Uncommon summer visitor.

Pheasant, *Phasianus colchicus.* Abundant resident; population greatly increased by commercially bred birds.

Water rail, *Rallus aquaticus.* Uncommon breeder; winter visitor in small numbers.

Spotted crake, *Porzana porzana.* Occasional; has bred at Tentsmuir.

[Baillon's crake, *P.pusilla.* A tiny crake caught in Tentsmuir in January 1889 was considered this species but little crake, *P.parva,* cannot be ruled out.]

Corncrake, *Crex crex.* Used to be a widespread breeding summer visitor; now only occasional on passage.

Moorhen, *Gallinula chloropus.* Locally common resident.

Coot, *Fulica atra.* Abundant resident.

Crane, *Grus grus.* Vagrant.

Little bustard, *Tetrax tetrax.* Vagrant; not since 19th century.

Oystercatcher, *Haematopus ostralegus.* Common resident, passage migrant and winter visitor.

Avocet, *Recurvirostra avosetta.* Vagrant.

Stone curlew, *Burhinus oedicnemus.* Vagrant.

Little ringed plover, *Charadrius dubius.* Very rare; has bred at least once in recent years.

Ringed plover, *C.hiaticula.* Local and declining breeder; common passage migrant and winter visitor.

Kentish plover, *C.alexandrinus.* Vagrant.

Dotterel, *C.morinellus.* Historically reported as a regular visitor; now rare passage migrant.

Golden plover, *Pluvialis apricaria.* Common winter visitor and passage migrant; bred regularly in W Fife last century and up to 1938 at Earlshall.

Grey plover, *P.squatarola.* Locally common winter visitor.

Lapwing, *Vanellus vanellus.* Common but declining resident and winter visitor.

Knot, *Calidris canutus.* Common winter visitor, locally abundant.

Sanderling, *C.alba.* Local winter visitor to sandy shores.

Little stint, *C.minuta.* Uncommon passage migrant, mainly in autumn.

Temminck's stint, *C.temminckii.* Occasional.

Pectoral sandpiper, *C.melanotos.* Vagrant.

Curlew sandpiper, *C.ferruginea.* Uncommon passage migrant, mainly in autumn.

Purple sandpiper, *C.maritima.* Winter visitor and passage migrant on rocky shores.

Dunlin, *C.alpina.* Common winter visitor and passage migrant; bred at Tentsmuir till 1937.

Broad-billed sandpiper, *Limicola falcinellus.* Vagrant.

Buff-breasted sandpiper, *Tryngitis subruficollis.* Vagrant.

Ruff, *Philomachus pugnax.* Winter visitor in small numbers and passage migrant, mainly in autumn.

Jack snipe, *Lymnocryptes minimus.* Winter visitor and passage migrant in very small numbers.

Snipe, *Gallinago gallinago.* Breeds locally, winter visitor and passage migrant.

Great snipe, *G.media.* Vagrant.

Long-billed dowitcher, *Limnodromus scolopaceus.* Vagrant.

Woodcock, *Scolopax rusticola.* Resident and passage migrant.

Black-tailed godwit, *Limosa limosa.* Winter visitor, mainly to the Eden Estuary.

Bar-tailed godwit, *L.lapponica.* Winter visitor, locally common.

Whimbrel, *Numenius phaeopus.* Passage migrant.

Curlew, *N.arquata.* Fairly common resident; commoner winter visitor and passage migrant.

Spotted redshank, *Tringa erythropus.* Uncommon passage migrant; occasional in winter.

Redshank, *T.totanus.* Breed in small numbers; common winter visitor and passage migrant.

Greenshank, *T.nebularia.* Passage migrant in small numbers; a few winter.

[Lesser yellowlegs, *T.flavipes.* Vagrant; only one record, probably correct, but not accepted by the Rarities Committee.]

Green sandpiper, *T.ochropus.* Regular on autumn passage in small numbers.

Wood sandpiper, *T.glareola.* Occasional passage migrant.

Common sandpiper, *Actitis hypoleucos.* Breed in small numbers, common passage migrant.

Turnstone, *Arenaria interpres.* Common winter visitor and passage migrant.

Wilson's phalarope, *Phalaropus tricolor.* Vagrant.

[Red-necked phalarope, *P.lobatus.* There are no authenticated records, though it is mentioned for 'Fifeshire' last century in at least one historical account without further detail.]

Grey phalarope, *P.fulicarius.* Occasional autumn and winter visitor.

Pomarine skua, *Stercorarius pomarinus.* Regular passage migrant in small numbers; occasional in winter.

Arctic skua, *S.parasiticus.* Regular passage migrant, especially in autumn; our commonest skua.

Long-tailed skua, *S.longicaudus.* Uncommon passage migrant in autumn.

Great skua, *S.skua.* Passage migrant, mainly in autumn.

Mediterranean gull, *Larus melanocephalus.* Occasional visitor.

Little gull, *L.minutus.* Uncommon and erratic throughout the year, may occur in large flocks.

Sabine's gull, *L.sabini.* Occasional autumn visitor.

Bonaparte's gull, *L.philadelphia.* Vagrant.

Black-headed gull, *L.ridibundus.* Resident; abundant in winter.

Common gull, *L.canus.* Common winter visitor and passage migrant; a few present all year.

Lesser black-backed gull, *L.fuscus.* Common summer visitor, breed on the islands in the Forth and in W Fife; some winter.

Herring gull, *L.argentatus.* Common resident, and common winter visitor from Scandinavia.

Iceland gull, *L.glaucoides.* Uncommon visitor, mostly in winter.

Glaucous gull, *L.hyperboreus.* Uncommon visitor, mostly in winter.

Great black-backed gull, *L.marinus.* Breed in small numbers on offshore islands; common winter visitor.

Kittiwake, *Rissa tridactyla.* Breed in numbers on I of May, present throughout the year.

Ivory gull, *Pagophila eburnea.* Vagrant.

Caspian tern, *Sterna caspia.* Vagrant.

Sandwich tern, *S.sandvicensis.* Common summer visitor and passage migrant; some breed; rare in winter.

Roseate tern, *S.dougallii.* Uncommon summer visitor, breed on off-shore islands in small numbers.

Common tern, *S.hirundo.* Summer visitor, breed in varying numbers, especially on I of May and other islands.

[Sooty tern, *S.fuscata.* Vagrant. A record of bird that was photographed and identified as this species on I of May in 1989 was initially rejected by the Rarities Committee on the grounds that it could have been a Bridled Tern; however the record is now being reconsidered.]

Arctic tern, *S.paradisaea.* Summer visitor, breed in varying numbers, especially on I of May and other islands.

Little tern, *S.albifrons.* Uncommon summer visitor, breed locally in small numbers.

Black tern, *Chlidonias niger.* Regular passage migrant in small numbers, especially in autumn.

White-winged black tern, *C.leucopterus.* Vagrant.

Guillemot, *Uria aalge.* Present

all year, breed in large numbers on I of May and other islands.

Razorbill, *Alca torda.* Present all year, breed on I of May and other islands.

[Great auk, *Pinguinus impennis.* Extinct; remains excavated recently on I of May, date of origin as yet unknown.]

Black guillemot, *Cepphus grylle.* Bred on I of May in early 19th century; recently recorded in the Forth throughout the year in very small numbers.

Little auk, *Alle alle.* Regular winter visitor, sometimes in large numbers.

Puffin, *Fratercula arctica.* Breed on I of May and other islands in the Forth; uncommon in winter.

Pallas's sandgrouse, *Syrrhaptes paradoxus.* Vagrant; two invasions 19th century, when bred on one occasion; two birds recorded on I of May in May 1975.

Rock dove (& feral pigeon), *Columba livia.* The true rock dove, ancestor to the feral pigeon, used to breed, but by end of 19th century the wild strain was considered rare and by 1935 no pure rock doves could be found in Fife.

Stock dove, *C.oenas.* Widespread resident, following colonisation in 19th century.

Woodpigeon, *C.palumbus.* Abundant resident; even more abundant winter visitor.

Collared dove, *Streptopelia decaocto.* Widespread resident, probably declined since its first influx in 1960s.

Turtle dove, *S.turtur.* Occasional on passage, has wintered and may have bred.

Rose-ringed parakeet, *Psittacula krameri.* Vagrant, feral origin.

Cuckoo, *Cuculus canorus.* Passage migrant; breed locally in small numbers; has probably declined.

Barn owl, *Tyto alba.* Breed locally in small numbers.

Scops owl, *Otus scops.* Vagrant.

[Eagle owl, *Bubo bubo.* Vagrant; not since 18th century, origins uncertain.]

Snowy owl, *Nyctea scandiaca.* Vagrant.

Little owl, *Athene noctua.* Vagrant; from introduced population in England.

Tawny owl, *Strix aluco.* Common resident.

Long-eared owl, *Asio otus.* Local resident and passage migrant.

Short-eared owl, *A.flammeus.* Winter visitor and passage migrant; has bred.

[Tengmalm's owl, *Aegolus funereus.* A bird in St Andrews January 1886 was probably of this species.]

Nightjar, *Caprimulgus europaeus.* Bred regularly last century and recorded as 'increasing' at Burntisland in 1926; now very rare visitor.

Swift, *Apus apus.* Common summer visitor; breed widely.

Little swift, *A.affinis.* Vagrant.

Chimney swift, *Chaetura pelagica.* Vagrant.

Kingfisher, *Alcedo atthis.* Local resident in very small numbers; more coastal in winter.

Hoopoe, *Upupa epops.* Occasional passage migrant.

Wryneck, *Jynx torquilla.* Occasional passage migrant.

Green woodpecker, *Picus viridis.* Local but widespread resident.

Great spotted woodpecker, *Dendrocopos major.* Local but widespread resident; occasional passage migrant from Scandinavia.

Short-toed lark, *Calandrella brachydactyla.* Vagrant; only at I of May.

Wood lark, *Lullula arborea.* Formerly occasional visitor; only one recent record.

Skylark, *Alauda arvensis.* Present all year; common breeder and passage migrant, variable numbers in winter.

Shore lark, *Eremophila alpestris.* Occasional winter visitor and passage migrant.

Sand martin, *Riparia riparia.* Summer visitor and passage migrant, breed locally in some numbers.

Swallow, *Hirundo rustica.* Common summer visitor and passage migrant, breed throughout Fife.

Red-rumped swallow, *H.daurica.* Vagrant; only at I of May.

House martin, *Delichon urbica.* Common summer visitor and passage migrant, breed throughout Fife.

Richard's pipit, *Anthus novaeseelandiae.* Occasional autumn migrant.

Tawny pipit, *A.campestris.* Occasional, mainly on I of May.

Olive-backed pipit, *A.hodgsoni.* Vagrant; only at I of May.

Tree pipit, *A.trivialis.* Uncommon passage migrant; breed locally in small numbers.

Meadow pipit, *A.pratensis.* Common breeding bird and passage migrant; a few winter.

Red-throated pipit, *A.cervinus.* Vagrant; only at I of May.

Rock pipit, *A.petrosus.* Common resident and winter visitor. The Scandinavian race *A.p.littoralis* occur in small numbers in winter.

Water pipit, *A.spinoletta.* Vagrant; only at I of May.

Yellow wagtail, *Motacilla flava.* Regular passage migrant in small numbers; has bred. The following races have been recorded: *M.f.flavissima; M.f.flava; M.f.cinereocapilla* and *M.f.thunbergii.*

Citrine wagtail, *M.citreola.* Vagrant; only on I of May.

Grey wagtail, M.cinerea. Local resident.

Pied wagtail, *M.alba yarrellii.* Common resident and passage migrant; the European sub-species *M.a.alba* or white wagtail occurs regularly on passage.

Waxwing, *Bombycilla garrulus.* Erratic winter visitor from Scandinavia.

Dipper, *Cinclus cinclus.* Local resident. The Scottish race *gularis* is sedentary, but the black-bellied race *C.c.cinclus* from Scandinavia is an occasional winter visitor.

Wren, *Troglodytes troglodytes.* Abundant resident.

Dunnock, *Prunella modularis.* Abundant resident and regular passage migrant.

Robin, *Erithacus rubecula.* Abundant breeding bird, winter visitor and passage migrant.

Thrush nightingale, *Luscinia luscinia.* Occasional passage migrant.

Nightingale, *L.megarhynchos.* Occasional passage migrant.

Bluethroat, *L.svecica.* Regular on spring passage; less frequent in autumn.

Red-flanked bluetail, *Tarsiger cyanurus.* Vagrant.

Black redstart, *Phoenicurus ochruros.* Regular passage migrant, occasional winter visitor; has probably bred on I of May.

Redstart, *P.phoenicurus.* Regular passage migrant; has bred.

Whinchat, *Saxicola rubetra.* Regular passage migrant; breed locally in small numbers.

Stonechat, *S.torquata.* Passage migrant and formerly bred in small numbers, occasional in winter; the Siberian races *S.t.maura/stejnegeri* occur on rare occasions in the autumn.

Wheatear, *Oenanthe oenanthe.* Common passage migrant; breed in small numbers.

Pied wheatear, *O.pleschanka.* Vagrant.

Black-eared wheatear, *O.hispanica.* Vagrant, only at I of May.

Siberian thrush, *Zoothera sibirica.* Vagrant, only at I of May.

Ring ouzel, *Turdus torquatus.* Regular but uncommon passage migrant.

Blackbird, *T.merula.* Abundant resident, passage migrant and winter visitor from Scandinavia.

Fieldfare, *T.pilaris.* Common passage migrant and winter visitor.

Song thrush, *T.philomelos.* Present all year; common breeder, passage migrant and winter visitor from Scandinavia.

Redwing, *T.iliacus.* Common passage migrant and winter visitor.

Mistle thrush, *T.viscivorus.* Local resident, occasional passage migrant.

Lanceolated warbler, *Locustella lanceolata.* Vagrant; only at I of May.

Grasshopper warbler, *L. naevia.* Uncommon passage migrant and summer visitor, breed locally in small numbers.

River warbler, *L.fluviatilis.* Vagrant.

Aquatic warbler, *Acrocephalus paludicola.* Occasional autumn passage migrant on I of May; no recent records.

Sedge warbler, *A.schoenobaenus.* Common breeding summer visitor and passage migrant.

Paddyfield warbler, *A.agricola.* Vagrant, only at I of May.

Blyth's reed warbler, *A.dumetorum.* Vagrant, only at I of May.

Marsh warbler, *A.palustris.* Occasional, mainly on I of May.

Reed warbler, *A.scirpaceus.* Occasional migrant, usually in autumn.

Great reed warbler, *A.arundinaceus.* Vagrant.

Olivaceous warbler, *Hippolais pallida.* Vagrant, only at I of May.

Booted warbler, *H.caligata.* Vagrant, only at I of May.

Icterine warbler, *H.icterina.* Uncommon but regular passage migrant.

Melodious warbler, *H.polyglotta.* Vagrant, only at I of May.

Subalpine warbler, *Sylvia cantillans.* Occasional passage migrant, mostly at I of May.

Sardinian warbler, *S.melanocephala.* Vagrant, only at I of May.

Barred warbler, *S.nisoria.* Regular but uncommon migrant on autumn passage.

Lesser whitethroat, *S.curruca.* Passage migrant, breed in very small numbers.

Whitethroat, *S.communis.*
Common passage migrant
and summer visitor; breed
widely.

Garden warbler, *S.borin.*
Common passage migrant
and summer visitor; breed
locally.

Blackcap, *S.atricapilla.*
Common passage migrant
and summer visitor, breed
locally; winter in small
numbers.

Greenish warbler, *Phylloscopus
trochiloides.* Occasional
passage migrant.

Arctic warbler, *P.borealis.*
Occasional autumn passage
migrant, mostly at I of May.

Pallas's warbler, *P.proregulus.*
Rare passage migrant in
autumn.

Yellow-browed warbler,
P.inornatus. Regular autumn
passage migrant in very
small numbers.

Radde's warbler, *P.schwarzi.*
Occasional autumn passage
migrant, mostly at I of May.

Dusky warbler, *P.fuscatus.*
Vagrant; only at I of May.

Wood warbler, *P.sibilatrix.*
Regular passage migrant,
recent breeding possible.

Chiffchaff, *P.collybita.* Common
passage migrant and
summer visitor; breed in
increasing numbers;
occasionally winters.

Willow warbler, *P.trochilus.*
Abundant passage migrant
and breeding summer visitor.

Goldcrest, *Regulus regulus.*
Common resident; abundant
passage migrant.

Firecrest, *R.ignicapillus.*
Occasional passage migrant,
now almost regular.

Spotted flycatcher, *Muscicapa
striata.* Passage migrant and
summer visitor; breed
locally in small numbers.

Red-breasted flycatcher,
Ficedula parva. Occasional
passage migrant, mainly in
autumn.

Pied flycatcher, *F.hypoleuca.*
Regular passage migrant.

Bearded tit, *Panurus biarmicus.*
Vagrant.

Long-tailed tit, *Aegithalos
caudatus.* Widespread local
resident.

Willow tit, *Parus montanus.*
Uncertain status; some old
records may have referred
to blackcaps; however
recent reports indicate that
it may occasionally winter
in W Fife and may have
bred.

Coal tit, *P.ater.* Common
resident.

Blue tit, *P.caeruleus.* Abundant
resident.

Great tit, *P.major.* Common
resident.

Treecreeper, *Certhia familiaris.*
Widespread local resident.

Golden oriole, *Oriolus oriolus.*
Occasional passage migrant;
has bred.

Isabelline shrike, *Lanius
isabellinus.* Vagrant.

Red-backed shrike, *L.collurio.*
Regular passage migrant in
small numbers.

Lesser grey shrike, *L.minor.*
Vagrant.

Great grey shrike, *L.excubitor.*
Uncommon passage migrant
and winter visitor.

Woodchat shrike, *L.senator.*
Vagrant.

Jay, *Garrulus glandarius.* Local
resident.

Magpie, *Pica pica.* Common
resident in W Fife,
occasional elsewhere.

Chough, *Pyrrhocorax
pyrrhocorax.* Said to have
occurred in the 19th
century; two recent records
are probably of escapes.

Jackdaw, *Corvus monedula.*
Common resident.

Rook, *C.frugilegus.* Common
resident.

Crow, *C.corone.* Carrion crow,
C.c.corone is a common
resident; hooded crow,
C.c.cornix was probably the
commonest crow in Fife last
century, now only
occasional and records
mainly of hybrids.

Raven, *C.corax.* Uncommon
visitor; formerly bred and
may be attempting to
re-establish itself.

Starling, *Sturnus vulgaris.*
Abundant resident.

Rose-coloured starling,
S.roseus. Occasional visitor.

House Sparrow, *Passer
domesticus.* Common
resident, perhaps declining.

Tree sparrow, *P.montanus.*
Local resident.

Chaffinch, *Fringilla coelebs.*
Abundant resident.

Brambling, *F.montifringilla.*
Regular passage migrant
and winter visitor in
varying numbers.

Greenfinch, *Carduelis chloris.*
Abundant resident.

Goldfinch, *C.carduelis.*
Widespread resident.

Siskin, *C.spinus.* Winter visitor
and passage migrant; breed
in small numbers.

Linnet, *C.cannabina.* Common
resident; winters in varying
numbers.

Twite, *C.flavirostris.* Winter
visitor in very small
numbers.

Redpoll, *C.flammea.* Local
resident and winter visitor
in small numbers.

Arctic redpoll, *C.hornemanni.*
Vagrant.

Crossbill, *Loxia curvirostra.* Occasional breeder in varying
numbers, following periodic

eruptions. Historical records of the Scottish crossbill, *L.scotica* in Fife may refer to the parrot crossbill, as the two species were separated at a later date.

Parrot crossbill, *L.pytyopsittacus.* Vagrant.

Common (scarlet) rosefinch, *Carpodacus erythrinus.* Occasional visitor; increasing.

Pine grosbeak, *Pinicola enucleator.* Vagrant, only at I of May.

Bullfinch, *Pyrrhula pyrrhula.* Local resident; occasional winter visitor from Scandinavia.

Hawfinch, *Coccothraustes coccothraustes.* Occasional visitor.

Lapland bunting, *Calcarius lapponicus.* Irregular passage migrant and winter visitor in very small numbers.

Snow bunting, *Plectrophenax nivalis.* Passage migrant and winter visitor in small numbers; has declined.

Yellowhammer, *Emberiza citrinella.* Common resident.

Cirl bunting, *E.cirlus.* Vagrant, only at I of May.

Ortolan bunting, *E.hortulana.* Occasional passage migrant, mostly at I of May.

Rustic bunting, *E.rustica.* Occasional passage migrant, only at I of May.

Little bunting, *E.pusilla.*

Occasional passage migrant, mostly at I of May.

Yellow-breasted bunting, *E.aureola.* Occasional passage migrant, mostly at I of May.

Reed bunting, *E.schoeniclus.* Locally common resident and passage migrant.

Black-headed bunting, *E.melanocephala.* Vagrant, origins uncertain.

Corn bunting, *Millaria calandra.* Locally common resident, now confined almost entirely to north and east Fife.

A number of other species that are commonly kept in captivity have been recorded. Some are obvious escapes, like the black swan and sulphur-crested cockatoos, but others are not so obvious:

White pelican, *Pelecanus onocrotalus.* One bird, probably of this species, on I of May was regarded as an escape.

Greater flamingo, *Phoenicopterus ruber.* Seen on various occasions, probably all escapes.

Chilean flamingo, *P.chilensis.* Several sightings, all regarded as escapes.

Black swan, *Cygnus atratus.* Several sightings of this Australian species, often kept in captivity; all escapes.

Red-breasted goose, *Branta ruficollis.* Only one record, of a ringed escape.

Lanner, *Falco biarmicus.* A species kept by local falconers.

Saker, *F.cherrug.* A falconer's species; some sightings also of reared hybrids.

Golden pheasant, *Chrysolophus pictus.* Vagrant; regarded as an escape.

Daurean redstart, *Phoenicurus auroreus.* One record from I of May; regarded as an escape (natural range E Asia).

Verditer flycatcher, *Eumyas thalassina.* One record from Fife Ness was regarded as an escape (natural range India and SE Asia).

Pallas's rosefinch, *Carpodacus roseus.* One record from I of May was regarded as an escape (natural range E Asia).

Chestnut bunting, *Emberiza rutila.* Only recorded from I of May, regarded as an escape (natural range E Asia).

Red-headed bunting, *E.bruniceps.* Only at I of May, regarded as an escape (natural range from E Russia to China, Iran to India).

Lazuli bunting, *Passerina amoena.* Only at I of May, regarded as an escape (natural range N America).

Amphibians and reptiles

All are predatory. The amphibians need fresh water for breeding but travel widely on land. For atlas of distribution in Fife see Smout and Pritchard (1995).

Common frog, *Rana temporaria.* Widespread.

Common toad, *Bufo bufo.* Widespread.

Smooth newt, *Triturus vulgaris.* Widespread but sparse.

Palmate newt, *T.helveticus.* The commonest newt.

Great crested newt, *T.cristatus.* Local, ponds.

Common lizard, *Lacerta vivipara.* Possibly extinct in Fife.

Slow worm, *Anguis fragilis.*
Formerly in W Fife,
possibly extinct.

Adder, *Vipera berus.* Formerly
in S and E, possibly extinct.
[Grass snake, *Natrix natrix.*
Occasional escapes.]

Leathery turtle, *Dermochelys
coriacea.* Vagrant in N Sea;
singles in Forth 1967, 1985
and 1997.

Fish

The fishes of the Firth of Forth
were documented in considerable detail by Richard Parnell
(1838), and much has been added
over the years including recent
studies of fish trapped at the in-
take of Longannet power
station. 159 species are listed
here. Names follow Wheeler
(1992).

Agnatha: jawless fish

Eel-like animals lacking true
jaws or bony skeleton; parasites
and scavangers on fish; in both
sea and fresh water.
Myxine glutinosa, Hagfish.
Marine; sometimes attack
cod.
Petromyzon marinus, Sea
lamprey. Breed in FW;
migrate to sea; now rare.
Lampetra fluviatilis, River
lamprey. Breed in FW;
migrate to sea.
L.planeri, Brook lamprey. FW
only; do not feed as adults.

Chondrichthyes: sharks,
dogfishes and rays

Marine fish with cartilaginous
skeletons; most of the larger
sharks generally stay well offshore.
Lamniformes: sharks with two
dorsal fins and an anal fin.
Lamna nasus, Porbeagle.
Occasional offshore.
Cetorhinus maximus, Basking
shark. Occasional offshore;
rare vagrant in Forth.
Alopias vulpinus, Thresher
shark. Usually far offshore,
occasional near coast.

Scyliorhinus canicula, Dogfish.
Common just offshore.
S.stellaris, Nursehound.
Occasional.
Prionace glauca, Blue shark.
Occasional; one washed up
N of Fife Ness 1991.
Galeorhinus galeus, Tope.
Young inshore.
Mustelus asterias, Starry
smooth hound. Occasional.

Squaliformes: sharks with two
dorsal fins and no anal fin.
Echinorhinus brucus, Bramble
shark. A 19th C record at
Elie.
Squalus acanthias, Spurdog.
Common, especially in deep
water.
Somniosus microcephalus,
Greenland shark. Occasional.
Squatina squatina, Monkfish.
Rare.

Rajiformes: rays and skates
Bottom-living.
Raja batis, Skate. Common in
deep water.
R.circularis, Sandy ray. Rare,
deep water.
R.clavata, Thornback ray.
Common; shallow water.
R.fullonica, Shagreen ray.
Occasional.
R.montagui, Spotted ray. Rare.
R.naevus, Cuckoo ray.
Occasional.
R.radiata, Starry ray.
Common; deep water.
[*R.oxyrinchus,* Long-nosed
skate. Doubtful.]
[*R.alba,* White skate. Old
records in Forth; doubtful.]

Dasyatis pastinaca, Sting ray. A
few records.

Osteichthyes: bony fish

The majority of fish.
Marine bony fish. Those that
migrate between fresh and salt
water are listed below with the
freshwater species (p.187).

Acipenseriformes
Acipenser sturio, Sturgeon. Rare
and dwindling.

Anguilliformes: eels
Muraena helena, Moray eel.
One record from mouth of
Tay, 1901.
Conger conger, Conger eel.
Shore pools to deep water.

Clupeiformes
Alosa alosa, Allis shad. Tay,
now rare.
A.fallax, Twaite shad. Tay,
now rare.
Clupea harengus, Herring.
Plankton-feeder, pelagic;
common in Forth.
Sardina pilchardus, Pilchard.
Erratic, occasionally
numerous in Forth.
Sprattus sprattus, Sprat.
Common in estuaries,
especially in winter.
Engraulis encrasicolus, Anchovy.
Rare.

Salmoniformes
Argentina sphyraena, Argentine.
Deep water.
Osmerus eperlanus, Sparling
(Smelt). Enters Tay and
Inner Forth estuary to
spawn; fishery based at
Newburgh.

Stomiformes
Maurolicus muelleri, Pearlside.
    Deep water, but
    occasionally stranded.

Gadiformes
Brosme brosme, Torsk. Rare.
Ciliata mustela, Five-bearded
    rockling. Common in pools
    on shore.
Enchelyopus cimbrius,
    Four-bearded rockling.
    Deep water; rare.
Gadus morhua, Cod.
    Widespread, in shallow and
    deep water; important
    nursery areas in Tay and
    Forth.
Gaidropsarus vulgaris,
    Three-bearded rockling.
    Occasional.
Melanogrammus aeglefinus,
    Haddock. Common on
    bottom 40–300m; a major
    component of the
    commercial catch.
Merlangius merlangus, Whiting.
    Shallow sandy water; a
    major commercial species.
Micromesistius poutassou, Blue
    whiting. Rare.
Molva molva, Ling. Deep
    water.
Phycis blennoides, Greater
    fork-beard. Young inshore.
Pollachius pollachius, Pollack.
    Common inshore.
P.virens, Saithe (Podles).
    Common offshore.
Trisopterus esmarki, Norway
    pout. Shallow water.
T.luscus, Bib. Common offshore.
T.minutus, Poor-cod. Common
    offshore; spawn in estuaries.
Raniceps raninus, Tadpole-fish.
    Occasional; shallow water.
Merluccius merluccius, Hake.
    Mainly deep water.

Lophiiformes
Lophius piscatorius, Angler
    (Monk). Bottom, at all
    depths.

Gobiesociformes
Diplecogaster bimaculata,
    Two-spotted clingfish. Rare;
    I of May.

Cyprinodontiformes
Belone belone, Garfish. Rare.
Scomberesox saurus, Skipper.
    Oceanic; occasional
    irruptions inshore.

Atheriniformes
Atherina presbyter, Sand-smelt.
    Kincardine.

Lampriformes
Lampris guttatus, Opah. Rare
    vagrant.
Regalecus glesne, Oar-fish. Rare
    vagrant.
Trachipterus arcticus, Deal fish.
    Rare, deep water.

Zeiformes
Zeus faber, Dory. Rare.
Capros aper, Boar-fish. Rare;
    near I of May.

Gasterosteiformes
Spinachia spinachia, Fifteen-
    spined stickleback. Rock
    pools and shallows,
    including estuaries.

Syngnathiformes
Entelurus aequoreus, Snake
    pipefish. Oceanic; rare in
    Forth.
[*Hippocampus ramulosus* ?,
    Seahorse. Four dead on
    beach, Elie, c.1980.]
Nerophis lumbriciformis, Worm
    pipefish. Rocky shores.
Syngnathus acus, Greater
    pipefish. Resident in Forth.
S.rostellatus, Nilsson's pipefish.
    Forth Estuary.
[*S.typhle*, Deep-snouted
    pipefish. Doubtful.]

Scorpaeniformes
Helicolenus dactylopterus,
    Blue-mouth. Rare, deep
    water.

Sebastes norvegicus, Redfish.
    Rare; deep water.
Aspitrigla cuculus, Red gurnard.
    Occasional.
A.obscura, Long-finned
    gurnard. Rare vagrant.
Eutrigla gurnardus, Grey
    gurnard. Common, migrates
    into estuaries in summer.
Trigla lucerna, Tub gurnard.
    Rare.
Myoxocephalus scorpius,
    Bull-rout. Common; pools
    and shallow water including
    estuaries.
Taurulus bubalis, Sea-scorpion.
    Common, rock-pools.
T.lilljeborgi, Norway bullhead.
    Deep water, occasional.
Triglops murrayi, Moustache
    sculpin. Rare.
Agonus cataphractus,
    Hook-nose. Common
    inshore.
Cyclopterus lumpus,
    Lumpsucker. Common,
    spawning on shore and in
    shallow water in spring.
Liparis liparis, Sea-snail.
    Shallow water, including
    estuaries.
L.montagui, Montagu's
    sea-snail. Common,
    rock-pools and shallow
    water.

Perciformes
Dicentrarchus labrax, Bass.
    Scarce; inshore in spring.
Serranus cabrilla, Comber. Rare
    vagrant from south.
Trachurus trachurus, Scad.
    Occasional.
Brama brama, Ray's bream.
    Erratic immigrant from
    Atlantic; sometimes
    stranded after storms.
Pagellus bogaraveo, Red
    sea-bream. Occasional.
Spondyliosoma cantharus, Black
    sea-bream. Rare vagrant.

Argyrosomus regius, Meagre. Rare vagrant from south.

Mullus surmuletus, Red mullet. Rare vagrant from south.

Chelon labrosus, Thick-lipped grey mullet. Rare.

Liza auratus, Golden grey mullet. Shoal 1935, St Andrews.

L.ramada, Thin-lipped grey mullet. Scarce.

Crenilabrus melops, Corkwing wrasse. Common in rock pools.

Ctenolabrus rupestris, Goldsinny. Rare, Forth.

Labrus bergylta, Ballan wrasse. Scarce; on rocky bottoms.

L.mixtus, Cuckoo wrasse. Shallow water; young occasional in pools.

Zoarces viviparus, Eelpout. Common, rock-pools and estuaries.

Chirolophis ascanii, Yarrell's blenny. Scarce.

Lumpenus lampretaeformis, Snake blenny. Rare, deep water in Forth.

Pholis gunnellus, Butterfish. Common, rock-pools.

Anarhichas lupus, Wolf-fish. Common, deep water.

Echiichthys vipera, Lesser weaver. Shallow water, on sand.

Trachinus draco, Greater weaver. Deep water, on sand.

Lipophrys pholis, Shanny. Common, rock-pools.

[*Parablennius gattorugine*, Tompot blenny. Old records, doubtful.]

Ammodytes marinus, Raitt's sand-eel. Offshore; abundant but over-fished.

A.tobianus, Sand-eel. Inshore, including estuaries.

Hyperoplus lanceolatus, Greater sand-eel. Common inshore.

Callionymus lyra, Dragonet. Common deep water; rare inshore.

Aphia minuta, Transparent goby. Occasional inshore.

Crystallogobius linearis, Crystal goby. Scarce, mid-water, Tay.

[*Gobius paganellus*, Rock goby. Old record, probably erroneous.]

Gobiusculus flavescens, Two-spotted goby. Amongst seaweed, on and off shore.

Pomatoschistus microps, Common goby. Pools on estuarine shores.

P.minutus, Sand goby. Common in shallow water on sand.

P.pictus, Painted goby. Rare; Tay.

Katsuwonus pelamis, Oceanic bonito. Oceanic; rare vagrant inshore.

Sarda sarda, Bonito. Rare vagrant.

Scomber scombrus, Mackerel. Common, in shoals, pelagic.

Thunnus thynnus, Blue-fin tunny. Common offshore; rare at coast.

Xiphias gladius, Swordfish. Rare vagrant.

Centrolophus niger, Blackfish. Vagrant from deep water.

Pleuronectiformes: flatfishes.

Lepidorhombus whiffiagonis, Megrim (Sail-fluke). Occasional, deep water.

Phrynorhombus norvegicus, Norwegian topknot. Rare.

Scophthalmus maximus, Turbot. Occasional.

S.rhombus, Brill. Common, shallow water on sand.

Zeugopterus punctatus, Topknot. Occasional.

Glyptocephalus cynoglossus, Witch. Deep water in Forth.

Hippoglossoides platessoides, Long rough dab. Common, including estuaries.

Hippoglossus hippoglossus, Halibut. Occasional.

Limanda limanda, Dab. Common inshore on sand.

Microstomus kitt, Lemon sole. Common, deeper water; an important component of the commercial catch.

Pleuronectes flesus, Flounder. Common, including estuaries, occasionally in fresh water.

P.platessa, Plaice. Common in shallow water, especially on sand.

Buglossidium luteum, Solenette. Common, moderate depths.

Solea solea, Sole. Common, shallow water.

Tetraodontiformes

Mola mola, Sunfish. Occasional oceanic vagrant.

Freshwater bony fish (including those that migrate between fresh and salt water; shad and flounders also enter fresh water to a limited extent.)

Anguilla anguilla, Eel. Widespread, arriving from the sea as young 'elvers' in spring and returning to sea to spawn and die.

Cyprinus carpio, Carp. Introduced, including Kinghorn L.

Gobio gobio, Gudgeon. Introduced and established in one pond in N Fife.

Phoxinus phoxinus, Minnow. Widespread in lochs, rivers and burns.

[*Scardinus erythrophthalmus*, Rudd. Introduced; current status uncertain.]

Tinca tinca, Tench. Introduced to ponds.

Rutilus rutilus, Roach. Lochs and sluggish rivers.

Barbatula barbatula, Stone

loach. Widespread in clean flowing water.

Esox lucius, Pike. Predator on other fish; in many lochs and reservoirs.

Oncorhynchus mykiss, Rainbow trout. Introduced (from N America) to many lochs and reservoirs but do not normally breed successfully.

Salmo salar, Salmon. Migrate through Forth and Tay estuaries; breed in Eden.

S.trutta, Trout. In all clear rivers and lochs, both resident populations and migrating 'sea-trout' which enter fresh water to breed.

Thymallus thymallus, Grayling. Introduced to R Eden.

Gasterosteus aculeatus, Three-spined stickleback. Widespread in burns, lochs and coastal water.

[*Pungitius pungitius*, Nine-spined stickleback. Old records; need confirmation.]

Gymnocephalus cernuus, Ruffe. Recently introduced from L Lomond.

Perca fluviatilis, Perch. Widespread in lowland lochs and rivers.

Invertebrates

CHORDATA (other than vertebrates)

Urochordata: tunicates, sea-squirts etc.

Colonial or solitary, filter-feeding marine invertebrates with tadpole-like larvae; all but the planktonic species remain fixed to rocks or seaweed as adults, many in rock-pools and on the lower shore.

Colonial sea-squirts

Clavelina lepadiformis. LW - offshore; OF,S.

Polyclinum aurantium. Offshore; I of May.

Sidnyum turbinatum. LW - offshore; OF,S.

Diplosoma listerianum. On and offshore, on algae and under stones; OF,S.

Botrylloides leachi. Common in kelp zone; OF,S.

Botryllus schlosseri. LW, especially amongst kelp holdfasts; OF,S.

Non-colonial sea-squirts

Ciona intestinalis. LW - offshore, on rocks; OF,S.

Corella parallelogramma. Offshore; I of May.

Ascidia conchilega. In pools; S.

Ascidiella scabra. LW - deep water; OF,S.

Dendrodoa grossularia. Common on and offshore; IF,OF,S.

Pelonaia corrugata. Offshore, in mud and sand; OF,S.

Molgula complanata. LW - shallow water; S.

Eugyra arenosa. Offshore on sand; OF,S.

Planktonic tunicates

Oikopleura dioica. Abundant, remaining tadpole-like as adults; S.

Fritillaria borealis. Common; S.

Salpa fusiformis. Abundant; S.

Cephalochordata: lancelets

Active, fish-like, marine invertebrates; only one species in British seas.

Branchiostoma lanceolatum, Lancelet or amphioxus. In stomachs of cod; S.

Hemichordata: acorn-worms

Marine worms with gill-slits, in sand and mud.

Glossobalanus marginatus. Offshore; OF.

ECHINODERMATA: ECHINODERMS

Wholly marine invertebrates that do not enter estuaries to any extent. Slow-moving but mostly predatory; large and moderately well recorded. Many of the offshore species can be found washed up on beaches after storms.

Asteroidea: starfish

All species are listed.

Astropecten irregularis. Offshore; OF,S.

Luidia ciliaris. Offshore on sand; I of May.

L.sarsi. Offshore on mud; S.

Hippasteria phryngiana. Offshore; OF,S.

Asterina gibbosa. Offshore; OF.

Crossaster papposus, Common sun-star. LW - offshore; OF,S.

Solaster endeca, Purple sun-star. Offshore; OF,S.

Henricia sanguinolenta. LW - offshore; OF,S.

Asterias rubens, Common starfish. Shore and offshore, abundant; OF,S,T.

Leptasterias muelleri. LW; S.

Ophiuroidea: brittle-stars

10 species, mostly offshore, but *Amphipholis squamata* is common under stones on shore.

Echinoidea: sea-urchins

All species are listed.

Echinus acutus. In deep water; S.

E.esculentus, Common sea-urchin. LW - offshore on hard ground; OF,S.

Psammechinus miliaris. Rocky
shores and offshore; OF,S.
Strongylocentrotus droebachiensis.
Mid-shore - offshore; OF.
Echinocyamus pusillus, Green
sea-urchin. Deep water, in
coarse sand; OF,S.
Spatangus purpureus, Purple
heart-urchin. Offshore in
coarse sand; S.
Echinocardium cordatum,
Sea-potato. On and offshore,
buried in sand, abundant;
OF,S.
E.flavescens. Offshore, rare;
OF,S.
Brissopsis lyrifera. Offshore; I of
May.

Holothurioidea: sea cucumbers

9 species recorded, mostly offshore but two occur around LW.

UNIRAMIA: INSECTS ETC.

Insecta (hexapoda): insects

By far the most abundant and
diverse group of invertebrates;
at least 2300 species have been
recorded in Fife and many more
are likely to occur.

Thysanura: bristletails

Active, wingless insects.
Lepisma saccharina, Silverfish.
Widespread indoors.
Petrobius brevistylis.
Widespread on sea-cliffs.
P.maritimus. I of May.

Diplura: two-tailed bristletails

Small white, wingless insects;
common in topsoil; 5 species
have been recorded, all in the
genus *Campodea,* but identification is difficult.

Collembola: springtails

Tiny insects that are often very
abundant in the leaf-litter, feed-

ing on fungi etc. The 43 species
recorded in Fife mostly derive
from Carpenter and Evans
(1899).

Ephemeroptera: mayflies

Insects with aquatic nymphs,
mainly herbivorous, and very
short-lived flying adults; 11
species recorded but several
more probably occur out of the
47 known in Britain.

Odonata: damselflies and dragonflies

Predators, both as larvae in fresh
water and as adults, which often
travel far from water. Fife atlas
by Smout and Kinnear (1993a).
Azure damselfly, *Coenagrion
puella.* Local in C & W Fife.
Common blue damselfly,
Enallagma cyathigerum.
Widespread.
Large red damselfly,
Pyrrhosoma nymphula.
Widespread but local.
Blue-tailed damselfly, *Ischnura
elegans.* Widespread.
Emerald damselfly, *Lestes
sponsa.* Widespread except S
coast.
Common hawker, *Aeshna
juncea.* Local, at ponds.
Golden-ringed dragonfly,
Cordulegaster boltonii. Rare
vagrant.
Four-spotted chaser, *Libellula
quadrimaculata.* Rare vagrant.
Black darter, *Sympetrum danae.*
Local at small pools.
Red-veined darter,
S.fonscolombei. Vagrant from
continent at I of May.
Common darter, *S.striolatum.*
Tentsmuir only.

Plecoptera: stoneflies

Insects with aquatic nymphs,
mostly herbivorous, some of the
larger predatory; mainly in
stony rivers and lochs; 19

species recorded – two or three
others might occur.

Orthoptera: grasshoppers etc.

These five are the only species
likely to occur in Fife; all but the
first feed on grass.
Tetrix undulata, Common
ground-hopper. Widespread
on dunes and in woodland,
feeding on moss and algae.
Omocestus viridulus, Common
green grasshopper.
Widespread; long grass.
Chorthippus brunneus, Field
grasshopper. Abundant on
coastal grassland, local
elsewhere.
C.parallelus, Meadow
grasshopper. Normally
flightless; only at Tentsmuir.
Myrmeleotettix maculatus,
Mottled grasshopper. Local;
short dry grass.

Dermaptera: earwigs

Omnivores; capable of flying but
rarely do so.
Forficula auricularia, Common
earwig (clip-shears).
Widespread and abundant.
Labia minor, Lesser earwig.
Recorded at Pettycur 1901;
[usually in dung or
compost].

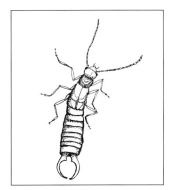
Common earwig

Dictyoptera: cockroaches etc.

Ground-living scavengers; none indigenous in Scotland.

Blatta orientalis, Common cockroach. Local indoors, including greenhouses.

Psocoptera: bark-lice

Small insects, with or without wings, living amongst vegetation, especially on the bark of trees; feed on pollen, fungi, algae etc. Poorly known; the 10 species recorded are probably a small proportion of those present. Other species live in stored foodstuffs, bird nests etc.

Mallophaga: biting lice

External parasites of birds and mammals, feeding on feathers, fur and skin; 33 species recorded on birds but many more are likely to occur. Only one record from a mammal, *Trichodectes retusus* on a weasel.

Anoplura: sucking lice

Blood-sucking external parasites of mammals; several additional species probably occur.

Echinophthirus horridus. On common seals.

Haemodipsus lyriocephalus. On brown hares.

Hoplopleura acanthopus. On field voles.

Pediculus humanus, Human head and body lice. Widespread.

Polyplax serrata. On wood mice.

P.spinulosa. On rats.

Pthirus pubis, Pubic louse. Local.

Hemiptera: bugs

Insects with sucking mouthparts, feeding on plants and/or animals. Poorly recorded in Fife.

Heteroptera (terrestrial). The majority are plant-feeders but some are predators and some are both. The only site in Fife that has been intensively studied is Tentsmuir Point with 90 species (Campbell, 1980), with casual records from elsewhere.

Acanthosomidae and Pentatomidae: shieldbugs

Dolycoris baccarum, Sloebug. Pettycur.

Elasmostethus interstictus, Birch shieldbug. Tentsmuir [birch].

Elasmucha grisea, Parent bug. Tentsmuir [birch].

Piezodorus lituratus, Gorse shieldbug. Cullaloe, Tentsmuir [gorse, feed on seeds].

Pentatoma rufipes, Forest bug. Tentsmuir [prey on caterpillars].

Picromerus bidens. Tentsmuir [woodland].

Rhacognathus punctatus. Tentsmuir [heaths, prey on heather beetles].

Lygaeidae: ground bugs; mostly dull-coloured, seed-eating bugs; 11 species recorded.

Berytinidae

Berytinus signoreti. Kincraig [legumes].

Piesmidae

Piesma quadratum, Beet leaf bug. Tentsmuir [saltmarsh].

Tingidae: lacebugs

Acalypta nigrina. Tentsmuir [moss].

A.parvula. Tentsmuir.

Derephysia foliacea, Ivy lacebug. Tentsmuir.

Tingis cardui, Spear thistle lacebug. Tentsmuir.

Reduviidae

Coranus subapterus, Heath assassin bug. Tentsmuir [heaths].

Nabidae

Nabis ferus, Field damsel bug. Tentsmuir [grassland predator].

Nabicula flavomarginata, Broad damsel bug. Tentsmuir [grass].

Cimicidae: flower bugs and bed-bugs

Anthocoris confusus. Tentsmuir, Kemback [woods].

A.nemoralis. Tentsmuir, Elie [woods].

A.nemorum, Common flower bug. Widespread.

A.sarothamni, Broom flower bug. Tentsmuir [broom].

Acompocoris pygmaeus. Tentsmuir [conifers].

Cimex lectularius, Bedbug. Sucks human blood; local.

Miridae: mirid or capsid bugs. The largest family of heteropteran bugs, with 60 species recorded in Fife, on all kinds of vegetation.

Dipsocoridae. Small bugs found on wet ground.

Ceratocombus coleoptratus. Tentsmuir, Dumbarnie Links [amongst moss].

Saldidae: shore bugs. Small bugs found in marshes, including salt-marshes; 6 species recorded.

Heteroptera (aquatic). In a wide variety of fresh-water habitats; 29 species recorded in Fife out of 45 in Scotland. Most of the following have been recorded since 1990.

Hydrometridae

Hydrometra stagnorum, Water-measurer. Otterston L.

Veliidae

Microvelia reticulata. Kilconquhar L, Gilston Pond.

Velia caprai. Widespread.
V.saulii. Clatto Res.

Gerridae: pond-skaters; 5 species of *Gerris* recorded.

Nepidae
Nepa cinerea, Water-scorpion. Kilconquhar L, Black L (Cleish).

Notonectidae: back-swimmers
Notonecta glauca,
    Water-boatman. Common.

Corixidae: diving bugs; 19 species recorded. The most widespread are *Callicorixa prae-usta* and *Sigara falleni.*

Homoptera
All are sap-suckers. The following represent a tiny proportion of the species likely to be present.

Cercopidae: froghoppers
Philaenus spumarius, Common spittle-bug. Widespread.

Cicadellidae: leafhoppers. Jumping bugs with long hind legs; 6 species recorded.

Psyllidae: jumping plant-lice Aphid-sized jumping bugs; 4 species recorded.

Pseudococcidae: scale insects
Chnaurococcus subterraneus. In ants' nest.
Rhizoecus halophilus. I of May.

Orthezidae
Arctorthezia cataphracta.
    Lomonds.

Aphididae: aphids
The familiar greenfly and blackfly; poorly recorded – only 18 species out of about 500 in Britain, including the following:
Brevicoryne brassicae.
    Widespread on crucifers.
Macrosiphum euphorbiae.
    Widespread on potatoes.

Myzus persicae. On brassicas and potatoes.

Adelgidae: aphids
Adelges abietis, Green spruce aphid. Widespread on conifers.

Pemphigidae: aphids
Forda formicaria. I of May, in ants' nests [on grass roots].
Paracletus cimiciformis. In ants' nest.

Thysanoptera: thrips (thunder-flies)

Tiny insects feeding on plant sap and on fungal hyphae and spores; can form troublesome swarms in hot weather; 11 species recorded in Fife, many more are likely to occur.

Neuroptera: lacewings

Larvae and most adults predatory, feeding mainly on aphids. A further 5 or 6 species are likely to be present.

Coniopterygidae; tiny insects easily mistaken for white-flies.
Conwentzia pineticola. One old record at St Andrews; [pine].

Hemerobiidae: brown lacewings; 11 species recorded.

Chrysopidae: green lacewings; 7 species recorded. *Chrysoperla carnea* is abundant and often hibernates in houses.

Megaloptera: alderflies

Large flies with predatory, aquatic larvae.
Sialis fuliginosa. Eden.
S.lutaria. Eden, Birnie L.

Mecoptera: scorpionflies and snow-fleas

Scavangers, adult scorpionflies visiting flowers. Only four species in Britain.

Panorpa communis. One record.
P.germanica. 2 sites.
Boreus hyemalis, Snow flea.
    Lomonds; Tentsmuir dunes.

Lepidoptera: butterflies and moths

Butterflies

Butterflies are by far the best recorded of the insects and include both resident and migrant species. 17 species breed regularly in Fife; a few more are regular or sporadic migrants. Fife atlas by Smout and Kinnear (1993b).

Pieridae
Clouded yellow, *Coleas croceus.* Eruptive immmigrant; may have bred.
Brimstone, *Gonepteryx rhamni.* Rare vagrant.
Large white, *Pieris brassicae.* Widespread; common pest on brassicas.
Small white, *P.rapae.* Widespread; caterpillars on wild and cultivated crucifers.
Green-veined white, *P.napi.* Widespread, usually the commonest white butterfly away from cultivation.
Orangetip, *Anthocharis cardamines.* Scarce; has recolonized Fife since 1983.

Lycaenidae
Green hairstreak, *Callophrys rubi.* Scarce: N & W Fife; larvae on blaeberry and *Erica.*
Small copper, *Lycaena phlaeas.* Widespread; larvae on sorrels and docks.
[Sooty copper, *L.tityrus.* Vagrant ?; one near Kincardine in 1960.]
Northern brown argus, *Aricia artaxerxes.* Two colonies on S coast; larvae on rockrose.
Common blue, *Polyommatus*

icarus. Widespread; larvae on bird's-foot trefoil.

Small blue, *Cupido minimus.* Rare on S coast, perhaps now extinct; larvae on kidney vetch.

Nymphalidae
Red admiral, *Vanessa atalanta.* Immigrant, arriving in spring and breeding on nettles.

Camberwell beauty, *Nymphalis antiope.* Rare vagrant, one recorded 1996.

Painted lady, *Cynthia cardui.* Immigrant, scarce in spring, increasingly frequent in autumn after breeding on thistles.

Small tortoiseshell, *Aglais urticae.* Widespread and abundant; larvae on nettles.

Peacock, *Inachis io.* Rare immigrant.

[Comma, *Polygonia c-album.* Extinct.]

[Pearl-bordered fritillary, *Boloria euphrosyne.* Extinct since 1930s.]

Small pearl-bordered fritillary, *B.selene.* Scarce local resident; caterpillars on marsh violet.

Dark green fritillary, *Argynnis aglaja.* Abundant Tentsmuir, local elsewhere; larvae on violets.

Marsh fritillary, *Eurodryas aurinia.* One old record at Falkland.

Grayling, *Hipparchia semele.* Confined to Tentsmuir; caterpillars of this and all following nymphalid species feed on grass.

Meadow brown, *Maniola jurtina.* Widespread and abundant.

Small heath, *Coenonympha pamphilus.* Widespread.

Large heath, *C.tullia.* Only on Cleish Hills.

Ringlet, *Aphantopus hyperantus.* Widespread except W Fife; expanding.

[Speckled wood, *Pararge aegeria.* Extinct.]

[Wall Brown, *Lasiommata megera.* Extinct.]

Danaidae
Monarch, *Danaus plexippus.* Rare vagrant from N America.

Moths
Names follow Emmet (1991) with minor changes. Larval food plants are those recorded in Fife. 674 species recorded in Fife.

Micropterigidae
Small day-flying moths that feed on pollen.
Micropteryx aruncella. Widespread.
M.aureatella. Widespread.

Eriocraniidae
Small moths with leaf-mining larvae, mostly associated with birch; 5 species of *Eriocrania* recorded.

Hepialidae: swift moths
Larvae feed on roots.
Hepialus fusconebulosa. Widespread in open woodland.
H.humuli. Widespread on rough ground.
H.lupulinus. Common.
H.sylvina. Local in open woodland.

Nepticulidae: pygmy moths
Very small moths (wingspan under 7 mm), most with leaf-mining larvae; 32 species recorded, including the very common *Stigmella aurella* on bramble.

Incurvariidae
Small day-flying moths, many with larvae starting as leaf-miners; 11 species recorded.

Heliozelidae
Very small day-flying moths; 3 species of *Heliozela* recorded.

Zygaenidae: burnet moths
Zygaena filipendulae, Six-spot burnet. Widespread on coast, larvae on *Lotus.*

Psychidae
Small moths with wingless females and larvae – 'bag-worms' – living in portable cases.
Dahlica lichenella. Widespread, larval cases on tree trunks.

Tineidae
Small moths with larvae feeding on dry material in birds' nests etc.; 7 species recorded, including the now less common 'common clothes moth' *Tineola biselliella.*

Ochsenheimeriidae
Ochsenheimeria urella, Cereal stem moth. Local in old pastures.

Lyonetiidae
Small moths with leaf-mining larvae; 7 species recorded.

Gracillariidae
Small, narrow-winged moths with leaf-mining larvae; 28 species recorded.

Sesiidae: clearwing moths
Sesia bembeciformis. Widespread, larvae in trunks of sallows.

Choreutidae
Anthophila fabriciana. Very common wherever there are nettles.

Glyphipterigidae
Glyphipterix simpliciella.

Common wherever there is cock's-foot grass.

G.thrasonella. Local amongst rushes.

Yponomeutidae
Small and medium moths; 20 species recorded, including:
Yponomeuta evonymella, Birdcherry ermine. Local, larvae on gean.
Argyresthia bonnetella. Widespread.
Plutella xylostella, Diamond-back moth. Common, especially on coast.

Epermeniidae
Phaulernis fulviguttella. Local, larvae in seeds of *Heracleum.*
Epermenia chaerophyllella. Widespread, larvae on leaves of *Heracleum.*

Coleophoridae
Small, narrow-winged moths; larvae make portable cases of silk and leaf-fragments; 23 species recorded, all in the genus *Coleophora.*

Elachistidae
Small moths with larvae forming mines in grasses and similar plants; 16 species recorded, mostly in *Elachista.*

Oecophoridae
A diverse family of small moths; 23 species recorded, including:
Hofmannophila pseudospretella, Brown house-moth. Common.
Endrosis sarcitrella, White-shouldered house-moth. Common.
Depressaria pastinacella. Very common, larvae on *Heracleum.*

Gelechiidae
Small moths; larvae mostly in spun-together leaves or shoots; 24 species recorded.

Blastobasidae
Blastobasis decolorella. Common, recent colonizer.
B.lignea. Widespread, recent colonizer.

Momphidae
Small moths, mostly associated with willow-herb; 5 species recorded.

Cosmopterigidae
Limnaecia phragmitella. Local, larvae in seed-heads of *Typha.*
Pancalia leuwenhoekella. Local.

Scythrididae
Scythris picaepennis. Local on coast.

Tortricidae
Small to medium moths; larvae often in rolled leaves; 95 species recorded, including:
Tortrix viridana. Local around oak.
Acleris emargana. Widespread amongst sallows.
A.variegana, Rose tortrix. Widespread, larvae on rosaceous trees.

Pyralidae
Mainly small moths, some well marked; 37 species recorded, including:
Crambus lathoniellus. Common in grassland everywhere.
Agriphila straminella. Common in grassland everywhere.
Catoptria pinella. Local, mostly on coast.
Pyrausta ostrinalis. Local, in short grassland.

Pterophoridae: plume moths
Small slender moths with wings divided and fringed; 5 species recorded, of which one is widespread:
Stenoptilia pterodactyla. Larvae on *Veronica.*

Lasiocampidae
Poecilocampa populi, December moth. Local, commonest at Tentsmuir.
Trichiura crataegi, Pale eggar. Single old record.
Macrothylacia rubi, Fox moth. Local, often common at Tentsmuir.

Saturnidae
Pavonia pavonia, Emperor moth. Local, only in heathy areas.

Drepanidae: hook-tip moths
Falcaria lacertinaria, Scalloped hook-tip. Tentsmuir.
Drepana falcataria, Pebble hook-tip. Local.

Thyatiridae
Thyatira batis, Peach blossom. Widespread.
Ochropacha duplaris, Common lutestring. Local.
Achlya flavicornis, Yellow horned. Widespread.

Geometridae
Medium to large moths with 'looper' caterpillars (inch-worms).
Alsophila aescularia, March moth. Local.
Geometra papilionaria, Large emerald. Local.
Cyclophora albipunctata, Birch mocha. Earlshall Muir.
C.porata, False mocha. Flisk, 1831.
Timandra griseata, Blood-vein. Tentsmuir.
Idaea aversata, Riband wave. Widespread.
I.biselata, Small fan-footed wave. Widespread.
I.dimidiata, Single-dotted wave. Occasional record.
Xanthorhoe designata, Flame carpet. Local.
X.fluctuata, Garden carpet. Surprisingly uncommon.

X.montanata, Silver-ground carpet. Common.

X.munitata, Red carpet. Local.

Scotopteryx chenopodiata, Shaded broad-bar. Widespread.

S.luridata, July belle. Widespread.

Catarhoe cuculata, Royal mantle. Reared from larvae, Auchtermuchty, 1854.

Epirrhoe alternata, Common carpet. Widespread, larvae on *Galium*.

E.tristata, Small argent and sable. Local.

Camptogramma bilineata, Yellow shell. Widespread; common on the coast.

Anticlea badiata, Shoulder stripe. Inchkeith, 1914.

A.derivata, The streamer. Newburn.

Mesoleuca albicillata, Beautiful carpet. Morton Lochs.

Pelurga comitata, Dark spinach. Local, including Tentsmuir and I of May.

Lampropteryx suffumata, Water carpet. Local.

Cosmorhoe ocellata, Purple bar. Local.

Eulithis populata, Northern spinach. Widespread in uplands, larvae on blaeberry.

E.prunata, The phoenix. Raith L.

E.pyraliata, Barred straw. Widespread.

E.testata, The chevron. Local.

Ecliptopera silaceata, Small phoenix. Local.

Chloroclysta citrata, Dark marbled carpet. Local.

C.miata, Autumn green carpet. Local, common on I of May.

C.siterata, Red-green carpet. Local.

C.truncata, Common marbled carpet. Widespread.

Cidaria fulvata, Barred yellow. Local amongst rose.

Plemyria rubiginata, Blue-bordered carpet. Local.

Thera cognata, Chestnut-coloured carpet. Flisk, 1831.

T.firmata, Pine carpet. Local, amongst pine.

T.obeliscata, Grey pine carpet. Widespread amongst pine.

T.britannica, Spruce carpet. I of May.

Electrophaes corylata, Broken-barred carpet. Widespread in woods.

Colostygia multistrigaria, Mottled grey. Earlshall Muir.

C.pectinataria, Green carpet. Widespread.

Hydriomena furcata, July highflyer. Common, larvae on trees and shrubs.

H.impluviata, May highflyer. Local, amongst alder.

Epirrita autumnata, Autumnal moth. Widespread.

E.dilutata, November moth. Widespread.

Operophtera brumata, Winter moth. Common, larvae on blaeberry etc.

O.fagata, Northern winter moth. Local, larvae on birch.

Perizoma affinitata, The rivulet. Flisk, 1831.

P.albulata, Grass rivulet. Widespread.

P.alchemillata, Small rivulet. Local.

P.bifaciata, Barred rivulet. Flisk, 1831 and Tayport, 1990.

P.blandiata, Pretty pinion. Local.

P.didymata, Twin-spot carpet. Common, larvae on blaeberry and low plants.

P.flavofasciata, Sandy carpet. Kinghorn.

P.minorata, Heath rivulet. Falkland area, 1895.

Eupithecia abbreviata, Brindled pug. Local.

E.absinthiata, Wormwood pug. Widespread (including form *goossensiata* (Ling pug) locally on moors).

E.assimilata, Currant pug. Local.

E.centaureata, Lime-speck pug. Widespread, larvae on *Atriplex*.

E.exiguata, Mottled pug. Flisk, 1831.

E.icterata, Tawny speckled pug. Local, larvae on *Artemisia*.

E.indigata, Ochreous pug. Lochgelly.

E.nanata, Narrow-winged pug. Local in heathy areas.

E.pulchellata, Foxglove pug. Local.

E.pusillata, Juniper pug. Local.

E.pygmaeata, Marsh pug. Local.

E.satyrata, Satyr pug. Local on heathland.

E.subfuscata, Grey pug. Widespread.

E.tenuiata, Slender pug. Local, amongst sallows.

E.tripunctaria, White-spotted pug. Tentsmuir.

E.trisignaria, Triple-spotted pug. Tentsmuir.

E.valerianata, Valerian pug. Tentsmuir.

E.venosata, Netted pug. I of May.

E.vulgata, Common pug. Local.

Chloroclystis rectangulata, Green pug. Earlshall Muir.

Gymnoscelis rufifasciata, Double-striped pug. Wemyss.

Chesias legatella, The streak. Amongst broom at Tentsmuir.

C.rufata, Broom-tip. Amongst broom at Tentsmuir.

Aplocera plagiata, Treble-bar. Widespread.

Odezia atrata, Chimney-sweeper. Local.

Venusia cambrica, Welsh wave. Local.

Hydrelia flammeolaria, Small yellow wave. Old record at Flisk.

Trichopteryx carpinata, Early tooth-striped. Local.

Abraxas grossulariata, The magpie. Local.

A.sylvata, Clouded magpie. Cullaloe, 1982.

Lomaspilis marginata, Clouded border. Widespread amongst sallows.

Semiothisa liturata, Tawny-barred angle. Tentsmuir.

S.clathrata, Latticed heath. Local.

S.wauaria, The V-moth. Tentsmuir and I of May.

Petrophora chlorosata, Brown silver-line. Local, amongst bracken.

Opisthograptis luteolata, Brimstone moth. Widespread.

Ennomos alniaria, Canary-shouldered thorn. Tentsmuir.

Selenia dentaria, Early thorn. Local.

S.lunularia, Lunar thorn. Tentsmuir.

S.tetralunaria, Purple thorn. Auchtermuchty, 1854.

Odontopera bidentata, Scalloped hazel. Local.

Crocallis elinguaria, Scalloped oak. Widespread.

Ourapteryx sambucaria, Swallow-tailed moth. Local.

Biston betularia, Peppered moth. Local.

Agriopis aurantiaria, Scarce umber. Local, larvae on birch.

A.marginaria, Dotted border. Wemyss Moss Wood.

Erannis defoliaria, Mottled umber. Widespread, larvae on birch.

Peribatodes rhomboidaria, Willow beauty. Widespread.

Alcis repandata, Mottled beauty. Widespread, larvae on low plants.

Ematurga atomaria, Common heath. Widespread, amongst heather.

Bupalus piniaria, Bordered white. Local, amongst pines.

Cabera exanthemata, Common wave. Local.

C.pusaria, Common white wave. Local.

Lomographa temerata, Clouded silver. Local.

Campaea margaritata, Light emerald. Local.

Hylaea fasciaria, Barred red. Local.

Gnophos obfuscata, Scotch annulet. Flisk, 1830s.

G.obscurata, The annulet. Local on Forth coast.

Perconia strigillaria, Grass wave. Culross Moor.

Sphingidae: hawk-moths
Large moths, many migratory.

Agrius convolvuli, Convolvulus hawk-moth. Regular immigrant.

Acherontia atropos, Death's-head hawk-moth. Occasional immigrant that briefly becomes established.

Laothoe populi, Poplar hawk-moth. Local.

Macroglossum stellatarum, Humming-bird hawk-moth. Regular immigrant.

Hyles galii, Bedstraw hawk-moth. Occasional immigrant.

Deilephila elpenor, Elephant hawk-moth. Local.

D.porcellus, Small elephant hawk-moth. Local.

Notodontidae
Phalera bucephala, Buff-tip. Local, larvae on oak.

Cerura vinula, Pussmoth. Local, larvae on sallows.

Furcula furcula, Sallow kitten.

Widespread, larvae on sallow.

Notodonta dromedarius, Iron prominent. Local, larvae on alder.

Eligmodonta ziczac, Pebble prominent. Local.

Pheosia gnoma, Lesser swallow prominent. Local, larvae on birch.

P.tremula, Swallow prominent. I of May and Wemyss.

Ptilodon capucina, Coxcomb prominent. Widespread, larvae on birch.

Ptilodontella cucullina, Maple prominent. Tentsmuir.

Clostera curtula, Chocolate-tip. 'Fife'.

Diloba caeruleocephala, Figure of eight. Local.

Lymantriidae
Orgyia antiqua, The vapourer. Local.

Dasychira fascelina, Dark tussock. Tentsmuir.

Arctiidae
Thumatha senex, Round-winged muslin. Local.

Nudaria mundana, Muslin footman. Local.

Eilema lurideola, Common footman. Local.

Parasemia plantaginis, Wood tiger. Lomonds.

Arctia caja, Garden tiger. Widespread on coast, larvae on low herbs.

Spilosoma lubricipeda, White ermine. Widespread.

S.lutea, Buff ermine. Local.

Phragmatobia fuliginosa, Ruby tiger. Lomonds, Tentsmuir.

Tyria jacobaeae, The cinnabar. Local on coast, larvae on *Senecio*.

Noctuidae
Euxoa cursoria, Coast dart. Tentsmuir.

E.nigricans, Garden dart. Widespread.

E.obelisca, Square-spot dart.
Only on coast.
E.tritici, White-line dart.
Widespread.
Agrotis clavis, Heart and club.
Local.
A.exclamationis, Heart and dart.
Common.
A.ipsilon, Dark sword-grass.
Local.
A.ripae, Sand dart. Local on
coast.
A.segetum, Turnip moth.
Widespread.
A.vestigialis, Archer's dart.
Local in E Fife.
Axylia putris, The flame. Local.
Actebia praecox, Portland moth.
Tentsmuir.
Ochropleura plecta, Flame
shoulder. Widespread.
Eugnorisma depuncta, Plain
clay. Boarhills.
Standfussiana lucernea,
Northern rustic. Local on
rocky coast.
Rhyacia simulans, Dotted rustic.
Local.
Noctua comes, Lesser yellow
underwing. Common.
N.fimbriata, Broad-bordered
yellow underwing. Local.
N.janthe, Lesser
broad-bordered yellow
underwing. Widespread.
N.orbona, Lunar yellow
underwing. Tentsmuir.
N.pronuba, Large yellow
underwing. Common.
Graphiphora augur,
Double-dart. Widespread.
Paradiarsia glareosa, Autumnal
rustic. Widespread.
P.sobrina, Cousin german.
Once at St Andrews.
Lycophotia porphyrea, True
lover's knot. Widespread.
Peridroma saucia, Pearly
underwing. I of May and
Tentsmuir.
Diarsia brunnea, Purple clay.
Local.

D.dahlii, Barred chestnut.
Local.
D.florida, Fen square-spot.
Earlshall Muir.
D.mendica, Ingrailed clay.
Widespread.
D.rubi, Small square-spot.
Local.
Xestia agathina, Heath rustic.
Tentsmuir, Raith L.
X.alpicola, Northern dart. I of
May, 1957.
X.baja, Dotted clay.
Widespread.
X.castanea, Neglected rustic.
Local.
X.c-nigrum, Setaceous hebrew
character. Widespread.
X.sexstrigata, Six-striped rustic.
Widespread.
X.triangulum, Double
square-spot. Widespread.
X.xanthographa, Square-spot
rustic. Common.
Naenia typica, The gothic.
Local.
Eurois occulta, Great brocade. I
of May.
Anaplectoides prasina, Green
arches. Local.
Cerastis rubricosa, Red chestnut.
Local.
Anarta myrtilli, Beautiful
yellow underwing.
Thornton (1895) and
Tentsmuir.
Hada nana, The shears. Local,
most abundant at Tentsmuir.
Polia bombycina, Pale shining
brown. An old record at
Kincardine.
P.hepatica, Silvery arches. An
old record at Tentsmuir.
P.nebulosa, Grey arches. Local
in W Fife.
Sideridis albicolon, White colon.
Tentsmuir.
Mamestra brassicae, Cabbage
moth. Widespread.
Melanchra persicariae, Dot
moth. Newburn and I of
May.

Lacanobia oleracea, Bright-line
brown-eye. Local.
L.thalassina, Pale-shouldered
brocade. Widespread.
Papestra biren, Glaucous
shears. Tentsmuir.
Ceramica pisi, Broom moth.
Widespread.
Hecatera bicolorata,
Broad-barred white.
Kinghorn.
Hadena bicruris, The lychnis.
Local.
H.confusa, Marbled coronet.
Along the Forth coast.
H.perplexa, Tawny shears.
Earlsferry, 1901.
H.rivularis, The campion.
Widespread.
Cerapteryx graminis, Antler
moth. Widespread.
Tholera cespitis, Hedge rustic.
Tentsmuir.
Orthosia cerasi, Common
quaker. Widespread.
O.gothica, Hebrew character.
Widespread.
O.gracilis, Powdered quaker.
Local.
O.incerta, Clouded drab.
Widespread.
Mythimna comma, Shoulder-
striped wainscot. Local.
M.conigera, Brown-line
bright-eye. Widespread.
M.ferrago, The clay.
Widespread.
M.impura, Smoky wainscot.
Common.
M.pallens, Common wainscot.
Widespread.
Cucullia chamomillae,
Chamomile shark. Balmuto,
1871.
C.umbratica, The shark. I of
May, 1913.
Brachylomia viminalis, Minor
shoulder-knot. Tentsmuir.
Dasypolia templi, Brindled
ochre. Widespread but
uncommon.

Aporophyla lutulenta, Deep-brown dart. Widespread.

A.nigra, Black rustic. Widespread.

Lithomoia solidaginis, Golden-rod brindle. I of May.

Xylena exsoleta, Sword-grass. Old records at I of May.

X.vetusta, Red sword-grass. Widespread but uncommon.

Allophyes oxyacanthae, Green-brindled crescent. Widespread, larvae on hawthorn.

Dichonia aprilina, Merveille du jour. Largo, 1895.

Mniotype adusta, Dark brocade. Widespread.

Antitype chi, Grey chi. Local.

Eupsilia transversa, The satellite. Local.

Conistra vaccinii, The chestnut. Local.

Agrochola circellaris, The brick. Widespread.

A.litura, Brown-spot pinion. Widespread.

A.lota, Red-line quaker. Widespread.

A.macilenta, Yellow-line quaker. Local.

Parastichtis suspecta, The suspected. Local.

Atethmia centrago, Centre-barred sallow. Newburn.

Omphaloscelis lunosa, Lunar underwing. Local.

Xanthia citrago, Orange sallow. Raith L.

X.gilvago, Dusky-lemon sallow. Tayport.

X.icteritia, The sallow. Common.

X.togata, Pink-barred sallow. Widespread.

Acronicta leporina, The miller. Fife Regional Park, 1984.

A.menyanthidis, Light knot-grass. Earlshall Muir.

A.psi, Grey dagger. Local, larvae often on rowan.

A.rumicis, Knotgrass. Local.

Cryphia domestica, Marbled beauty. Local, larvae on lichen on walls.

C.muralis, Marbled green. Once on I of May.

Amphipyra tragopogonis, Mouse moth. Widespread, often indoors.

Mormo maura, Old lady. Local.

Rusina ferruginea, Brown rustic. Widespread.

Thalpophila matura, Straw underwing. Local.

Euplexia lucipara, Small angle shades. Local.

Phlogophora meticulosa, Angle shades. Widespread.

Cosmia trapezina, The dun-bar. Widespread.

Apamea crenata, Clouded-bordered brindle. Common.

A.furva, The confused. Local.

A.lithoxylea, Light arches. Widespread.

A.monoglypha, Dark arches. Common.

A.phiogramma, Double-lobed. Tentsmuir.

A.remissa, Dusky brocade. Widespread.

A.sordens, Rustic shoulder-knot. Widespread.

A.unanimis, Small clouded brindle. Anstruther, 1993, and old record at I of May.

A.zeta assimilis, Northern arches. Cullaloe (1995) and Kincardine.

Oligia fasciuncula, Middle-barred minor. Widespread.

O.latruncula, Tawny marbled minor. Local.

O.strigilis, Marbled minor. Widespread.

O.versicolor, Rufous minor. Widespread.

Mesoligia literosa, Rosy minor. Local.

M.furuncula, Cloaked minor. Local.

Mesapamea secalis, Common rustic. Widespread.

M.secallela, Lesser common rustic. Newburn.

Photedes elymi, Lyme grass. Tentsmuir.

P.minima, Small dotted buff. Widespread.

P.pygmina, Small wainscot. Widespread.

Luperina testacea, Flounced rustic. Widespread.

Amphipoea crinanensis, Crinan ear. Local.

A.lucens, Large ear. Widespread.

A.oculea, Ear moth. Widespread.

Hydraecia micacea, Rosy rustic. Common.

H.petasitis, The butterbur. Local.

Gortyna flavago, Frosted orange. Local.

Celaena haworthii, Haworth's minor. Local.

C.leucostigma, The crescent. Tentsmuir.

Nonagria typhae, Bulrush wainscot. Morton Lochs.

Rhizedra lutosa, Large wainscot. Local.

Hoplodrina alsines, The uncertain. Local.

H.blanda, The rustic. Widespread.

Caradrina clavipalpis, Pale mottled willow. Local.

C.morpheus, Mottled rustic. Widespread.

Stilbia anomala, The anomalous. Tentsmuir.

Pyrrhia umbra, Bordered sallow. Local on coast.

Nycteola revayana, Oak nycteoline. Brunton.

Colocasia coryli, Nut-tree tussock. Widespread, larvae on birch.

Diachrysia chrysitis, Burnished brass. Common.

Polychrysia moneta, Golden plusia. Local.

Plusia festucae, Gold-spot. Widespread.
P.putnami gracilis, Lempke's gold spot. Tentsmuir.
Autographa bractea, Gold spangle. Local.
A.gamma, Silver Y. Common, frequent immigrant.
A.jota, Plain golden Y. Widespread.
A.pulchrina, Beautiful golden Y. Common.
Syngrapha interrogationis, Scarce silver Y. Newburn.
Abrostola triplasia, The spectacle. Local.
Catocala fraxini, Clifden nonpareil. Occasional immigrant.
Callistege mi, Mother shipton. Local.
Scoliopteryx libatrix, The herald. Widespread.
Hypena proboscidalis, The snout. Common.
Herminia grisealis, Small fan-foot. Local.
H.tarsipennalis, The fan-foot. Local.

Trichoptera: caddis flies

Insects with aquatic larvae that mostly make portable cases of stones or plant debris; 35 species recorded but mostly from rivers; many others probably occur in standing water.

Diptera: two-winged flies

A huge assemblage of flies, some with aquatic, some with terrestrial larvae.

Trichoceridae: winter gnats
Trichocera hiemalis. I of May.
T.regelationis. Widespread, forming swarms in winter.

Ptychopteridae
Small flies resembling craneflies, with aquatic larvae.
Ptychoptera albimana. Aberdour.

Tipulidae: craneflies
Mostly large flies – 'daddy-long-legs'– with larvae in soil (leatherjackets), mud, or rotting wood; 25 species recorded, probably many more present. The commonest one in gardens and pasture is *Tipula paludosa*.

Culicidae: mosquitoes etc.
Aedes detritus. Salt-marshes.
Anopheles plumbeus. Larvae in tree-holes; Aberdour.
Culex pipiens. Widespread, feeding on birds.
Culiseta annulata. Often indoors.

Ceratopogonidae: biting midges
15 species recorded, all but one in a study at Newburgh in 1960.

Chironomidae: non-biting midges
Larvae aquatic; 26 species recorded; many more probably present.

Mycetophilidae: fungus-gnats
Larvae mostly in fungi.
[*Allodia silvatica*. Carriston Res.; needs confirmation.]

Sciaridae
Trichosia coarctata. Kinkell Braes.

Bibionidae
Black hairy flies with larvae in leaf-litter and soil.
Bibio lepidus. Benarty Hill.
B.marci, St Mark's fly. Widespread.
B.nigriventris. Aberdour.
B.pomonae. Leven, Thornton.

Scatopsidae
Larvae in dung etc.
Reichterella geniculata. I of May.

Cecidomyidae: gall-midges
Small flies with larvae forming galls in many plants; 30 species recorded.

Stratiomyidae: soldier flies.
Includes several large, boldly

coloured flies; larvae in soil, rotting wood etc., some aquatic.
Beris vallata. Widespread.
Chloromyia formosa. Widespread.
Microchrysa flavicornis. Earlshall.
Nemotelus uliginosus. Cocklemill Marsh; Charlestown.
Sargus flavipes. Earlshall Muir.

Xylophagidae
Large, slender flies; larvae in dead wood.
Xylophagus ater. Woodland; W Fife.

Rhagionidae
Large boldly marked flies; larvae in leaf-litter, dead wood etc.
Chrysopilus cristatus. Wetlands.
Rhagio lineola. Aberdour.
R.scolopacea. L Gelly.

Tabanidae: horse flies etc.
Females suck blood; larvae predatory in wet soil, rotting wood etc.
Chrysops caecutiens. Widespread.
C.viduatus. I of May.
Haematopota pluvialis, Cleg. N Fife.

Bombyliidae: bee-flies
Bee-like flies, some parasitic on bees.
Villa paniscus. Leven, Elie.

Asilidae: robber flies
Adults prey on other insects; larvae in decaying vegetation.
Dysmachus trigonus. Tentsmuir.
Leptogaster guttiventris. Tentsmuir.
Philonicus albiceps. Coastal dunes.
Rhadiurgus variabilis. Tentsmuir.

Therevidae
Thereva annulata. Tentsmuir.
T.nobilitata. Tentsmuir.

Empididae: dance flies
Adults are predators on other

dipterous flies; larvae in soil or mud; 17 species recorded; the largest is the widespread *Empis tesselata*.

Dolichopodidae: long-headed flies
Predators on small insects and larvae; 7 species recorded.

Platypezidae: flat-footed flies
Larvae mostly in fungi.
Platypeza ornata. Aberdour.

Pipunculidae: big-headed flies
Larvae parasitic in insects.
Cephalops obtusinervis.

Syrphidae: hoverflies
Active flies, many with bold yellow and black patterns; adults visit flowers. 102 species recorded in Fife out of c.270 in Britain, but few sites have been sampled.

Syrphinae
Hoverflies with predatory, mostly aphid-eating, larvae; 50 species recorded of which the following are the most widespread:
Chrysotoxum arcuatum. Woodland edge etc.
Epistrophe grossulariae. Woodland edge, often on umbels.
Episyrphus balteatus. Often in gardens; boosted by migrants.
Eupeodes luniger. Widespread and migratory.
Melanostoma mellinum. Especially in grassland.
M.scalare. Especially in grassland.
Meliscaeva cinctella. Woodland.
Playcheirus clypeatus. Grassland.
P.cyaneus. Common in gardens.
P.manicatus. Especially in grassland.
P.peltatus. Widespread.
P.scutatus. Especially woodland edge.

Pyrophaena granditarsa. Damp meadows.
Scaeva pyrastri. Gardens, and migrant at I of May.
Syrphus ribesii. Abundant in gardens; also a migrant.
S.vitripennis. A common migrant.

Milesiinae
Hoverflies with larvae in water, mud, dead wood or, in a few cases, bulbs or stems of plants; 48 species recorded of which the following are widespread:
Cheilosia albitarsis. Larvae feed on living plants.
C.illustrata. A bee-mimic, often on umbel flowers.
Eristalis arbustorum. Larvae in drains etc.
E.horticola. Widespread.
E.intricarius. Widespread.
E.pertinax. Like next species, bee-mimics, common in gardens.
E.tenax. Widespread.
Helophilus pendulus. Larvae in manure etc.
Merodon equestris. Larvae in bulbs, e.g. of wild hyacinth.
Rhingia campestris. Larvae in cowdung.
Sericomyia silentis. Wetland.
Syritta pipiens. Gardens; small, slim; larvae in compost etc.
Volucella pellucens. Large, black; larvae in nests of bees and wasps.
Xylota segnis. Larvae in dead wood.

Pipizini
Hoverflies with larvae that feed on waxy aphids.
Neocnemodon verrucula. Tentsmuir.
Pipiza austriaca. Dunfermline.
P.luteitarsus. Lundin Links.
P.viduata. Luthrie.

Otitidae: picture-winged flies
Small flies with patterned wings.

Herina frondescentiae. Oakley.

Sepsidae
Larvae mainly in dung; 12 species recorded in Fife.

Psilidae
Larvae in roots and stems.
Chyliza fuscipennis. Tentsmuir.
Psila fimetaria. Aberdour, I of May.
P.pallida. I of May.
P.rosae, Carrot-fly. I of May.

Lauxaniidae
Lyciella rorida. Aberdour.
Minettia longipennis. Aberdour.

Sciomyzidae: marsh flies
Larvae mostly aquatic.
Pelidnoptera fuscipennis. Oakley.
Pherbellia griseola. Tentsmuir.
Tetanura pallidiventris. Kinghorn.

Chamaemyiidae
Larvae prey upon aphids.
Chamaemyia juncorum. I of May.

Pallopteridae
Small picture-winged flies.
Palloptera modesta. Lochgelly.
P.saltuum. W Wemyss.
P.trimacula. Cullaloe.
P.umbellatarum. Oakley.

Tephritidae: picture-winged flies
With gall-forming larvae.
Paroxyna absinthii. Charlestown.
Trypeta artemisiae. Charlestown.
Tephritis neesi. Near Dunfermline.
Xyphosia miliaria. Charlestown, I of May.

Coelopidae: kelp flies
All in rotting seaweed, St Andrews.
Coelopa frigida. Also I of May.
C.pilipes.
Orygma luctuosa. Also I of May.

Helcomyzidae
Helcomyza ustulata. In rotting seaweed.

Heterocheila buccata. In rotting seaweed, St Andrews.

Heleomyzidae
Larvae in decaying material and fungi.
Heleomyza serrata. Indoors.
H.borealis. I of May.
Suillia pallida. Aberdour.
S.notata. Aberdour.

Opomyzidae
Larvae in grass stems.
Geomyza venusta. I of May.
Opomyza florum. I of May.
O.germinationis. I of May.

Ephydridae: shoreflies
Notiphila cinerea. Two sites.
Parydra coarctata. Aberdour.
Scatella stagnalis. Aberdour.
S.palludum. Aberdour.

Sphaeroceridae
Pteremis fenestralis. I of May.
Thoracochaeta zosterae. In rotting seaweed; I of May.

Drosophilidae: fruit-flies
Drosophila funebris. In decaying seaweed.

Agromyzidae: leaf-mining flies
Larvae in mines in leaves or occasionally stems; 31 species recorded. The following are especially common:
Agromyza alnibetulae.
    Widespread; on birch.
Liriomyza amoena. Common; on elder.
P.flavicornis. Widespread; mines in stems of nettles.
P.heracleana. Common; on hogweed.

Chloropidae
Tiny flies; larvae herbivorous.
Chlorops hypostigma. I of May.
Goniopsita palposa. Tentsmuir.
Oscinella frit, Frit fly. A pest of cereals.

Tachinidae: parasitic flies
Larvae mostly in insects, especially caterpillars; 5 species recorded.

Calliphoridae: blow-flies etc.
Bellardia vulgaris. Kinkell Braes.
Calliphora vicina. Widespread; larvae in carrion.
Cynomya mortuorum.
    Widespread; larvae in carrion.
Lucilia sericata. I of May.
Pollenia griseotomentosa.
    Carlingnose.
P.rudis, Cluster-fly. Enters houses in autumn to hibernate; larvae parasitic in earthworms.

Rhinophoridae
Melanophora roralis. I of May.

Sarcophagidae: flesh-flies
Larvae in carrion.
Heteronychia vagans. Tentsmuir.
Metopia argyrocephala.
    Tentsmuir.
M.campestris. Earlshall.
Pierretia nigriventris.
    Carlingnose, Ruddons Point.
Sarcophaga carnaria. I of May.
S.subvicina. Carlingnose.

Hypodermatidae: warble-flies
Parasites in skin of cattle; two species formerly present, now probably extinct; presence is a notifiable disease.
[*Hypoderma bovis.*]
[*H.lineatum.*]

Scathophagidae: dung-flies etc.
Includes species with dung-feeding, herbivorous and predatory larvae; 7 species recorded including the common yellow dung-fly of cowpats, *Scathophaga stercoraria.*

Anthomyiidae: flower-flies
Adults often on flowers; larvae varied, in fungi, rotting wood and plants, including some pest species such as the wheat bulb fly, *Delia coarctata*; 34 species recorded.

Fanniidae: lesser house-flies
Larvae in manure etc; 12 species of *Fannia* recorded, including the widespread lesser house fly, *F.canicularis.*

Muscidae: house-flies etc.
Larvae varied, in dung, compost etc.; 60 species recorded, including the common house fly, *Musca domestica,* now much less common than previously.

Hippoboscidae: flat-flies
Blood-sucking parasites of birds and mammals.
Crataerina hirundinis.
    Widespread on house martins.
Ornithomya chloropus. On many birds, especially passerines.

Siphonaptera: fleas
Adults blood-sucking parasites of mammals and birds. Little studied in Fife but 25 out of 53 British species recorded, 18 on mammals, 7 on birds.

Hymenoptera: wasps, bees, ants etc.
A very large and diverse group. Only the bumble-bees, social wasps and ants are moderately well known. Other groups have been little recorded in Fife although there are likely to be many hundreds of species.

Symphyta: sawflies
With herbivorous or wood-boring caterpillar-like larvae; records of only 5 species plus the following wood-boring species have been found so far, although many other species undoubtedly occur.
Sirex juvencus. Largo.
S.noctilio. Sporadic, in imported timber.

Urocerus gigas, Horntail. In imported timber.
Xiphydria camelus, Alder wood-wasp. One record.

Formicidae: ants
Mostly predators on other insects, especially aphids.
Formica lemani. Widespread.
Lasius flavus. Mainly coastal.
L.mixtus. I of May.
L.niger. Scattered, including towns.
Leptothorax acervorum. Moorland.
Monomorium pharaonis, Pharaoh's ant. Sporadic in heated buildings.
Myrmica lobicornis. Coastal.
M.rubra. 2 coastal sites.
M.ruginodis. Widespread.
M.sabuleti. I of May.
M.scabrinodis. Several coastal sites.

Apidae: bumble- and honey-bees
Colonial bees feeding on nectar and pollen.
Apis mellifera, Honey bee. Widespread.
Bombus hortorum. Widespread.
B.lapidarius. Widespread.
B.leucorum. Widespread.
B.monticola. Moors and coast.
B.muscorum. Scarce, coastal.
B.pascuorum. Widespread.
B.pratorum. Widespread.
B.terrestris. Widespread; usually the first to appear in spring.
Psithyrus barbutellus. One coastal record. This and other *Psithyrus* are parasites of *Bombus* spp.
P.bohemicus. Widespread.
P.campestris. 3 sites.
P.sylvestris. 4 sites.

Vespidae: social wasps
Predators on insects and other invertebrates.

Dolichovespula norvegica. Old records W Fife.
D.sylvestris. Widespread.
Vespula austriaca. Scarce; parasite of *V.rufa.*
V.germanica. Widespread.
V.rufa. Widespread.
V.vulgaris. Widespread.

Solitary wasps
Eumenidae: mason wasps
Ancistrocerus oviventris. One record.
A.pictus. I of May.
A.trimarginatus. I of May.

Sphecidae: digger wasps
Crabro cribrarius. Lundin Links.
Gorytes tumidus. N Queensferry.
Pemphredon inornatus. Inverkeithing.
P.lethifer. Kinghorn.

Pompilidae: spider-hunting wasps
Ceropales maculata. Thornton.

Solitary bees
Andrenidae
Andrena tarsata. Thornton.
A.wilkella. Kinghorn.

Megachilidae
Megachile circumcincta. Kinghorn.

Anthophoridae: cuckoo solitary bees
Nomada obtusifrons. Thornton.

Parasitic wasps
Very poorly recorded; several hundred species are likely to occur.

Ichneumonidae
Larvae parasitic in other insects; 21 species recorded, very many more likely to be present.

Chrysididae: ruby-tailed wasps
Parasitic, mainly in nests of solitary wasps and bees.
Chrysis ignita. Widespread on coast.
C.ruddi. S coast.

Braconidae
Apanteles glomeratus. In caterpillars of large white butterflies.
A.limbatus. In caterpillars of magpie moths.
Mesochorus angustatus. In caterpillars of magpie moths.

Pteromalidae
Pteromalus maerens. Hyperparasite in caterpillars of magpie moths.

Mymaridae
Caraphractus cinctus. Parasitoids in eggs of water beetles.

Chalcidae
Stenomalus muscarum. Parasite on two-winged flies.
Torymus affinis. Parasite in oak-apple galls.

Cynipidae: gall-wasps
Larvae stimulate plants to form galls; 8 species recorded including:
Andricus kollari, Marble-gall wasp. On oak.
Diplolepis rosae, Robin's pin-cushion. Widespread on rose.
Neuroterus quercusbaccarum, Common spangle gall. On oak.

Coleoptera: beetles

Beetles are extremely varied in both appearance and ecological niche. Well recorded only in some coastal sites. Although records of 685 species have been located, many more are likely to be present.

Terrestrial beetles (families with most species terrestrial – a few aquatic members are included).

Carabidae: ground beetles
Mainly predatory, nocturnal and active at ground level; 85 species recorded; the following are

amongst the more widespread or easily recognized:

Agonum dorsale. Widespread, including gardens.

Broscus cephalotes. Coastal; Tentsmuir.

Carabus violaceus, Violet ground beetle. One record but probably widespread.

Cicindela campestris, Green tiger beetle. Local; sandy heaths.

Cychrus caraboides. Widespread.

Elaphrus cupreus. Water margins; Cameron Res., Tentsmuir.

Loricera pilicornis. Widespread.

Notiophilus biguttatus. Widespread; an active diurnal species.

Pterostichus madidus. Widespread.

Ptiliidae
Very small beetles living under bark, in rotting seaweed etc.; 5 species recorded.

Leptinidae
Leptinus testaceus. In fur of wood mouse, *Apodemus sylvaticus.*

Leiodidae
Small beetles, many associated with fungi; 21 species recorded.

Histeridae
Predators in carrion and dung.

Aetholus deodecimstriatus. Tentsmuir.

Baeckmanniolus dimidiatus. Dunes; Tentsmuir, Earlsferry.

Hister impressus. Earlshall.

Silphidae: burying beetles etc.
Scavangers and predators.

Nicrophorus humator. Widespread.

N.interruptus. Tentsmuir.

N.investigator. Widespread.

N.vespillo. Tentsmuir.

N.vespilloides. Ruddons Point, Tentsmuir.

Silpha atrata. Widespread.

Thanatophilus rugosus. I of May, Tentsmuir.

Scydmaenidae
Neuraphes angulatus. Tentsmuir.

Stenichnus collaris. Tentsmuir.

Staphylinidae: rove beetles
Predators and scavangers with short wing-cases and projecting abdomens; 210 species recorded, many very small; the following are large and easily recognized:

Creophilus maxillosus. One record but probably widespread.

Ocypus olens, Devil's coach-horse. Widespread.

Pselaphidae
Brachygluta helferi. Kincardine; saltmarsh.

Reichenbachia juncorum. Tentsmuir; [waterside].

Geotrupidae
Large irridescent dung beetles.

Geotrupes stercorarius. I of May.

Scarabaeidae: scarabs and chafers
Includes many large beetles, some feeding on dung (*Aphodius* spp.), others herbivorous, feeding on roots.

Aegialia arenaria. Dunes; Earlsferry, Tentsmuir.

A.sabuleti. Tentsmuir.

Anomala dubia. Dunes; Tentsmuir.

Aphodius ater. Tentsmuir.

And 7 other *Aphodius.*

Calyptomerus dubius. Tentsmuir.

Melolontha melolontha, Cockchafer. Kinghorn, I of May.

Onthophagus joannae. Kincraig; on carrion.

Serica brunnea. Widespread on coast.

Byrrhidae
Byrrhus fasciatus. Tentsmuir.

B.pilula. Tentsmuir.

Cytilus sericeus. Tentsmuir.

Morychus aeneus. Tentsmuir; [waterside].

Simplocaria semistriata. I of May, Tentsmuir.

Dryopidae
By water; larvae aquatic.

Dryops ernesti. Dumbarnie Links, Tentsmuir.

D.luridus. Morton L.

Elateridae: click beetles
Larvae (wireworms) in soil or wood; 7 species recorded; *Agriotes obscurus* is a widespread pest on pasture and arable land.

Cantharidae: soldier beetles
Predators, often active, and actively copulating, on flowers by day; 15 species recorded.

Dermestidae: carpet beetles etc.
Larvae feed on hair, leather etc.

Attagenus pellio. Leven.

Ptinidae: spider beetles
Small, rather globular beetles found in stored food.

Niptus hololeucus. I of May.

Ptinus tectus. Dunfermline.

Nitidulidae
Small beetles with truncate wing cases, often on flowers; 10 species recorded.

Sphindidae
Aspidophorus orbiculatus. Tentsmuir.

Cryptophagidae
Small beetles, in decaying vegetation; 24 species recorded.

Endomychidae
Mycetaea hirta. Thornton; in poultry house.

Coccinellidae: ladybirds
Adults and larvae of many species prey upon aphids.

Adalia bipunctata. Widespread.

A.decempunctata. Widespread.

Anatis ocellata. On pines; Tentsmuir.

Aphidecta obliterata. Tentsmuir.

Colvia 14-guttata. Keil's Den.

Coccidula rufa. Dumbarnie Links, Tentsmuir.

Coccinella hieroglyphica. Tentsmuir; [heather].

C.septempunctata, Seven-spot ladybird. Ubiquitous and often very abundant.

C.undecimpunctata. Widespread on coast.

Exochomus quadripustulatus. Tentsmuir, Kinkell.

Myrrha octodecimguttata. Tentsmuir.

Myzia oblongoguttata. Tentsmuir; [on pine].

Nephus redtenbacheri. Tentsmuir.

Scymnus femoralis. Tentsmuir; [grassland].

S.nigrinus. Tentsmuir; [pines].

S.schmidti. Dumbarnie Links.

S.suturalis. Tentsmuir.

Lathridiidae
Tiny beetles on foliage and in leaf-litter; 9 species recorded.

Mycetophagidae: fungus beetles
Typhaea stercorea. Tentsmuir.

Colydiidae
Orthocerus clavicornis. Tentsmuir; dunes.

Tenebrionidae
Includes the mealworm beetle, *Tenebrio molitor,* often bred for bird-food etc.

Isomera murina. I of May.

Melanimon tibialis. Tentsmuir; dunes.

Cerambycidae: longhorn beetles
Large beetles with wood-boring larvae.

Acanthocinus aedilis. Kirkcaldy; probably in imported timber.

Nacerdes melanura. Recorded

on a pleasure boat off Methil, 1914.

Rhagium bifasciatum. Blairadam and Cullaloe; pines.

Scraptiidae
Anaspis maculata. Tentsmuir; [on flowers].

A.rufilabris. Tentsmuir.

Chrysomelidae: leaf beetles
Herbivores, often found on foliage as larvae and adults; 34 species recorded. *Lochmaea suturalis* is the common heather beetle; *Phyllotreta undulata* is a striped flea beetle that can be a pest on garden crucifers.

Attelabidae
Rhynchites nanus. Tentsmuir; [on sallows and birch].

Apionidae
Similar to weevils; on herbs and shrubs; 9 species recorded.

Curculionidae: weevils
Herbivores, often seed-eating; 44 species recorded.

Scolytidae: bark beetles
Hylastes ater. N Queensferry; pine.

H.brunneus. Tentsmuir; [pine].

Hylastinus obscurus. Cardenden; broom.

Hylurgops palliatus. Cullaloe; conifers.

Water beetles (there are also a few aquatic species in the families Chrysomelidae and Curculionidae)

Gyrinidae: whirligig beetles
Predators, on surface of water; 6 species of *Gyrinus* recorded of which *G.substriatus* is widespread.

Haliplidae
Small yellow beetles, usually in still or slow water; 10 species recorded, mostly in genus *Haliplus.*

Noteridae
Small brown beetles living in rafts of vegetation.

Noterus clavicornis. Kilconquhar L.

N.crassicornis. Lindores L, one of two Scottish sites.

Dytiscidae: diving beetles
Larvae and adults predatory; 58 species recorded, including:

Agabus bipustulatus. Widespread.

Dytiscus marginalis, Great diving beetle. Occasional in ponds and vegetated loch edges.

D.semisulcatus, Black-bellied diving beetle. In shallower habitats, often in slow running water.

Hydroporus palustris. Commonest species of vegetated edges of lochs etc.

Laccophilus minutus. Frequent in man-made ponds and reservoirs; occasional in lochs.

Oreodytes sanmarkii. Common in streams, rivers and loch shores.

Helophoridae
Small beetles; larvae predatory, adults herbivorous; 10 species recorded of which *Helophorus brevipalpis* is the commonest water beetle.

Hydrophilidae
Globular beetles associated with aquatic vegetation or wet litter; 22 species recorded.

Hydraenidae
Very small, aquatic beetles; 13 species recorded.

Dryopidae
Dryops ernesti. On damp vegetation; St Andrews, Morton L.

D.luridus. Common in muddy margins of lochs.

Elmidae: riffle beetles
Mainly in fast streams; 6 species recorded.

Scirtidae
Larvae aquatic; adults terrestrial; 7 species recorded.

Chilopoda: centipedes
Predators living mainly on and under the ground. Fairly well recorded.

Geophilomorpha
Very elongate, blind centipedes living in the soil, dead wood etc.; 8 species recorded.

Lithobiomorpha
Shorter, surface-active centipedes; 8 species recorded including the common garden centipede, *Lithobius forficatus.*

Diplopoda: millipedes
Feed mainly on dead vegetation; important creators of humus-rich soil. Well recorded.
Polyxenida: bristly millipedes
Polyxenus lagurus. A short, bristly species, recorded only on 2 churchyard walls.

Glomeridae: pill millipedes
Can roll into a ball.
Stygioglomeris crinita. A rare subterranean species known at 2 sites, on limestone.

Chordeumatida
Craspedosoma rawlinsii. Cullaloe Reservoir only.
Nanogona polydesmoides. Widespread in calcareous sites.
Melogona gallica. Riverside Park, Glenrothes.
M.scutellare. Sparse, in woodland leaf-litter.
Nemasoma varicorne. Kenly Den, under dead bark.

Julida: snake millipedes
In leaf-litter and top-soil; 17

species recorded including the large, yellow-striped *Ommatoiulus sabulosus* which is abundant in many coastal habitats.

Polydesmida: flat-backed millipedes
In leaf-litter and top-soil; 6 species recorded, including the widespread *Polydesmus angustus.*

Symphyla
Small white centipede-like animals with twelve pairs of legs; feed mainly on decaying vegetation.
Scutigerella immaculata. Probably widespread.
Symphylellopsis subnuda. I of May.
Symphyella vulgaris. I of May.

Chelicerata

Arachnida: spiders etc.

Araneae: spiders
Predators on other invertebrates, mostly on insects; in all terrestrial habitats. In Fife 232 species recorded out of c.650 in Britain. Recording has been strongly biased towards coastal sites.

Amaurobiidae
Amaurobius fenestralis. Widespread, especially under bark; sometimes indoors.
A.ferox. On buildings and walls.
A.similis. Widespread, especially in and around buildings.

Dictynidae
Dictyna arundinacea. Widespread in grassland.

Oonopidae
Oonops pulcher. In and around buildings.

Dysderidae
Dysdera crocata. Widespread, mainly on old walls, preying upon woodlice.
Harpactea hombergi. A few coastal records.

Segestriidae
Segestria senoculata. Widespread, especially on walls and rocks.

Gnaphosidae
Hunting spiders; 7 species recorded.

Clubionidae
Nocturnal hunters spending day in silken cell; 14 species recorded.

Zoridae
Zora spinimana. Widespread.

Thomisidae: crab-spiders
Feed by waiting and pouncing on insects, mainly on vegetation; 8 species recorded; *Xysticus cristatus* is very abundant in grassland.

Salticidae: jumping spiders
6 species recorded; the zebra spider, *Salticus scenicus,* is common on buildings.

Lycosidae: wolf-spiders
Active, diurnal hunters; the most conspicuous spiders on open ground; 16 species recorded; *Pardosa pullata* and *P.amentata* are widespread, including gardens.

Agelenidae
Mostly large house spiders.
Cryphoeca silvicola. Widespread in woodland.
Tegenaria atrica. One record.
T.domestica. In buildings.
T.saeva. The largest of the house spiders.
Textrix denticulata. Widespread in and around buildings.

Hahniidae
Small spiders making sheet webs at ground level.
Antistea elegans. In marshes.
Hahnia helveola. One record.
H.montana. Carlingnose.
H.nava. Earlshall Muir.

Mimetidae
Small spiders preying on other spiders.
Ero cambridgei. Two coastal sites.
E.furcata. Widespread on coast.

Theridiidae: comb-footed spiders
Small spiders with globular abdomen, often abundant on foliage; 17 species recorded.

Nesticidae
Nesticus cellulanus. Two old records.

Tetragnathidae: orb-web spiders.
Metellina mengei. Widespread.
M.merianae. Widespread in damp places.
M.segmentata. Widespread.
Pachygnatha clercki. Widespread.
P.degeeri. Abundant and widespread.
Tetragnatha extensa. Scattered records.
T.montana. Barnyards Marsh.

Araneidae: orb-web spiders
Araneus diadematus. Widespread in gardens etc.
A.quadratus. On coastal dunes.
Araniella cucurbitina. Widespread.
Atea sturmi. Tentsmuir.
Cyclosa conica. One record, W Fife.
Hypsosinga albovittata. Tentsmuir.
Nuctenea umbratica. Woodland.
Zygiella atrica. Widespread, on bushes.

Z.x-notata. Widespread around buildings.

Linyphiidae: money spiders
Small, usually dark spiders making small sheet webs responsible for the 'gossamer' noticeable in grassland on damp mornings; 127 species recorded, in many habitats.

Opiliones: harvestmen
Predators and scavengers in all terrestrial habitats. 16 species recorded out of 23 in Britain.

Pseudoscorpiones: false scorpions
Small, elusive predators in leaf-litter, bird nests and in stored foodstuffs. Little studied in Fife, with 7 out of 25 British species recorded.

Acari: mites and ticks
A vast assemblage of terrestrial and aquatic invertebrates, many very small. They have been little studied in Fife and no attempt has been made to search the specialist literature.

Hydracarina: water mites
Predatory mites, many very colourful, preying upon crustaceans, insects etc. in fresh water. Very poorly recorded in Fife with only 20 out of about 320 British species.

Halacaridae: sea mites
Nine species were recorded from rock pools in St Andrews Bay and one offshore.

Ixodoidea: ticks
Temporary, blood-sucking parasites of birds and mammals; other species are likely to be present.
Ixodes caledonicus. On birds; I of May.
I.ricinus. On most birds and

mammals; Tentsmuir, I of May.

Parasitidae
Predatory mites, in spite of the name; mainly in leaf-litter etc., but some frequently carried by insects.
Parasitellus fucorum. Carried by bumble bees.
Poecilochirus carabi. On burying beetles; I of May.
Vulgarogamarus kraepelini. I of May.
V.remberti. On rabbits.

Dermanyssidae
Hirstionyssus oryctolagi. On rabbits.

Oribatidae
Nannohermannia nana. One record.

Listrophoridae: fur mites
Tiny mites that cling to individual hairs on mammals.
Listrophorus gibbus. On brown hares and rabbits.

Psoroptidae
Otodectes cynotis. Ears of cats and rabbits, causing otodectic mange.
Psoroptes ovis. Causes sheep-scab.

Sarcoptidae
Notoedres cati. Causes mange in cats and dogs.

Trombiculidae
Neotrombicula autumnalis, Harvest-mite (berry bug). On rabbits etc. and a pest on people in autumn.

Trombidiidae
Trombidium holosericeum, Red velvet mite. Widespread.

Demodicidae
Demodex canis. Causes red mange in dogs.

Eriophyidae: gall-mites
A large group of mites causing galls in many species of trees and herbs; 5 species recorded, including:
Aceria fraxinivora. On ash.

Tetranychidae
Bryobia praetiosa. On herbaceous plants, sometimes swarming on buildings.

Cheyletidae
Cheyletiella parasitivorax. On rabbits and dogs; predators on other mites.

Tardigrada: water-bears
Microscopic animals ubiquitous in moss (on which most species feed), with a few species on the sea-shore. Poorly recorded in Fife.
Macrobiotus hufelandii. L Gelly.
Hypsibius angustatus. Thornton; in moss.
H.chilenensis.
H.scoticus. Thornton.

CRUSTACEA: CRUSTACEANS

A vast group of mainly aquatic invertebrates, ranging from microscopic forms in the plankton to the large crabs and lobsters. The base-line for knowledge of the crustaceans of the Forth and south Fife is the catalogue of Scott (1906).

Branchiopoda

Cladocera: waterfleas
Small, free-swimming crustaceans, mainly in fresh water; 26 fresh-water and 2 marine species recorded.

Ostracoda: ostracods
Minute crustaceans with a bivalved shell, very abundant and diverse in both fresh water and the sea; 25 fresh-water and 83 marine species recorded.

Copepoda
Marine and freshwater crustaceans. Most are very small, less than 1 mm. Many are planktonic but others are parasitic in fish and in invertebrates; 306 species were recorded from the Forth area by Scott (1906), most from Fife waters.

Calanoida
Mostly free-swimming planktonic copepods including *Calanus finmarchicus*, the principal food of herring; 24 marine species recorded; freshwater species probably also present.

Poecilostomatoidea
Parasites and commensals of fish and invertebrates.
Mytilicola intestinalis. Parasite of mussels; IF,OF.

Harpacticoida
Tiny copepods in many marine and brackish habitats; an important component of meiobenthos, i.e. living in the spaces between sand-grains; 116 species recorded.

Cyclopoida
Mostly free-living copepods in fresh and salt water; some parasitic.

Cyclopidae
10 marine and 8 freshwater species recorded.

Notodelphyidae
Notodelphys allmani. In sea-squirts; OF.

Ascidicolidae
Ascidicola rosea. In sea-squirts; OF.
Aplostoma affinis. In sea-squirts; OF.

Poecilostomatoida
Parasitic copepods on marine invertebrates and fish; 24 species recorded.

Monstrilloida
Adults pelagic, young parasitic; 5 species recorded in Forth.

Siphonostomatoida
Parasitic on fish and invertebrates; 32 species recorded.

Cirripedia: barnacles etc.
Attached to rocks etc. as adults; including both filter-feeding barnacles and parasitic species.

Thoracica: barnacles
Scalpellum scalpellum. On hydroids offshore; S.
Lepas anatifera. Occasional, on floating timber etc.: S.
Conchoderma auritum. On timber; OF.
Verruca stroemia. Abundant on shore; OF, S.
Balanus balanus. Offshore; OF.
B.crenatus. LW - offshore, on crabs and rock; OF,S,T.
B.hameri. Offshore; OF,S.
Chthamalus stellatus. Offshore; OF.
Semibalanus balanoides. Abundant on rocky shores; IF, OF, S, T.
Elminius modestus. On shore, introduced from New Zealand; T.

Rhizocephala
Parasitic species

Peltogaster paguri. On hermit crabs; OF,S.

Sacculina carcini. On shore crabs; S.

Malacostraca

The majority of the larger crustaceans.

Leptostraca

Small marine crustaceans with a bivalved carapace.

Nebalia bipes. Under stones on shore; S.

Cumacea

Small, tadpole-like marine crustaceans, found on sandy shores as well as offshore on the bottom and in the plankton; 24 species recorded.

Tanaidacea

Small, flattened, marine, crustaceans found on shore and in shallow water; 9 species recorded.

Mysidacea

Small, shrimp-like, marine crustaceans; 18 species recorded, mostly offshore but a few, including the chameleon shrimp, *Praunus flexuosus,* common in shore pools.

Isopoda

Terrestrial isopods: woodlice
Woodlice feed mainly upon dead vegetation, fungi and other organic detritus, especially in the leaf-litter but also on tree trunks and in the soil. They are sensitive to dessication and are active mainly at night. Moderately well recorded, with 15 species recorded in Fife out of 20 in Scotland; the following are very widepread or distinctive:

Ligia oceanica. Rocky shores around HWM.

Trichoniscus pusillus. Ubiquitous and usually abundant in leaf-litter, both woodland and grassland.

Oniscus asellus. The most abundant and ubiquitous of the larger woodlice.

Philoscia muscorum. Widespread, especially in grassland.

Armadillidium vulgare, Pill woodlouse. A few coastal, calcareous sites.

Porcellio scaber. Widespread, especially in dead wood and under bark.

Freshwater isopods
Asellus aquaticus. Widespread, including moderately polluted burns and ditches.

Marine isopods
Woodlouse-like crustaceans, found amongst algae, under stones etc. on and offshore; 26 species recorded, of which two are parasitic, on hermit crabs and barnacles.

Amphipoda: sandhoppers etc.
Small crustaceans with the body flattened from side to side. Shore or bottom living; a few in fresh water.

Marine amphipods; 165 species recorded; the commonest sandhoppers on the tideline are *Orchestia gammarellus* and *Talitrus saltator* while *Corophium volutator* is very abundant in estuarine mud.

Freshwater amphipods

Gammaridae
Crangonyx pseudogracilis. R Eden, R Leven; an introduction from N America.

Gammarus lacustris. R Ore.

G.pulex. Widespread.

Decapoda: prawns, crabs etc.
Mostly large, active crustaceans; some predatory, many detritus feeders, some filter-feeders.

Prawns, shrimps and lobsters; 17 species recorded, including the following:

Crangon crangon, Common shrimp. Mid-shore - offshore, on sand; IF,OF,S.

Homarus gammarus, Lobster. LW - offshore; OF,S.

Nephrops norvegicus, Norway lobster (Scampi). Offshore, burrowing in mud and sand; a major target of fisheries; OF,S.

Pandalus montagui, Aesop prawn. Common LW - offshore; OF,S.

Paguridae: hermit crabs
In discarded gastropod shells.

Anapagurus laevis. Offshore; OF,S.

Pagurus bernhardus. Abundant on and offshore; OF,S,T.

P.cuanensis. Offshore; OF,S.

P.pubescens. Offshore; OF.

Galatheidae: squat lobsters
Mostly offshore; 7 species.

Porcellanidae
Pisidia longicornis. On and offshore; OF,S,T.

Porcellana platycheles, Porcelain crab. On shore; OF,S.

Brachyura: crabs
Atelecyclidae
Atelecyclus rotundatus, Circular crab. Offshore; OF.

Cancridae
Cancer pagurus, Edible crab. Mid-shore - offshore; OF,S,T.

Corystidae
Corystes cassivelaunus, Masked crab. LW - offshore; OF,S.

Geryonidae
Geryon tridens. Offshore on mud; OF.

Leucosiidae
Ebalia tuberosa, Nut crab.
  Offshore; I of May.
E.cranchii. Offshore; OF,S.

Lithodidae
Lithodes maja, Stone crab.
  Offshore; I of May.

Majidae
Eurynome aspera, Strawberry
  crab. Offshore; S.
Hyas araneus, Great
  spider-crab. LW - offshore;
  OF,S,T.
H.coarctatus. Offshore; OF,S.

Inachus dorsettensis, Scorpion
  spider-crab. Offshore; S,T.
I.leptochirus, Slender-legged
  spider-crab. Offshore; OF.
I.phalangium, Leach's
  spider-crab. Offshore; S.
Macropodia rostrata,
  Long-legged spider-crab.
  Offshore; OF,S.

Portunidae
Carcinus maenas, Shore crab.
  Abundant on shore; OF,S,T.
Liocarcinus depurator, Harbour
  crab. LW - offshore; OF,S,T.
L.holsatus. Offshore; OF,S.
L.marmoreus, Marbled

swimming crab. Offshore on
  sand; I of May,S.
L.pusillus, Offshore; OF,S.
Necora puber, Velvet crab.
  Offshore; OF,S,T.
Pirimela denticulata, LW; S.
Portumnus latipes, Pennant's
  swimming crab. Offshore on
  sand; OF,S.

Pinnotheridae
Pinnotheres pisum, Pea crab.
  Parasitic in mussels etc.;
  OF,S,T.

MOLLUSCA: MOLLUSCS

Molluscs are extremely diverse and abundant in both terrestrial and aquatic habitats. The lists of marine species are based primarily upon McKay and Smith (1979) which includes maps of most species, with names updated from Smith and Heppel (1991).

Caudofoveata

Worm-like molluscs without a shell.
Chaetoderma nitidulum. On muddy gravel; OF.

Polyplacophora: chitons

Limpet-like grazing molluscs, with the shell in 8 segments. Entirely marine; 8 species recorded of which *Lepidochiton cinereus* is the only common one on shore.

Gastropoda: snails and slugs

Land snails and slugs
Mainly herbivorous, but many feed on dead vegetation and fungi, and a few are predatory. Names follow Kerney and Cameron (1979), updated.

Snails (with prominent shell)
Carychium minimum. Local; marshes.
C.tridentatum. Widespread; woodland litter.
Oxyloma elegans. Widespread; marshes.
Cochlicopa lubrica. Common in many habitats.
C.lubricella. Local, mainly coastal.
Columella edentula. Local in woodland.
C.aspera. Local in damp woods and grassland.
Vertigo antivertigo. Wetland, old records only.
V.pygmaea. Very local, mainly calcareous grassland by coast.
V.substriata. Very local in wetland.
Pupilla muscorum. Local, mainly coastal and calcareous sites.
Leiostyla anglica. Mainly old woodland; old records only.
Lauria cylindracea. Common in a variety of habitats.
Vallonia costata. Locally

common, mainly around coast.
V.excentrica. Common in a variety of habitats but mainly in woodland.
Acanthinula aculeata. Common in woodland.
Ena obscura. Local, usually woodland.
Punctum pygmaeum. Common, mainly woodland.
Discus rotundatus. Very common in many habitats.
Vitrea crystallina. Common, especially in woodland.
V.contracta. Local, particularly woodland on calcareous sites.
Nesovitrea hammonis. Local, wetland and wet woodland.
Aegopinella nitidula. Common in a variety of habitats.
A.pura. Common in woodland, usually in low numbers.
Oxychilus alliarius. Common in a variety of habitats.
O.cellarius. Common in a variety of habitats.
O.draparnauldi. Local, mainly in disturbed habitats.
Euconulus fulvus. Common in woodland.

Clausilia bidentata. Local, mainly coastal and in woodland.

Cochlodina laminata. Old record, W Fife.

Balea perversa. Very local in a variety of habitats.

Candidula intersecta. Common on coast and a few inland calcareous sites.

Helicella itala. Dunes from Largo to St Monans.

Monacha cantiana. Formerly Tentsmuir and Largo Bay; perhaps extinct.

Ashfordia granulata. One old record.

Zenobiella subrufescens. Old woodland; old records only.

Trichia hispida. Common in many habitats.

T.striolata. Common in many habitats.

Arianta arbustorum. Common in woods and wetland.

Cepaea hortensis. Fairly common in many habitats.

C.nemoralis. Common in many habitats.

Helix aspersa. Common around coasts and some inland sites.

Slugs.

These represent four separate families, each more closely related to shelled snails than to each other; 19 species recorded, including:

Arion ater. The familiar large black slug; widespread.

Limax marginatus. Common in woods, often climbing trees.

L.maximus. Common in many habitats.

Deroceros reticulatum. Ubiquitous and abundant.

Freshwater snails
All herbivorous.

Valvata cristata. Old records only.

V.piscinalis. Common.

Potamopyrgus antipodarum. Common; also in estuaries.

Physa fontinalis. R Leven only.

Lymnaea auricularis. Shells locally common; current status uncertain.

L.palustris. Local, including R Leven.

L.peregra. Widespread.

L.stagnalis. Common, often introduced in garden ponds.

L.truncatula. Common.

Planorbis carinata. Locally common.

P.planorbis. Local.

Anisus leucostoma. Rivers; old records only.

A.vortex. Local; L Fitty.

Bathyomphalus contortus. Common.

Gyraulis albus. Local.

G.laevis. Local.

Armiger crista. Old records only.

Hippeatis complanatus. Old records only.

Ancylus fluviatilis, River limpet. Common in running water.

Acroloxus lacustris, Lake limpet. Old records only.

Marine snails
Herbivores, grazing on algae, predators and a few parasites. All are found on fully marine rocky shores unless otherwise indicated.
Predominantly herbivorous species.

Fissurellidae: slit-limpets
Emarginula fissura. In deep water on rocks; OF,S.

Puncturella noathina. Off I of May.

Acmaeidae: tortoise-shell limpets
Tectura testudinalis. M - LW; IF,OF,S,T.

T.virginea. Pools at LW; OF,S.

Patellidae: limpets
Patella vulgata, Common

limpet. Abundant on all rocky shores.

P.ulyssiponensis, China limpet. Pools on exposed shores; IF,OF,S.

Helcion pellucidum, Blue-rayed limpet. On kelp and wrack; OF,S,T.

Trochidae; topshells
7 species, of which the grey topshell, *Gibbula cineraria*, is abundant on rocky shores.

Turritellidae
Turritella communis, Screw shell. Common offshore; IF,OF,S.

Littorinidae
Lacuna crassior, a chink shell. Offshore; OF,S.

L.pallidula. Common in brown algae; OF,S,T.

L.vincta. Widespread on shore; OF,S,T.

Littorina littorea, Common periwinkle. Abundant on shore.

L.obtusata, Flat periwinkle. Abundant on shore.

L.mariae. Common on shore.

L.neglecta. Common on shore; OF,S.

L.saxatilis, Rough periwinkle. H-MW; IF,OF,S,T.

L.nigrolineata. Common on shore; OF,S.

Melarhaphe neritoides. HW, on exposed rocks; OF,S.

Skeneopsidae
Skeneopsis planorbis. In pools and offshore; OF,S,T.

Rissoidae
With small conical shells up to 5 mm; 9 species recorded, including *Rissoa parva* which is abundant on and offshore.

Iravadiidae
Ceratia proxima. Doubtful in Forth.

Hyala vitrea. Common offshore in Forth.

Hydrobiidae
Hydrobia ulvae. Very abundant on estuarine mud, feeding mainly on diatoms.

Caecidae
Caecum glabrum. Rare, dead shells only; OF.
C.imperforatum. E of I of May.

Predominantly predatory species of marine snails.

Aporrhaidae
Aporrhais pespelecani, Pelican's-foot shell. Offshore; OF,S,T.

Capulidae
Capulus ungaricus, Fool's cap. Offshore, rare; OF,S.
Trichotropis borealis. Rare offshore; S.

Triviidae: cowries
Trivia arctica. LW and offshore; OF,S.
T.monacha. Rare, E Neuk.

Lamellariidae
Lamellaria perspicua. Under stones LW; OF,S.
L.latens. LW; OF.
Velutina velutina, Velvet shell. LW and offshore; OF,S.
V.plicatilis. Rare: fresh shells at Crail.

Naticidae: necklace shells
Polineces catena. Offshore on sand; St Andrews and Tentsmuir.
P.polianus. MW-offshore on sand; OF,S,T.
P.montagui. Offshore, shells rare on tideline; OF,S.

Eulimidae
With long, slender shells; ecto-parasitic on echinoderms; 3, perhaps 4 species recorded.

Muricidae
Boreotrophon truncatus. Offshore; dead shells common; OF,S.
Trophonopsis barvicensis. Rare offshore; OF.
Nucella lapillus, Dog whelk. Abundant on all rocky shores, feeding on barnacles.
Ocenebra erinacea. Rare offshore; OF.

Buccinidae
Buccinum undatum, Whelk. Pools and offshore, abundant, widespread.
Colus gracilis. Offshore, shells rare on shore; OF,S.
C.jeffreysianus. Deep water; one record E of I of May.
Neptunea antiqua, Buckie. Common offshore; OF,S.
Hinia incrassata, a dog-whelk. Common LW; OF,S.
H.pygmaea. Rare, off I of May, worn shells only.

Turridae
With small, spindle-shaped shells; 7 species recorded, mostly rare and offshore.

Omalogyridae
With a tiny shell (1 mm), on algae in shore pools.
Omalogyrus atomus. MW ; OF,S.

Pyramidellidae
Ectoparasites with small conical shells, up to 10 mm; 14 species recorded, mostly rare and off-shore, but *Brachystomia scalaris* is a common parasite on mussels.

Cephalaspidea
Predators, many with shell re-duced and internal; 11 species recorded, including:
Acteon tornatilis, Beer barrel. LW, muddy gravel; OF,S.

Marine slugs

Saccoglossa
Herbivores, grazing on algae.

Placida dendritica. On green algae; S.
Hermaea bifida. MW pool, Aberdour.
Limapontia capitata. Pools high on shore; OF,S.
L.depressa. Eden Estuary, salt-marsh.

Anaspidea
Aplysia punctata. LW, pools, grazing on algae; S.

Notaspidea
Berthella plumula. MW pools, preying on sea-squirts; S.

Thecosomata
Limacina retroversa. Planktonic; OF.

Gymnosomata
Planktonic.
Clione limacina. OF.

Nudibranchia
Predatory sea-slugs, feeding mainly on sedentary animals such as sponges, sea-mats and hydroids; 33 species recorded of which the following are common on shore:
Onchidoris bilamellata. Feeding on barnacles; OF,S,T.
Acanthodoris pilosa. OF,S.
Aegires punctilucens. Under boulders on shore; OF,S.
Cadlina laevis. Widespread on and offshore; OF,S.
Archidoris pseudoargus. Common on and offshore; OF,S.

Scaphopoda: elephant-tooth shells

Detritus feeders, living offshore in mud and sand.
Antalis entalis. Common; OF,S.

Pelecypoda: bivalves

Filter-feeding molluscs, most living buried in soft sediments; fresh water, intertidal and off-shore.

Fresh-water bivalves

Margaritifera margaritifera, Pearl mussel. Formerly in rivers Leven and Eden; possibly now extinct.

Anadonta anatina, Duck mussel. R Leven only.

A.cygnaea, Swan mussel. Old records only.

Sphaerium corneum. Common.

S.lacustre. Old records only.

Pisidium spp. 10 species recorded, of which *P.amnicum* is the largest and *P.nitidum* the most widespread.

Marine bivalves

Nuculoidea

Nucula nitidosa. Common offshore in mud; IF,OF,S.

N.nucleus. Common offshore in mud; IF,OF,S.

Nuculoma tenuis. Offshore; OF,S.

Jupiteria minuta. Common offshore; OF.

Arcoidea

Arca tetragona, Ark shell. Offshore; OF.

Glycymeris glycymeris, Dog-cockle. Far offshore, on sand; OF,S.

Mytiloidea: mussels

Mytilis edulis, Common mussel. Abundant on all shores, including estuaries.

Modiolus modiolus, Horse-mussel. Common offshore, and in shore pools; IF,OF,S,T.

Modiolula phaseolina, Bean horse-mussel. Near I of May.

Crenella decussata. Locally abundant offshore; OF.

Modiolarca tumida. LW - offshore, especially in sea-squirts; OF,S.

Musculus discors. Common on shore; OF,S.

M.niger. Rare; dead shells near I of May.

Limoidea

Limaria loscombi. Rare; dead shells near I of May and in stomach of cod; S.

Limatula subauriculata. Dead shells only; S.

Ostreoidea: oysters and scallops

Ostrea edulis, Common oyster. Formerly fished in Forth; now rare or extinct.

Crassostrea gigas, Portuguese oyster. Dead shells; IF.

Chlamys distorta. LW - offshore, on rock; IF,OF,S.

C.varia. Offshore; I of May, OF.

Pecten maximus, Great scallop. Occasional offshore; S,T.

Aequipecten opercularis, Queen scallop. Common offshore, fished commmercially in Forth at times; IF,OF,S,T.

Palliolum striatum. Occasional offshore; OF.

P.tigerinum, Tiger scallop. Offshore; dead shells common; OF,S.

Similipecten similis. Offshore; dead shells only; OF,S.

[*Anomia ephippium,* Saddle oyster. Records probably erroneous.]

Heteranomia squamula. Common on and offshore, under boulders etc.; OF,S,T.

Pododesmus patelliformis. LW - offshore, common; OF,S.

Veneroidea

Lucinacea

Lucinoma borealis. Offshore in sand and gravel; OF,S.

Thyasira flexuosa. Common offshore in sand and gravel; IF,OF,S,T.

Galeommatacea

Kellia suborbicularis. On and offshore, in muddy debris.

Lasaea adansoni. On shore, E Neuk.

Semierycina nitida. Rare; dead shells E Neuk.

Montacuta substriata. Rare, on echinoderms; Fife Ness.

Tellimyia ferruginosa. Deep water; OF,S.

Mysella bidentata. LW - offshore; IF,OF,S,T.

Astartacea

Astarte sulcata. Rare, offshore; OF.

Goodallia triangularis. Rare, E Neuk.

Tridonta elliptica. Near I of May.

T.montagui. Offshore in muddy gravel; OF.

Cardiacea: cockles

Acanthocardia echinata, Prickly cockle. Common offshore; IF,OF,S,T.

Parvicardium minimum. Rare; OF.

P.ovale. Common in gravel offshore; OF,S.

P.scabrum. Offshore; OF,S.

Laevicardium crassum, Smooth cockle. Scarce, offshore; S.

Cerastoderma edule, Common cockle. Common on sandy shores; IF,OF,S,T.

Mactracea

Mactra stultorum, Rayed trough-shell. In sand around LW; OF,S,T.

Spisula elliptica. Offshore, OF.

S.solida. Common in sand LW - offshore; IF,OF,S,T.

S.subtruncata. Common in sand LW - offshore; OF,S,T.

Lutraria lutraria, Otter-shell. Offshore, shells common on tide-line; OF,S,T.

Solenacea: razor-shells

Ensis arcuatus. Offshore; OF,S.

E.ensis. Offshore; OF,S.

E.siliqua. The commonest razor, around LW in clean sand; OF,S,T.

Phaxas pellucidus. Common offshore; OF,S.

Tellinacea: tellins

Angulus tenuis, Thin tellin. In clean sand around LW; OF,S,T.

Arcopagia crassa. Offshore, scarce; OF,S.

Fabulina fabula. On and offshore, in silty sand; OF,S,T.

Moerella pygmaea. Scarce, offshore; OF,S.

Macoma balthica, Baltic tellin. Abundant on shores with muddy sand; IF,OF,S,T.

Donax vittatus, Banded wedge-shell. Common LW and shallow water, in sand; OF,S,T.

Gari tellinella. Offshore, in coarse sand; OF.

G.fervensis. Offshore, in sand; OF,S,T.

Abra alba. Abundant offshore, in sand; IF,OF,S,T.

A.nitida. LW - offshore, in mud; IF,OF,S,T.

A.prismatica. Offshore, in clean sand; OF,S,T.

Scrobicularia plana. Estuaries, in mud; IF,S,T.

Arcticacea

Arctica islandica. Widspread offshore.

Veneracea

Circomphalus cassina. Offshore, in coarse sand; S.

Gouldia minima. Offshore, in gravel; E Neuk.

Chamelea gallina, Striped venus. On and offshore, widespread in sand.

Clausinella fasciata, Banded venus. Offshore, in gravel; OF,S.

Timoclea ovata, Oval venus. Offshore in sand; OF,S.

Tapes rhomboides, Banded carpet-shell. Offshore; IF,OF,T.

Venerupis senegalensis, Pullet carpet-shell. On and

offshore, in crevices; IF,OF,S.

Dosinia lupinus. Common on and offshore, in sand; OF,S,T.

D.exoleta. Offshore; OF,S.

Turtonia minuta. Rocky shores; OF,S.

Mysia undata. Common offshore; OF,S.

Myoidea

Mya truncata, Blunt gaper. LW-offshore, abundant in muddy gravel; IF,OF,S.

M.arenaria, Sand gaper. Shore and shallow water, in sand; IF,OF,S,T.

Corbula gibba. Common offshore in muddy gravel; OF,S.

Hiatella arctica. LW - offshore, under boulders etc; OF,S.

Saxicavella jeffreysi. Rare as dead shells on tide-line, E Neuk.

[*Pholas dactylus*, Common piddock. Doubtful; OF,S.]

Barnea candida, White piddock. Burrowing in soft rock; OF,S.

Zirphaea crispata, Oval piddock. LW, burrows in soft rock; OF,S.

Xylophaga dorsalis, Wood piddock. Occasional, burrowing in driftwood; S.

Teredo navalis, Shipworm. In driftwood; S.

Psiloteredo megotara. In driftwood, one record E Neuk.

Pholadomyoidea

Thracia convexa. Offshore in muddy gravel; OF.

T.phaseolina. On and offshore; OF,S.

T.villosiuscula. Offshore in muddy gravel; OF.

T.distorta. Rare; OF.

Cochlodesma praetenue. Offshore; OF,S.

Cephalopoda: cuttlefish, squid and octopus

Large active predatory molluscs, without external shell (in local species).

Sepia officinalis, Common cuttlefish. Cuttlebone common on tideline; OF,S.

Sepiola aurantiaca. Old records from Forth.

S.atlantica, Dumpling squid. Common offshore; OF,S.

Loligo forbsii, Long-finned squid. Commonest squid, sometimes fished commercially; OF,S.

Alloteuthis subulata. S.

Todarodes sagittatus. Common offshore, occasional mass strandings; OF,S.

Eledone cirrhosa, Curled octopus. Common offshore, on rocky bottoms; OF,S.

BRYZOA: SEA-MATS

Sessile, colonial, filter-feeding animals, forming crusts on rocks, seaweed etc., or plant-like fronds; mostly marine.

Cyclostomatida

Calcified, encrusting or erect; 12 species recorded, mostly off-shore.

Cheilostomatida

Calcified, encrusting or erect; 51 species recorded; the following are conspicuous on the tideline:

Membranipora membranacea. On kelp etc.; OF,S.

Flustra foliacea, Hornwrack. Abundant in shallow water; seaweed-like fronds, often abundant on tide-line.

Ctenostomatida

Fleshy or gelatinous, encrusting or erect; 10 species recorded, including:

Alcyonidium gelatinosum.

Branching fronds on algae on shore; OF,S.

Flustrellidra hispida. On shore, on *Fucus* and stones; OF,S.

PHORONA

Sedentary, filter-feeding marine invertebrates.

Phoronis muelleri. Offshore in sand; OF,S.

P.ovalis. Offshore; OF.

ANNELIDA: SEGMENTED-WORMS

Segmented worms, abundant in marine, fresh water and terrestrial habitats.

Polychaeta: multi-bristled worms

A very diverse group of detritus feeders and predators. Pioneering studies were undertaken at the Gatty Marine Laboratory, St Andrews by Professor W C McIntosh between 1883 and 1917.

Predominantly active polychaetes

Aphroditidae

Aphrodita aculeata, Seamouse. Common offshore in sand and often washed ashore; OF,S.

Polynoidae: scale worms
Predatory, often rather short worms with overlapping scales on the back; 16 species recorded.

Pholoidae
Pholoe inornata. LW and offshore; IF,OF.

P.synophthalmica. Offshore; IF.

Sigalionidae
Active predatory worms in sand.
Sigalion mathildae. Common offshore; OF,S.

Sthenelais boa. Under stones on shore; S.

S.limicola. Offshore; OF,S.

Eunicidae
Long slender worms with an evertible proboscis; 8 species recorded.

Glyceridae
Predatory worms burrowing in sand and mud; 7 species recorded.

Hesionidae
Active, centipede-like worms.
Kefersteinia cirrata. Under stones, in pools and offshore; OF,S.

Nereimyra punctata. LW - offshore [kelp holdfasts etc.]; S.

Nephtyidae
Large, active, pallid worms.
Nephtys hombergi. In sand and under stones on and offshore; IF,OF,S,T.
Plus 5 other species of *Nephtys.*

Nereidae: ragworms
Large worms, some over 30 cm; predators and scavengers.
Hediste diversicolor, Common ragworm. Muddy sand on shore; IF,OF,S,T.

Neanthes fucata. Offshore, often in *Buccinum* shells with hermit crabs; S.

N.virens, King rag. On shore; OF,S,T, common in Eden Est.

Nereis longissima. Offshore in mud; IF,OF,S.

N.pelagica. Abundant LW and offshore; IF,OF,S,T.

Perinereis cultrifera. Under stones on mud; S.

Platynereis dumerillii. LW - offshore, in crevices and kelp holdfasts; S.

Phyllodocidae: paddle worms
Active, predatory worms, some large (up to 45 cm); 20 species recorded; *Paranaitis maculata* is abundant on and offshore.

Sphaerodoridae
Sphaerodorum flavum. LW - offshore amongst algae; OF,S.

Syllidae
Predators, some feeding on hydroids; 9 species recorded.

Tomopteridae
Active planktonic worms.
Tomopteris helgolandica. Abundant; S.

Predominantly sedentary polychaetes
Ampharetidae
Offshore worms, in a membranous tube in sand; 6 species recorded.

Arenicolidae
Arenicola marina, Lugworm. Abundant in sand on lower shore; IF,OF,S,T.

A.defodiens, Black lugworm. On shore in deep, black zone of sediment.

Capitellidae
Capitella capitata. In mud amongst rock, LW - offshore; IF,OF,S,T.

Notomastus latericeus. LW - offshore [in sand]; OF,S.

Chaetopteridae
In tough, permanent tubes in sand and mud; 5 species recorded offshore.

Cirratulidae
Cirratulus cirratus. In mud and muddy sand, on and offshore; IF,S.

Cirriformia tentaculata. Mud at LW; IF,S.

Dodecaceria concharum. LW - offshore, in kelp holdfasts; IF,OF,S.

Tharyx marioni. Offshore; IF,OF.

Flabelligeridae
Diplocirrus glaucus. Offshore;
    OF,S.
Flabelligera affinis. On and
    offshore; S; [associated with
    sea-urchins].
Pherusa plumosa. Mud/rock on
    and offshore; IF,OF,S.

Magelonidae
Burrow in sand.
Magelona alleni. Offshore; OF.
M.filiformis. Offshore; OF.
M.mirabilis. Offshore, in
    gravelly sand; OF,S,T.
Poecilochaetus serpens. Offshore;
    S.

Maldanidae
In tubes in sand and mud.
Nicomache lumbricalis. Under
    stones on shore - offshore; S.

Opheliidae
Ophelia borealis. Offshore; S.
O.limacina. On and offshore; T.
Ophelina acuminata. On mud;
    IF,OF.

Orbiniidae
Orbinia sertulata. Sandy shore;
    S.
O.latreilli. Sandy shore; S.
Scoloplos armiger. Under stones
    on sand, LW - offshore;
    OF,S,T, common in Eden
    and Tay estuaries.

Oweniidae
In tubes encrusted with sand.
Myriochele heeri. Offshore in
    mud; S.
Owenia fusiformis. Offshore;
    OF, S.

Pectinariidae
In tubes in sand.
Amphictene auricoma. Offshore
    in sand; S.
Lagis koreni. LW - offshore in
    sand; OF,S.
Pectinaria belgica. Abundant
    offshore [in muddy sand];
    OF,S.

Scalibregmidae
Scalibregma inflatum. Offshore;
    IF,OF,S.

Spionidae
Usually in U-shaped burrows in
sand or mud; 20 species recorded.

Terebellidae
In tubes in sand and mud, feeding on detritus; 11 species
recorded including:
Lanice conchilega, Sand mason.
    Abundant on sandy shores
    and offshore, making tubes
    of sand grains; IF,OF,S,T.

Sabellariidae
In tubes often cemented
together in colonies.
Sabellaria spinulosa. Abundant
    on and offshore, on rock;
    IF,OF,S.

Sabellidae
In tubes in sand and mud; a
crown of feeding tentacles; 7
species recorded, the following 2
very abundant in estuaries:
Fabricia stellaris. Abundant on
    muddy shores and mussel
    beds; OF,S.
Manayunkia aestuarina.
    Abundant in mud; IF,OF.

Serpulidae
In calcareous tubes; feed on suspended particles; 6 species
recorded, one abundant on rocky
shores:
Pomatoceros triqueter. In
    calcareous tube on rocks, on
    and offshore; OF,S,T.

Spirorbidae
In small spiral calcareous tubes
encrusting seaweed etc.
Circeis spirillum. Offshore on
    hydroids etc.; S.
Jugaria granulata. Common in
    pools; S.
Spirorbis spirorbis. On algae; S.

Oligochaeta: earthworms etc.
Apart from earthworms, many
more freshwater and marine
species are likely to be present.

Lumbricidae: earthworms
Predominantly terrestrial
worms but including a few in
fresh water; 13 species recorded,
including:
Allolobophora chlorotica.
    Widespread.
Aporrectodea caliginosa.
    Abundant in cultivated soil.
A.longa. Abundant in
    cultivated land.
Eiseniella tetraedra. In fresh
    water; widespread.
Lumbricus castaneus.
    Widespread.
L.rubellus. Widespread, often
    under dung.
L.terrestris. Most common in
    grassland.
Satchellius mammalis.
    Widespread.

Enchytraeidae: potworms
Small pale mainly soil-dwelling
worms, with a few species in
fresh water; ubiquitous but
rarely recorded; 14 species recorded.

Lumbriculidae
Small worms in fresh water.
Lumbriculus variegatus.
    Widespread.
Stylodrilus heringianus. Eden.

Tubificidae
Small worms, in both fresh and
salt water, some very abundant
in estuarine mud; 14 species recorded.

Naididae
Small worms, under 2 mm; 3
freshwater species recorded,
plus:
Nais communis. Intertidal mud;
    OF.

Hirudinea: leeches

Aquatic worms, mostly external parasites but some predatory.

Marine leaches; all are parasitic on fish; 5 species recorded.

Freshwater leaches; predators on invertebrates; some parasites on fish, amphibians and water birds; 7 species recorded.

ECHIURA

Unsegmented marine worms living in mud and sand.
Echiurus echiurus. Offshore mud; OF,S.
E.pallasii. Common; S.

CHAETOGNATHA: ARROW-WORMS

Actively swimming, marine, planktonic, predatory worms.
Sagitta elegans. In plankton; S.
S.setosa. In plankton; S.

PRIAPULA

Almost radially symmetrical, unsegmented marine worms.
Priapulus caudatus. Intertidal mud; OF.

SIPUNCULA

Unsegmented marine worms burrowing in mud and sand.
Golfingia vulgaris. Offshore; OF.
Nephasoma minuta. Rock-pools - offshore, amongst algal holdfasts; S.
Thysanocardia procera. Offshore; OF.
Phascolion strombi. In gastropod shells offshore; OF,S.

PYCNOGONIDA: SEA-SPIDERS

Small, short-bodied, predatory, marine animals with four pairs of long jointed legs. Usually amongst seaweed holdfasts or under stones; 12 species re-corded; *Pycnogonum littorale* is common on shore.

NEMERTEA: RIBBON-WORMS

Wholly marine, predatory, un-segmented worms, some reaching extraordinary lengths (e.g. *Lineus longissimus* up to 30 metres); mostly under stones on muddy shores or amongst the holdfasts of seaweeds; 27 species recorded.

ENTOPROCTA

Sessile, filter-feeding marine animals, many colonial.
Pedicellina cernua. Abundant on red algae and on sea-squirts; OF,S.

ROTIFERA: ROTIFERS

Microscopic but complex animals, ubiquitous in fresh water, including wet moss, with a few species marine (and some both); 119 species recorded in Fife, mostly by John Hood, an ama-teur microscopist in Dundee in the late 19th century.

KINORHYNCHA

Tiny, segmented, spiny worms in marine sediments; 4 species recorded.

NEMATODA: ROUNDWORMS

Unsegmented worms, many very small or microscopic; ubiq-uitous and abundant but little studied. The specialist literature has not been systematically sear-ched.

Dorylaimida

Longidoridae
Parasitic on roots of plants; 4 species widespread in Fife soils.

Trichodoridae
External parasites on roots of plants; 7 species recorded.

Tylenchida

Criconematidae
Tiny roundworms in soil, under 2 mm; parasitic on plant roots, especially woody plants; 6 species recorded.

Hoplolaimidae
Plant parasites.
Rotylenchus goodeyi. Widespread.
R.robustus. Widespread.

Mononchida
Soil-living roundworms, preda-tory on those parasitic on roots of plants.

Anatonchidae
Anatonchus tridentatus. Widespread in soil.

Rhabditida
Bunonema reticulatum. In bog moss; Thornton.
B.richtersi. In bog moss; Thornton.

Trichinellida
Trichurus muris. In house mice; I of·May.

NEMATOMORPHA: HORSEHAIR WORMS

Slender, wire-like worms; adults in fresh water, immature stages parasitic in insects and other invertebrates; probably wide-spread, and recorded from I of May and elsewhere, but only one fully identified record:
Parachordodes violaceus. Aberdour.

ACANTHOCEPHALA: SPINY-HEADED WORMS

Small worms, parasitic in the gut of vertebrates; 3 species re-corded.

PLATYHELMINTHES: FLATWORMS

Flat, unsegmented worms; many parasitic.

Turbellaria: non-parasitic flatworms

Predatory worms.
Terrestrial
Artioposthia triangulata, New
   Zealand flatworm.
   Widespread in gardens; first
   recorded in Fife early 1980s.
Microplana terrestris. Gardens
   and woodland.

Freshwater; 6 species recorded.
Marine; 12 species recorded;
many more likely to be present.

Trematoda: flukes

Parasites, mainly in vertebrates
but many with intermediate invertebrate hosts. Little studied
other than those in marine fish
at St Andrews.

Monogenea
Mainly on gills of fish; 4 species
recorded.

Digenea
Mostly in stomach or intestines
of fish, one in porpoise, one in
birds; 30 species recorded; the
sheep liver-fluke, *Fasciola hepatica*, occurs occasionally in
imported sheep but is not en-
demic.

Cestoda: tapeworms

Parasites; adults mainly in gut of
vertebrates; larvae in invertebrates   or   in   muscle   of
vertebrates.   Records   are   of
adults in the intestine of the final
host unless otherwise stated.

Pseudophyllidea
Four species recorded, in fish
and porpoise.

Proteocephalidea
Proteocephalus longicollis. In
   trout.

Spathebothriidea
Bothrimonus sturionis. In
   gammarid crustaceans and
   (experimentally) in fish.

Cyclophyllidea
Nine species recorded, in birds;
larvae in invertebrates.

CNIDARIA: COELENTERATES

Predatory invertebrates, mostly
marine (*Hydra* spp. in fresh
water).

Scyphozoa: jellyfish

Large, pelagic jellyfish, except
for *Haliclystus*.
Cyanea capillata. Large, brown,
   commonly stranded in
   autumn; IF,OF,S.
C.lamarckii. Large, bluish; OF,S.
Aurelia aurita. Small, bluish,
   commonly stranded; enter
   estuaries; IF,OF,S,T.
Haliclystus auricula. LW -
   shallow water, attached to
   algae and sea-grass; S.

Hydrozoa: hydroids and medusae

Hydroida
Mostly small, branching, colonial, sessile coelenterates –
'polyps' – with a free-swimming
medusa (jellyfish-like) stage in
the life-cycle. Most abundant in
shallow water.

Athecata (Anthomedusae)
Feeding polyps cannot be contracted   within   a   protective
'theca'; 35 species recorded of
which 7 are known only in the
medusoid form.

Thecata (Leptomedusae)
Feeding polyps can usually be
contracted within cup-like 'the-

cae'; 69 species recorded of
which 14 are known only as medusae.

Limnomedusae
Medusae with reduced hydroid
stage.
Gonionemus vertens. Medusae;
   Aberdour [probably
   introduced].
Proboscidactyla stellata.
   Medusae; S.

Trachymedusae
Pelagic medusae without a polyp
stage.
Aglantha digitale. S.

Narcomedusae
Oceanic   medusae   without   a
polyp stage.
Solmaris corona. S.

Siphonophora
Floating colonies of polyps with
no free medusa stage.
Muggaiea atlantica. In
   plankton; S.

Anthozoa: sea-anemones etc.

Stolonifera
Colonial;   polyps   arising   from
branching, encrusting stolon.
Sarcodictyon roseum. Offshore;
   OF.

Alcyonacea: soft corals
With fleshy colonies.
Alcyonium digitatum, Dead
   men's fingers. Abundant
   offshore on rocks and shells;
   OF,S.

Pennatulacea: sea-pens
Large, feather-like colonies of
polyps, anchored in soft sediment.
Pennatula phosphorea. In mud
   and sand; OF.
Virgularia mirabilis. Offshore in
   mud; OF.

Cerianth;aria
Solitary anemones in a tube in
soft sediment.

Cerianthus lloydii. LW - offshore; OF,S.

Scleractinia: stony corals
Caryophyllia smithii, Cup-coral. Offshore; I of May.

Actinaria: sea-anemones
Large, solitary polyps; 16 species recorded. The following are the most distinctive ones on shore:
Actinia equina, Beadlet anemone. Widespread on rocky shores.
Urticina felina, Dahlia anemone. LW - offshore; OF,S,T.
Metridium senile, Plumose anemone. LW - offshore; OF,S.
Sagartia elegans. Pools and offshore; S.
S.troglodytes. Abundant LW, often in sand with stones; OF,S,T.

CTENOPHORA: COMB-JELLIES

Planktonic predators, like spherical jellyfish.
Pleurobranchia pileus. OF,S.
Bolinopsis infundibulum. Abundant; IF,OF,S.
Beroe cucumis. S.

PORIFERA: SPONGES

Sedentary, filter-feeding animals; mainly marine, a few in fresh water.

Calcarea

With skeleton of calcareous spicules.
Clathrina coriacea. Offshore; I of May.
Leucosolenia botryoides. Common on rocky shores, on wrack; IF,OF,S.
Sycon ciliatum. On kelp stems, LW; OF,S.
Scypha compressa. Abundant on shore, especially under overhanging rocks; OF,S.
Leuconia nivea. In rock pools; OF,S.

Demospongiae

With skeleton of siliceous spicules; 18 species recorded, including the following:
Halisarca dujardini. Yellow incrustation in pools, LW; OF,S.
Halichondria panicea, Bread-crumb sponge. LW - offshore, on rocks and shells; OF,S,T (up to Rail Bridge).
Euphydatia fluviatilis. Freshwater; upper Tay.

Bibliography
(for Part II)

This includes the principal sources used in compiling the lists, along with the publications followed with respect to names and classification. A more detailed bibliography is included on the accompanying disk available from Fife Nature (p. 223).

Alexander, W B (1932). The natural history of the Firth of Tay. *Transactions and Proceedings of the Perthshire Society of Natural Science* 9 (2), 35–41.

Ballantyne, G H (1970). *The flowering plants of Kirkcaldy and district.* Kirkcaldy, Kirkcaldy Naturalists' Society.

Ballantyne, G H (1978). *The flowering plants of Kinross.* Kirkcaldy, Scottish Wildlife Trust. 2nd ed.1985.

Ballantyne, G H (1982). Wild flowers. In Ballantyne, G H (ed.) *The wildlife and antiquities of Kirkcaldy District,* 81–104. Kirkcaldy Naturalists' Society.

Ballantyne, G H (1990). Flowers of west Fife: a select annotated list. *Forth Naturalist and Historian,* 12, 67–98.

Ballantyne, G H (1991). The wild flowers of Balmerino Parish, Fife: 150 years of change. *Forth Naturalist and Historian,* 14, 65–83.

Bennett, T L (1989). *Littoral and sublittoral survey of the Isle of May, Fife.* Nature Conservancy Council, CSD report 907.

Campbell, J K (1980). The true bugs (Heteroptera) of Tentsmuir Point, Fife. *Forth Naturalist and Historian,* 5, 72–85.

Carpenter, G H and Evans, W (1899). The Collembola and Thysanura of the Edinburgh district. *Proceedings of the Royal Physical Society of Edinburgh,* 14, 221–266.

Corbet, G B and Smout, A-M (1994). *The mammals of Fife: A provisional atlas.* Fife Regional Council.

Emmet, A M (1991). Life history and habits of the British Lepidoptera, in Emmet, A M and Heath, J (eds) *The moths and butterflies of Great Britain and Ireland,* vol.7, part 2, pp 61–301.

Hayward, P J and Ryland, J S (1990). *The marine fauna of the British Isles and north-west Europe.* Clarendon Press, Oxford.

Hayward, P J and Ryland, J S (1995). *Handbook of the marine fauna of north-west Europe.* Oxford University Press.

Kerney, M P and Cameron, R A D (1979). *A field guide to the land snails of Britain and north-west Europe.* Collins, London.

Khayrallah, N and Jones, A M (1975). A survey of the benthos of the Tay Estuary. *Proceedings of the Royal Society of Edinburgh (B),* 75, 113–135.

Kingston, P F (1980). *Firth of Forth benthic faunal survey 1976–1977.* Heriot-Watt University, unpublished report.

Kloet, G S and Hincks, W D (1964). *A checklist of British insects,* 2nd ed., part 1. Royal Entomological Society, London.

Laverack, M S and Blackler, M (1974). *Fauna and flora of St Andrews Bay.* Scottish

Academic Press, Edinburgh, 310 pp.

Leslie, G and Herdman, W A (1881). *The invertebrate fauna of the Firth of Forth.* Edinburgh.

Maitland, P S (1977). *A coded checklist of animals occurring in fresh water in the British Isles.* Institute of Terrestrial Ecology, Edinburgh.

McKay, D W and Smith, S M (1979). *Marine Mollusca of east Scotland.* Royal Scottish Museum, Edinburgh.

Parnell, R (1838). Fishes of the Firth of Forth. *Memoirs of the Wernerian Natural History Society* 7: 161–460.

Scott, T (1906). A catalogue of land, fresh-water and marine Crustacea found in the basin of the river Forth and its estuary. *Proceedings of the Royal Physical Society of Edinburgh*, 1906, 97–190; 267–382.

Smith, S M and Heppell, D (1991). *Checklist of British marine Mollusca.* National Museums of Scotland, Edinburgh.

Smout, A-M (1986). *The birds of Fife. An outline of their status and distribution.* Donald, Edinburgh, 274 pp.

Smout, A-M and Kinnear, P (1993a). *The dragonflies of Fife/ A provisional atlas.* Fife Regional Council.

Smout, A-M and Kinnear, P (1993b). *The butterflies of Fife/ A provisional atlas.* Fife Regional Council.

Smout, A-M and Pritchard, S (1995). *The amphibians and reptiles of Fife: A provisional atlas.* Fife Regional Council.

Stace, C (1991). *New flora of the British Isles.* Cambridge University Press.

Wheeler, A (1992). A list of the common and scientific names of fishes of the British Isles. *Journal of fish biology*, 41, supplement A, 37 pp.

Young, W (1936). A list of the flowering plants and ferns recorded from Fife and Kinross (V.C.85). *Transactions Botanical Society of Edinburgh*, 32, 1–173.

APPENDIX 1

Sites to visit

The following list includes nature reserves and other sites of special interest. All have unrestricted public access unless otherwise stated, but attention should be paid to any local restrictions, for example by keeping to marked paths. Grid references refer to the principal access points. Many other coastal sites could be added – almost the entire coastline is rich in wildlife and is accessible from the Fife Coastal Path and other points. The following abbreviations are used:

CP: Country Park
FC: Forestry Commission
LA: Local Authority Land
LNR: Local Nature Reserve (controlled by the local authority)
NNR: National Nature Reserve (controlled by Scottish Natural Heritage)
RP: Regional Park.
SWT: Reserve controlled by Scottish Wildlife Trust.
WT: Woodland Trust.

Auchtermuchty Common. NO 236134. A rich mixture of woodland, scrub and grassland.

Bankhead Moss. SWT. NO 447106. Raised bog, birch woodland, wet grassland.

Barnyards Marsh, Kilconquhar. SWT. NO 484021. A small fen with a good variety of wetland plants.

Birnie Loch and Gaddon Loch, Collessie. CP. NO 283124. Former gravel pits; waterside plants, breeding black-headed gulls.

Cameron Reservoir. NO 479113. Disused reservoir. Waterfowl, roosting geese in winter.

Carlingnose, N Queensferry. SWT. NT 725596. Cliffs and coastal vegetation.

Cleish Hills. NT 097963. Upland pasture, bogs and lochs.

The Clink, Pitmedden Forest. FC. NO 223128. Mixed woodland.

Coul Reservoir, Glenrothes. LA. NO 269038. Disused reservoir, willow scrub, marsh.

Craighall Den, Ceres. LA. NO 399108. Wooded den with burn.

Cullaloe Reservoir. SWT. NT 186973. Disused reservoir, marsh.

Devilla Forest. NS 959869. Private conifer plantations with some deciduous woodland, lochs and raised bogs.

Dunnikier Park, Kirkcaldy. LA. NT 285940. Woodland walks.

Eden Estuary. LNR. NO 497195 and 451192 (public hide and visitor centre). Estuarine mud and saltmarsh; waders and waterfowl.

Fife Ness. NO 631098. Vantage point for seabird movements.

Fife Ness Muir. SWT. NO 637097. Scrub planted to give refuge for small migrant birds.

Formonthills. WT. NO 262033. Recently planted woodland.

Heatherhall Wood, Ladybank. FC. NO 292093. Mixed-aged conifers, good for red squirrels.

Isle of May. NNR. Limited access by advertised boat trips from Anstruther. Cliffs, sea-bird colonies, seals.

Gillingshill Nature Reserve. LA. NO 510062. Redundant reservoir and den woodland.

Keil's Den, Upper Largo. WT. NO 414042. A good example of a wooded den.

Kennoway Den. LA. NO 347027. A wooded den with a rich variety of habitats.

Kilminning Coast. SWT. NO 630389. Rocky coast, grassland and scrub.

Kilrenny Common. NO 573050. Scrub, grassland and wet woodland.

Letham Glen, Leven. LA. NO 382016. Wooded den.

Levenmouth. View from carpark at NO 382004. Excellent vantage point for waders and waterfowl.

Lielowan Meadow. SWT. NT 092926. Species-rich meadow.

Lindores Loch. NO 268165. Visible from the public road.

Loch Gelly. NT 207927. A shallow loch, good for wildfowl and waders, visible from road on E side.

Lochore Meadows. CP. NT 170951. Loch, woodland, marsh, visitor centre, displays.

Lomond Hills. RP. NO 228063. Upland grassland and heather moorland.

Morton Lochs. NNR. NO 460262. Shallow lochs, wildfowl, wetland vegetation, public hide.

Pittencrieff Glen, Dunfermline. LA. Wooded park.

Ravenscraig Park, Kirkcaldy. LA. NT 292925. Woodland and seaside walks.

Riverside Park, Glenrothes. LA. NO 265016. River Leven, estate woodland.

Ruddon's Point. Access from Shell Bay Caravan Park at NO 463005 (charge for parking). Flower-rich promontory; good vantage point for wildfowl of Largo Bay.

Saline Den. NT 023924. Wooded den with burn.

Tentsmuir Forest. FC. NO 498241. Mature coniferous plantations with clearings.

Tentsmuir Point. NNR. NO 498241. Expanding dunes and dune-slacks; seals on sand-banks.

Torry Bay. LNR. NS 990859, NT 023859. Estuarine mudflats; waders and waterfowl.

Townhill Park, Dunfermline. CP. NT 103891. Loch, conifer wood and grassland.

Valleyfield Woods. NT 008869. Wooded den and estate woodland.

West Quarry Braes, Crail. SWT/LA. NO 597088. Scrub, woodland; refuge for small migrant birds.

Getting organized

Many voluntary and statutory organizations are concerned with 'The Nature of Fife':

Scottish Wildlife Trust (SWT)

The SWT was established in 1964 as a voluntary body to protect Scotland's wildlife. It is affiliated to The Wildlife Trusts, a UK-wide network of 47 trusts. The SWT has around 15,000 members, with a core staff at Cramond, Edinburgh and other regional staff throughout Scotland.

The SWT:

- Owns or manages over 100 Wildlife Reserves throughout Scotland.
- Surveys other 'Wildlife Sites' without statutory protection, and encourages their owners to manage them in a way sympathetic to wildlife.
- Operates training courses in wildlife surveying and practical conservation in collaboration with local authorities and enterprise companies (including one unit based at Kirkcaldy).
- Campaigns to protect raised bogs from peat extraction; to minimize damage to wildlife sites from the construction of roads; and on many other topical issues.
- Collaborates with statutory and other voluntary bodies to document and conserve species and habitats.
- Operates an urban wildlife project – the Green Machine – to enable local people to save wildlife and green space in urban areas.
- Involves thousands of children in activities relevant to the conservation of wildlife through its junior wing, Scottish Wildlife Watch.

The Fife & Kinross Branch holds meetings and outings throughout Fife and Kinross, and collaborates closely with Fife Council and other bodies in implementing the above activities locally. There are eight reserves in Fife, all included in Appendix 1.

Enquiries to: Scottish Wildlife Trust, Cramond House, Cramond Glebe Road, Edinburgh EH4 6NS; phone 0131 312 7765.

Fife Nature

Fife Nature is the biological records centre for Fife, established in 1992, and is an integral part of the Planning Service of Fife Council. Its objectives are:

- To gather, organize and store all relevant information on Fife's biodiversity, including information on wildlife habitats and sites of natural history interest, and on as many species of animals and plants as possible.
- To publish guides, distribution atlases and other material relating to Fife's wildlife.
- To make information available for conservation, education, planning, research and the general public.
- To encourage and co-ordinate systematic recording of biological data, e.g. through a network of recorders.
- to work with everyone to promote environmental sustainability and a better understanding of all apsects of the countryside.
- To help conserve Fife's habitats and species by providing quality information to decision makers.

Records are stored on a computer database which currently holds over 150,000 records relating to about 4000 species, as well as details of habitats and sites. Further records are always welcome and anyone can contribute.

Enquiries to: Fife Nature, Fife

House, Glenrothes, KY7 5LT; phone 01592 413793.

Farming and Wildlife Advisory Group (FWAG)

A farmer-led organization to encourage the integration of sound, profitable farming and forestry with the conservation and enhancement of wildlife habitat and landscape.
Fife office: 33 Castlefield, Cupar, KY15 4DB; phone 01334 656546.

Fife Bird Club

Produces newsletters with recent bird records and the annual *Fife Bird Report*. Holds indoor and field meetings and operates bird hides.
Enquiries: Rab Shand, 33 Liddle Drive, Bo'ness, EH51 0PA; phone 01506 825101.

Kirkcaldy Naturalists' Society

Holds meetings in Kirkcaldy and organizes excursions. Enquiries: c/o Kirkcaldy Museum, Kirkcaldy.

Largo Field Studies Society

Holds meetings in Upper Largo and organizes excursions.
Enquiries: Mrs P Smith, Auchendownie, Upper Largo, KY8 5QH.

Royal Society for the Protection of Birds (RSPB)

Has reserves at nearby Vane Farm, Loch Leven (Kinross) and on the (Lothian) Forth islands of Inchmickery and Fidra.
Enquiries to: RSPB, Vane Farm, Kinross, KY13 7LX; phone 01577 862355.

Scottish Natural Heritage (SNH)

The statutory body, responsible to the Secretary of State for Scotland, concerned with the conservation and enhancement of Scotland's natural heritage – the wildlife, habitats and landscape.
Fife office: 46 Crossgate, Cupar, Fife, KY15 5HS; phone 01334 654038.

Scottish Ornithologists' Club (SOC)

Has Fife branch which meets in St Andrews, arranges excursions and issues a newsletter.
Enquiries to: 21 Regent's Terrace, Edinburgh, EH7 5BT.

Woodland Trust

Aims to protect the woodland heritage by acquiring woods through purchase and as gifts, and to acquire land to plant new woods. Has four woodlands in Fife in addition to most of the woodland in Glenrothes. All but one have public access (detailed in appendix 1).
Enquiries to: Glenruthven Mill, Abbey Road, Auchterarder, Perthshire, PH3 1DP; phone 01764 662554.

The Nature of Fife on disc

The annotated lists of species comprising Part II of this book, detailing about 3000 species, have been derived from a more comprehensive annotated list of about 8000 species. This full list is available from Fife Nature on a 3½" AppleMac or PC compatible disc for £7 (post-free). The PC version for Windows 3.1 and 95 comes with a free, easy-to-use browser. Additional formats may also be available on request.
Orders should be sent directly to: Fife Nature, Fife House, Glenrothes, KY7 5LT.

Index